KANT'S THINKER

KANT'S THINKER

Patricia Kitcher

Oxford University Press is a department of the University of Oxford.
It furthers the University's objective of excellence in research, scholarship,
and education by publishing worldwide.

Oxford   New York
Auckland   Cape Town   Dar es Salaam   Hong Kong   Karachi
Kuala Lumpur   Madrid   Melbourne   Mexico City   Nairobi
New Delhi   Shanghai   Taipei   Toronto

With offices in
Argentina   Austria   Brazil   Chile   Czech Republic   France   Greece
Guatemala   Hungary   Italy   Japan   Poland   Portugal   Singapore
South Korea   Switzerland   Thailand   Turkey   Ukraine   Vietnam

Oxford is a registered trade mark of Oxford University Press
in the UK and certain other countries.

Published in the United States of America by
Oxford University Press
198 Madison Avenue, New York, NY 10016

© Oxford University Press 2011

First issued as an Oxford University Press paperback, 2014.

All rights reserved. No part of this publication may be reproduced, stored in a retrieval system,
or transmitted, in any form or by any means, without the prior permission in writing of Oxford
University Press, or as expressly permitted by law, by license, or under terms agreed with the appropriate
reproduction rights organization. Inquiries concerning reproduction outside the scope of the above
should be sent to the Rights Department, Oxford University Press, at the address above.

You must not circulate this work in any other form
and you must impose this same condition on any acquirer.

Library of Congress Cataloging-in-Publication Data
Kitcher, Patricia.
Kant's thinker / Patricia Kitcher.
p.   cm.
ISBN 978-0-19-975482-3 (hardcover); 978-0-19-936372-8 (paperback)
1. Kant, Immanuel, 1724–1804.
2. Self-knowledge, Theory of. I. Title.
B2799.S37K58 2011
193—dc22   2010011177

For C.P.E.K and S.-Y.A.

Preface

After arguing in 1990 that Kant's theory of cognition could not be fully understood or appreciated without taking his 'transcendental psychology' seriously, I thought that it would be the work of a few years to fill out the sketch of his theory offered there. When I took up the problems of working out how Kant thought the categorial principles arose from the (*a priori*) activities of the mind and why he believed that conscious synthesizing was necessary for cognition, however, I found that I could not produce interpretations that were faithful to the text, and reasonably detailed and consistent. Agreeing to do more administrative work than was wise in the 1990s and 2000s made it difficult to find time to work on the large, interconnected set of problems that need to be considered in interpreting the transcendental deduction where the cognitive theory is laid out. This book does not offer a complete interpretation of the deduction, but it aims at a reasonably thorough account of the deduction's theory of the unity of apperception.

Although I wrote up various pieces over the years, I was able to engage in the sustained effort required to make significant progress on the whole only on a sabbatical leave from Columbia University that I spent at the Wissenschaftskolleg zu Berlin in 2007–8. I am very grateful to both these wonderful institutions for support during that year. Having finally figured out how I thought Kant's account of mental activity, conscious synthesis, and rational cognition went, I read pilot versions of the central elements of the book to a number of helpful audiences. I'm very grateful to Joel Smith and to the late Mark Sacks for inviting me to participate in their series on transcendental philosophy, naturalism, and the mind in November of 2007 where I met Sebastian Rödl. We were both surprised to discover that we had been thinking along similar lines on a number of topics that are central to my interpretation of Kant's theory of cognition. It's been enormously helpful to discuss these issues with Sebastian on later occasions that brought us together.

I'm also grateful to Bernard Thöle for pressing me very hard on some central claims at a session organized by Thomas Sturm at the Max Planck institute in Berlin in December 2007 and to Tobias Rosefeldt for offering a clear and insightful challenge to my Kantian theory of rational cognition at a conference he organized in Konstanz in June 2008. As is evident in the book, my research has profited enormously from Wolfgang Carl's studies of Kant's silent decade and of the A and B deductions. We have also had a number of very helpful conversations as I was finalizing some details of my account. Finally, I'm grateful to my colleague Chris Peacocke. I don't think it is coincidental that my views began to take their present form shortly after he joined the Columbia department in 2004 and we began to talk fairly regularly. He has been both the gentlest and clearest of critics and many discussions in the book have been improved by his interventions.

Despite his waning patience with Kantian epistemology, Philip Kitcher has been extremely patient in helping me with the manuscript. His careful reading of the penultimate draft was invaluable. Our children Andrew and Charles—and more recently, our daughter-in-law Sue, have also been supportive and very patient with my obsession with this project. I had hoped to dedicate it to Charles and Sue on the occasion of their marriage in July 2008. At least I've managed it before their second anniversary.

New York City, February 2010

Contents

Abbreviations, xiii

1. *Overview*, 3
   1. Searching for Kant's Thinker, 3
   2. Interpretive Framework, 5
   3. Preview, 7
   4. Current Work on Kant's 'I-Think', 10

PART I: Background

2. *Locke's Internal Sense and Kant's Changing Views*, 15
   1. Locke's Influence, 15
   2. Locke's Complex Theory of Internal Sense, 16
   3. Kant's Varied Reactions, 18
   4. 'Inner Sense' in Relation to Kantian 'Apperception', 21
   5. Kant's Use of 'Inner Sense', 25

3. *Personal Identity and Its Problems*, 27
   1. Locke's Problems, 27
   2. Leibniz's Criticisms and Additions, 28
   3. Kant and Hume, 31
   4. Tetens (and Hume), 32

4. *Rationalist Metaphysics of Mind*, 39
   1. The Role of Rationalism, 39

2. Leibniz's Elegant I-theory, 40
  3. Faculties, Powers and Substances, 43
  4. Rational Psychology, 47

5. *Consciousness, Self-consciousness, and Cognition*, 54
  1. Introduction, 54
  2. Locke's 'Reflection' and Leibniz's 'Apperception', 54
  3. Self-consciousness and Object Cognition, 57
  4. Self-consciousness through Self-Feeling, 62
  5. Summary, 64

6. *Strands of Argument in the* Duisburg Nachlaß, 66
  1. Introduction, 66
  2. Kant's Objection to the *Inaugural Dissertation*, 66
  3. Principles of Appearance and Thought in the *Duisburg Nachlaß*, 68
  4. What is the *Duisburg Nachlaß*'s Notion of 'Apperception'?, 72
  5. From the *Duisburg Nachlaß* to the *Critique*, 76

Part II: Theory

7. *A Transcendental Deduction for* A Priori *Concepts*, 81
  1. Kant's Goal, 81
  2. Clues to the Nature of the Argument, 84
  3. The First Premise of the Transcendental Deduction, 89
  4. Apriority and Activity, 93
  5. A 'Transcendental' Deduction, 95

8. *Synthesis: Why and How?*, 98
  1. Problems to Be Solved, 98
  2. Kant's Definition, 100
  3. Synthesis and Objective Reference, 108
  4. Five Syntheses and Their Relations, 114

9. *Arguing for Apperception*, 115
  1. Introduction, 115
  2. 'I-Think' as the '*Cogito*'; The One-step Deduction from Judgment, 115

3. What Kind of Cognition Is at Issue in the
      Transcendental Deduction?, 118
   4. What Is the Principle of Apperception?, 121
   5. The Apperceptive Synthesis of Recognition
      in a Concept, 126
   6. Combination and Self-consciousness
      in the B Deduction, 142
   7. Arguing from the Unity of Apperception to the
      Necessary Applicability of Categories to
      Intuitions, 152
   8. Transcendental Apperception, Empirical
      Apperception, and 'Mineness', 157
   9. Summary, 159

10. *The Power of Apperception*, 161
    1. Introduction, 161
    2. What is the Power/Faculty of
       Apperception?, 162
    3. Does the Faculty of Apperception Endure? Is it
       the 'Inner Principle' of a Substance?, 164
    4. Does the Power of Apperception Initiate Causal
       Chains or Provide Impressions of Necessary
       Connection?, 166
    5. 'Is It an Experience That I think?', 173
    6. Root Powers, Scientific Ideals, and the Ground
       of Appearances, 175

11. *'I-Think' as the Destroyer of Rational
    Psychology*, 180
    1. Understanding Kant's Criticisms, 180
    2. Kant's Earlier and Later Treatments of Rational
       Psychology, 182
    3. 'I-Think' as the Vehicle of the Categories, 187
    4. 'I-Think' as Analytically Contained in the
       Concept of Thought, 189
    5. Does the Analysis of Cognition Imply the
       Existence of a Thinker?, 193
    6. Why Can't Thinkers Know Themselves as
       Such?, 197

PART III: Evaluation

12. Is *Kant's Theory Consistent*?, 203
    1. The Old Objection, 203
    2. The Most Problematic Passage (A251–52), 205

3. Confusions about the Causes of Sensations, 206
4. A Second Look at the Most Problematic Passage, 210
5. Criticizing Rationalist Confusions, 213
6. What Kant's Epistemology and Metaphysics Imply, 215

13. *The Normativity Objection*, 217
    1. Psychologism or Noumenalism?, 217
    2. Scrutinizing Sensations and Adding 'Transcendental Content', 219
    3. Forming Concepts and Acquiring the I-Representation, 223
    4. Making *A Priori* Principles Explicit and Testing Instances, 227
    5. Normativity and the I-Rule, 231

Appendix to Chapter 13: Longuenesse on Concept Formation, 234

14. *Is Kant's Thinker (as Such) a Free and Responsible Agent?*, 238
    1. Introduction, 238
    2. Texts Linking Theoretical and Practical Reason, 241
    3. Autonomy and Accountability, 245
    4. Intellectual Accountability, 247

15. *Kant Our Contemporary*, 249
    1. Supporting and Showing Relevance, 249
    2. Transcendental Arguments, 250
    3. Must Rational Cognition involve Self-consciousness?, 253
    4. A Second Hard Problem of Consciousness?, 265
    5. Other 'I's, 268

Notes, 271
Bibliography, 293
Index of Quoted and Cited Passages, 301
General Index, 305

Abbreviations

C1755   Walford, David, with Ralf Meerbote, trans. and eds. (1992). *Immanuel Kant. Theoretical Philosophy 1755–1770*. The Cambridge Edition of the Works of Immanuel Kant, P. Guyer and A. W. Wood, gen. eds. New York: Cambridge University Press.

C1781   Allison, Henry, and Peter Heath, eds. (2002). *Immanuel Kant. Theoretical Philosophy after 1781*. The Cambridge Edition of the Works of Immanuel Kant, P. Guyer and A. W. Wood, gen. eds. New York: Cambridge University Press.

CJudge Guyer, Paul, and Eric Matthews, trans. (2000). *Immanuel Kant. Critique of the Power of Judgment*. The Cambridge Edition of the Works of Immanuel Kant. P. Guyer and A. W. Wood, gen. eds. New York: Cambridge University Press.

CLet   Zwieg, A. trans. and ed. (1999). *Immanuel Kant. Correspondence*. The Cambridge Edition of the Works of Immanuel Kant, P. Guyer and A. W. Wood, gen. eds. New York: Cambridge University Press.

CLog   Young, J. Michael, trans. and ed. (1992). *Immanuel Kant. Lectures on Logic*. The Cambridge Edition of the Works of Immanuel Kant, P. Guyer and A. W. Wood, gen. eds. New York: Cambridge University Press.

CMet   Ameriks, Karl, and Steve Naragon, trans. and eds. (1997). *Immanuel Kant. Lectures on Metaphysics*. The Cambridge Edition of the Works of Immanuel Kant, P. Guyer and A. W. Wood, gen. eds. New York: Cambridge University Press.

CNotes Bowman, Curtis, Paul Guyer, and Fred Rauscher, trans. (2005). *Immanuel Kant. Notes and Fragments*. P. Guyer, ed. The Cambridge Edition of the Works of Immanuel Kant, P. Guyer and A. W. Wood, gen. eds. New York: Cambridge University Press.

CPract Gregor, Mary, trans. and ed. (1996). *Immanuel Kant. Practical Philosophy*. The Cambridge Edition of the Works of Immanuel Kant. P. Guyer and A. W. Wood, gen. eds. New York: Cambridge University Press.

CRel   Wood, Allen W., and George Di Giovanni. trans. and eds. (1996). *Immanuel Kant. Religion and Rational Theology*. The Cambridge Edition of the Works of Immanuel Kant, P. Guyer and A. W. Wood, gen. eds. New York: Cambridge University Press.

KANT'S THINKER

1
Overview

1. Searching for Kant's Thinker

Kant's theory of the cognitive subject is complex, subtle, and immensely fruitful. My aim is to get somewhat closer to a comprehensive understanding of the theory. I situate his claims about the thinker in the context of then contemporary problems and in the context of his attempt to defend the categories in the *Critique of Pure Reason*. Since the theory is presented in the transcendental deduction of the categories, I don't see how one can be confident of understanding it without investigating this pivotal and infamously opaque chapter of the *Critique*. Much of the book consists in assembling the necessary materials for reading the Deduction chapter in a way that enables us to see its theory of thinking in considerable detail. Because the transcendental deduction lies at the center of the *Critique*, getting a better grasp on its elusive main character should lead to a clearer and richer picture of many of Kant's doctrines. But the principal rationale for the effort is to provide a "new" source of illumination for current attempts to understand the nature of cognition and of the mind.

The project of advancing our understanding of the cognitive subject through examining Kant's theory of cognition has been on the philosophical agenda at least since the publication of P. F. Strawson's seminal work *The Bounds of Sense* in 1966. I take up a Strawsonian project, but I depart from the usual way in which it has been pursued. In *The Bounds of Sense*, Strawson provided a *Bauplan* for interpreting Kant's distinctive contribution to understanding the expression 'I-think'.

> And now we come to the fact that lies at the root of the Cartesian illusion. It may be put as follows. When a man (subject of experience) ascribes a current or directly remembered state of consciousness to himself, no use whatever of any criteria of personal identity is required to justify his use of the pronoun 'I' to refer to the subject of that experience . . . (I think it could be said, without serious exaggeration, that it is because Kant recognized this truth that his treatment of the subject is so greatly superior to Hume's). (1966, 165)

In the intervening forty-plus years, numerous interpreters have embraced and elaborated his interpretive insight. The 'criterionless self-ascription' reading of Kant's critique of Rational Psychology, and of his positive treatment of the 'I', is pervasive, if not dominant, across Anglo-American students of Kant and has also been very influential in Germany.[1]

Chapter 11 offers an alternative view of Kant's diagnosis of the errors of Rational Psychology. Here I try to give my non-Strawsonian approach to Strawson's quest some initial plausibility by noting the lack of surface credibility of interpreting Kant's positive doctrine in terms of the ascription of mental states without criteria of identity. The 'I-think' principle concerns multiple states:

> The synthetic proposition that all the varied **empirical consciousness** must be combined in <u>one</u> single self-consciousness is the absolutely first and synthetic principle of our thought as such. (A117n., my underscoring)[2]
>
> The **I think** must be **capable** of accompanying all my representations . . . Hence everything manifold in intuition has a necessary reference to the **I think** in the <u>same</u> subject in whom this manifold is found. (B132, my underscoring)
>
> The supreme principle for the possibility of all intuition in reference to understanding is that everything manifold in intuition is subject to conditions of the original synthetic <u>unity</u> of apperception. (B136, my underscoring)

He insists that the principle concerns the necessity of taking diverse representations to belong to a single or unified subject. It is focused on what we might call the 'togetherness' of different mental states. By contrast the phenomenon of self-ascription without criteria of identity concerns what might be described as the 'mineness' of mental states. When I am in a mental state, I am entitled to self-ascribe it without employing any criteria of identification.

Further, when Gareth Evans considered the problem of how to fit cases which involve identity across different states into the framework of criterionless self-ascription, he produced an account that was markedly different from Kant's. Evans considers the case of tracking an object:

> When a subject keeps track of an object . . . as he or it moves (or not), I think we should regard the slightly varying forms of the judgment ['It's ϕ here', 'It's ϕ there' . . .] he is disposed to make as manifestations of a single persisting belief . . . I cannot see the latter members of the series of judgments . . . as based upon an identification. (1982, 236)

Evans's solution to the problem of attributing the latter judgments to the same subject as earlier ones ('I judge it to be ϕ here,' then 'I judge it to be ϕ a little further on') is to sweep the judgments into a single persisting belief that can be self-ascribed without criteria. That single belief underlies the various judgments: It is a disposition to make judgments of this sort.

Although I do not argue for the interpretation until much later, I will try to give a sense of how different Kant's approach is by sketching the way that he would understand a case that is similar to Evans's. Suppose that I am keeping an eye on our puppy, 'Teddy.' As Kant would analyze the situation, I believe or continue to judge that Teddy is in the room, because I occasionally check on a necessary condition for that judgment, *viz.* that he is at some determinate place in the room. Since I cannot believe that Teddy is in the room unless I believe that he is at a particular location in the room, Kant thinks that my capacity to make the *rational* judgment that Teddy is here depends on my ability to recognize that my state of judging that he is here depends on, and so is necessarily connected to, another mental state, in this case, the state of perceiving him to be somewhere in the room. (I could also believe that he is at a determinate place in the room on another ground, perhaps through hearing a report that he is behind a chair. But since, in this case, I believe that he is in the room through perception, my current belief is rational only by virtue of its dependency on the state of perceiving him.) And since I recognize these states as necessarily connected I understand them as meeting the condition for belonging to a single 'I.'

Where Evans's idea is that different states can be ascribed to a common subject because they emanate from a common criterionlessly self-ascribed belief, Kant argues that a subject understands different mental states as belonging to a common 'I' only through recognizing the sort of necessary connections that obtain between, for example, reasons and beliefs. In short, I resist the popular view that Kant's theory of the I-think anticipated the discovery of the phenomenon of self-ascription without criteria for two reasons. First, they involve different issues: the 'togetherness' as opposed to the 'mineness' of mental states. Second, when a very gifted philosopher tried to deal with the togetherness problem within the framework of self-ascription without criteria of identity, he produced an account that runs in the opposite direction from Kant's. Evans presents observations as the expression of a belief understood as a disposition; Kant is concerned with the special dependence of beliefs on perceptual evidence that exemplifies the necessary connection of different states in a single subject.

Strawson appreciated that Kant's criticisms in the Paralogisms chapter were not directly connected to the insight with which he credits him.

> Instead he connects that [delusive use of the 'I'] with the philosophical employment which he has already made of the first personal pronoun in expounding the doctrine of the necessary unity of consciousness, the transcendental unity of apperception. (1966, 166–67)

I explain the doctrine of the necessary *unity* of consciousness that Kant expounds in relation to the 'I-think' and use the resulting account to make sense of, among other doctrines, his critique of Rational Psychology in the Paralogisms chapter.

2. Interpretive Framework

The framework of my interpretation of Kant's theory is what he would call 'scientific metaphysics' and what contemporary philosophers usually characterize as his 'epistemological turn.' How his epistemological turn works is, roughly, by turning widely recognized metaphysical theses into epistemological ones. Putting the matter in a friendlier way, the epistemological turn is effected by revealing apparently metaphysical theses as disguised epistemological assumptions. Most famously, he argued that the thesis of determinism was no insight into the way reality must be, but an implicit assumption that cognizers must make if they are to acquire any empirical cognition, even of the course of their own mental lives.

Kant is explicit about how he understands metaphysics or 'scientific metaphysics.' He begins the 'Second Reflection [*Betrachtung*]' of his 1764 'Inquiry concerning the distinctness of the principles of natural theology and morality' with the following equation:

> Metaphysics is nothing other than a philosophy of the basic principles [*ersten Gründe*] of our cognition. (2.283, C1755 256)[3]

More than twenty years later, between the editions of the *Critique*, he offered a more elaborate account in the *Metaphysical Foundations of Natural Science*:

> All true metaphysics is drawn from the essence of the faculty of thinking itself, and is in no way fictitiously invented on account of not being borrowed from experience. Rather, it contains the pure actions of thought, and the *a priori* concepts and principles, which first bring the manifold of *empirical representations* into the law-governed connection through which it can become *empirical* **cognition**, that is experience. (4.472, C1781 187)[4]

More simply, true metaphysics concerns *a priori* concepts and principles that are required for empirical cognition. More bluntly, true metaphysics is *a priori* epistemology.[5]

A letter that Kant wrote to Christian Garve in August of 1783 confirms that he understood the relationship between the Critical project and traditional metaphysics as just described:

> Be so kind as to have another fleeting glance at the whole and to notice that it is not at all <u>metaphysics</u> that the **Critique** is doing but a whole new science . . . the critique of **an *a priori* judging** reason. Other men have touched on this faculty, for instance, Locke and Leibnitz, but always with an admixture of other faculties of cognition . . . Absolutely no other science attempts this, that is, to develop *a priori* out of the mere concept of a cognitive faculty (when that concept is precisely defined) all the objects, everything that can be known about them . . . Logic . . . would be the science most similar to this one . . .
>
> I believe I can demonstrate formally that not a single <u>truly metaphysical</u> proposition, torn out of the whole system, can be proved except by showing its relation to the sources of all our pure rational knowledge and, therefore, that it would have to be derived from the concept of a possible system of such cognitions. (10.340–41, CLet 198–99, my underscoring)[6]

Given the second mention of 'metaphysics,' the first should be read as implicitly modified by 'traditional' or some equivalent. The *Critique* is not engaged in traditional metaphysics, but in true metaphysics or *a priori* epistemology.

It carries out the epistemological turn in two ways. Negatively, it shows why metaphysical principles cannot be established by the methods used by Kant's predecessors. Positively, it reveals that principles that were mistakenly understood as metaphysical are *a priori* principles that are both necessary for cognition and that arise through actions of the mind. (I consider these actions in Chapters 7 and 13.) His work on the principle of apperception is of a piece with his general reform project in metaphysics. Although the relations between traditional metaphysics and his various claims about the 'I' are complex, his argument is, roughly, that the metaphysical principle that representations are necessarily states of simple thinking substances is, in fact, a confused and misleadingly cast version of a principle that thinkers must assume in cognition, *viz*., 'it must be possible for representations to belong to a common "I-think."' In the Paralogisms chapter, he explains why the original metaphysical principle could not be established through the methods of Rational Psychology.

Beyond this systematic Kantian framework, I explore the argumentative moves of the transcendental deduction against the background of two then contemporary issues. At that time, there was much confusion about how self-consciousness should be modeled and a vigorous debate about the relative priority of self or object consciousness. The Deduction argument offers elegant solutions to both: Self-consciousness and object consciousness mutually condition each other—and that is how self-consciousness is possible.

3. Preview

I begin with four short historical chapters that lay out key elements of the context of Kant's discussion. Chapter 2 examines the Lockean faculty of 'internal sense,' which Kant first accepts as essential to rational cognition and then demotes in relation to the newly introduced faculty of 'apperception.' Chapter 3 presents four theories of mental unity, those of Locke, Leibniz, Hume, and J. N. Tetens. The failings of these theories give a sense of what he was reacting against—which is not to say that his theory makes good on all their shortcomings. Chapter 4 details the metaphysical theories of the mind offered by Leibniz and by Rational Psychology that he rejects and tries to replace with 'scientific' versions. Chapter 5 charts the debates about how self-consciousness should be understood and about the priority relations between self-consciousness and object consciousness.

It is hardly news that the Deduction chapter is a tough slog. Chapters 6–8 are intended to make the going easier. Chapter 6 examines a set of 'Reflections,' the so-called '*Duisburg Nachlaß*.' These are unbound sheets that were found among Kant's literary remains and are usually dated around 1775 (R4674–84, 17.643–673).[7] They are widely believed to offer the most sustained pre-*Critique* sketch of a transcendental deduction. By looking at these notes, which try to demonstrate the place of categorial principles (described as 'titles of the understanding') in cognition with only an undeveloped theory of apperception, we can get a better appreciation of the features of his 'I-think' theory that are critical to his mature account of cognition. Chapter 7 handles some basic questions about the structure of the transcendental deduction so that Chapter 9 can concentrate on the argument itself. What are its premises/conclusions? I offer a synthetic account of the nature of the argument that incorporates advances made by Dieter Henrich (1976, 1989b), Manfred Kuehn (1997), and Wolfgang Carl (1989b). Chapter 8 also provides an essential preliminary to following the Deduction argument by clarifying two terms that are ubiquitous in the text, 'synthesis' and *a priori.*'

Chapter 9 is the center, because it presents the Deduction argument and so Kant's account of thinking and the thinker. In briefest compass, the argument is this: Rational cognition of objects given in experience requires the combination of sensory elements from diverse representations in concepts and the combination of different concepts in further concepts and that the cognizer understand these combinations as such. For a rational cognizer to judge that x is a body, for example, she must see her judgment 'x is a body' as having as 'partial grounds,' 'x is extended,' 'x is impenetrable,' and so forth. That is, she must recognize that her judgment depends on and would be impossible without the representations that are its grounds and that those representations would be impossible as grounds of cognition unless they were the basis of the judgment. Thus, in recognizing that she can and does assert 'x is a body' only because she can assert, for example, 'x is extended,' she also recognizes that the two representations, *qua* representations, must belong together and so are instances of the rule governing the representation 'I,' namely, the rule that different representations must belong to some common 'I.' More generally, in any case where a cognizer can engage in rational cognition—in any case where she knows the grounds of her judgment—she must understand the representations involved as necessarily connected to each other (and so to a common subject).

Since Kant's argument for apperception is complex and takes slightly different forms in the two editions, I postpone discussion of important related issues until Chapter 10. What is the 'faculty' or 'power' of apperception that is introduced in the transcendental deduction? What is the relation between Kant's 'thinker' and the 'Psychological Idea,' and between those two notions and that of an alleged 'noumenal self'? Chapter 9 also passes over most alternative interpretations of the argument for apperception. In Chapter 10, I try to bring my account into sharper relief by contrasting it with somewhat similar-sounding analyses offered by Henry Allison (1983) and Eric Watkins (2005).

It is natural to think that the teachings of the Paralogisms chapter are entirely negative. But I argue in Chapter 11 that when we see the details of Kant's criticisms of the Rational Psychologists, we gain a deeper appreciation of his positive theory through the contrast with the erring ways of his predecessors. Chapter 11 also argues that he does not just criticize Descartes' *cogito* but recasts the argument for his own purposes.

The last four chapters evaluate Kant's theory. Chapter 12 addresses the oldest objection to transcendental psychology: His cognitive theory is inconsistent with his metaphysics. The problem might seem to be internal to the Kantian system. But the way the objection is developed, it threatens to undermine the cognitive theory. Given his division of the world into phenomena and noumena, the subjects and objects of cognition must be one or the other. Seemingly, however, they cannot be phenomenal, so they must be noumenal. I suggest that Kant becomes confused about a confusing topic: how to describe the initial stages of cognition. But I argue that the confusion does not threaten his basic account of thought and the thinker. He is not engaged in the impossible project of noumenal epistemology.

Chapter 13 addresses another venerable objection: Transcendental psychology is an inappropriate method for normative epistemology. Either it provides no explanation for cognitive normativity or the foundation it offers is psychologistic. I defend Kant by laying out more of the cognitive theory (in particular, the theory of concept formation) and by considering his view of how ordinary cognizers manage to improve their cognition through 'natural' as opposed to 'scientific' logic. My concern is to defend his claim that the apperceptive principle, the principle that different representations must belong to a common 'I-think,' is both *a priori* and a *norm* of cognition. I turn the tables on the objection that apriority cannot be a source of normativity by arguing that the apperceptive principle is a norm that is required by any other cognitive norm—and that it can only be *a priori*. (In an appendix I contrast my view of Kant's theory of concept formation with that offered by Béatrice Longuenesse in *Kant and the Capacity to Judge*.)

Chapter 14 moves from rebutting traditional criticisms of Kant's transcendental psychology to evaluating it in relation to current work. I begin in a slightly odd way, by arguing that one contemporary invocation of Kant is mistaken. Although he focuses on the spontaneity of thought and the spontaneity of action, he understands these two sorts of freedom very differently. He is not a forerunner of those who would assimilate cognitive subjects to moral agents, but an opponent.

Chapter 15 looks at Kant's theory in relation to four additional issues of great current interest. I begin by contrasting his transcendental argument for a thinker with recent attempts at constructing transcendental arguments. I show that his argument for apperception works in a different and more successful way than latter-day transcendental arguments because of features that are unique to the I-concept and unique to his theory of cognition. So the result is somewhat mixed. He offered a good argument for apperception but he did not invent a new and generalizable form of argument for defending other *a priori* concepts.

Chapter 15 also takes up an issue that is both crucial to the overall evaluation of Kant's position and very prominent in contemporary philosophy of mind. It is a central part of his theory that rational cognition requires self-consciousness. Having accepted his argument for this view in Chapter 9, I weigh likely objections here. Part of my defense consists in showing that we can understand the self-knowledge of beliefs where the subject knows the reason (I believe that *p*, because I believe that *q*) only by appealing to his theory of cognition and that that theory implies that rational cognizers are not 'self-blind' (in Sydney Shoemaker's terminology [1996]) but necessarily self-conscious. That is, I defend Kant's claim that cognition requires self-consciousness by showing how his theory can advance the cause of those who think that self-blindness is impossible.

Where Locke took cognizers to be conscious *of* mental acts, it is an essential part of Kant's view that they are conscious *in* thinking (or synthesizing). Chapter 15 considers this act-consciousness in relation to current theories of consciousness. I argue that if he is right about thinking, then it is not just sensory states such as being in pain or seeing a purple haze (Levine, 2001) that pose a problem for completing a science of mind. Rational cognition seems very difficult to model with current resources. Finally, I argue that Kant's theory of the thinker implies that the recent flurry of work on the problem of reading the minds of others has omitted something essential to understanding others as 'I's.

In drawing out the implications of Kant's theory for issues of the normativity of cognition, the relation between thought and action, the efficacy of transcendental arguments, self-knowledge of beliefs, the nature of consciousness, and the requirements of 'mind-reading,' these later chapters offer the proof for my opening claim about its fertility.

4. Current Work on Kant's 'I-Think'

My study falls within the broad Strawsonian tradition of looking to Kant for a sophisticated theory of the cognitive subject—even though I reject the central interpretive claim of that tradition. If we turn to work that focuses on Kant's texts, we see that my approach is also at odds with the seminal work in English, Karl Ameriks's *Kant's Theory of Mind* (1982), reissued with a new preface and postscript in 2000. Ameriks deliberately focuses on metaphysical questions raised in the Paralogisms chapter. He notes that he

> minimize[s] attention to the general cognitive activity of the self as subject, since that topic . . . involves the entirety of Kant's theory of knowledge rather than the self as such. (2000, vi)

I concentrate on the aspect of Kant's theory that Ameriks left open to other scholars, the cognitive activity of the subject. Because I start with the 'I-think' of the transcendental deduction and Ameriks starts with the Rationalist tradition, we read the Paralogisms chapter in different ways. In Chapter 11, I try to explain why both approaches seem attractive, though I defend mine as preferable.

German scholars have also taken the epistemology to be the royal road to the Kantian consciousness—and vice versa. In *Identity and Objectivity: A Study of Kant's Transcendental Deduction* (1976) and in subsequent works (especially 1989a), Dieter Henrich provides close readings of key Deduction texts, and subtle and forceful interpretations of key doctrines. Although my work is much indebted to Henrich's, I disagree with him on a crucial point: his insistence that the Deduction is concerned with Cartesian certainty about the thinker (e.g., 1976, 58–59, 69–70). My view is closer to that defended by Dieter Sturma in *Kant über Selbstbewußtsein* (1985). Sturma argues that the theory of self-consciousness emerged from the analysis of the preconditions for cognition (e.g., 1985, 30). We differ because Sturma views criterionless self-ascription to be central to Kant's insights about the mind and I do not. Wolfgang Carl's (1992) commentary on the long and complex discussion of the relations between cognition and consciousness in the A deduction is an unparalleled resource for all who venture into these difficult passages. His shorter treatment of the B deduction is also full of insights into the philosophical issues at stake (1998). My position is like his in taking the 'I-think' to be a thoroughly cognitive subject; my major disagreement concerns the status of this doctrine. Where Carl takes the theory of 'transcendental apperception' to be asserted dogmatically (1992, 178), I find arguments for it in both editions of the Deduction chapter.

Hansgeorg Hoppe's *Synthesis bei Kant* (1983) is a starting place of my discussion of this topic in Chapter 8. Hoppe resisted the then current assumption that Kant's transcendental psychology must be avoided in understanding his theory of object cognition. On the other hand, he believed that it was possible to reconstruct the Deduction argument for the categories just by talking about the operation of 'synthesis' and without appealing to Kant's theory of the thinking self—his '*Egologie*,' as he stigmatizes it (1983, 119–21). In Chapters 8 and 9 I explain how this truncated transcendental psychology falls short of Kant's goals (as Hoppe realized) and how a richer version can meet them. Heiner Klemme's *Kants Philosohie des Subjekts* (1996) offers a rich history of Kant's and his predecessors' attempts to come to grips with 'I-representation.' He traces Kant's changing views about the cognitive subject through the student lecture notes on Anthropology and Metaphysics as well as his published writings. I draw on Klemme's historical materials to fill out some of the background to Kant's philosophical queries.

Locating this study on the map of current work then, I emphasize Kant's epistemological rather than metaphysical concerns about the thinker (in contrast to Ameriks). Within the group of scholars concerned with his analysis of the necessary conditions for cognition, I find his central contribution in the theory of the unity of the self rather than in a theory of the self-ascription of mental states (in contrast to most Strawsonians). Although my analysis is closest to those of Dieter Henrich (1989a) and Wolfgang Carl (1992), both give Kant a dogmatic starting place: The 'I-think' principle expresses the form of cognition (Henrich, 1989a, 266ff., Carl, 1992, 101ff.). By contrast I maintain that Kant *argues* that implicit use of the 'I-think' principle is a necessary condition for cognition of the distinctive sort exhibited in human judgment.

Finally, this book differs in many ways from my earlier treatment in *Kant's Transcendental Psychology*. That book's range was too narrow. I was very taken with the potential of Kant's theory of synthesis to offer a principled account of the unity relation for persons: The states of one person must be connected, because later states depend on the contents of earlier states for their contents. I think that this interpretation is partly correct, but very incomplete. It doesn't give sufficient weight to the importance that Kant places on mental acts and on the need for those acts to be conscious. *Kant's Transcendental Psychology* was also too centered on Hume. I was struck by the fact that Kant's apparent references to Hume's denial of personal identity were not used by interpreters as a tool to plot some of the twists and turns of the Deduction argument. It is now clear that Kant was aware of Hume's discussion of personal identity and freshly reminded of it just a few years before the A edition.[8] Below I suggest a more detailed timeline for Hume's possible influence on the shape of Kant's theory. Regardless of the effect of the encounter with Hume, I should have taken more account of Locke's influence. As will be clear in Chapters 2 and 9, Kant's important contrast between inner sense and apperception can be understood by tracing his changing attitudes towards Locke's theory of inner sense. One project of *Kant's Transcendental Psychology* was to argue that it was philosophically useful (as well as textually necessary) to follow Kant's cognitive psychological descriptions of the necessary conditions for cognition. I don't pursue that methodological project further here, because it no longer seems necessary.

Part I
Background

2

Locke's Internal Sense and Kant's Changing Views

1. Locke's Influence

Some of the 'illustrious Locke's' (Aix) contributions to the *Critique*'s cognitive theory are apparent. Kant's opening move of section 1 of the Transcendental Aesthetic is to divide the human ability to receive representations—sensibility—into an outer and an inner sense (A22/B37). Scholarship over the last thirty years has revealed that Locke's influence on Kant and his philosophical community was more pervasive than previously thought. Reinhard Brandt reports that Locke was officially approved by all German faculties as a text to follow in metaphysics (1981, 45). According to Kuehn's new biography, one of Kant's most influential teachers, Martin Knutzen, was incorrectly classified as a 'Wolffian'; his epistemology came from Locke and the Lockeans (2001, 78–80). Many of Kant's early critics, including the editor of the notorious 'Göttingen Review' of the A edition, J. G. H. Feder, were also Lockeans (Sassen, 2000, 20). One critic, Gottlob August Tittel, presented his objections in the form of a contrast between Locke's views and Kant's (Sassen, 2000, 227–30).

Beyond the *Critique*'s flattering references, Kant apparently often mentioned Locke in his Logic and Metaphysics lectures. Brandt (1981, 46) draws attention to a discussion that appears in student notes from the Logic lectures and that is highly relevant to my topic.

> Locke had taken the most essential step of all to prepare the way for understanding . . . He had sought the descent and source of concepts . . . Wolff had asked: what is a soul? Locke: where does the idea of the soul in my mind come from? ('Phillipi Logic,' May 1772, 24.338)

Although Kant admired Locke and credited him with introducing the important issue of the descent of concepts, he pushed back against his signature theories of internal sense, self-consciousness, and the moral identity of persons. This chapter considers his ambivalent attitude to his predecessor's hypothesis of an internal sense.

2. Locke's Complex Theory of Internal Sense

After Book 1's critical remarks about innate principles and ideas, Book 2 of *An Essay Concerning Human Understanding* takes up the challenge of providing a sensory descent for large classes of ideas. Locke introduces the hypothesis of an additional and 'internal' sense for this purpose:

> The other Fountain, from which Experience furnisheth the Understanding with *Ideas*, is the Perception of the Operations of our own Minds within us, as it is employ'd about the *Ideas* it has got; which Operations, when the soul comes to reflect on, and consider, do furnish the Understanding with another set of *Ideas*, which could not be had from things without: and such are *Perception, Thinking, Doubting, Believing, Reasoning, Knowing, Willing*, and all the different actings of our own Minds; which we being conscious of, and observing in our selves, do from these receive into our Understanding, as distinct *Ideas* as we do from bodies affecting our Senses. This source . . . though it be not Sense, as having nothing to do with external Objects; yet it is very like it, and might properly enough be call'd internal Sense[1] . . . The term *Operations* here, I use in a large sense, as comprehending not barely the Actions of the mind about its *Ideas*, but some sort of Passions arising sometimes from them, such as is the satisfaction or uneasiness arising from any thought. (ECHU 2.1.4, 105)[2]

Where the notion of an internal sense is, I think, novel, one phenomenon that underlies its introduction was familiar. Many in the logical tradition maintained that people are aware of the cognitive acts they perform. Taking the most prominent example, the authors of the *Port Royal Logic* assume that anyone can tell when he is conceiving, imagining, judging, and so forth (Arnauld, 1662/1964, e.g., 32).

Since this phenomenon is much less remarked today, I provide an anecdotal example to make it vivid. Years ago my partner in a game of Trivial Pursuit managed to find his way to an answer. The question was: What is the most common last name in Russia? By his own account, he reasoned as follows. He knew that Russian surnames are patronymics. Then he surmised that the most common first name in the United States would be John. He remembered that 'Ivan' is the Russian equivalent of 'John.' Then he applied the standard rule for making patronymics, producing 'Ivanov' from Ivan and inferred that 'Ivanov' must be most common surname in Russian. This example involves several steps, but the point is equally clear in a simple inference:

All men are mortal.
Caius is a man.
Therefore, Caius is mortal.

Normal humans are aware both of the conclusion and of the movement of their minds from the premises to the conclusion. With no effort at all, they can distinguish acts of inferring from cases where they see no relation and have to be told what follows from the premises. This distinction would be obvious even if someone were to say the conclusion as quickly as the mind might infer it; it would be obvious even if a neurosurgeon could induce the production of subvocal speech, 'Caius is mortal,' as quickly as the mind could infer that conclusion.

Although 'logical' acts are hardly a current topic of discussion, Christopher Peacocke has worked on modeling mental act awareness and on investigating its significance for epistemology (2008, Chapter 7). Nonphilosophical evidence for the presumption of mental act awareness can be found in the clinical literature on schizophrenia. Schizophrenics sometimes describe their condition in terms of a feeling that thoughts have been 'inserted' into their minds (Frith and Johnstone, 2003, 131). The psychologist Garry Young appeals to Kant's views on mental spontaneity to frame a possible explanation for this phenomenon (2006). My claim is more circumspect. Whatever is going on in the minds of schizophrenics, the clinicians who treat them try to fathom their condition against the background of their understanding of normal minds, and that understanding includes the assumption that people can tell whether or not they have judged or inferred. I mention current work to forestall any suggestion that mental act-consciousness is like Freudian 'hysteria,' which seems to have been a time-limited phenomenon. The logicians' use of mental acts in presenting their subject and Locke's hypothesis of internal sense may be relics of early modern philosophy, but one phenomenon that inspired them doesn't seem to be.

The phenomenon of mental act awareness does not justify Locke's introduction of an inner sense on analogy with the 'outer' senses.[3] I highlight mental act awareness not to support Locke's introduction of 'internal sense,' but to draw attention to one phenomenon that it was meant to illuminate, a phenomenon that is central to Kant's theory of thinking.

Locke's list of the types of mental acts of which humans are conscious matches almost perfectly the actions that Descartes claimed to be inseparable from thinking.[4] His goal, presumably, was to make plausible a sensory descent for ideas of the recognized varieties of thinking. After the initial description, he significantly expands the range of ideas supplied by the internal sense. The topic is the 'original' of the ideas of 'duration' and 'succession':

> 'Tis evident to any one who will but observe what passes in his own mind, that there is a train of *Ideas*, which constantly succeed one another in his Understanding ... *Reflection* on these appearances of several *Ideas* one <u>after</u> another in our Minds, is that which furnishes us with the *Idea* of *Succession*. For whilst we are thinking, or whilst we receive successively several *Ideas* in our Minds, we know that we do exist; and so we call the Existence or Continuation of the Existence of our selves, or anything else, Commensurate to the succession of any *Ideas* in our minds, the *Duration* of our selves, or any such other thing co-existent with our Thinking. (ECHU 2.14.3, 182, my underscoring)

Locke's comments are wide-ranging and raise many puzzles, one of which, the nature of 'reflection,' I discuss further in Chapter 5.

In Locke's view ideas appear in human minds, either through thinking or through being received (presumably by outer sense). These ideas can be 'observed' through the human capacity for 'reflection' (which the previous citation identifies with 'internal sense'). Combining these remarks with the first description, 'internal sense' would refer to a capacity to be aware of both acts of mind and the changing contents of a mind. In being aware of these changing contents, the internal sense is also aware of their succession—the train of thought—which is how the mind acquires its idea of succession.[5]

How does thinking or receiving ideas enable humans to know of their own existence? The context strongly implies internal sense. Humans are aware through internal sense of their mental acts and of constantly changing mental contents. Locke's assumption seems relatively straightforward: Awareness of acts or of contents is *ipso facto* awareness of something that acts or of something that possesses those contents; since the awareness is through internal, rather than external, sense, it is the mind's awareness of *its* acts or contents and *ipso facto* an awareness of the mind or self.

Locke makes a further important addition to the stock of ideas acquired through internal sense, that of 'active power.' First he notes the distinction between the idea of an 'active power,' that which makes changes, and that of a 'passive power,' that which receives changes (ECHU 2.21.2, 234). Then he explains that he is not sure that the external senses can supply a clear idea of active power. For this reason

> [he] thought it worth while to consider here by the way, whether the mind does not receive its *Idea* of *active Power* clearer from reflection on its own Operations, than it doth from any external sensation. (ECHU 2.21.4, 236)

The operations that are to supply the clearer idea of active power are those of understanding and willing.

Without trying to sort out the complexities or unclarities of Locke's view, I just summarize some central claims. 'Internal sense' senses:

1. Mental acts or operations (and so active powers).
2. The train of mental contents or ideas (and also their succession).
3. The self (through sensing its acts and/or ideas).

We can get a better understanding of several Kantian doctrines by seeing them in the context of his evolving reactions to the different elements in Locke's hypothesis of an internal sense.

3. Kant's Varied Reactions

For much of his career Kant was an internal or, as he calls it, 'inner,' sense enthusiast. He lauds the power of inner sense in *The False Subtlety of the Four Syllogistic Figures* (1762) as he criticizes Georg Friedrich Meier for suggesting that animals possess concepts.[6] He objects to Meier as follows:

> [Meier's] argument runs like this: an ox's representation of its stall includes the clear representation of its characteristic mark of having a door; therefore, the ox has a distinct concept of its stall. It is easy to prevent the confusion here. The distinctness of a concept does not consist in the fact that that which is a

characteristic mark of the thing is clearly represented, but rather in the fact that it is recognized [*erkannt*] as a characteristic of the thing. The door is something which does, it is true, belong to the stall and can serve as a characteristic mark of it. But only the being who forms the judgment: **this door belongs to this stable** has a distinct concept of the building, and that is certainly beyond the powers of animals.

I would go still further and say: it is one thing to **differentiate** things from each other, and quite another thing **to recognize** [*erkennen*] the difference between them. (2.59–60, C1755 103–4)

The context of the criticism is a discussion of the relation between distinct concepts and judging. Kant's position is that a cognizer can have a distinct concept only through judging, in particular, only through recognizing a 'characteristic mark'—a concept contained in a distinct representation of another concept[7]—as such (2.58, C1755 102). Animals offer an illuminating contrast, because they can distinguish objects on the basis of their characteristic marks, that is, by marks that humans can recognize as characteristic marks. But they can't recognize the characteristic marks as such, as the means by which they make the distinction or apply the concept.

The essay continues by offering a hypothesis about how humans or rational animals more generally are able to recognize characteristic marks as such and so employ (distinct) concepts: Perhaps they do it through

> the faculty of inner sense, that is to say, the faculty of making [*zu machen*] one's own representations the objects of one's thought. This faculty cannot be derived from any other faculty. It is, in the strict sense of the term, a fundamental faculty, which in my opinion, can only belong to rational beings. But it is upon this faculty that the entire higher faculty of cognition is based. (2.60, C1755 104)

Why must a rational animal who recognizes characteristic marks as such be able to think about her *representations*? Kant's view of rational cognition is that in applying concepts, rational animals know the basis or ground or reason for the application—hence they must be aware of their own representations, because those are the grounds of the application. Since reasoning as well as judging requires that human cognizers recognize their grounds as such, inner sense is the basis of the 'higher faculties' of cognition: understanding (the faculty of judging) and reason (the faculty of inference). By contrast, animals differentiate things only 'blindly,' without any idea of the basis of their differential behavior. I belabor this point, because the cognition that is the prime subject matter of the *Critique* is the rational cognition just described.

Kant's *Logic*,[8] which Benjamin Jäsche prepared for publication in 1800, presents the same contrast with animals and virtually the same *differentiae* of human cognition as the 1762 essay:

> The **first** degree of cognition is to **represent** something;
> The **second degree** is to represent something with consciousness, or **to perceive** (*percipere*);

> The **third**: to be **acquainted** (*kennen*) with something (*noscere*), or to represent something in comparison with other things, both as to **sameness** and as to **difference**;
>
> The **fourth**: to be acquainted with something with **consciousness**, i.e., to cognize it (*cognoscere*). Animals are **acquainted** with objects too, but they do not **cognize** them.
>
> The **fifth: to understand** something (intelligere), i.e., to cognize something **through the understanding by means of concepts** . . . (9.64–65, CLog 567–78, cf. 24.845–46, CLog 299–300)

I'm not sure exactly what Kant (or, perhaps, Jäsche) intends as the difference between the fourth and fifth degrees, but the basic distinction between the human and animal cases remains the same. Human cognition goes beyond mere differentiation, because it is conscious and conceptual.

Student lecture notes present Kant as continuing to believe that inner sense is essential to cognition and to the higher faculties at least through the middle 1770s.

> Animals will have all the representations of the outer senses; they will forgo only those representations which rest on inner sense, on the consciousness of oneself, in short, on the concept of the I. Accordingly, they will have no understanding and no reason, for all actions of the understanding and reason are possible only insofar as one is conscious of oneself. (28.276, CMet 87)

Appealing to student notes is a delicate matter. The student notes from his lectures are not exactly student lecture notes.[9] They are later transcriptions that are usually hard to date and often difficult to trace to a particular author. With those *caveats* in mind, I claim only that he appears to favor inner sense as the basis for rational cognition long after the *False Subtleties* essay.

By contrast Kant dissents from one Lockean thesis about inner sense very early. Locke and Leibniz are wrong: Inner sense can intuit states—but not the succession of states. His explicit target in the *Inaugural Dissertation* (1770) is Leibniz, but the point applies equally well to Locke.

> They [one sort of realist about time] conceive of it as something real that has been abstracted from the succession of internal states—the view maintained by Leibniz and his followers. Now the falsity of [this] . . . opinion clearly betrays itself by the vicious circle in the commonly accepted definition of time. (2.400–401, C1755 394)

Kant did not specify which definition he had in mind, but two pages before he had explained that

> it is only through the idea of time that it is possible for the things which come before the senses to be represented as simultaneous or successive. Nor does succession generate the concept of time; it makes appeal to it. And thus the concept of time, regarded as if it had been acquired through experience, is very

badly defined, if it is defined in terms of the series of actual things which exist one **after** the other. For I only understand the meaning of the little word **after** by means of the antecedent concept of time. (2.399, C1755 392)

If 'internal states' from the first citation replaces 'actual things' in the second, the position criticized would be Locke's—including the incautious use of the term 'after' (see p. 17 above).

Beyond rejecting inner sense as the source of the human representation of succession, Kant also denies that it is the origin of the idea of 'power.' His objection is straightforward. Since the idea of 'power' or 'cause' involves that of 'necessary connection,' it is not possible to acquire this idea through any sense, inner or outer (e.g., A91/B123–24).

4. 'Inner Sense' in Relation to Kantian 'Apperception'

Kant sharply distinguishes inner sense from apperception in the *Critique*, but discussions of the two faculties in the *Duisburg Nachlaß* (1776–78) and in roughly contemporaneous notes are murky about their functions.

> Apperception is the consciousness of thinking, that is, of representations insofar as they are set in the mind. There are three exponents: 1. the relation to subject, 2. the relation of following to each other, 3. composition. (R4674, 17.647, CNotes 160)

How are we to understand the equation between consciousness of thinking and consciousness of representations? The objects of the former seem to be acts, those of the latter to be mental states. In that case, Kant would be changing the relevant faculty from 'inner sense' to 'apperception,' but agreeing with Locke that one faculty is aware of both mental actions and mental contents. In a subsequent passage, inner sense is again presented as an essential contributor to cognition:

> We perceive something only by being conscious of our apprehension, consequently of the existence in our inner sense . . .
> The intellectual element of perception pertains to the power of inner sense. (R4681, 17.667–68, CNotes 174)

The first part of the citation again seems to conflate consciousness of an act (apprehension) with consciousness of existing items (presumably representations), and to attribute both to inner sense. The claim of the second part is expressly denied in the *Critique*:

> This apperception is what must be added to pure imagination in order to make its function intellectual. (A124)

A fragment dated slightly later than the *Duisburg* notes suggests continuing uncertainty about inner sense:

[Crossed out: Inner sense] Consciousness is the intuition of oneself. It would not be consciousness if it were sensation. (R5049, 18.72, CNotes 208)

The second sentence presents a reason for distinguishing 'consciousness' from 'inner sense,' by denying that the former can be a matter of sensation. But the first indicates a temptation to attribute an awareness or intuition of oneself, and so consciousness, to inner sense.

Kant berates his contemporaries for confusing inner sense and apperception in the B deduction (B152–53):

We intuit ourselves only as we are inwardly **affected**; and this seems contradictory, because we would then have to relate to ourselves as passive. And this is the reason why people in their systems of psychology usually prefer to pass **inner sense** off as being the same as the power of **apperception** (which we carefully distinguish form inner sense). (B153, cf. 7.142)

Some of the criticism may be self-directed. He seems to struggle with the distinction himself. In the A edition transcendental deduction, he carefully distinguishes inner sense from apperception, but along a somewhat different dimension from the active/passive contrast mentioned here. 'Inner sense' is presented in the Transcendental Aesthetic as a faculty by which humans are aware of their own states and so of themselves. The A deduction introduces the faculty of 'apperception' by explicit contrast with the faculty of 'inner sense': Inner sense provides humans with an empirical consciousness of their states and empirical consciousness cannot ground any claim for the necessity of a single subject of consciousness (A107). These distinctions may track each other, because the data accumulated through a passive faculty could not provide a basis for claims of necessity. What is less obvious is how an active faculty can provide such a basis.

Although Kant contrasts apperception with inner sense in respect to active/passive and necessary/empirical in the *Critique*, his most elaborate discussion of the differences between the two occurs in a note to his published *Anthropology* lectures:

If we consciously imagine for ourselves the inner action (spontaneity), whereby a concept (a thought) becomes possible we engage in reflection; if we consciously imagine for ourselves the susceptibility (receptivity), whereby a perception (*perceptio*), i.e. empirical observation, becomes possible, we engage in apprehension; however, if we consciously imagine both acts, then consciousness of the self (*apperceptio*) can be divided into that of reflection and that of apprehension. Reflection is a consciousness of the understanding, while apprehension is a consciousness of the inner sense; reflection is pure apperception, and apprehension is empirical apperception; consequently the former is falsely referred to as the inner sense. (7.134)

This rich account requires a fuller discussion than I give it here. I note just two points that are important for the present issue. The first is a clarification. Kant adds an extra layer: He asks his readers to perform two mental acts: Imagine yourself thinking and imagine yourself perceiving (7.133, 134n.). His interest does not lie in these imaginative exercises themselves, but in their presumed results. By performing these acts of imagination, his students and readers can experience for themselves that it is quite different to be conscious in thinking than to be conscious of the contents that they receive through perception. In this way, they are supposed to see for themselves Locke's error of attributing both sorts of consciousness to a single faculty of inner sense.

A question still seems wide open. Even if being conscious in thinking is very different from being aware of a perceptual content, why not assume that the difference is that between an act and a content so that one faculty might be involved in the awareness of both? Alternatively, Kant's fundamental break with Locke comes in the restriction of inner sense to a faculty that can provide information about mental states and not information about both states and acts; even if cognition requires an active faculty of understanding, why can't inner sense provide information about its acts as well as about the contents of perceptual states?

Although this question won't be fully answered until much later, I offer a hypothesis that would solve two closely related puzzles. How does Kant become so much clearer between the period of the *Duisburg Nachlaß* and the *Critique* that inner sense is too restricted to be the essential faculty supporting cognition? What convinces him that understanding is not just an active faculty, but some type of self-conscious faculty as well? Although other influences may be at work, both changes can be explained by his well-documented study[10] of Johann Nicholas Tetens's *Philosophische Versuche über die menschliche Natur und ihre Enwicklung* (*Philosophical Investigations concerning Human Nature and Its Development*).

Tetens introduces the topic of inner sense under the following heading:

> The representations of inner sense have the same distinguishing characteristic [*Unterscheidungsmerkmal*] of representations. Proof of this through observations. (1777/1979, 1.45).[11]

His opening remarks echo Locke in taking inner sense to provide consciousness of activity and also consciousness of states or representations:

> With the representations that we have of ourselves, of our inner alterations, of our activities and faculties, in general with the kind of things that belong to the representations of inner sense we encounter great obscurity. (1777/1979, 1.45)

He then raises the basic question:

> Should these representations also even be called representations in, that is, the sense that representations of outer objects [are]? (1777/1979, 1.45)

In examining the possible parallels, he takes Christian Wolff's position to be that the representations of outer sense represent objects, because sensations arise in the mind as effects of those objects. In the case of inner sense, what can the sensory impressions be that are made in the mind and that remain there to be later called up by the mind's powers?

Tetens thinks he has found the key to the problem in the fact that the mind cannot perceive and perceive that it perceives at the same time (1777/1979, 1.48). He then offers a positive proposal.

> No change can arise in representations that is not connected to a certain modification in the brain [those who identify brain and soul can substitute 'soul'] . . . Then if from an outwardly directed effort of the thinking power a change is caused in the representations, that change is herewith bound together with a change in the organ [brain or soul], which [change] can again be sensed by the soul. In this way it is comprehensible how a sensation of action on ideas in the soul itself can arise in, that is, the manner that a sensation is caused by an impression that an external object brings forth on the [sensory] organ. (1777/1979, 1.49)

The precise *differentiae* of representations cover those of both inner and outer sense. As objects cause impressions in sensory organs that give rise to sensations that represent the objects, (mental) acts cause impressions on the mind/brain organ that give rise to sensations—which then represent the actions. In light of his analysis, Tetens accepts a criticism of the *cogito* that he attributes to Johann Bernard Merian (1732–1807): Descartes should not have said 'I think,' but 'I have thought' (1777/1979, 1.47).

T. H. Weldon assimilates Tetens's reasoning to Ryle's famous 'one-step-behind' analysis of conscious thought (1958, 256–70) and uses that analysis to explain Kant's position on inner sense. I agree with Henry Allison that the texts do not support this interpretive suggestion. As he notes, one of the few clear doctrines of the *Critique*'s theory of self-consciousness is that it is not inner sense, but apperception, that accounts for awareness in acts of thinking (1983, 260). I would go further. Kant vacillated on the assignment of functions to inner sense and to apperception in the period not much before the *Critique*. It seems more reasonable to think that, in reading Tetens's efforts to spell out the way in which a sense would provide awareness of mental acts, he came to see why an internal sense would be insufficient on its own to explain cognition. A sense could provide only a 'one-step-behind' awareness of thinking and, as will be clear in later chapters, that is too late. So he must assume that the faculty that acts, the understanding, is also conscious in acting.

Kant doesn't lay all this out in his discussion of the 'confusions' of psychologists in the *Critique*, so the reasoning is somewhat mystifying. Psychologists confuse apperception with inner sense, but apperception or understanding is an active faculty, whereas inner sense is a passive faculty. Both claims could be true and psychologists could unconfusedly believe that inner sense is passively aware of acts of understanding. It is only the realization that inner sense is incapable of the sort of action awareness required for cognition that leads him to assume not just an active understanding, but one that also involves some type of awareness, which should then be contrasted with an inner sense that is merely aware of states.

5. Kant's Use of 'Inner Sense'

Beyond denying that humans are aware of thinking through inner sense, Kant also rejects Locke's hypothesis that inner sense offers additional representational contents for cognition. He is explicit that the proper (*eigentlichen*) materials of inner sense are representations that come from outer sense (B67). Further, although he claims that time is the 'form' of inner sense, he denies that inner sense senses temporal relations. He distinguishes the representations of inner sense from the materials that it receives. He agrees with his predecessors and contemporaries that inner sense represents a temporally ordered sequence of mental contents as outer sense represents a world of objects. On his view, however, neither the temporal order of the mental contents, nor the objecthood of the objects is received by these senses. It is these gaps between what the senses receive and what they represent that he believes an account of cognition needs to explain.

Kant maintains that his opponents assume the reality of time, because they think that they are directly aware of the succession of their mental states through inner sense. He argues in the *Critique* that this is wrong. There is no direct awareness of temporal relations. Rather, the representation of the temporal order of the contents of inner sense is derived from the mind's representations of the order of events. For the purpose of this key argument, he needs to assume only what all will grant: Humans are aware of a 'train of thought,' a succession of mental states. He does not assume—but denies—that the awareness of mental succession comes from inner sense.

Nevertheless, for all of the *Critique*'s unfavorable contrasts between the active faculty of apperception that can support claims of necessity and the passive faculty of inner sense that cannot, it is clear from the discussion of Meier that he views inner sense as essential to rational cognition. Humans must be able to represent their representations as such. Kant adopts a then current hypothesis to explain this ability: They are aware of their representations through inner sense. The question is how much this move undermines the resulting theory. Objections to the 'inner sense' theory are legion, but they center on three features. Traditional objections concern the related issues of sense data foundationalism and infallibility. More recently, Shoemaker and others have objected to a perceptual model of self-knowledge on the grounds that it (incorrectly) allows for the possibility of self-blindness (1996).

It is a singular feature of transcendental epistemology in comparison to previous theories that it rejects both sense data foundationalism and infallibility. Kant's reason for clarifying the distinction between inner sense and apperception in the Deduction chapter and in the *Anthropology* is to defend his unorthodox doctrine that the objects of inner sense are just as much 'appearances' as those of outer sense. He explicitly rejects the view of his contemporaries that inner sense is a prior and more reliable source of information than outer sense.[12]

On the other hand, in accepting Locke's theory of inner sense, Kant seems to permit a situation where, roughly, inner sense would malfunction and cognizers might end up self-blind. On the other hand, it follows directly from his theory of cognition that cognizers must be self-conscious. Shoemaker has argued that since malfunction is always a possibility, it is inconsistent to hold that cognizers *must* be self-conscious and to take their source of self-knowledge to be inner sense (1996). As far as I can tell, Kant doesn't see the tension in his views.

Because Kant takes inner sense to be a 'fountain' of self-knowledge of sensations and thoughts, he sees no further need to explain the 'mineness' of representations—how cognizers are aware of representations as theirs. Although he does not focus on this issue, parts of his theory of cognition offer indications of how he could have developed an alternative to inner sense for the case of thoughts or beliefs or judgments. I discuss this alternative in Chapters 9 and 15. What is far less clear is how to craft a distinctively Kantian account of the self-ascription of sensations such as pain.

3

Personal Identity and Its Problems

---

1. Locke's Problems

This chapter lays out several crucial pieces of background to Kant's reflections on the unity of a mind and a person. I begin with Locke's seminal account, a view that Kant criticizes as a theory of the unity of the cognitive subject in the transcendental deduction and criticizes as an account of the continuity of a moral person in the Third Paralogism. Section 2 presents Leibniz's 'friendly amendments' to Locke and so sets up the metaphysical disagreement between them. Section 3 returns to a theme of my earlier work, the role of Hume's denial of the self in the development of Kant's theory of cognition and self-consciousness (1990, Chapter 4). Section 4 develops this theme further by examining Tetens's attempts to counter Hume's scandalous claims.[1] The case won't be complete until we look at the progress made in defending the categories in the *Duisburg Nachlaß*, but I offer a theory of the general shape and timeline of Hume's influence.

Despite the familiarity of these passages, I cite Locke's opening account of what 'person' stands for and his presentation of the 'memory' criterion for easy reference:

> A thinking intelligent being, that has reason and reflection, and can consider itself as itself, the same thinking thing, in different times and places; which it does only by that consciousness which is inseparable from thinking . . . For since this consciousness always accompanies thinking, and 'tis that, that makes every one to be, what he calls *self*; and thereby distinguishes himself from all other thinking things, in this alone consists *personal Identity*, i.e., the sameness of the rational Being: And as far as this consciousness can be extended backwards to any past Action or Thought, so far reaches the Identity of that *Person*; it is the same *self* now as it was then; and 'tis by the same *self* with this present one that now reflects on it, that that Action was done. (ECHU 2.27.9, 335)

Chapter 5 examines issues surrounding the notions of 'consciousness' and 'reflection.' Here I concentrate on identity through time.

Because he rejected the scholastic notion of 'substantial form,' Locke needed to find some alternative means of specifying the identity conditions for individuals through time.[2] He appears to settle on the uniform solution of using the nominal essence attached to sortal terms: Resolving issues of individuation requires attention to our notions of things (ECHU 2.27.7, 332). He argues that humans rank individuals into sorts by nominal and not by real essences by noting that sorting practices are different for different groups (ECHU 3.6.26, 453). He exemplifies the point by considering how different nominal essences of 'man' would classify hard cases.

Locke seems to take the same approach to persons when he prefaces the passage above with the remark that

> To find wherein *personal Identity* consists, we must consider what *Person* stands for. (ECHU 2.27.9, 335)

But there is a special problem about persons, because a nominal essence appears to introduce an intolerable arbitrariness into human and Divine judgment. Whether someone receives earthly or heavenly rewards or punishments for a deed would depend on local linguistic practice.

In a way, Locke's solution to the problem with finding the principle of individuation for persons is brilliant. In the case of 'person,' the nominal essence is given by the consciousness that accompanies thinking and can access previous mental states through recollection. The real basis for the use of the term 'person' (though not the real essence of persons) thus guarantees that no one will be punished for a deed of which his conscience does not accuse him. Still, the problem of unacceptable arbitrariness has not been resolved. It is surely not accidental that he illustrates the changeable character of nominal essences by reference to the term 'man' and not 'person.' Since he spends the rest of this chapter trying to ease worries about arbitrariness, while admitting he could not solve them (ECHU 3.6.28–51, 455–71), he seems to recognize the difficulty quite clearly.

2. Leibniz's Criticisms and Additions

Leibniz's discussion of Locke's proposal in the *New Essays* shows a clear awareness of the arbitrariness problem. It concludes with Theophilus (representing Leibniz) remarking:

> But we have devoted ourselves in this conference to discussions more important than the meaning of words. (1765/1996, 2.27.29, 257)[3]

When Philalethes (representing Locke) repeats (with a few additions) the familiar passage above, Theophilus greets the same consciousness theory with warm agreement:

> I am also of the opinion that consciousness or perception of the ego proves a moral or personal identity. (1765/1996, 2.27.9, 236)

He goes on to note that this difference establishes an important difference between animal souls, which, as monads, are unceasing, and human souls, which are immortal. Both cases exhibit physical and real identity through time, but only the latter case possesses a moral identity that is apparent to the individual. I return to the disagreement (here presented as agreement) about real identity below.

Leibniz's enthusiasm for Locke's position is both honest and a little disingenuous. It's disingenuous, because he had made essentially the same proposal in the *Discourse on Metaphysics*, which appeared four years before Locke's *Essay*. Leibniz differentiated between different forms of immortality. Any substance would persist forever; but the immortality required for spirits must include memory.

> The chief difference [between other substances and spirits] is that they do not know what they are or what they do . . . because they lack reflection about themselves, they have no moral quality. Hence, though animals may pass through a thousand transformations like that which we see when a caterpillar changes into a butterfly, yet from the moral or practical point of view the result is just as if they had perished . . . But the intelligent soul, knowing what it is and being able to say this little word 'I' which means so much, not merely remains and subsists metaphysically . . . but also remains the same morally and constitutes the same character. For it is memory or the knowledge of this 'I' which makes it capable of punishment and reward. (*Discourse on Metaphysics* §34, 325)[4]

Theophilus's 'response' to Philalethes is simply a reiteration of this view, with no claim to priority.

Although Locke and Leibniz agree on the importance of continuity of consciousness to persons, there is a deep metaphysical disagreement. The difference becomes apparent as Theophilus/Leibniz turns to what Locke envisions in contemplating the divergence of personal and real or substantial identity. Leibniz's concern is not with the familiar case of the prince and the cobbler who switch souls, but with the underlying assumption that substantial identity does not matter and so could change while consciousness persisted or vice versa. Setting aside the possibility of an appeal to the power of God, a power that could accomplish anything, Leibniz did not see how Locke thought it possible for personal identity to continue in the absence of real identity.

> [he] should have thought that, according to the order of things, an identity which is apparent to the person concerned—one who senses himself to be the same—presupposes a real identity obtaining through each immediate [temporal] transition accompanied by reflection, or by the sense of *I*; because an intimate and immediate perception cannot be mistaken in the natural course of things. If a man could be a mere machine and still possess consciousness, I would have to agree with you sir; but I hold that that state of affairs is not possible—at least not naturally. (1765/1996, 2.27.9, 236)

Leibniz thought that a person's contemporary consciousness could not err (1765/1996, 2.27.13, 238). To see why he may have thought that awareness of mental transitions was also unerring, we may consider his well-known 'mill' analogy, which also deals with the difference between conscious beings and machines:

> If we pretend that there is a machine whose structure enables it to think, feel, and have perception, one could think of it as enlarged yet preserving its same proportions, so that one could enter it as one does a mill. If we did this, we should find nothing within but parts which push upon each other; we should never see anything which would explain a perception. So it is in the simple substance, and not in the composite substance or machine, that perception must be sought. (*Monadology* §17, 644)

Margaret Wilson analyzes this passage in relation to Kant's contemplation in the Second Paralogism of the parts of a verse scattered among different subjects. Wilson glosses Kant's reasoning (and so indirectly Leibniz's) as follows:

> Let us suppose that the subject of thought is complex and divisible. Then each part of the complex thought will inhere in a different part of the subject. But then the *part* of the subject in which a given part of the thought inheres may be taken as the subject of that (part of the) thought. But then the original must be regarded as divided among a plurality of subjects . . . the supposition that the subject of thought is material . . . leads to the absurd and contradictory consequence that every single thought is constituted of thoughts belonging to a *plurality* of consciousnesses. (1974, 510–11)

Wilson also offers a memorable illustration. She imagines herself to be seeing something green while also experiencing an odor like the smell of cooking cabbage. Leibniz's argument against materialism is then to be understood as claiming that, if one of these sensations were in one consciousness, and the other in another, then nothing would explain the fact that seeing-green-and-smelling-cabbage is one experience with different components (1974, 511).

In Chapter 10, I argue that that is not how to understand Kant's argument for the unity of the subject, though it may be a way of understanding the argument that he criticizes in the Second Paralogism. Wilson's quarry was more Leibniz than Kant and perhaps this is the best way to understand the mill argument. The interpretive suggestion can be extended from the synchronic case to the diachronic case of 'unerring' transitions. As experiencing green-plus-cabbage-smell requires a single unified consciousness, so too would experiencing the transition from thinking A to thinking B. When dealing with moral beings, it is necessary to explain not merely the transition from one state to another (as with all substances), but the *consciousness* of the transition from thinking A to thinking B. This consciousness would be possible only for a simple unified substance; otherwise there would be no experience of transition from one state to another. Hence—barring the miraculous—it is not possible to have consciousness of mental unity in the absence of substantial identity. On this reading the objection to Locke is direct. Locke takes a person to be someone who can, through consciousness, consider himself to be the same across transitions. In Leibniz's view, this implies that a person must have a unitary consciousness and that in turn requires that he be a simple (and identical) substance.

Kant did not adopt either Locke's or Leibniz's theories of mental or personal unity. One way to understand his position is to see him as denying the parameters of their 'debate.' Leibniz presumes that it is necessary to determine the (suitable) relations among Divine and human moral practices, the human way of knowing identity (through consciousness), and the underlying metaphysical reality. Kant rejects the metaphysical debate as insoluble and also as irrelevant to the issues of how humans know their identity and how moral personality should be understood.

3. Kant and Hume

Locke's theory of personal identity was much discussed both by followers and by opponents. In *A Treatise of Human Nature*, Hume alludes to the change in the intellectual agenda after the theory in a less than fully positive way:

> We now proceed to explain the nature of personal identity, which has been so great a question in philosophy, especially of late in England where all the abstruser subjects are studied with ardour and application. (1739/1978, 259)

By placing Locke's theory among the 'abstruser' subjects, Hume situates it in the realm of epistemology and metaphysics as opposed to its original home in practical questions of morality. His substantive discussion of the issue is limited to Book 1 of the *Treatise*, whose topic is the understanding, and to the famous *mea culpa* of the Appendix (1739/1978, 633).

Hume's notorious conclusion is that there is no continuing self:

> The question concerning the substance of the soul is unintelligible . . .
> What we call a *mind* is nothing by a heap or collection of different perceptions . . . which succeed each other with inconceivable rapidity, and are in a perpetual flux and movement . . . There is properly no simplicity in the mind at one time, nor identity in different [times], whatever natural propension we have to imagine that simplicity and identity . . . They are successive perceptions only that constitute the mind. (1739/1978, 250, 252, 253)

Kant makes no references to Hume's no-self theory and scholars believed for many years that he was unaware of the view.[5] That position no longer seems tenable. I (1982a, 1990) have presented evidence that he would have encountered Hume's denial of a continuing self in two books that we have good reason to believe he read: James Beattie's *Essay on the Nature and Immutability of* Truth (1772)[6] and Tetens's *Versuche* (1777/1979). The excerpts about selves presented above are from Beattie's citations from the *Treatise* (1772/1809, 79, 249–50). Kuehn explains that Kant would have had many opportunities to think about Hume's views. Two of his close friends, J. G. Hamann and C. J. Kraus, knew the *Treatise* very well. By Kuehn's report, Kraus, a frequent partner on Kant's daily walks, had practically memorized it; Hamann had translated some of it (1987, 178–89). He also notes that Kant would also have encountered Hume in reading J. C. Lossius (1987, 92–93, 92–93n.). In their survey of the reception of Hume's work in Germany, Günter Gawlick and Lothar Kriemendahl observe that his opinion on personal identity was barely discussed despite its incendiary relation to ongoing disputes (1987, 90n.). On the other hand, they note that it was discussed both by Dietrich Tiedemann and by Tetens in books published in 1777. They take Tiedemann's reaction to be quite superficial; as we shall see below, Tetens's was more far-reaching.

Still, the most compelling evidence for Hume's influence on the *Critique* comes from the text. Two crucial passages from the transcendental deduction present clear echoes of his views on the self:

> There is, in inner perception, a consciousness of oneself in terms of the determinations of one's state. This consciousness of oneself is merely empirical and always mutable; it can give us no constant or enduring self in this flow of inner appearances. (A107)
>
> Otherwise [if I didn't unite different representations in one consciousness] I would have a self as many-colored and varied as I have representations of which I am conscious. (B133)

The strongest evidence against any impact concerns timing. Kant probably learned of Hume's singular opinion through Beattie shortly after the German translation appeared in 1772. As Heiner Klemme observes, he continued to discuss the substantially, simplicity, and identity of the soul in his Metaphysics and Anthropology lectures, however, through the late seventies (1996, 47–48).

Although it seems clear that there was no immediate appreciation of Hume's position, the possibility remains that it exerted an important influence later in the decade as Kant worked on the doctrines of the *Critique*. Henry Allison argues that proving that Kant had access to Hume's views falls short of establishing influence. He also sets a high bar for proof:

> it would be necessary to show from Kant's discussions of apperception during the 'silent decade'—more specifically, from the time of the *Duisburg'she Nachlaß* to the publication of the *Critique*—that Kant was concerned with the Humean problem. (1996, 191, n. 15)

I don't think it is possible to meet Allison's challenge as posed: Kant did not take up Hume's concerns.[7] Instead, I argue in the next section that when he reencountered Hume through reading Tetens in 1777, he drew on his predecessor's insights to advance his own concerns in establishing the categories and in curtailing metaphysical speculation.

4. Tetens (and Hume)

According to the above chronology, Kant encountered Hume's rejection of a continuing self in 1772 and again in 1777 in Tetens's *Versuche*. One reason to think that these engagements produced different reactions is their differing contexts. By the time he read Tetens's investigations, Kant had sketched some lines of argument for the categorial principles in the *Duisburg Nachlaß*. A second reason is the context in which Hume's denial of the self appears in the *Versuche*. Having considered the nature of representations, feeling and sensations, perception and consciousness, thinking and the thinking power in the first four inquires, Tetens turns to his fifth 'Inquiry':

> On the origin [*Ursprung*] of our cognition [*Kenntnisse*] of the objective existence of things. (1777/1979, 1.373)

It is reasonable to think that Kant would have had considerable interest in this topic. The fifth section of the fifth inquiry comes even closer to his interests. Its topic is

> of the origin of the fundamental concepts [*Grundbegriffe*] of the understanding, those required for judgments on the existence of things. Concepts of a subject and of specific properties [*Beschaffenheiten*]. The concept of our I, as a thing. (1777/1979, 1.388)

Tetens explained that this section would address the following overstuffed question:

> How do general representations and concepts arise, [representations and concepts] of things, of specific properties that are in things, of substance and of accidents, of an actual thing or object, of our I, and of outer objects, and of the inherence of a property in the former or the latter, of subjective and objective existence? (1777/1979, 1.388)

Feeling perhaps that he was overreaching, Tetens retreats. He will just lay out the basic lines of a fruitful investigation; he refers his readers to Locke and to Leibniz for the remainder that he is unable to cover.

Tetens assumes, following Locke, that the basic answer to the question must lie in abstraction from sensed materials. He takes perception to be the source of material for concepts of things and of their properties. In this discussion, he elaborates the brief account of the first of three representing activities that he had presented in Inquiry 1, section 13 (1777/1979, 1.104–7). Section 5 of Inquiry 5 provides the following account of perception. When someone has an image, this sensation may consist in a multitude (*Menge*) of uncountable small feelings that follow each other. Even though that feeling may contain many simpler simultaneous ones in it, it is, for the human, a unitary feeling. The same act of consciousness that has joined these small feelings in the one distinguishes it as one sensation. And as a sensation, it is simple, unified, and without parts. Although the whole sensation of an image contains different colors, [e.g.], these are different parts of it only in a limited sense, for humans don't see it that way, but as an undivided whole. Since the sensation has been singled out, it is easily apperceptible (1777/1979, 1.378–79, 1.389–90).

In this section, Tetens lays out an Empiricist abstraction theory of concept formation, suitably modified by an appreciation of Leibniz's recognition of imperceptible or 'small' perceptions. The similarities between the description of the first phase of perception and the A deduction's 'first' synthesis of apprehension in intuition are too striking to be coincidental. Kant posits an act of synthesis that 'runs through' a multitude and holds it together in a single intuition. As a single intuition occurring at a single moment in time, it possesses 'absolute unity' even though it contains a manifold of representation (A99). The parallels suggest that he studied this piece of Tetens's lengthy work with some care.

Tetens continues by sketching some possibilities about how the concepts of thing as 'subject' and property as 'predicate' might arise from these original sensations. Then he turns immediately to Hume, the author of the 'beguiling work on human nature' (1777/1979, 1.392).

Hume had presented the idea that we have of our soul or self:

> as [having] a content of a particular multitude [*Menge*] of impressions that follow each other, but are separate and scattered [*zerstreuter*], out of whose combination by the imagination is made the idea of a single whole as one subject, which contains [*in sich halten*] the single impression [*das einzelne Empfundene*] as its specific property. (1777/1979, 1.392)[8]

He reports Hume as drawing the conclusion with which his opponents charge him: He denies the existence of the soul; humans have evidence only of immediately felt states and changes and not of the self as a single thing, a whole thing, a real thing (1777/1979, 1.392).

Tetens thought that the familiar rejoinder of Reid and Beattie—the view runs counter to human understanding—was basically correct. Still, he believed that it would be better to provide an alternative way to ground the belief in a self, an alternative that would reveal where Hume had erred. Tetens maintained that Hume had underestimated the materials available for solving the problem of continuing identity:

> I feel a representation; and another one, also an activity of thinking, an expression of will and so forth, and these feelings are different and actual. However, I also feel still more. (1777/1979, 1.393)

Tetens's view was that Hume's focus on the objects of consciousness led him to overlook an important circumstance: Whenever someone feels or senses a representation and is directly conscious of it, she is also conscious that this feeling of modification is merely a noticeable landmark in a much larger, extended, stronger, although for the most part obscure or, perhaps, somewhat clear, feeling. The concept of the identity of the I arises from the comparison of the present feeling of our I as a subject with a similar feeling in its previous property, a feeling that has been reproduced (and so can be compared). It follows that the idea a man has of himself is not that of a collection of individual representations that have been made into a whole by the imagination, like soldiers in a regiment. Rather, the connection lies in the feeling itself, in its nature, and not in a connection made by the self through the imagination (1777/1979, 1.393–94).[9]

Rational Psychology is discussed in greater detail in the next chapter. To appreciate how Kant might have reacted to reading these passages in Tetens, however, we need to consider part of the theory here. Oddly, from our post-Kantian perspective, Rational Psychology was supposed to be founded upon Empirical Psychology. Empirical Psychology would work out the faculties required for cognition and that material would be the subject matter of Rational Psychology. In particular, Empirical Psychology would establish the soul's existence and Rational Psychology would appeal to considerations about being in general to determine its particular properties of substantiality, simplicity, and identity. Against this background, Tetens is presenting Hume as maintaining that the first (and essential) part of this research program cannot get off the ground. Empirical Psychology cannot establish the soul's existence.

Tetens is not a Rational Psychologist but a follower of Locke. Still, he is clearly worried about providing an Empirical basis that is capable of supporting the theories of Rational Psychology. After presenting his alternative account of the origin of the concept of an 'I' in terms of 'same feeling' in section 5, he begins the next section by observing that it is radically incomplete. As it stands, the concept of a subject and its properties is not yet a complete concept of a thing as an object; it is even further from the concept of a substance. In particular, the concepts of being or actuality, subsisting [*Bestehen*] or continuing [*Fortdauern*], and subsisting for itself need to be added to it (1777/1979, 1.395). Presumably Kant appreciated the problem as well as Tetens did.[10] What Tetens's discussion makes clear is that the façade of Rational Psychology cannot be built on the Empirical foundation standardly assumed for it. An Empirical derivation of the 'I-representation' yields far too little.

In the 1770s, Kant had apparently claimed in both his Metaphysics and his Anthropology lectures that humans have an intuition of a self (28.265, 25.10, 25.244, 25.473–74). Reading the *Versuche* should have brought home to him that this is simply incorrect. Hume's ironic thought experiment of 'looking' for an impression of the self and Tetens's suggestion of a self 'feeling' rather than an impression of a self make a self-intuition claim highly implausible. The status of the apperceptive-I in the *Duisburg Nachlaß* is controversial. Some interpreters suggest that it is a substantial subject, others an empirical subject. Oddly, from the perspective of the *Critique*, Kant never focuses on the question of the origin of the representation 'I' or on the necessity of this representation for cognition. Rather, consciousness is characterized as the model and/or ground of *a priori* representations—of objects (R4674, 17.647, CNotes 160, R4676, 17.656, CNotes 166, R4678, 17.660–61, CNotes 168–69).

The *Duisburg Nachlaß* casts *a priori* concepts as, roughly, rules for judging objects that are necessary for any experience. Given this new and fundamentally different approach to the *a priori* and Tetens's (unintentionally) convincing demonstration that there is a serious problem about the origin of the I-representation, it would have been natural for him to begin to think of the 'I' along these lines: 'I' can only be an *a priori* representation that therefore needs justification and justification that can only be provided by showing its necessity for the experience of objects.

Wolfgang Carl has pursued a line of research that casts some doubts on the connections just drawn between Tetens's discussions in the *Versuche* and the development of Kant's thought. I take a brief look at his objections, because it is an important part of my reading of the Deduction argument for apperception that the case is made on the basis of the lack of an 'I' intuition. And that reading is made more plausible by the historical background offered in this chapter. The Tetens materials provide a basis for rejecting the claims of Rational Psychology and they are often thought to have led to Kant's 'discovery' of the Paralogisms. Carl offers reasons for thinking that this straightforward scenario is not quite right.

The issue concerns the contents and dating of a set of student notes from Kant's Metaphysics lectures, a set now referred to as 'L_1.' These notes are interesting, because Carl takes them to show that Kant had already embraced the theories of cognitive capacities that will fill the A deduction and which are generally traced to Tetens's influence. Yet the notes also present what seems to be the standard Rational Psychology line on the simplicity, substantiality, and identity of the subject.[11] The dating of the notes has varied. At one point, they were thought to be early, partly because of the presence of the doctrines of Rational Psychology. Carl's careful analysis places them somewhere between 1777–78 and 1779–80, and so between Kant's reading of the *Versuche* and the A edition. He argues further that a very important *Nachlaß* sketch of the Deduction dating from 1780 ('B12,' 23.18, CNotes 258–60) need not presuppose the discovery of the Paralogisms (Carl, 1989a, 119).

Carl documents that Kant saw Tetens's influence on him as limited. He concedes that Kant described Tetens as one of a small group (the others were Moses Mendelssohn and Marcus Herz) who might be able to understand the new method of doing philosophy presented in the *Critique*.[12] He observes, however, that Kant sharply constrains the inspiration that Tetens could have provided:

> **Tetens** investigates the concept of pure reason merely subjectively (human nature), I investigate them objectively. The former analysis is empirical, the latter transcendental. (R4901, 18.23, CNotes 199, cited by Carl, 1989a, 116 and 120)

More broadly Carl's argument is that it is a mistake to understand Kant's cognitive theory as having been freed from Rational Psychology only through coming to rest on Tetens's empirical psychology (1989a, 115–26 and 183). This assimilation is especially tempting because of an issue that I have not mentioned: the theory of productive imagination, an imagination that does not merely repeat the data of sense, but 'enhances' it. Although this crucial element of Kant's view is usually also traced to Tetens,[13] I agree with Carl's overarching point. Kant's analyses of the necessary conditions for cognition are entirely different from Tetens's attempt to work out Lockean derivations for key concepts.[14]

On the other hand, the fact that Kant's approach to philosophy differs at a fundamental level from Tetens's hardly implies that he learned nothing from his extensive reading of the *Versuche*. In the preceding chapter, I made a case that Tetens's attempt to work out why inner sense was a sense could well have led him to see that it was unsuitable as the central faculty responsible for rational cognition. Tetens didn't provide Kant with a positive account of the faculty of apperception; he characterized 'inner sense' in a way that allowed him to see that it could not be the key faculty in cognition. Here I make a parallel claim: Tetens's efforts to fill in the details of an Empirical descent for the 'I' that could serve as the needed input to Rational Psychology made the question of the source of this representation prominent, while simultaneously showing that neither Empiricism nor Rational Psychology had a plausible answer to the question and so were ripe for criticism on this issue.

Much later I explain how the absence of an I-intuition is critical both to Kant's argument for the 'I' of apperception and to his diagnosis of the errors of Rational Psychology. But even at this point, we can see that his close study of the *Versuche* would account for the odd way in which he chose to present his distinctive 'I' theory in the A deduction (already cited in part above, on p. 32).

> There is, in inner perception, a consciousness of oneself in terms of the determinations of one's state. This consciousness of oneself is merely empirical and always mutable; <u>it can give us no constant or enduring self in this flow of inner appearances.</u> But what is to be represented **necessarily** as numerically identical cannot be thought as such through empirical data. <u>A condition that is to validate such a transcendental presupposition must be one that precedes all experience and that makes experience itself possible.</u> (A107, my underscoring)

Kant's main point is that insofar as the numerical identity of the self is represented as necessary, then no empirical derivation of that identity is possible. On the other hand, no philosopher on either the Empiricist or Rationalist side of the origins of ideas debate had to be reminded that Empirical data could not be a source of necessity. He prefaces this Leibnizian chestnut with the (highlighted) claim that an Empirical derivation cannot produce a representation of a continuing self at all. Tetens's compounding of Hume's failure to find a plausible Empirical basis for knowledge of a continuing self presented him with an argumentative opening. Since no one in his right mind doubted that continuing selves exist, these failures provide some space for Kant to introduce his *prima facie* implausible view that the identity of the self can be established only as a necessary condition for cognition. And that is the approach that he immediately lays out in the last sentence of the passage.

Although I agree with Carl about the gulf in methodology between Tetens and Kant, I am not convinced by his argument about timing. Kant writes to Marcus Herz in April 1778 about his exhausting reading of Tetens. Carl's argument is that if he had discovered the Paralogisms from the *Versuche*, then L_1, possibly from lectures during the next academic year or the year after that, should not contain doctrines of Rational Psychology. These notes also present him as repeating the claim that humans intuit themselves (28.224, CMet 44). So the objection can be made that there is no influence: If he'd been influenced by Tetens's discussion of Hume's denial of a self, then he would not maintain in the lectures reported in L_1 that the self is intuited.

My resistance to this line of reasoning is that it rests on the assumption that the 'discovery' of the Paralogisms and the acceptance of the lack of any intuition of a self were something like 'Eureka' experiences. Karl Ameriks has argued that Kant's full appreciation of the ramifications of his position on the 'I' is evident only in the B edition of the *Critique* (2000, 217–20). For reasons I give in the next chapter, I think that timeline is too slow. Yet, Ameriks's suggestion that Kant took some time to come to grips with his radical doctrine of the 'I' seems plausible. Further, it is reasonable to believe that he would not immediately start to lecture on the philosophically notorious and theologically parlous Humean position on intuiting the self. If he believed that Hume's position was also fundamentally wrong—because humans do know themselves to be continuing subjects—then there would be additional reason to delay until he could provide a positive account of the consciousness of self-identity.

Cognitive capacities are introduced in the lectures reported in L_1 that are similar to the A deduction's 'synthesis of apprehension' (the 'formative' faculty that produces images, 28.235–36, CMet 53–54) and 'synthesis of reproduction' (the 'faculty of imitation,' 28.236, CMet 54), but there is no hint of a faculty of apperception. In the 'third' slot, Kant talks about a 'faculty of anticipation.' So the L_1 notes do not present the *Critique*'s theory of the 'I' that can fill the void that is left once the lack of an intuition of the 'I' is acknowledged. I do not accept the thesis Carl aims to deflate—that Tetens is the (total) source of Kant's 'discovery' of the Paralogisms. In my view, Tetens's investigation led Kant to see that the 'I' representation does not arise from any intuition, but can only be *a priori* and, consequently, that Rational Psychology is inadequately based. More important, they led him to see the source of the I-representation as an important philosophical problem and one that holds the key to solving his long-standing difficulty with justifying the categories. But much further work is required to figure out how exactly this representation figures in cognition and then to see, from that work, where Rational Psychology went wrong.

Finally, although L_1 presents the claims for the substantiality, simplicity, and immateriality of the soul, it also provides evidence of doubt. In relation to the argument about immateriality, Kant is reported as saying:

> This works only insofar as this main category proves the consciousness of a subject, which is distinguished from the body, thus proves a soul; therefore we can already speak of a soul to that extent:
>
> 1. of my subject and my state;
> 2. of things outside me. (28.226, CMet 46)

If the note-takers were accurate enough to capture nuance, then he was offering a *caveat*—this chain of reasoning stands or falls depending on whether the consciousness of a subject *qua* substance can be assumed.

4

Rationalist Metaphysics of Mind

1. The Role of Rationalism

Chapter 1 offers a sketch of Kant's ambivalent relation to Rationalist metaphysics. This is particularly evident in the letter to Christian Garve: Having first asserted that the *Critique* does no metaphysics, Kant writes that the only way that a truly metaphysical proposition can be proven is by showing its relation to the sources of pure cognition. Despite the appearance of tension, the claims are consistent. Revealing that a metaphysical principle has an essential role to play in the development of cognition is not 'doing metaphysics'; it is doing epistemology. One plan for the *Critique* is to trace various claims of Rationalist metaphysics back to one of two 'higher' faculties, 'understanding' and 'reason.' The principles that can be traced to the *necessary* activities of the understanding in constructing cognition will be vindicated. Those laid at reason's door have a mixed fate. Some will also be vindicated, though only in the guise of 'regulative' principles; others will be dismissed as thwarting cognition. The metaphysical principle dearest to Kant—freedom—has a different fate. It is reassigned to the realm of practice.

This chapter presents Leibniz's metaphysics of the cognitive subject and several further Rationalist principles. Seeing these principles in their original context adds detail to Chapter 1's sketch, by illuminating the radical nature of Kant's transformation of metaphysics. The chapter also lays out the basic claims of Rational Psychology, the alleged discipline that he exposes as no discipline at all in the Paralogisms chapter. Although it mainly provides background materials for later discussions, the chapter also details some of Kant's objections to the theses discussed. These objections provide constraints for interpreting his theories, since it is reasonable to believe that he would eschew Rationalist positions whose weaknesses he clearly understood.

2. Leibniz's Elegant I-Theory

Leibniz takes monads to be the fundamental constituents of reality. In the *New Essays*, he tries to carry out his dispute with Locke without presupposing his own metaphysics (1765/1996, 1.1.1, 74). Still, his views are never far from the surface. After criticizing Philalethes' same organization criterion for numerical sameness, Theophilus continues:

> As for substances which possess in themselves a genuine, real, substantial unity . . . and as for substantial beings, which are sustained by a single spirit: one can rightly say that they remain perfectly 'the same individual' in virtue of this soul or spirit which makes the *I* in substances which think. (1765/1996, 2.27.4, 231–32)

The *New Essays* idea of a 'substantial being that is sustained by a single spirit' appears to be the same as the *Monadology*'s notion of a 'living body with a dominant entelechy or monad' (*Monadology* §70, 650). How a dominant monad dominates is unclear. The suggestion is that, since what monads do is represent, the body that a particular monad dominates represents the world in a distinctive way (presumably, from a unique apparent spatial location) (*Monadology* §63, 649). The soul has a particular mode of representing the world and the body it dominates uses the same mode of representation, although its representations are more obscure (*Monadology* §60, 62, 63, 648–49).

Even if representational isomorphism partly explains, or at least characterizes, the vital unity of the different monads in a living body, Leibniz still needs to explain how the dominant monad or single spirit retains its identity through time (and so that of the substantial being it sustains). His account of this crucial notion is somewhat clearer. As a created being, a monad must change through time. He explains how a monad remains the same through time, by explaining how it changes through time.

> (*Monadology* §11, 643–44) The natural changes in monads come from an *internal principle*, since an external cause could not influence their interior.
>
> (*Monadology* §12, 644) But besides the principle of change there must be some distinguishing *detail in that which changes*, which constitutes the specific nature and the variety, so to speak, of the change.
>
> (*Monadology* §13, 644) This detail must enfold a multitude in the unity or the simple.
>
> (*Monadology* §14, 644) The passing state which enfolds and represents a multitude in unity or in the simple substance is merely what is called *perception*.
>
> (*Monadology* §15, 644) The action of the internal principle which brings about change or the passage from one perception to another can be called *appetition*.

The first thesis expresses the doctrine from which he abstracts in the *New Essays*. Since substances cannot interact, thoughts cannot be acquired from the interaction of outer senses and objects. As Leibniz sees it, he can explain the way a monad changes through time (and hence the way it preserves its identity through change) by making use of two elements, one which changes, the perception, and one which initiates changes, an 'internal principle' that is understood on the model of 'appetite,' a tendency to go towards a goal.

Although Leibniz's metaphysics of the soul was simple in a way—a soul is a substance whose accidents change through time *via* the operation of its internal principle—his account of the continuity of rational souls, or spirits, was complex. As we saw in Chapter 3, the continuity of spirits—as opposed to animals—requires both substantial unity (through an internal principle) and memory. We also saw the importance of awareness of transitions from one state to another, an awareness that ruled out error. The *New Essays* offers yet a further bond carrying identity. In considering whether a spirit could lose all perceptions of past existence, Theophilus demurs:

> [A] spirit retains impressions of everything which has previously happened to it . . . but these states of mind are mostly too minute to be distinguishable and for one to be aware of them . . . It is this continuity and interconnection of perceptions which make someone really the same individual. (1765/1996, 2.27.14, 239)

That is, self-identity is carried by the train of '*petites perceptions*.' Leibniz's position is consistent. The internal principle would be the ground of the continuous series of unconscious perceptions, the immediate transitions that are consciously accessible, and the memories that are consciously accessible. All three latter conditions hold because of the sort of internal principles that spirits have; the latter two also provide epistemic access to their identities for spirits.

Kant reportedly discussed the Leibnizian notion of an 'internal principle' in Metaphysics lectures presented in notes L_1 (the set of student notes described in the preceding chapter). The topic is freedom of the will and he is alleged to have used the notion of an internal principle to explicate what he means by 'transcendental' freedom or spontaneity.

> But it is asked: do the actions of the soul, its thoughts, come from the inner principle which is determined by no causes, or are its actions determined by an external principle? If the latter, then it would have only spontaneity in some respect, and thus not freedom in the transcendental sense. (28.268, CMet 80)

On the eve of composing the A edition of the *Critique* (1778–1780) Kant seems to be tempted by the idea that an internal principle offers a useful way of thinking about transcendental freedom. But he is also represented as suspicious. He is said to maintain that as long as he is conscious to himself of an active action, to that extent I act from an inner principle of activity according to the power of free choice, without an outer determination; only then do I have absolute spontaneity (28.269, CMet 80)

According to the note-takers, however, he also raised a devastating objection. How can *created* beings be free of external influence? Even if they act freely by their inner principles, they would still be determined in their thoughts and actions by the creator who provided them with the internal principle. Allegedly he used the same metaphor of a 'turnspit' that he invokes in an unusual display of pique in the *Critique of Practical Reason* when he criticizes Leibniz for explaining freedom in terms of an *automaton spirituale* (5.97, CPract 218).[1] He is reported as resolving the issue in the same way that he does there: Even though a transcendentally free, but dependent being cannot be conceived through reason, it cannot be refuted either (28.268, CMet 80).

Besides his recognition that internal principles could not solve the problem of the transcendental freedom (and so moral responsibility) of a created being, Kant also opposes the doctrine of substantial internal principles on metaphysical grounds. In one of his earliest philosophical writings, the *Novo Dilucidatio* of 1755, he objected that an internal principle that worked as Leibniz claimed would be metaphysical nonsense. The problem is that

> It is necessary that whatever is posited by a determining ground be posited simultaneously with that determining ground. For having posited the determining ground, it would be absurd if that which was determined by the determining ground were not posited as well . . . it follows that . . . change cannot take place by means of those factors which are to be found within the substance. If, therefore, a change occurs it must be the case that it arises from an external connection. (1.411, C1755 37–38)

Kant's point is sound. If a simple, causally isolated substance contains the determining ground or sufficient condition for its own changing perceptions, then at T_1 it must contain the determining ground for whatever perception it would have at T_2. If it contained the sufficient condition for this perception at T_1, however, then it must have that perception at T_1. Unless time is efficacious, the instant that a sufficient condition for an effect comes into being, the effect must come into being. In that case, however, an internal principle could not account for the changes in representations in a mind through time. From this metaphysical argument, Kant argues further in the *Nova Dilucidatio* that changes in the soul establish the existence of objects outside the soul with which it stands in reciprocal connection and that it is necessary for souls to be connected with bodies (1.412, C1755 39).

Kant never gave up his opposition to the thesis that the internal principle of a simple substance could account for alteration in that substance. As Paul Guyer notes, this metaphysical view stands behind the *Critique*'s central arguments for the causal principle in the Second Analogy and against idealism in the Refutation of Idealism (1987, 11–12). The internal principle provides the metaphysical glue that binds the separate parts of Leibniz's theory. It accounts for the real (and so moral identity) of a soul and explains the transition of the soul from one state to the next. By contrast, Kant will explain the transition from one representation to another in a very different way, by appealing to the activities of the understanding that are required for cognition.

3. Faculties, Powers and Substances

Beyond the theory of monads, Leibniz offers further metaphysical principles that concern the study of the mind. He also offers a bit of background for questions about the soul's faculties and powers in the *New Essays*:

> The question of whether there is a real distinction between the soul and its faculties has long exercised the Scholastics. The realists have said Yes, the nominalists No; and the same question has been debated concerning the reality of various other *abstract beings* which must stand or fall with faculties . . . Faculties or qualities do not act, rather, substances act through faculties. (1765/1996, 2.21.6, 174)

This passage occurs in a discussion of how to understand the 'power' of willing. In a sense Leibniz agrees with Locke that 'freedom of the will' is a misnomer. The will isn't free; the person is (ECHU 2.21, 6–21).

Leibniz also considers powers and faculties in a passage where Theophilus draws a sharp distinction between his position and that of Philalethes. Philalethes has just ventured the 'blank slate' metaphor and Theophilus pounces:

> It may be said that this 'blank page' of the philosophers means that all the soul possesses, naturally and inherently, are bare faculties. But inactive faculties—in short the pure powers of the Schoolmen—are also mere fictions, unknown to nature and obtainable only by abstraction. For where will one ever find in the world a faculty consisting in sheer power without performing any act? There is always a particular disposition to action, and towards one action rather than another. And as well as the disposition there is an endeavour towards action—indeed there is an infinity of them in any subject at any given time, and these endeavours are never without some effect . . . (1765/1996, 2.1.2, 110)

In Leibniz's view, Locke's effort to make the mind plastic to experience falls into metaphysical error. Even a receptive power or faculty must be understood as receiving in some way or other; a capacity that is just receptivity would be impossible.

The issue of the proper way to understand mental capacities was also addressed by Christian Wolff, who has sometimes been considered a systematizer of Leibniz's scattered views. Wolff considered this question in *Rational Thoughts on God, the World, and the Soul of Humans, and all things in general* (1751), better known as the 'German Metaphysics.' Wolff objects that the mere disposition to do something—the possibility of doing it—does not suffice to explain any actual doing. For that, it is necessary to consider a power that acts.

> A power [*Kraft*] should not be confounded with a mere faculty [*Vermögen*]: for a **faculty** is only a possibility of doing something: on the other hand, since a power is a source of alteration, an endeavor to do something must be encountered with a power. (Meta. §117, 61)[2]

Wolff's claim might be understood as an elaboration of Leibniz's: A disposition to do something needs to be supplemented by an account of the disposition becoming effective.

Metaphysics L_1 presents Kant as chastising Wolff for thinking that powers are fundamental:

> **Wolff** assumes one basic power and says: the soul itself is a basic power which represents the universe. It is already false when one says: the soul is a basic power . . . the soul is falsely defined, as Ontology teaches. Power is not what contains in itself the ground of the actual representation, but rather the relation of the substance to the accident, insofar as the ground of the actual representations is contained in it [i.e., in the substance]. **Power is thus not a separate principle, but rather a relation.** Whoever thus says: the soul is power maintains that the soul is not separate substance, but rather only a power, thus a phenomenon and accident. (28.261, CMet 75)

On this point, Kant's position seems closer to Leibniz's. He thinks that Wolff has erred, because properly understood, a 'power' is not the ground of an accident; rather 'power' refers to the relation of a substance to an accident, when the substance contains the ground of the accident.

On the other hand, Kant goes on to agree with Wolff that there is a basic power in the soul from which the others are derived:

> Because the soul is indeed a unity, which will be demonstrated later, and which the I already proves, then it is obvious that there is only one basic power in the soul, out of which all alterations and determinations arise. But **this is a wholly other question: whether we are capable of deriving all actions of the soul, and its various powers and faculties, from one basic power.** This we are in no way in the position [to do], for we certainly cannot derive effects which are actually different from one another from one basic power. (28.261–62, CMet 75)

Notice the direction of argument. From the assumption that the soul is a unity, it can be inferred that it has only one basic power. I return to the highlighted *caveat* below.

The discussions of power and substance in L_1 might be read as evidence that Kant's 'epistemic turn' was not as thorough as his self-descriptions present it to be. He seems to revert to 'old-style' metaphysical principles. In the discussion of power and substance, he makes explicit appeal to ontology; the discussion of basic powers also seems to involve a move straight from the playbook of Rationalist metaphysics, the move from the unity of the soul to its possessing a single power. But if he relied on metaphysical assumptions in L_1—lectures given just one or two years before the A edition—then perhaps the more obviously epistemological claims of the *Critique* also rest on less obvious metaphysical assumptions.[3]

I read L_1 differently. In an earlier section of the notes, Kant allegedly explained that just as there are *a priori* principles of intuition

> likewise we have also ascertained *a priori* principles of thinking. What is the necessary condition of thinking belongs to the objective, and what is a necessary condition of cognition also belongs to things. Objects must conform to the conditions under which they can be cognized; this is the nature of the human understanding. (28.239, CMet 57)

The principles he is referring to are the pure concepts of the understanding. So he is laying out his strategy of characterizing objects not in terms of some fundamental metaphysics, but in terms of the 'objective' conditions under which they can be cognized.

Given that Kant seems to have been self-conscious about his metaphilosophy in L_1, an alternative explanation for the presence of these principles is that he thought that they could be defended by scientific metaphysics. Some evidence that he held such a belief is that he provides warrants for them in the A edition published one or two years later—although the warrants are somewhat different.

According to the L_1 'ontological' definition, references to powers are references to the relations of substances to alterations. After the main event of establishing the principle of determinism is over, the Second Analogy takes up the task of providing a justification for treating 'action' as a 'criterion' of 'empirical' 'permanence' and so of 'substance.' This is a curious passage, because Kant begins by saying that he is leaving the proof of subordinate principles as exercises for the reader—except in this case where he will do it himself.

> How, from action on something, are we to infer at once **the agent's permanence**? (A205/B250)

That is, how can we infer from action to substance? Since action implies power one inference to be established is that from power to substance. He quickly dismisses attempts to provide a defense in terms of definitions as circular.

> Where there is action and hence activity and force [or power, *Kraft*], there is also substance, and in substance alone is to be sought that fertile source of appearances. That is nicely said; but if we are to explain what we mean by substance and want to avoid the fallacy of circular reasoning, then the answer is not so easy. How, from action on something, are we to infer at once **the agent's permanence**—this permanence being, after all so essential and peculiar a characteristic of substance ([as] phenomenon)? (A204/B250)

He resolves the problem by drawing on what has already been established:

> Action already means the relation of the causality's subject to the effect. Now any effect consists in what occurs, and hence in the mutable that designates time in terms of succession. Therefore the ultimate subject of the mutable is the **permanent** as the substratum of everything that varies, i.e., substance. For according to the principle of causality actions are always the first basis of all variation by appearances; hence actions cannot reside in a subject that itself varies, since otherwise other actions and another subject determining that variation would be required. By virtue of this does action prove, as a sufficient empirical criterion, the substantiality of a subject, without my needing first of all to search for the subject's permanence by perceptions that I have compared. (A205/B250–51)

Action is indicated through alteration. This might seem to show only that the before and after states of the thing altered must be states of a permanent against which change can be cognized. But actions are changes in the agent. This point is underscored in L_1's account of power as a relation: substance A changes substance B from state 1 to state 2. But substance A does not always stand in that relation to substance B; rather it does so only for the time from B being in state 1 to its being in state 2. Since A's altering of the states of B is an alteration in A, from not doing the altering to doing it, by the argument of the First Analogy, that alteration can be cognized only on the assumption that it is a change in a substance. I am not going to defend Kant's arguments in the Analogies. My claim is only that since he was able to provide what *he* took to be a Critical defense of the 'power to substance' 'ontological' principle in the course of arguing for his derivative 'action to substance' epistemological principle 1781,[4] his use of it in the immediately preceding period need not indicate the continuing influence of Rationalist metaphysics. Since he also briefly introduces his new approach in L_1, it seems more reasonable to assume he was self-conscious in his handling of metaphysical issues and principles in those lectures.

In the case of the second 'metaphysical' principle of L_1, Kant was reportedly careful about how it needed to be treated. We can infer from the unity of the subject to a basic power underlying its various faculties, but we must beware. We may not infer that it is possible to derive all actions of the soul and its powers from one basic power. Rather, we must look and see whether the powers are reducible to one. This apparently 'ontological' principle of one subject-one basic power is thus an early statement of the 'regulative' principle of reason to seek homogeneity in diversity that is also defended in the *Critique* (A682/B710)—although only as a regulative principle. Indeed, if the notes are to be believed, he seems to have made the special status of this principle clear in his succeeding remarks:

> Now since in the human soul we meet real determinations or accidents of essentially different kinds, the philosopher strives in vain to derive these from one basic power. It is indeed this which is the main rule of the philosopher: that he strive to bring everything to one principle, so far as it is possible, so

that the principles of cognition are not increased too much; but whether we also have cause to reduce various powers in the human mind to one power does not follow from that. (28.262, CMet 76)

4. Rational Psychology

Wolff explains the principles and methods of Rational Psychology in both the *German Metaphysics* and in the *Prolegomena to Empirical and Rational Psychology*. My discussion of the latter draws on Robert J. Richards's illuminating analysis (1980). After laying out Wolff's view, I consider Kant's discussions of Rational Psychology in his Metaphysics and Anthropology lectures.

Wolff opens the *German Metaphysics* in Cartesian fashion with an account of the indubitable basis of human knowledge:

> We are conscious of ourselves and other things, of this no one can doubt; . . . For, how would he deny or bring something into doubt to me if he is not conscious of himself or other things? . . . Whoever is conscious of that, which he denies or brings into doubt, is the same as the one [who is so conscious]. (Meta. §1, 1)

Although Wolff seems to begin where Descartes left off at the end of the Second Meditation, there is a crucial difference. For Wolff, the first items of consciousness are the self—and other things. As we shall see in the next chapter, much turns on this difference.

Again echoing Descartes, Wolff maintains further that knowledge so obtained is certain:

> These truths, which are certified [*bestätiget*] through unerring [*untrueglich*] experiences, are the ground of the rules, according to which the powers of the soul are directed in cognition, as in willing or refraining, consequently [rules] of logic, ethics and politics (Meta. §191, 107)

Because its foundations are thus secure, knowledge of the soul originates in Empirical Psychology.

Empirical Psychology works out the various faculties required for cognition. Its data then become the basis for Rational Psychology; for this reason Rational Psychology is less reliable than Empirical Psychology. The former discipline proceeds by bringing the

> **occurrences in our souls of which we are conscious...** (*Prolegomena to Empirical Psychology*, no. 2, cited in Richards, 1980, 231)

under accurate definitions and then determining the sufficient reason for their occurrence. The sufficient reason is the operation of a power. Any performance of an action implies that in the subject features exist through which actions are able to be distinctly explained, so that one may understand how they were able to occur (Wolff's *Ontologica*, no. 716, note, cited in Richards [1980, 235, n. 5])

Rational Psychology is also somewhat unreliable, because it rests on ontology and cosmology. Starting from the fact of the soul's existence and its various powers, Rational Psychology appeals to ontology to establish propositions about it that are true of being in general; it appeals to cosmology to understand the soul in relation to the theory of body (*Prolegomena to Rational Psychology*, no. 3, Richards, 1980, 234–35).

We can see this methodology in operation in a brief discussion in the *German Metaphysics*. Wolff starts with the metaphysical (rational) view that all change in bodies happens through motion (Meta. §738, 460). He then explains that thinking cannot be explained by the motions of different bodies (Meta. §739–42, 461–63). This enables him to conclude that the soul must be simple and so a substance (Meta. §742, 463, §743, 463). From these claims, he is able to infer further that the various powers of the soul, that is, imagination, memory, the capacity to reflect, understanding, sensible desire, and will, must all be expressions of a single power of representation (Meta. §747, 465–66).[5]

We have already encountered a further Wolffian doctrine:

the basic power of the soul is to represent the world. (Meta. §784, 488)

That power is what accounts for all of the soul's effects, from cognition to action. This theory provides him with a striking (if not very plausible) version of Leibniz's doctrine that real identity is carried through the internal principle that produces the changes in a substance from one state to another. On Wolff's view, it is the basic power of representation that accounts for both the continuity and the substantiality of a soul.

We encounter in the soul nothing further than a power to represent the world, and this [power] is that in the soul that endures and that makes it a self-standing being. (Meta. §784, see also §127, 66, §743, 463–64)

Where Leibniz had powers dependent on substances, amounting to nothing more than (apparent) relations between substances, Wolff has substances dependent on (their) enduring powers. This is the view Kant is reported as criticizing for ontological unsoundness in L_1.

Doctrines of Rational Psychology appear in notes from both Kant's lectures on Anthropology and his lectures on Metaphysics. This is helpful, because, of the two extant sets of pre-*Critique* Metaphysics lecture notes (CMet xxii), only L_1 is reasonably well-ordered.[6] Fortunately, several pre-*Critique* Anthropology lecture notes present the Rational Psychology theses of the substantiality, simplicity, spontaneity, and personality. In lectures during the winter of 1772–73, Kant is reported as saying:

It is remarkable, that we are able to represent so much under the I, for by analysis of it we find that we can think the following parts: the simplicity, the substantiality, a rational substance . . . I reflect over the faculties that lie in the soul. The freedom of the soul. (25.244, 245)

Similar remarks appear in notes from the course given in the winter term of 1775–76.

This concept of I . . . from which much can be derived. Substantiality . . . Simplicity . . . Spontaneity . . . (25.473)

Notes from later Anthropology lectures have Kant still talking about the special quality of the representation 'I,' but tying it to practical matters. Although the 'I' is what distinguishes men from the animals, if a horse could say 'I,' then a man must regard him as part of his society (25.859) (as opposed to regarding him as a substantial, simple, spontaneous being). Metaphysics lecture notes after 1781 have Kant mentioning arguments of Rational Psychology only to criticize them (e.g., 29.904, CMet 270).

As Ameriks observes, a reader who comes to the lectures on Rational Psychology from the Paralogisms will be shocked at the inclusion of an argument about freedom (2000, 190). Not only is the topic present, it receives by far the most extensive treatment. After discussing practical freedom, which involves the capacity to act independently of sensory stimuli, and which is described as sufficient for morality (28.267, CMet 80), Kant offers the considerations about inner principles that are to establish transcendental freedom discussed above. Ameriks raises a pressing interpretive question. Given the centrality of freedom to Rational Psychology, as Kant lectured on it, why is there no Paralogism involving spontaneity? Ameriks's hypothesis is that he was not prepared to surrender the possibility of establishing transcendental freedom through the spontaneity required for thought. In his view, the A edition presents a mixed message. Several passages, most prominently a dramatic and oft-quoted remark in the Antinomy's discussion of the regulative use of cosmological ideas, suggest that thinkers have a kind of absolute spontaneity:

In animate but merely animal nature, we find no basis for thinking any power as being other than merely sensibly conditioned. Only the human being . . . cognizes himself also through mere apperception—*viz.* in actions and inner determinations that he cannot class at all with any impressions of the senses. (A546/B574)[7]

On the other hand, Kant makes it fairly clear in both editions that he has

not sought to establish the **actuality** of freedom . . . or even . . . the **possibility** of freedom. (A558/B586)

Ameriks sees a marked shift between the editions, a shift that he thinks was occasioned by Kant's recognition, recorded in the *Critique of Practical Reason*, that his attempt to deduce freedom in the *Groundwork of the Metaphysics of Morals* fails (2000, 203 ff.). The new view is expressed in the General Comment to the second edition Paralogisms chapter:

> Thought, taken by itself, is merely the logical function, and hence is wholly spontaneity in the combination of the manifold of a merely possible intuition . . .
> But insofar as the proposition **I think** says the same as **I exist thinking**, it is not a mere logical function. Rather it determines the subject (which is then taken simultaneously an object); and it cannot take place without inner sense, whose intuition always provides us with the object . . . merely as appearance. (B429)

Ameriks takes this passage to express for the first time a consistently Critical view of self-knowledge: Thinkers cannot know themselves as they are in themselves, even through representing the spontaneity of their thought (2000, 218). He notes that at the end of his life, Kant conceded that only his theoretical philosophy was critical; his practical philosophy was dogmatic, assuming rather than establishing freedom of the will (2000, 218).

Ameriks's claim that it took Kant some time to come to grips with the implications of his theory for self-knowledge seems right. Many additions to the second edition address the issue of what we can know about the self—whether we can know that it exists or its nature (B67–68, B152–53, B157–58, and B157–58n., B422n.).[8] But the case seems different for freedom. As we have seen, he understood the problem of created free beings in L_1. He alludes to the difficulty in a passage that is common to both editions:

> But whether reason is not, even in these actions through which it prescribes laws [of freedom], determined in turn by other influences, and <u>whether what in regard to sensible impulses is called freedom may not in regard to higher and more remote efficient causes in turn be nature</u>—this further question does not concern us in the practical [realm]. (A803/B831, my underscoring)

Although the reference is inexplicit, I agree with Heiner Klemme's suggestion that the 'higher and more remote' cause is God (1996, 93). Kant's solution is that such questions are irrelevant in the realm of practical reason. Shortly before this passage, he is not allusive, but direct in observing the lack of relation between freedom and matters of cognition:

> Accordingly, if these three cardinal propositions [the existence of God, the freedom of the will, and the immortality of the soul] are not at all necessary to us for **knowledge**, and are nonetheless urgently commended to us by our reason, then—I suppose—their importance will properly have to concern only the **practical**. (A799–800/B827–28)

He is blunter in the B edition, suggesting that reason's refusal to answer such questions is its own hint to turn to the practical realm for solutions (B421). Still the common passage is barely less explicit that philosophers should accept and ponder the implications of their inability to resolve these issues theoretically—and that includes the issue of freedom.

The absence of a Paralogism about spontaneity in both editions can be explained without assuming that Kant continues to be tempted by this approach to proving freedom. It is widely agreed that his criticism of Rational Psychology is that its proponents mistakenly believe that they can argue from the prerequisites of thought to the nature of a thinking thing as a simple, identical substance. Had he added a parallel criticism of the spontaneity argument, then his objection would be that the Rational Psychologists wrongly believe that they can infer from the prerequisites of thinking to an absolutely spontaneous, simple, identical substance. At least from L_1 onwards, however, his principal objection to this Rationalist picture was very different: It's internally inconsistent. A simple, identical, *created* substance cannot be understood as absolutely free. Further, it is reasonable to believe that this case is similar to that of the absence of a denial of a self-intuition in L_1. He does not wish to raise a devastating objection to a standard proof for freedom before he has had a chance to lay out the positive *practical* case in its favor.

The L_1 notes present Kant as offering unequal treatment of the other three arguments of Rational Psychology, those concerning substantiality, simplicity, and singleness. The arguments that the soul is a substance and is single are brief and unconvincing.[9]

> The I is the **general subject** of all predicates, of all thinking, of all actions, of all possible judgments that we can pass of ourselves as a thinking being. I can only say: I am, I think, I act. Thus it is not at all feasible that I would be a predicate of something else... I cannot say: another being is the I. Consequently the I, or the soul through which the I is expressed, is a substance. (28.266, CMet 79)

> I am not conscious of myself as several substances. For if there were several thinking beings in a human being, then one would have to be conscious oneself of several thinking beings... I am conscious of myself as one subject. (28.267, CMet)

The difficulty with the first argument is that Kant does not explain why different predicates must be attributed to a general or common subject. Even if we grant that 'I' can't be a predicate, because it is necessary to have a subject for being, thinking, and acting, and that the division between those predicates and subjects is exclusive and exhaustive, nothing follows about attributing more than one predicate to the same subject/substance. In the case of singleness, he dismisses multiple subjects by noting that a cognizer is not conscious of himself as several substances. His positive claim that subjects are conscious of themselves as one subject [not substance] is consistent with his discussion in the Paralogisms chapter, though it is left undeveloped in these lecture notes.

If L_1 is accurate, Kant lays out the argument for simplicity in somewhat more detail. It is the same argument that he later criticizes in the Second Paralogism. For a thought or a representation to be possible, the soul must be simple:

> For if the parts of the representations should be divided among many subjects, then each subject would have only one part of the representation, therefore no single subject would have the whole representation. (28.266, CMet 79–80)

In this case, Kant's students were apparently given a serious argument and one that rests on the possibility of thought and cognition. Because the *Critique* illustrates the point with the words of a verse, I'll refer to this as the 'verse' argument.[10]

According to L_1, Kant also explored the implications of the verse argument for immaterialism. He disagrees with Wolff that simplicity establishes immateriality, because the soul could be simple and material. Instead, he is supposed to have argued that philosophy can establish immateriality

> from nothing more than the expression: **I** . . . Immateriality thus lies in the concept of the **I**. **We cannot prove a priori** the immateriality of the soul, but rather **only so much: that all properties and actions of the soul cannot be cognized from materiality.** (28.272–73, CMet 84)

That is, Wolff is wrong in believing that the philosophy can prove that the soul is immaterial. Its purview is limited to the more modest epistemological point that it is impossible to understand the actions of the soul from a material standpoint. He claims, but does not elaborate, that immateriality can be proven by appeal to the expression 'I.'

So far, we have looked at different pieces separately. By putting them together, we can get a sense of how Kant saw the logic of the arguments of Rational Psychology in the immediately pre-*Critique* period—at least as reported in L_1. Inner principles, transcendental freedom, and the difficulty that humans are creatures are presented under the heading 'Introductory Concepts.' The next large section covers topics in 'Empirical Psychology.' A subsection on the interaction between soul and body offers the argument from the unity of the soul to its having a single power. Recall that Kant is reported as explaining that the assumption of unity will be defended later. That promise is redeemed in the section on Rational Psychology, where he gives the argument for the singleness of the soul. He goes on to argue for spontaneity on the basis of thinking and acting. This discussion does not contradict the earlier treatment. Rather, it repeats the problem flagged in the section on 'Introductory Concepts.'

> Do I have transcendental spontaneity or absolute freedom?
> Here the I must again help out. It is true, the absolute spontaneity cannot be conceived through reason in a dependent being. (28.268, CMet 81)

Slightly later he is reported as reflecting that:

> All practical propositions would have no sense if human beings were not free. (28.269, CMet 81)

Then he repeats the problem of dependent beings a third time. In a subsequent section dealing with Rational Psychology that compares the human soul to other things, he ruminates on the issue of immaterialism.

Far from endorsing the views of Rational Psychology, L_1 raises a number of flags that are left as markers of potential difficulties. In the case of spontaneity, L_1 displays the agonized ambivalence that Ameriks sees in the A edition. Kant seems not to be able to resist offering the argument from the spontaneity of thought and action to absolute freedom—or pointing out its fatal flaw. I have taken a fairly close look at this material, because contemporary readers have been tempted to see Kant as arguing from an analysis of thought to 'freedom' in a weighty sense.[11] It seems to me that both editions move beyond this temptation and present the basic Critical line that the question of freedom cannot be settled by metaphysics or epistemology, but is left open for a decision on practical grounds.[12]

5

Consciousness, Self-consciousness, and Cognition

1. Introduction

The argumentation of the transcendental deduction centers on the relations among consciousness, self-consciousness, and cognition. This chapter traces some debates about these relations from Locke's *Essay* through the period just prior to the A edition. Sometimes the 'debate' is within the thought of a single contributor as he struggles to make sense of these separately difficult notions and of the complex relations among the phenomena they are intended to capture. I begin again with Locke and Leibniz and their proposals for understanding self-consciousness or apperception. I then turn to the debate about Christian Wolff's claim that self-consciousness presupposes object cognition. Drawing partly on recent studies by Udo Thiel and Falk Wunderlich, I present several reactions to Wolff's thesis. H. J. Paton expressed the sense of hopelessness readers feel in trying to follow the 'windings and twistings' of the transcendental deduction (1965, 1.547). Knowing some of the issues about consciousness and cognition that were in play as Kant wrote makes it possible to anticipate a few of the turns. It is also easier to see what he is doing with these issues by contrasting his handling of them with some close alternatives.

2. Locke's 'Reflection' and Leibniz's 'Apperception'

Chapter 2 considers only two aspects of Locke's discussion of 'internal sense.' What are the objects of this sense and how can it be a sense? Despite the use of the term 'internal *sense*,' Locke's remarks can be viewed from a different perspective, as introducing a *sui generis* notion of 'reflection.' The passage below is a piece of the text cited earlier with elided material restored:

> the other fountain is,—*the Perception of the Operations of our own Minds* within us, as it is employ'd about the *Ideas* it has got;—<u>which Operations, when the</u>

soul comes to reflect on, and consider, do furnish the understanding with another set of *Ideas*, which could not be had from things without: and such are, *Perception, Thinking, Doubting, Believing, Reasoning, Knowing, Willing*, and all the different actings of our own Minds. (ECHU 2.1.4, 105, my underscoring)

How does the internal sense or reflection work? This passage, particularly the part I underscore, suggests a two-stage process. Cognizers perceive mental operations and then reflect on what they have perceived to form the idea of, say, 'willing.' Just after the passage, however, Locke gives an explicit account of his understanding of 'reflection' that suggests it happens in a single stage. Reflection is that notice which the mind takes of its own operations (ECHU 2.1.4, 105). That is, it is the perception of the mind's operations.

Locke began the second book of the *Essay* with the declaration that every man is conscious to himself that he thinks. This need not imply that whenever a man thinks, he is conscious of doing so, but Locke shortly avers that

> it [is] . . . hard to conceive that anything should think and not be conscious of it. (ECHU 2.1.11, 110)[1]

Further, in the familiar passage already partially cited in Chapter 3 he explains that 'person' stands for

> a thinking intelligent Being, that has reason and reflection, and can consider itself as itself, the same thinking thing, in different times and places; which it does only by that consciousness which is inseparable from thinking, and as seems to me essential to it: It being impossible for any one to perceive, without perceiving, that he does perceive. (ECHU 2.27.9, 335)

On the Lockean view, a person listening to Schubert's Wanderer Fantasy would have three objects of consciousness: the music, her hearing, and herself.

In an early theological writing, *The Confession of Nature against Atheists* (1669), Leibniz also claimed that the mind perceived its perceptions:

> If one of the actions of a being is thinking, one of its actions is immediately perceptible, without supposing any parts in it.
>
> For thought is (1) a thing that is immediately perceptible, mind being immediate to itself when it perceives itself thinking. (2) Thought is a perceptible thing without being aware of its parts. (1969, 113)

His goal was to appeal to the lack of perceived parts to argue for immortality, but his argument was *via* an appeal to the same phenomenon that Locke (later) noted in the *Essay*: thinkers perceive their thinking. Unpublished notes on metaphysics from April 1676 show Leibniz wavering on the perceptual model.

> In our mind there is perception or a sense of itself as of a certain specific thing; this is always in us, because, as often as we use the name, we at once recognize

it. As often as we will, we recognize that we perceive our thoughts, that is, that we have thought a little earlier. Therefore intellectual memory consists not in what we sense but in that we sense—that we are those who sense. This is what we commonly call identity. (1969, 161–62)

He starts by asserting the perception of both the self and thoughts, though the latter is presented not as automatic, but voluntary. From these claims, however, he concludes that the kind of perception cognizers have of their states is not a matter of sensing. Rather, it is a matter of recognizing that they think and perceive. In another note from the same time, he remarks that

I have noticed . . . that this perception of perception also occurs without characters and therefore that memory does also. For to perceive perception, or to sense that I have sensed, is to remember, as Hobbes says. I do not yet adequately experience how these different acts of mind take place in this continually reciprocating reflection, as it were, in the intervals between these acts . . . perception of perception goes on perpetually in the mind to infinity. In it consists the existence of the mind per se and the necessity of its continuation. (1969, 161)

Although still presenting a perception model of self-consciousness, Leibniz also raises some problems with it. If such perception is quality-less, is it a form of perception? Assuming that they are different acts of mind, the perceiving and the perceiving of the perceiving, cognizers seem to be launched on an infinite regress.

By the time of the *New Essays*, Leibniz recognizes that the perception of perception model that he takes Locke to defend is hopeless:

It is impossible that we should always reflect explicitly on all our thoughts; for if we did, the mind would reflect on each reflection, ad infinitum. (1765/1996, 2.1.19, 118)

He goes on to develop a complex account of 'reflection' insofar as it includes consciousness of self. In the *Monadology* and the *Principles of Nature and Grace*, he provides nearly identical accounts of the very indirect route that leads through a specialized type of reflection to the ability to say 'I.' The *Monadology* passage is more compact:

It is also by knowledge of the necessary truths and by their abstractions that we rise to *reflective acts*, which enable us to think of what is called *I* and to consider this or that to be in us; it is thus, as we think of ourselves, that we think of being, of substance, of the simple and the compound, of the immaterial, and of God himself, conceiving of that which is limited in us as being without limits in him. These reflective acts provide the principal objects of our reasonings. (*Monadology* §30, 646, cf. *Principles of Nature and Grace* §5, 638)

The *Principles of Nature and Grace* labels the reflective knowledge 'apperception' (§5, 637). Although humans have the capacity for apperception, they do not start to reflect and become aware of themselves with the dawn of perceptual awareness. Beyond mere perception, rational animals have the capacity to attain knowledge of necessary truths. Knowledge of necessary truths is a prerequisite for reflective acts, because human beings could not reflect on themselves without the necessary concepts or, perhaps, propositions with which to carry out the reflection. Prior to understanding what simple substances are, people lack the ability to reflect on themselves, because they are not equipped to think about what are, in fact, their selves.

The reference to thinkers reflecting on themselves by also thinking about God explains both why the capacity for apperception differentiates men from the beasts and how it simultaneously informs them of their special status. The difference cannot be a matter of being substances or even being simple substances, since human beings share those qualities with the lowest of animals. Rather, when thinkers attain knowledge of the necessary truths, they know, among other things, that God is the author of an intelligible world, and that they are like God, though in a very limited degree, in having a capacity to make the world partly intelligible. Having come to recognize themselves as intelligent simple substances, they are capable of self-reflection. They can apperceive. They also know wherein they differ, in kind, from the beasts which can perform none of the prerequisites to reflection. The Leibnizian reflection that enables thinkers to think of themselves is no mere perception, but a highly sophisticated cognitive achievement to which cognizers must rise. To return to the example used above: In Leibniz's view, Locke would take listening to the Wanderer Fantasy to involve perception of the hearing (as well as of the music), and consciousness of the self; but the correct analysis of the latter, complex achievement requires understanding yourself as a simple intelligent substance.

Locke would have none of this. He believed that humans constantly reflected and that they were incapable of knowing their natures. Still, Leibniz has a reasonable point: How can a thinker reflect on herself if she is clueless about the object of her reflection? Locke could reply that the object is just the thinker of a current thought who also remembers other thoughts. If the contrast between Lockean reflection and Leibnizian apperception is that between having within one's purview just a subject of thinking and having within one's purview a metaphysically elaborated self, then it is tempting to believe that Kant's doctrine of 'apperception' employs a Leibnizian term to express a Lockean position. But he rejects both Locke's claims for reflection and Leibniz's view that in apperceiving thinkers are aware of themselves as simple substances. He finds a third way between simple awareness of mental states and actions and a full metaphysical understanding of their subject.

3. Self-Consciousness and Object Cognition

The initial foray in the debate over the priority of self-consciousness and object cognition is Descartes' famous claim that the first items of knowledge anyone could have concerned himself: 'I think,' 'I exist.' Wolff began the *German Metaphysics* with what appears to be a straightforward endorsement of the Cartesian position. Chapter 4 cited this passage in a slightly different context. I repeat it for easy reference:

> No one can doubt that he is conscious of himself and other things; . . . For, how can he deny to me or bring into doubt if he is not conscious of himself or other things? . . . Whoever is conscious of the one, which he denies or brings into doubt, is the same as that one. (Meta. §1, 1)

The slight difference from the *cogito*—conscious also of other things—is important. On Wolff's view, cognizers come to self-consciousness in discerning other objects. It is not sufficient for consciousness of something merely to differentiate its different pieces (as say the parts of a mirror); rather, consciousness requires an act of differentiating that thing from others.

> This difference [between ourselves and other things] appears directly as we are conscious of other things. For should we be conscious of that which we cognize through the senses, we must recognize the difference between that thing and others . . . This differentiation is an effect of the soul, and we cognize therefore through it the difference between the soul and the things that are represented. (Meta. §730, 455–56)

If thinkers can discern themselves only in the act of differentiating between other things, then they can have knowledge neither of their thinking nor of their existence (if those are different) prior to having at least some representations of objects. Since Wolff maintains that the soul's substantiality and identity are carried by its power to represent, it was perhaps natural for him to take self-consciousness to require an awareness of the activity of representing. Regardless of the plausibility of Wolff's metaphysics, his doctrine that humans cannot be self-conscious until they begin to think enjoys considerable surface plausibility. It is also implied by Locke's position. It was, however, strongly resisted by a number of critics.

I begin with Christian August Crusius's *Sketch of Necessary Truths of Reason in so far as they are opposed to the contingent*, originally published in 1745. Kant owned the third edition of 1755 (Warda, 1922, 47).[2] Crusius argues that materialists err, because they do not distinguish representations, which could be physical images, from thoughts that require consciousness. He offers a striking analogy: as the sun differs from a representation of the sun, so too does the idea of the sun in the sense of the action through which it is thought differ from the representation of the sun (1745, §444, 863–64). He continues by noting that consciousness is a fundamental faculty through which it is possible to represent the sun with consciousness.

> Consciousness is thus according to nature prior to differentiation and is the effective cause of the differentiation. It is a mistake to think of an idea as having a higher degree of liveliness. And so little can it be right that consciousness arises through the comparison of ideas. Rather, we are not conscious of things through differentiating them, but we can differentiate them because we are conscious of them. Consciousness is by nature prior to differentiation and is an efficient cause of differentiating. Differentiation is possible through powers of abstraction and consciousness. (1745, §444, 863–64)

Although this passage seems to be directed against Wolff, there is a reply to make on his behalf. Crusius may be talking about consciousness as a power or faculty—indeed he describes it as a special power (1745, §443, 912). Wolff could agree that the power of consciousness is required for differentiation, but still maintain that self-consciousness cannot precede the acts of differentiating made possible through the power of consciousness.[3]

Wolff's position was also criticized by Johann Bernhard Merian in a small essay that Udo Thiel (1996) has very helpfully brought to the attention of scholars. Merian's paper on apperception appeared in French in 1749 and was translated into German in 1778. Thiel has no direct evidence that Kant read Merian, but he would have seen some of his ideas discussed in Tetens (1777/1979, 41–42). One focus of Merian's essay is what he takes to be Descartes' antiskeptical *cogito* argument. As Thiel notes the argument in question is a Wolffian syllogistic version of the *cogito* (1996, 221ff.):

Everything that thinks exists.
I think.
Therefore I exist. (Merian 1749/1778, 98)

In a sense, Merian's argument is very simple. In (allegedly) presenting knowledge of one's existence as a conclusion, Descartes is incorrectly making it mediate. Merian replies with his own syllogism: either consciousness of the self is direct or indirect, and since it cannot be indirect, then it must be direct (1749/1778, 96ff.).

As Merian notes, there are two ways in which knowledge of one's own existence could be mediate, *viz.*, if it is known through reasoning or if it is known through reflection (1749/1778, 97). He has many objections to the Descartes-Wolff claim that the *cogito* is an inference, including that it could not be certain. In relation to Wolff's position on self-knowledge through acts of differentiating, however, the more interesting considerations concern reflection.

Oddly, Merian does not set up this discussion in relation to Wolff, but in relation to someone

> who would be so little a philosopher that he would like to derive the consciousness of self from reflection. (1749/1778, 116)

Thiel observes, however, that Wolff is explicit that consciousness of objects requires reflection (*Überdenken*; Meta. §733, 458; 1996, 219). On Wolff's model, the mind compares and differentiates objects and then is conscious of itself through recognizing (comparing and differentiating) the difference between things and its act of differentiating (Meta. §730, 455–56).

Merian does not see how reflection could enable a subject to discern an 'I' or to discern the same 'I' through time. Either the mental condition that is the target of reflection includes or lacks a consciousness of the self. If it lacks such consciousness, then so will the reflection; if it has a consciousness of self, then the reflection is unnecessary (1749/1778, 117). Suppose we consider not the object of reflection, but the act of reflecting. Reflecting presupposes a consciousness of self, because the mind stands in a determinate relation to some representation A. For example, it attends to

A. But how can this 'reflecting I' establish its sameness across different representations if consciousness of self is not directly given? Abstraction will not work unless the 'reflectings' have a common element. In that case, however, the same 'I' must already be represented. Since the 'I' cannot come to be represented through this indirect route (or through inference), the only alternative is that subjects are directly conscious of their existence as a self (1749/1778, 117–18). Whether or not Kant was aware of this discussion, he makes a related argument against Lockean reflection in the B deduction (B133).

When Merian addresses Wolff's theory later in the essay, he is more circumspect. After laying out the theory of apperceiving through differentiating, he explains that he wants to examine it giving all due respect to the merits of the famous men who made the theory current and who have earned the highest regard of the entire philosophical world (1749/1778, 125). He explains that according to the order of nature, and usually also of time, differentiation presupposes apperception. His reasoning is more explicit than Crusius's. It is not simply that differentiation requires consciousness,[4] but that it requires apperception.

> It is contradictory to say that one can differentiate before one apperceives. For if one should ask in this case: what does one then differentiate? I do not believe that one could ever answer. A clear mark that one has not differentiated. To differentiate A from B is to apperceive that A is not B, and B not A; when at the same time to have apperceived neither A nor B. (1749/1778, 127)

Merian's point is that differentiating A from B requires first that one attend to or focus on A and on B. But then if a cognizer can answer the question of what (things) are to be differentiated, namely A and B, then he must already take them to be objects of his consciousness—he must already have apperceived them.

Merian goes on to consider whether God could make a creature capable of differentiation, but not of apperceiving the objects differentiated:

> Undoubtedly, he would be able to do so, if apperception depended on the capacity to differentiate; he cannot, however, where differentiation depends on apperception. Such a thinking creature would be able to have only abstract concepts of numbers; all of arithmetic and its ideas would have to be just numerals. (1749/1777, 127)

This discussion is interesting in two respects. First, Merian rules out a third possibility by fiat. Perhaps apperceiving and differentiating are mutually dependent. Second, his view that the capacity to do arithmetic requires an ability to single out instances of arithmetic concepts is very like Kant's claim that humans cannot have even mathematical knowledge without sensory representations to which concepts can be applied:

> The mere form of . . . space is as yet no cognition at all. Rather in order to cognize some thing or other—e.g. a line—in space, I must **draw** it . . . so that an object (a determinate space) is thereby first cognized. (B137)

Merian's and Kant's common objection is that knowledge must be of some thing and the representation of that thing must be an object of one's consciousness—it must be apperceived.

Thiel highlights a further relevant theme from Merian.[5] After the anti-*cogito* argument, Merian claims that apperception is original (*'ursprüngliche Apperzeption'* in the German translation) and completely fundamental:

> It is presupposed by all other knowledge and cannot be subordinate to any prior thought . . . the apperception of oneself is the first act, and an essential act of an intelligent being, as intelligent being, considering that it is presupposed by all cognitions, while it alone does not presuppose anything. (Thiel's translation from the French edition, 1996, 225)

The *Critique*'s references to apperception as 'original' and as presupposed in all cognition (A107, B132, A116) suggest that Kant may have known about a position very like Merian's, if not the view itself.

Wunderlich's examination of eighteenth-century theories of self-consciousness presents further theories of the relations between the self and the capacity to differentiate objects/representations. One development is common to Martin Knutzen and Marcus Herz. Knutzen was on the faculty at Königsberg when Kant was a student and is thought to have had a strong influence on his development; Herz was one of his best known students (Kuehn, 2001, 78–79, 161).

Wunderlich cites Knutzen's proof that differentiation establishes the simplicity of the soul:

> Three cardinal elements [*Hauptstücke*] particularly belong to the differentiation of things: 1) That representations of several things are attended. 2) That these are in a single subject. 3) That the holding up against each other [of these several things] is brought about in or through the exercise of this subject. (cited in Wunderlich, 2005, 48, n. 155)

Wunderlich offers the plausible gloss that the second condition is meant to rule out the possibility of the representations of the different things being divided among different subjects (2005, 48).

Wunderlich also cites Herz's similar line of reasoning from two different passages:

> In every relation some kind of subject must necessarily be presupposed, which compares these objects with each other and which, from the difference that it perceives in the impressions of the two, produces a simple result.
>
> This subject which engages in the comparison must necessarily be a simple substance. (2005, 60)

The common view of Kant's teacher and his student is interesting in being close to his position, while also being entirely different. Both Knutzen and Herz see the need to appeal to comparing in the explanation of cognition as providing grounds for a metaphysical conclusion about the simplicity of the self. Kant agrees that cognition requires combining several representations in a single resulting representation, but he denies that this operation requires a simple self.

According to Wunderlich, Kant's sometime nemesis, Johann August Eberhard, follows Wolff in holding that both the soul and its basic power are simple. Like Wolff, he thinks the simplicity of this power is necessary to explain the preservation of one and the same 'I' through time. But how is a subject aware of its identity?

> For the preservation of the I and of personality depends entirely on the consciousness of its unbroken continuity. In order to recognize this *Identity* of itself, it must think itself as the subject of all of its alterations, of which it is conscious up to present moment of thought. (cited in Wunderlich 2005, 57)

And this presupposes the consciousness of something constant in the transition from one representational condition to another:

> It is thus easily seen that it is merely the consciousness of the constancy (*Städtigheit*) in our representations, through which our soul can recognize its numerical identity, and assure itself that it is still always the same I or moral individual that continues. (cited in Wunderlich 2005, 57)

Wunderlich offers the plausible interpretive hypothesis that Kant's familiarity with the Wolffian tradition stands behind his criticisms at A107 and B133 that empirical apperception divulges nothing constant across different representations and cannot be the basis of any claim to identity (2005, 163–64). Eberhard's claim of a consciousness of constancy would seem to be an especially likely target for such an objection. I resist this interpretation, because both criticisms deal with the *necessity* that attaches to the representation 'I think.' That suggests an anti-Empiricist rather than an anti-Rationalist target. Still he may well be arguing against both simultaneously, using the Empiricists' result of no constant 'I' across representations to dismiss Eberhard, while simultaneously criticizing their project of looking for empirical evidence for a necessary proposition.

4. Self-Consciousness through Self-Feeling

Kant's predecessors offered further models of self-consciousness beyond Lockean reflection and complex Leibnizian apperception. I have already briefly considered Tetens's appeal to a common self-feeling to oppose Hume's skepticism about personal identity. The French psychologist Charles Bonnet also understood self-consciousness in terms of a feeling of perceiving:

> Perception is inseparable from feeling [*sentiment*] of perception . . . The feeling of a perception is only of the thinking being as existing in a certain manner. (1755/1978, 115)

Bonnet's physiological approach to the mind led him to a remarkable view about willing. As a sensation must be a motion that takes place at some point in the brain, so too must willing take place somewhere. These two points could not be the same, however, or that location would have, simultaneously, a thought motion and a willing motion (1755/1978, 115). He concludes that

> The I that wills is not the I that apperceives. (1755/1978, 115)

The German translation renders this in even more shocking terms:

> The I that wills is not the same as the I that thinks. (1755/1773, 83)[6]

Kant dismisses this sort of physiological speculation (7.136), so there is no reason to believe that he would have taken Bonnet's odd theory seriously. I mention it only to show the wide range of speculation surrounding the issue of self-consciousness.

Thiel offers a brief history of theories of inner sense that includes several philosophers who also held self-feeling theories. He thinks that the original usage comes from Bernhard Basedow and was picked up by Johann Georg Feder (Thiel, 1997, 62). Thiel's focus is on the ideas of Christoph Meiners (1747–1810) and Michael Hißmann (1752–1784) as presented in their essays of 1773, 1775, and 1777 (1997, 59, n. 4). One interesting doctrine that they share is that apperception is distinct from self-consciousness. If apperception is consciousness of perceptions or of mental operations, then it could exist without self-consciousness, a feeling of existence, or consciousness of the self. On the other hand, they do not see how self-consciousness could exist without apperception (Thiel, 1997, 69ff.). Further, Meiners and Hißmann distinguish a feeling of existence from a feeling of personality. The latter requires memory and involves the combining of present and past perceptions; the former does not. Still, they do not believe that a feeling of existence is possible in men of sound organs without a feeling of personality (Thiel, 1997, 73). Thiel notes some tensions in their views, because Meiners and Hißmann take self-consciousness to be an immediate feeling and yet they also follow the Wolffian tradition in making it dependent on other processes (1997, 70). Again, I do not present these views either because they are plausible or because they might have influenced Kant. My point is, rather, to show the lengths to which his predecessors went to try to characterize self-consciousness.

Against this background, we can see that Tetens was presenting a synthesis of then current views. He combines the differentiation view and the feeling view of self-consciousness:

> To be conscious of something expresses a persisting situation in which one feels a differentiating of an object or its representation, and feels in addition one's self. Consciousness is from one side a feeling, but a clear feeling, clear sensation, a feeling combined with a differentiation of the felt thing and one's self. Feeling and apperception [*Gewahrnehmung*] are the two constituents of consciousness. (1777/1979, 1.263)

Locke simply asserted an awareness of states, actions, and the self. Wolff explained that cognizers are aware of themselves as differentiators, in contrast to the objects (or their representations) that are differentiated. Tetens tries to fill out these accounts while fully acknowledging the Humean point that there is no awareness of a continuing self. He does so in terms of a feeling of differentiating. One problem is that unless the feeling is somehow located in the qualitative characteristics of the object/representation perceived, the theory will fall afoul of Leibniz's plausible observation that the perception of perceptions is quality-less. But locating the 'feel' in the representations of objects runs counter to the idea that what is involved in differentiating is a *self*-feeling.

5. Summary

Although Tetens's account is highly problematic, the difficulty that he was trying to resolve was real. After Wolff, it was widely believed that cognizers recognized themselves as differentiators; but no one had a very good account of what such recognition might involve. Since I have covered a number of figures, it may be helpful to provide a summary of the different views:

Descartes: Thinkers are conscious of themselves as existing through thinking.

Locke: Thinkers perceive their mental acts and themselves through inner sense; they reflect on these acts.

Leibniz: Thinkers are conscious of themselves through being conscious of innate truths about simple substances and God.

Crusius: Differentiation of objects presupposes consciousness.

Merian: Thinkers are conscious of themselves independently of any consciousness of any other act or object or faculty of thought.

Bonnet: Thinkers are conscious of themselves through a fundamental feeling that accompanies perceiving.

Meiners/Hißmann: Apperception of perceptions and mental activities is different from consciousness of self and of personality, even if these always occur together.

Tetens: Thinkers are conscious of themselves through a feeling that arises when differentiating objects.

Knutzen/Herz: Consciousness of objects requires differentiation, which presupposes a simple soul.

Eberhard: Consciousness of objects requires consciousness of something constant across transitions from one representation to another; it involves consciousness of one's own actions in making those transitions.

All of these authors were confident that cognizers are self-conscious, but they struggled to find a plausible model of such consciousness. Is it like perception? Does it involve later reflections on acts? Must the existence of the self simply be recognized as a first truth? Must the self simply be taken to be a primitive element in thought? Is self-consciousness merely a feeling of one's existence? And crucially, how does self-consciousness relate to awareness of the self's activities in differentiating objects? We can follow Kant's exploration of the relations between cognition and self-consciousness in the *Critique* more easily if we see it against the background of these two intertwined contemporary problems: the priority issue between self-consciousness and object consciousness and the puzzle about how to model a quality-less self-consciousness where no self can be perceived.

6

Strands of Argument in the *Duisburg Nachlaß*

1. Introduction

This chapter offers a final piece of historical background intended to make the *Critique*'s theory of apperception more comprehensible. Its topic is a set of Kant's pre-*Critique* notes from around 1775. The *Duisburg Nachlaß* (R4674–84, 17.643–673) have been regarded as especially important by DeVleeschauwer, Guyer, Carl, and others, because they include a relatively sustained discussion of relevant issues in the otherwise 'silent decade' of the seventies. For reasons that will be clear, the *Duisburg* notes are often described as presenting an early version of the transcendental deduction of the categories. Some of the notes are written on the reverse side of a dated letter (May 20, 1775) and others seem very similar to these, so the dating is more secure than for most of the literary remains (Guyer, 1987, 430–31, n. 1).

For anyone who has looked at the notes, appealing to them for illumination—rather than just trying to make some sense of them for the historical record—may seem bizarre. They are extremely fragmentary and filled with crossings out. I do not try to make sense of all or even most of the discussions, but consider them only in relation to two important issues, the preview they offer of the transcendental deduction of the categories and their ruminations about 'apperception.' The next section places these notes in the context of the problem Kant tries to solve in the *Critique*. Section 3 lays out some elements of the solution that are worked out in the notes. In section 4, I look at the debate between Carl and Guyer about the 'soul' who appears in these notes: Is it Empirical or Rational? In the last section, I consider important changes between the *Duisburg* accounts of apperception and the necessary identity of apperception featured in the *Critique*—and offer a hypothesis about the drivers of the change.

2. Kant's Objection to the *Inaugural Dissertation*

To understand the *Duisburg Nachlaß*, we need to consider them as an episode in the development of Kant's thinking about the problem of *a priori* concepts or categories.

Kant wrote the *Inaugural Dissertation* on demand and on reasonably short notice. He was appointed Professor at Königsberg on March 31, 1770, and offered the required public defense of his *Inaugural Dissertation* less than six months later, on August 21 (Kuehn, 2001, 189). The *Inaugural Dissertation* provided a metaphysical account of two different worlds, that of sense and that of intellect. It explained that sensory representations represent things only as they appear. Further,

> empirical concepts do not, in virtue of being raised to greater universality, become intellectual in the **real** sense, nor do they pass beyond the species of sensitive cognition; no matter how high they ascend by abstracting, they always remain sensitive. (2.394, C1755 386)

By contrast intellectual concepts apply to the real or intelligible world.

Beginning in Chapter 1, I have presented Kant as holding a different view of metaphysics—the view that metaphysical principles are nothing but principles of human reason. In the *Inaugural Dissertation*, he seems to assume the more traditional position that metaphysical concepts (and principles) characterize the real world. They are part of a real metaphysics. In fact, the *Inaugural Dissertation* is exceptionally clear about the origins of metaphysical concepts. They

> are given by the very nature of the understanding; they contain no form of sensitive cognition and they have been abstracted from no use of the senses. (2.394, C1755 386)

> Since, then, **empirical** principles are not found in metaphysics, the concepts met with in metaphysics are not to be sought in the senses but in the very nature of the pure understanding, and that not as **innate** concepts but as concepts abstracted from the laws inherent in the mind (by attending to its actions on the occasion of experience), and therefore as **acquired** concepts. To this genus belong possibility, existence, necessity, substance, cause, etc. (2.395, C1755 387–88)

Although Kant is clear about the link between metaphysical concepts and the understanding, he makes a further assumption. He assumes that if the understanding figures out from the phenomena how the world must be for the phenomena to be as they are, then that suffices to establish the truth of the metaphysical claim that the world is that way.

We can see this assumption in Kant's debate with the Newtonians about whether a real space could explain the interaction of objects (Friedman, 2009). What is important for present purposes is not the issue itself, but how he approaches it:

> Accordingly, the following question which can only be solved by the understanding remains untouched; '**what is the principle on which this relation of all substances itself rests** . . .?' (2.407, C1755 401)

His assumption is that since only the understanding could solve it, then that resolution will not only be satisfying to the understanding—but also correct. The

Inaugural Dissertation reflects Kant's continuing belief that metaphysical concepts originate in the nature of the understanding, but from his later perspective in the *Critique*, its reasoning is too loose in two respects. It not only glides from 'resolved according to the principles of understanding' to 'true of an intelligible world,' it also links the concepts that would be found by examining acts of the understanding to traditional metaphysical categories without having made any serious effort to demonstrate such a connection.

By early 1772, Kant was clear that there was a fundamental problem with his theory of the intelligible world. Why should principles given by the nature of the human understanding be considered as true of the real world of objects? In a letter to Marcus Herz of February 21 that is often cited to clarify the *Critique*'s goals, he explained that

> I asked myself this question: What is the ground of the relation of that in us which we call 'representation' to the object? If a representation comprises only the manner in which the subject is affected by the object, then it is easy to see how it is in conformity with this object, namely, as an effect accords with its cause, and it is easy to see how this modification of our mind can **represent** something, that is, have an object . . . However, our understanding, through its representations, is neither the cause of the object (save in the case of moral ends) nor is the object the cause of our intellectual representations in the real sense. Therefore the pure concepts of the understanding . . . though they must have their origin in the nature of the soul, they are neither caused by the object nor do they bring the object into being. In my dissertation I . . . silently passed over the . . . question of how a representation that refers to an object without being in any way affected by it can be possible . . . If such intellectual representations depend on our inner activity, whence comes the agreement that they are supposed to have with objects—objects that are nevertheless not possibly produced thereby? (10.130–31, CLet 133)

Although it does not use the canonical formulation of the *Critique* and the *Prolegomena*—how are synthetic *a priori* propositions possible?—the letter raises a directly related problem. How is it possible to apply an *a priori* concept to objects?

3. Principles of Appearance and Thought in the *Duisburg Nachlaß*

The initial sheet of *Duisburg* notes distinguishes time as the principle of appearance in general from principles of thought and from principles for the 'exposition' of what is given in sensation:

> [A.] The principles of appearance in general are merely those of form, namely time.
>
> The **principium** of the exposition of appearances is the ground of the exposition in general of that which is given. <u>The exposition of that which is thought</u>

depends solely on consciousness, but the exposition of that which is given, if one regards the matter as undetermined, depends on the ground of all relation and of the concatenation of representation (sensations). The concatenation is grounded ... not on the mere appearance, rather it is a representation of the inner action of the mind in connecting representations, not merely for placing them next to one another in intuition, but for constituting a whole as regards its matter. Thus there is here a unity not by means of that wherein but rather by means of that through which the manifold is brought into one, hence universal validity. Hence it is not forms but rather function on which the **relations** of appearances depend. The exposition is thus the determination of the ground on which the interconnection of them in sensation depends. (R4674, 17.643, CNotes 158, my underscoring; I label the *Duisburg* citations alphabetically for easy reference)

In the first underscored sentence pure thinking is contrasted with the 'exposition' of what is thought insofar as the materials for thought are supplied by sensation. The claim is that what is supplied by sensation is concatenated by 'an inner action of the mind' in relation to relation to forming a whole with respect to the matter in the sensations. The second underscored sentence claims that the unity involved the concatenating is not the unity of time (that 'wherein' appearances are represented), but that of something else, perhaps that of the mind or power that does the concatenating or perhaps the unity of the function that concatenates the parts into one. In any case, we seem to have moved from the two worlds of the *Inaugural Dissertation* to three distinct types of ordering of materials: the general order of time, the order of thought that can be explicated merely in terms of concepts (which Kant refers to in terms of 'consciousness'), and the exposition or ordering of the materials given in sensation.

The notes proceed by connecting sensible data to concepts. Their focus is not just the relation of data to concepts, but also the relation of the concept of sensation to concepts that are applied in virtue of sensory data:

[B.] By a universal concept of a sensible **dati**, in which the reality and at the same time its relation to the sensible condition in general is indicated, we understand the action of sensibly determining an object in accordance with such conditions; e.g, that which happens signifies the action of determining something in accordance with its succession in time. Now **x** is this determinable, which contains the conditions of determination [*was die Bedingungen der determination enthalt*]; **a** however signals only the action of determining in general. (R4674, 17.643, CNotes 158, my underscoring)

Kant makes several moves here. First, he notes that the concept of a sensation is that of something that is related both to reality and to the form of sensibility in general, that is, to time. So the concept of a sensation is the concept of something that is an indicator of reality and that occurs in time. I take 'x' to denote a sensation that has neither been brought under any concept nor been determined in respect of its temporal location; 'a' indicates a determining of 'x' presumably through a concept 'a' or an act 'a'—or through an act that determines the sensation in relation to the concept 'a.'

The cryptic account in this passage is filled in a bit in two further passages:

[C.] For the origination of a rule three elements are required: 1. **x**, as the **datum** for a rule (object of sensibility or rather sensible real representation). 2. **a**. the **aptitude** for a rule or the condition, through which it [the representation] is in general related to a rule. 3. **b**, the exponent of the rule. (R4676, 17.656, CNotes 166)[1]

Here, as in the *Critique*, concept-application and bringing under rules are treated as equivalent. The 'aptitude' of the rule is some condition through which the undetermined sensation **x** can be brought under a rule.[2] In his handwritten logic notes (of uncertain date), Kant explains that the 'exponent' of the rule is a relation among concepts (R3063 16.636, CNotes 60).[3] Given his usage in other *Duisburg* notes, I take the relation among concepts to be that specified by the rule that is presented as the exponent, for example, the relation of the concept 'representation' to that of a 'subject.' The idea that the condition of a rule, or the mark of a concept, can be fulfilled by something that is itself not a concept, but a sensory *datum*, is ruled out again in another passage on the same page:

[D.] Now if a norm for the rule of appearances in general or of experiences is to arise—e.g. everything existent is in substance—then **x** is sensation in general as the **specif**[ication, Kant abbreviates here] of reality. <u>By being represented as reality it becomes the material of a rule or sensation becomes capable of a rule</u>, and **a** is only a function of the apprehension of appearance as given in general. Now since everything must be given in time, which therefore comprehends everything in itself, thus **b** is an **actus** of apperception, namely the consciousness of the subject which apperceives as that which is given in the whole of time is necessarily connected with it, for otherwise the sensation would not be represented as belonging to me. (R4676, 17.656, CNotes 166, my underscoring)

The piece I emphasize clarifies that a sensation *per se* is not the condition of a rule for applying concepts; the condition is a sensation understood or represented as reality, which is accomplished by some function **a**. One question is whether the reality at issue is that of what the sensation represents or the real existence of the sensation itself. A third possibility is that the concept of a sensation is the concept of something that is both an indication of reality and also a part of the real in time. Combining these passages, Kant's view is that the concept of a sensation is the concept of something that is real and so takes place in time, and that indicates the real. It does the latter by being 'determined'—by being taken to be the indicator of a certain kind of reality.[4] In the simplest case, a sensation might be understood as indicating through its quality the quality of an object, for example, yellowness.

When represented as real, a sensation is understood as a *datum* in general, as something through which a conceptual rule could be applied. When represented as a sensation of yellow, the sensation as so represented can be the condition for the application of some concept through a rule. For example, it could be the condition for the application of the concept 'gold' to a piece of metal.

Passage D makes two further important points. Since everything exists in a substance (according to metaphysics), the sensation must also. Further, anything that is given must exist in time, so the rule for sensations as such (rather than as indicators of other realities) must include location in time. If the sensation could not be located in time, then it could not be real, could not be part of a substance, and could not belong to the human subject. This act is said to be 'apperceptive' because the subject who acts in representing the sensation as reality can locate the sensation in a (whole) time. It is not clear why this act is sufficient for 'apperception,' meaning the subject's awareness of the sensation as hers.

With its exploration of the concept of 'sensation' passage D fills in some crucial points merely assumed in the *Critique*. Sensations are both real and indicators of reality. They can be understood as providing a basis for concept application only when they are understood or represented as both real and as indicators of reality. They relate to two different orders, the order of time and the order of thought under concepts. Another Reflection indicates how the two orders might relate:

> [E.] Thus we represent the object to ourselves through an analogy of construction, namely that it allows of being constructed in inner sense, namely that something always follows something else, so when something happens it follows something else, or that this representation is one of the universal actions of the determination of appearance, which thus yield a rule, just as a triangle is constructed only in accordance with a rule and serves as a rule for all. (R4684, 17.670, CNotes 176)

That is, the object of a representation is constructed according to the rule of causation (something always follows something else) and this construction permits the construction of sensations (of the items) as following one another in inner sense. When we bear in mind that Kant was clear in the *Inaugural Dissertation* that time could not be perceived, he seems very close to a major piece of the *Critique*'s argument for the category of 'cause.' Sensations are constructed (in their temporal order) in inner sense; this is done in virtue of rules for the exposition of appearances, which concatenate the sensations in a determinate order. The gap in the *Inaugural Dissertation* was that it offered no reason to believe that the principles of the understanding applied to real objects. In the *Duisburg* notes Kant seems to have found a line of solution for the category of cause. For sensations to be understood as real, they must belong to a substance. So, they must be assigned a determinate place in time. This construction in inner sense could be carried out by the rule of causation, the rule that something always follows something else in time, being applied to the appearances represented through the sensations.[5]

4. What Is the *Duisburg Nachlaß*'s Notion of 'Apperception'?

One Reflection sketches what seems to be a formal account of 'apperception':

> [F.] Apperception is the consciousness of thinking, that is, of representations insofar as they are set in the mind. There are three exponents: 1. the relation to subject, 2. the relation of following to each other, 3. composition . . . (R4674, 17.647, CNotes 160–61, also cited in Chapter 2, section 4)

I take the 'exponents' to be rules governing the use of 'apperception.' But how did Kant understand these rules?

The notes offer two clues about what the 'relation to subject' is. Kant goes on to discuss the three exponents in terms of the actions of thinking (R4674, 17.647, CNotes 161). In the next Reflection, he claims that he could not represent anything outside of himself unless he could refer those representations to something that is parallel to the I. Both the reference to action and the reference to a substance outside the subject that is parallel to the I suggest that the relation at issue is one of an accident belonging to a substance. The rule governing 'apperception' would be that representations relate to an apperceptive subject as accidents to a substance. These passages lend considerable credence to Wolfgang Carl's view that the subject of the notes is that of Rational Psychology.

Carl's position is given considerable support by two other passages.

> [G.] That in the soul there lies a *principium* of disposition as well as of affection. That the appearances can have no other order and cannot otherwise belong to the <u>unity of the power of representation</u> except that they are in accord with the common *principio* of disposition. For all appearances with their common determination must still have unity in the mind, consequently must be subject to such conditions by means of which the unity of representation is possible. (R4678, 17.660–61, CNotes 168–69, my emphasis)

As Alison Laywine observes (2006), '*principium*' here should be understood as equivalent to the German '*Grund*' (basis or ground or reason). The idea would be that just as what is represented in sense depends on the nature of the sense organs, so too what is 'set in' or 'concatenated' in the mind depends on the acts of concatenation that the mind is disposed to perform.

Another passage, which immediately precedes the discussions of requirements for rules and the concept of sensation already considered (passages B and C, pp. 69, 70), provides further support for Carl's position:

> [H.] If something is apprehended, it is taken up in the function of apperception. I am, I think, thoughts are in me. These are all relations, which to be sure do not provide rules of appearance, but which make it such that all appearance is to be represented as contained under a rule. The I constitutes the substratum for a rule in general, and apprehension relates every appearance to it. (R4676, 17.656, CNotes 166, cited by Carl, 1989a, 91. See also R4675, 17.649, CNotes 162)

Seemingly only the substantial unity of a '*res cogitans*' could be a ground or a *substratum* of the organization of representations in the mind according to rules (Carl, 1989a, 92).

Yet when we turn to the second exponent, the relation of representations following one another, the focus shifts to time and we seem to be considering an empirical subject of thought. That was the interpretation staked out by Paul Guyer, against whom Carl proposed his *res cogitans* reading. Guyer sums up his interpretation as follows:

> It seems to be Kant's intention just to discover what conditions the objects which cause our empirical intuitions must satisfy **when and if** we are to be capable of a unified experience of them and/or ourselves. (1987, 61)

He finds strong support for it in the passage labeled D above, which I repeat (in part) for easy reference:

> [D.] Now since everything must be given in time, which therefore comprehends everything in itself, thus **b** is an **actus** of apperception, namely the consciousness of the subject which apperceives as that which is given in the whole of time is necessarily connected with it, for otherwise the sensation would not be represented as belonging to me. (R4676, 17.656, CNotes 166)

He interprets this passage as follows:

> [It] tries to establish the transcendental theory of experience by arguing that the interpretation of any particular sensation (x) as an object of experience requires that it be governed by both the general function of appearances as given—that is the rules of sensibility—and by the rule that an act of apperception represent its particular object as part of its representation of a unified self. The representation of a unified self, in turn, is identified with the consciousness of the self in the whole of the time through which it has experience: Apperception is clearly the consciousness of the identity of the self through time. (1987, 50)

I read the passage more narrowly. Kant does not raise the issue of the identity of the self through time, but claims only that it is necessary for a sensation to belong to a (temporal) subject that the sensation be able to be given a temporal position that is, of necessity, related to all other temporal positions. Still, it is clear that the apperceptive subject is one that exists in time.

Kant's third exponent, 'composition,' probably means something like the relations of different parts to a whole. As such it doesn't seem to lend weight to either a Rationalist or an empirical reading.

Carl buttresses his interpretation by appealing to the claim of the notes that the self offers a 'model' of a substance:

> [I.] **x** is the object. This can be given *a priori* in the construction, but in the exposition (which is something completely different from observation, which

has not combined anything *a priori* with a) the *a priori* conditions of the subject can be cognized under which **a** in general is related to an object, namely, something real. This object can only be represented in accordance with its relations and is nothing other than the subjective representation of the subject itself, but made general for <u>I am the original of all objects</u> . . .

There are three functions of apperception, which are met with in . . . the thought of our state in general and under which all appearance must on that account fit, because in it there would lie no synthesis in itself if the mind did not add it or make it out of the **datis** of appearance. <u>The mind is thus the archetype [*Urbild*] of such a synthesis</u> through original and not through derivative thinking. (R4674, 17. 647, CNotes 160, my underscoring)

The mind is presented as a model for synthesizing. As Carl understands Kant's position, the mind is a Rationalist substance that is the ground of the rules of thought and whose rules of combining representations of objects reflect its nature (1989a, 91–92, 97). He believes that the *Duisburg* notes thus offer a 'subjective' deduction of the rules for cognizing objects, a deduction that traces them to the nature of the mind and so explains how they and cognition are possible.[6]

Appealing to a different Reflection, Guyer thinks the model or analogy between the 'exponents' or 'titles' or 'functions' for thinking about objects and the apperceptive subject goes in the opposite direction:

[J.] Thus these propositions [titles of the understanding, e.g., in all intuition there is magnitude, in all appearance substance and accident . . .] are valid of all objects of experience. The very same propositions also hold for the mind with regard to the generation of its own representations are moments of *genesis*. But all appearances must be brought under the title of apperception, so that they are constructed in accordance with intuition as well as [breaks off] (R4679, 17.664, CNotes 172, see Guyer, 1987, 43)

That is, the titles for representing objects are primary and the rules for representing apperception are analogical (Guyer, 1987, 43).

An obvious solution for resolving the debate between these knowledgeable and careful scholars is that both are right. The *Duisburg Nachlaß* contains reflections on both Guyer's empirical subject and Carl's Rationalist subject. From the perspective of the *Critique* what is most interesting about these discussions is the absence of any considerations about the necessary identity of apperception. The notes focus on several necessary conditions for empirical cognition. Sensations are essential and these must occur as part of a whole temporal order. But there is no claim that cognition requires a consciousness of necessary *identity* of apperception (cf. A116). This point is somewhat obscured in Carl's and Guyer's discussions. In Guyer's interpretation (quoted above) of passage D, p. 73, he refers to the 'transcendental theory of experience and the 'representation of a unified self.' More bluntly, he maintains that

Apperception [in the *Duisburg* notes] is clearly the consciousness of the identity of the self through time. (1987, 50)

Carl also links apperception to identity:

> Apperception itself as the consciousness of such a subject is the knowledge of an identity, which can only be thought in relation to a multiplicity. (1989a, 89)

But the *Duisburg* notes never use the term 'identity' or any related form in discussing apperception[7] and, *a fortiori*, they raise no questions about how such identity can be established or how it can be known by the subject.

This absence might seem insignificant, because the notes discuss many sorts of unities, and 'unity' could be read as a stylistic variant of 'identity.' So passage I above refers to unity of the power of representations that makes possible the unity of representations; passage D indicates that sensations must be posited at a time in a whole of time. Another note considers the relation between a unity of mind and the collective unity of representations:

> [K.] In the unity of the mind a whole is only possible insofar as the mind determines one partial representation reciprocally from the other and all are collectively comprehended in an action that is valid for all of them. (R4679, 17.663, CNotes 171)

The relation between partial and whole representations and their relation to self-identity will be a theme of Chapter 9's account of the transcendental deduction. Perhaps this passage contains an early statement of the theme, but it may refer to the 'unity of the mind' only as the power that forms whole representations from partial ones. My point is that if notes are said to address the status of the identity of the apperceptive subject and its relation to cognition, then that claim must be an interpretive one,[8] because the notes make no explicit mention of this central doctrine of the *Critique*.

Further, insofar as Guyer and Carl are right about the subjects of the *Duisburg* notes, we can appreciate why identity would not be an issue. The ability to place the mental states of a temporal cognizer in a sequence would be necessary for grasping those states as states of a single thinker. But temporal sequencing doesn't make states to belong a thinking subject. More simply, none of the Reflections' claims about the ordering requirements for states of a temporal cognizer addresses the issue of the necessary identity of thinker *per se* (rather than that of a spatiotemporal thinker). Similarly, the issue of necessary identity of the subject is screened off by considering a substantial thinker.[9]

The *Duisburg* notes also raise an issue considered in Chapter 4. One Reflection expresses qualms about the action to substance inference that Kant defends in the Second Analogy:

> [L.] Why is that which acts regarded as if it were continuous as if only the actions, effects, and juxtapositions vary[?] (R4679, 17.664, CNotes 172)

It is easy to read too much into these fragments, but he seems to be questioning a standard metaphysical principle and so suggesting that it needs to be put on a firmer foundation than what has previously been offered for it.

5. From the *Duisburg Nachlaß* to the *Critique*

Carl argues that the important changes in the treatment of apperception between the sketches of the *Duisburg Nachlaß* and the doctrines of the *Critique* can be traced to the discovery of the Paralogisms. Once Kant appreciates that the apperceptive subject cannot be known to be a substance, he drops the idea of it as a model for objects and moves from an ontological theory to an epistemological one. The identity of the self is not a reflection of its substantial character but a necessary condition for the possibility of experience. Although Carl's basic claim seems incontrovertible, a more fine-grained diagnosis seems possible.

In reading Tetens's *Versuche* two or three years after the period of the *Duisburg Nachlaß*, Kant would have been presented with considerations that rule out the subject of thought as a model or paradigmatic object. In particular, the lack of an intuition of the I as permanent makes it inappropriate as a model for the concept 'substance.' He would also have been given plenty of evidence to see that Rationalist complacency about the continuing identity of a thinking substance-subject was unwarranted. It was far from obvious how anyone could know even that he continued to exist as the same self, let alone as a substantial one. The *Duisburg* notes present elements of a Rationalist subject and elements of an empirical one. Tetens (and Hume) confront Kant with the problem of the identity of both subjects. Yet Hume is plainly wrong: People know that they are self-identical. Since the representation 'I' has nothing to do with sensation, it must be *a priori*. In that case, its status, like that of the titles or categories, should be established as a necessary condition for experience. In arguing not merely that any sensation that belongs to an apperceptive self must be orderable in time—but that it is necessary for experience that any representation belongs to such a self—he is able to establish a broader principle of scientific metaphysics. All representations *per se* must belong to a thinker *per se*. From that conclusion, he is in a position to argue that every representation must meet whatever conditions are necessary for belonging to that self. And that is the *Critique*'s basic argumentative strategy.

No commentator doubts that the absence of an intuition of time is essential to Kant's defense of the universal applicability of the category of cause. My interpretive claim is that the absence of an intuition of the subject of thought plays a similarly important role in his argument for the categories in general. As the inability to intuit time leaves the field open to the laws of understanding to order sensations in time, so too the lack of an I-intuition leaves the field open for the understanding to be the source of the representation 'I' and for the actions of the understanding to relate representations to a common 'I.'

Finally, the *Duisburg* notes offer a rumination about self-consciousness and object consciousness along Wolffian lines:

> [M.] We are conscious of ourselves and of our own actions and of appearances insofar as we become conscious of the apprehension of them, either by coordinating them or by apprehending one sensation through the other. (R4679, 17.662, CNotes 170)

That is, we can become conscious of ourselves and of other things in that we apprehend an appearance. A note that is not part of this set, but apparently from the same time, is even clearer:

> The mind can become conscious of itself only through appearances, appearances that correspond to its dynamic functions, and of the appearances only through its dynamic functions, (R4686, 17.675)

Self-consciousness is possible only because the mind can recognize its 'dynamic functions' in the appearances, presumably appearances that can represent objects only because the mind's dynamic functions have ordered them in some way.

On the Empiricist picture of self-consciousness that Tetens tries to sketch, Wolff must be wrong: Humans are not aware of themselves as (substantial) agents of differentiation through differentiating representations, because they are not aware of themselves as substantial agents at all. Crusius and Merian had pursued a different line of objection to Wolff. Self-consciousness is necessary for object cognition, not vice versa. After reading Tetens Kant would be cognizant of three theses that together point towards the *Critique*'s picture of the unity of apperception: Object consciousness is necessary for self-consciousness, self-consciousness is necessary for object consciousness, and humans have no intuition of an I before or after object consciousness. With intuition removed, humans must represent themselves as 'I's—a condition that is necessary for object consciousness—in some other fashion.

Part II
Theory

7

A Transcendental Deduction for *A Priori* Concepts

1. Kant's Goal

The purpose of this chapter is to clarify the goal or conclusion of the transcendental deduction, its manner of argument and opening premise, and the location of the 'I-think' doctrine within it. This material will prepare the way for an analysis of the deduction in Chapter 9.

Kant states his goal in the *Critique* clearly and succinctly. He wants to answer a very general question:

How are synthetic *a priori* judgments possible? (B19)

He highlights this formulation in the B edition and the *Prolegomena* (4.276, C1781 72) and presents it in passing in the A edition (A9). The transition to the transcendental deduction offers a somewhat different formulation.

> The difficulty . . . is namely how **subjective conditions of thinking** should have **objective validity**, that is, yield conditions for the possibility of all cognition of objects. (A89–90/B122).[1]

Prima facie, the second formulation is closer to the problem of the *Inaugural Dissertation* that he worked on in the *Duisburg* Reflections than the first. The difficulty was to explain how rules of the understanding could apply to objects of the senses. Equating 'rules of thought' (or 'consciousness' or 'intellect')' with 'subjective conditions of thinking,' one half of the problem description is identical; for the second half, he now describes the goal as one of showing how such rules present conditions for any object cognition. This claim is similar to a striking assertion in one of the notes of the *Duisburg* group (which uses 'principle' for 'rule' or 'category'):

> [N.] The principles of exposition must be determined on the one side by the laws of apprehension, on the other by the unity of the faculty of understanding. <u>They are the standard for observation and are not borrowed from perception, but from their ground as a whole</u> . . . (R4678, 17.660, CNotes 169, my underscoring)

The *Duisburg* formulation is less cryptic and so more helpful. What is crucial about the rules of thinking—how they supply the conditions for the possibility of cognition of objects—is that they provide standards by which an observation can be judged an observation.

This section offers a preliminary clarification of the goal of the transcendental deduction, by explaining why Kant's two formulations of his problem are equivalent, that is, why the problem of 'subjective' conditions that are to be shown to be 'objective' is the same problem as that of defending synthetic *a priori* judgments. To see the connection, we need to consider the notion of 'apriority' and its relation to subjectivity. Up to this point I have followed standard practice and used '*a priori*' as if it had a well-understood meaning. In fact, Kant has a unique theory of 'apriority,' which he takes care to present with a contextual definition in the opening paragraphs of the B Introduction.

> That all our cognition begins with experience, of this there can be no doubt. For what else might rouse our cognitive power to its operation if objects stirring our senses did not do so? In part these objects by themselves bring about representations. In part they set in motion our understanding's activity . . .
> But even though all our cognition starts **with** experience, that does not mean that all of it arises **from** experience. <u>For it might well be that even our experiential cognition is composite, consisting of what we receive through impressions and what our own cognitive power supplies from itself (sensory impressions merely prompting it to do so)</u> . . .
> The question, then, whether there is such a cognition that is independent of experience and even of all impressions of the senses, is one that cannot be disposed of as soon as it comes to light, but that at least still needs closer investigations. Such cognitions are call ***a priori* cognitions**; they are distinguished from **empirical** [ones], whose sources are *a posteriori*, namely in experience. (B1–2, my underscoring, amended translation)

The sentence I highlight lays out the possibility that Kant spends the rest of the *Critique* developing and demonstrating. He will try to show that empirical cognition must be a conjoint product of the contributions of objects through the sensory impressions they cause in cognizers, and the contributions of cognitive faculties in response to sensory stimulation.

Interestingly, the B edition definition of 'apriority' is closer to the formulations of the Herz letter and the *Duisburg* notes than that offered in the A edition. It is also closer to the terminology of the Transition passage. Since *a priori* aspects of representations arise from the activities of the mind in response to sensory stimulation, they are 'subjective' in that they come from the nature of the subject's mind. So the question arises as to how these subjectively generated representations can relate to objects. By contrast, the A edition defines 'apriority' in relation to universality and necessity:

> Yet experience is far from being the understanding's only realm and our understanding cannot be confined to it. Experience does indeed tell us what is, but not that it must necessarily be so and not otherwise. And that is precisely why experience gives us no true universality; and reason, which is so eager for that kind of cognitions, is more stimulated by experience than satisfied. Now, such universal cognitions, which are at the same time characterized by intrinsic necessity, must be independent of experience, clear and certain in themselves. Hence they are called *a priori* cognition; by contrast, what is borrowed solely from experience is, as we put it, cognized only *a posteriori*, or empirically.
> Now, it turns out—what is extremely remarkable—that even among our experiences there is an admixture of cognitions that <u>must originate *a priori*</u>, and that serve perhaps only to give coherence to our representations of the senses. (A1–2, my underscoring)

Both commentators and philosophers with a systematic interest in the '*a priori*' have emphasized the A edition definition in preference to the later one. This partiality reflects their concerns and their resistance to Kant's formulations in terms of psychological faculties.[2] Notice, however, that even in A, it is not possible to escape the subjective aspect of the *a priori* for Kant: He draws attention to the remarkable fact of the *a priori* origin (*Ursprung*) of some cognitions. Because '*a priori*' expresses a subjective origin, the goal of the transcendental deduction can be formulated either in terms of proving that subjective conditions can be objective or in terms of proving that synthetic *a priori* cognitions—cognitions of objects that involve representations that come from the activities of the mind—are legitimate or possible.

Universality and necessity also feature prominently in the second edition, but only as characteristics (*Merkmale*) by which *a priori* cognitions can be correctly distinguished from *a posteriori* ones (B3–4). Since, again, neither universality nor necessity can be gleaned from experience, if cognizers make universal and necessary judgments, then (part of) their origin must be *a priori*, that is, in the mind. Notice, however, that where it is clear that universal and necessary judgments could not be supported by empirical evidence, it is far from obvious how they can be rest on activities of the mind. I return to this issue in section 4 where I explain how Kant sees universal and necessary propositions as arising from mental activities.

The Introduction raises a further question about necessary and universal propositions: Does the *Critique* presuppose that there are such propositions or not? The textual evidence that Kant presupposes Euclidean geometry seems clear:

> Now it is easy to show that in human cognition there actually are such judgments, judgments that are necessary and in the strictest sense universal, and hence are pure *a priori* judgments. If we want an example from the sciences, we need only to look to all the propositions of mathematics. (B4)

As we see in the next section, however, Kant's characterization of the *Critique*'s argument structure as 'synthetic' precludes this type of presupposition. Although the interpretive problem seems vexed, he provides the solution himself in the continuation of the discussion in the Introduction:

> But we do not need such examples in order to prove that pure *a priori* principles actual[ly exist] in our cognition. We could, alternatively, establish that these principles are indispensable for the possibility of experience as such, and hence establish [their existence] *a priori*. For where might even experience gets its certainty if all the rules by which it proceeds were always in turn empirical and hence contingent, so that they could hardly be considered first principles? (B5)

In this passage Kant presents himself as employing a method of argumentation that has recently been labeled 'reflective equilibrium' in honor of John Rawls. It is widely agreed that propositions of mathematics are necessary and universal (though not synthetic), and so *a priori*. So he could make that assumption. But he can also argue from a different direction, by showing that *a priori* propositions must supply standards for empirical cognition. The two approaches do not represent vacillation, but consilience. There are good reasons from mathematics to assume that synthetic *a priori* propositions are actual, so possible; the same point can be established by an independent line of reasoning; the availability of both lines reinforce each other and so establish the conclusion all the more securely. We'll see a similar pattern with the 'I-think' doctrine.

2. Clues to the Nature of the Argument

Kant explains his method in a number of passages. I begin with his contrast between the methods of the *Critique* and the *Prolegomena*. In the former

> I worked on this question [Is metaphysics possible? Are synthetic *a priori* propositions possible?] **synthetically**, namely by inquiring within pure reason itself, and seeking to determine within this source both the elements and the laws of its pure use, according to principle . . . *Prolegomena* should by contrast be preparatory exercises . . . They must therefore rely on something already known to be dependable, from which we can go forward with confidence and ascend to the sources, which are not yet known, and whose discovery will not only explain what is known already, but which will also exhibit an area with many cognitions that all arise from the same sources. The methodological procedure of prolegomena . . . will therefore be **analytic**. (4.275, C1781 70)

He also contrasted the synthetic and analytic methods in prefatory remarks to the *Groundwork of the Metaphysics of Morals*. He explained that its argument would proceed analytically from common [moral] cognition to the determination of its supreme principle and then synthetically from the examination of this principle and its sources back to common knowledge in which we find it used. (4.392, CPract 47).[3]

When we put these descriptions together, we can agree with Kemp Smith's observation that the analytic and synthetic methods do not seem completely distinct (1923/1962, 44ff.). Both trace cognition back to its sources and then move in the contrary direction from the sources back to other cognitions.

Kemp Smith saw the key difference between them in their assumptions: The analytic method accepts, at least provisionally, a body of knowledge from which it 'regresses' to its necessary conditions; the synthetic method does not. That is why it is tendentious to interpret the *Critique* as presuming the truth of Euclidean geometry, since its method is supposed to be synthetic. Rather, a synthetic argument starts from ordinary experience, perhaps just the consciousness of time. And it simultaneously explains and validates its starting place. This is not, however, exactly what Kant says. He claims that the synthetic method starts not with ordinary experience, but with reason. The idea that the transcendental deduction is a synthetic argument, and one that starts from reason itself, may suggest that its opening move is 'I-think,' the *cogito*.

Chapter 9 offers considerations that weigh against taking Kant's opening premise to be the *cogito*. But how can an argument start from 'pure reason' itself?[4] His audience consists exclusively of those with reason. Still his readers must be reminded or led to think explicitly about what having reason involves. Kemp Smith tried to cut through the methodological confusions he saw with the suggestion that the *Critique*'s argument is a back and forth between the analytic and synthetic methods (1923/1962, 44–45). He also highlighted the feature of that made Kant's transcendental method genuinely novel. The new method was to examine the necessary conditions not for this or that body of knowledge, but for the possibility of experience. Kemp Smith believed that this novel feature of the argument was tied to its synthetic status. That would be correct if the way that Kant got his readers to focus on their rational capacities was by asking them to think about the necessary conditions for any possible experience.

The view that the transcendental deduction is an exploration of the necessary conditions for experience is widely shared and strongly supported by two key texts.

> Hence the transcendental deduction of all *a priori* concepts has a principle to which the entire investigation must be directed: viz., the principle that these concepts must be recognized as *a priori* conditions for the possibility of experience (whether the possibility of the intuition found in experience, or the possibility of the thought). (A94/B126)

The second text contains his most explicit account of the transcendental deduction's method of proof. In the Discipline of Pure Reason in Regard to its Proofs, he explains that in a transcendental proof

> as long as [the] . . . cognition deals merely with concepts of understanding this outside guideline is possible experience. For the proof here does not show that

the given concept (e.g., the concept of what occurs) leads straightforwardly to another concept (that of cause), because such a transition would be a leap that could not at all be justified; <u>the proof shows, rather, that experience itself and hence the object of experience would be impossible</u> without the connection. (A783/B811, my underscoring)

Unfortunately, the broad agreement that the assumption from which the transcendental deduction regresses is that of the 'possibility of experience' does not settle everything. Section 3 will look at two very different views of what that possibility is.

Kant began the Principles of a Transcendental Deduction as Such by explaining why a special deduction was needed.

We employ a multitude of empirical concepts without being challenged by anyone. And we consider ourselves justified, even without having offered a deduction, to assign to these empirical concepts a meaning and imagined signification, because we always have experience available to us to prove their objective reality . . .

But there are, among the various concepts making up the highly mixed fabric of human cognition, some that are determined for pure *a priori* use as well (i.e. for a use that is completely independent of experience); and their right to be so used always requires a deduction. For proofs based on experience are insufficient to establish the legitimacy of using them in that way; <u>yet we do need to know how these concepts can refer to objects even though they do not take these objects from any experience.</u> Hence when I explain in what way concepts can refer to objects *a priori*, I call that explanation of them the **transcendental deduction** of these concepts. (A84–85/B116–17, my underscoring)

These introductory remarks make three important points. The simplest is the underscored reiteration of the problem left over from the *Inaugural Dissertation*, that of relating concepts that did not arise through experience with objects to such objects. That is the problem to be solved by a transcendental deduction. The second point was foreshadowed in *Duisburg* notes cited above, but it is clearer here. Given the special use to which the concepts will be put—namely of applying to all objects, or of supplying a standard for all object cognition—they need to be established in some nonempirical fashion. Their *a priori* status is not a deficit to be overcome, but a necessary feature of their use. The third point is equally important. It is contained in the first paragraph. Kant explains the need for a transcendental deduction for *a priori* concepts by citing the contrastive case of *a posteriori* representations. No special argument needs to be given for the latter, because their objective reality (their applicability to objects) can be established by turning to experience to find instances.

The contrast between the situations of *a priori* and *a posteriori* representations implies that the transcendental deduction is not meant as a reply to a general skeptical challenge. It is not hyperbolic Cartesian skepticism, but Humean skepticism of the *a priori* that must be overcome.[5] Given his worries about the *Dissertation*, this is what we should expect and I think the view is almost correct. What, however, are we to make of the odd expression that cognizers feel themselves justified in assigning meaning and an 'imagined' (*eingebildete*) signification to *a posteriori* concepts? Are *a posteriori* representations to be revealed as merely imaginary? In *Kantian Humility*, Rae Langton sees the source of Kant's idealism in his recognition that all cognition depends on indirect access to objects through sensory representations (1998, 43ff.).[6] If that is the problem to be solved by transcendental idealism, then the *a posteriori* would be as questionable as the *a priori*. Kant's continual focus on the *a priori* makes that interpretation less plausible. I think there is a way to interpret 'imagined' here without adopting something like Langton's representational skepticism. 'Imagined' can be seen as setting up a *tu quoque*. Since the problem all along with *a priori* representations is that they (in contrast to the *a posteriori*) do not arise from sensory contact with objects, an appropriate standard of proof would be to show that they have the same status as *a posteriori* representations, whatever that desirable status is surmised to be.

Besides the *Prolegomena*'s methodological observations, the most striking and, prior to 1989, least used clue about the nature of the transcendental deduction was the famous analogy with legal deductions. In that year, Dieter Henrich explained the practice of legal deduction writing to which Kant alludes. According to Henrich, the practice arose because some means were needed to settled disputes about property and inheritance among the various entities that had constituted the Holy Roman Empire. He explained how they worked:

> In order to determine whether an acquired right was real or only presumption, one must legally trace the possession somebody claims back to its origin. The process through which a possession or a usage is accounted for by explaining its origin, such that the rightfulness of the possession or the usage becomes apparent, defines the deduction. (Henrich 1989b, 35)

As he notes, the analogy with legal deductions provides considerable insight into the transcendental deduction's numerous references to the 'origins' of representations. In this preparatory section, Kant discusses the sources of various kinds of representations and characterizes the objective of the deduction as one of providing for the categories

> a <u>certificate of birth</u> quite other than descent from experience (A86/B199, my underscoring)

Why such a certificate is needed is the subsequent use as a standard of observation.

Henrich concludes that, if the transcendental deduction is like a legal deduction, then we shouldn't expect a single line of argument. Lawyers are trained to make their cases by including all the relevant considerations on their side of the issue. In that case, we should anticipate a weaving together of considerations. If this is the method of argumentation, then method, rather than haste or an attachment to old arguments, could explain the 'patchwork' quality that earlier scholars thought they saw in the text (Kemp Smith, 1923/1962, xix–xxv).

Manfred Kuehn criticizes Henrich for placing so much stress on the allusion to legal deductions (1997, 245). In his view, Kant's project in the transcendental deduction and some of his views about analytic and synthetic method derive from Wolff. Wolff understood philosophy as

> the science of all possible objects, how and why they are possible. (Wolff cited in Kuehn [1997, 229])

On Kuehn's account, Wolff's goal was to prove that certain concepts were possible, by showing that objects falling under the concepts were possible (1997, 232). He observes that Meier's logic text, which Kant used as a basis for his lectures, laid out the basics of the Wolffian program:

> A learned concept which has been created by arbitrary conjunction must be proved or disproved. We can achieve this either by (i) experience, if we show that their concepts are real or not real, or (ii) by reason, either directly or indirectly by showing that and how their objects can become real or that they cannot become real. (Kuehn, 1997, 232)

That is, a concept can be shown to be real by finding an object that instantiates it or by reasoning from objects that are cognized to general principles that permit an inference to the existence of objects that instantiate the concept.

Kuehn argues that Kant equates 'real possibility' with 'objective validity' and 'objective reality' (1997, 240). Given the Wolffian meaning of 'real possibility of a concept'—that it can be demonstrated to apply to objects—the equation seems plausible. If we accept it, then Wolff's view is echoed in the *Critique*'s explanation of the uncontroversial status of *a posteriori* concepts. Their objective reality can always be proved.

Although Kuehn's historical case is plausible, trying to understand the transcendental deduction in terms of Wolffian efforts to establish the possibility of concepts has an evident limitation: Neither of his methods can be applied to the categorial concepts.[7] Kuehn casts his claims for historical influence in opposition to Henrich's, but there is no incompatibility between the analogy with legal deductions and the description of its goal in terms of demonstrating the 'objective reality,' 'objective validity,'[8] or 'real possibility' of the categories. Since available methods for establishing 'objective reality' are not applicable, an obvious hypothesis is that Kant looks to the model of legal deductions for a different approach. The model would be especially appropriate, because the difficulty about intellectual concepts is their source. On analogy with legal deductions, he would trace these contested concepts back to their source. Except that is not what happens. Rather, in line with the goal of establishing parity between the *a priori* and *a posteriori*, he tries to regress from empirical aspects of cognition, from perception, from the use of empirical concepts, from the thought of any object at all, from the consciousness of mental states, to activities of the mind that are necessary for the possibility of these cognitive tasks. The progressive or synthetic step (detailed in section 4) then shows how these necessary activities give rise to the applicability of the contested concepts, the categories. Such a deduction would provide an origin for the concepts that is suitable to their role, which is that they are applicable to all objects of empirical cognition. An empirical derivation could show that the concept in question applies to only some objects, but a transcendental deduction is supposed to show why the categories can be applied to any object that can be perceived or thought at all.

Henrich's and Kuehn's theories of the historical precedents of the transcendental deduction can thus be seen as complementary to a certain degree. Where they disagree is on the question of a single or multiple lines of argumentation. To a first approximation, lawyers throw the kitchen sink at a case, where philosophers often have the ideal of a linear argument. Despite their seeming incompatibility, these strategies can work together. The transcendental deduction has an overall line of argument from the assumption that cognition is possible to the activities of the mind that are needed to support it, and then to the universal applicability of the categories. Since empirical cognition is itself complex, the regress involves a number of elements. Kant explores the necessary conditions for perception and for empirical concept use. But consciousness of mental states is also a form of empirical cognition, so he also regresses from it. And he regresses from empirical cognition to the necessity of this consciousness. The dual appearance of consciousness does not indicate a second line of argument, but the complex contours of a single line. The complexity arises in part, because he makes his argument stronger by both assuming cognitions that are taken to be obvious (the basic theorems of Euclidean geometry or consciousness of mental states) and also offering arguments in their favor. But the more fundamental source of complexity is the circumstance that various aspects of empirical cognition depend on each other. So he explores the interdependency of object cognition and subject cognition. The overall line of argument is to show how the interdependent capacities involved in empirical cognition all depend on the ability to use the contested *a priori* concepts.

3. The First Premise of the Transcendental Deduction

Section 2's discussion of Henrich and Kuehn makes some assumptions about what is presupposed in the transcendental deduction. Here I try to defend them. There is wide agreement that the argument regresses from the 'possibility of experience.' But what is that?

Kant's remarks on this topic seem clear and consistent. The possibility of 'experience' should be understood as the possibility of 'empirical cognition':

> The categories serve only for the possibility of **empirical cognition**. Such cognition, however, is called **experience**. (B147)

> Because experience is empirical cognition . . . (7.141)

By the 'possibility of empirical cognition,' he means the possibility of cognizing objects through receiving information about them *via* the senses (cf., e.g., Hoppe, 1983, 29). The opening phrase of the B Introduction (already cited) thus presents the first premise of the *Critique*'s principal argument:

> That all our cognition begins with experience, of this there can be no doubt. (B1, amended translation)

Kant's terminology is awkward, because here he uses 'experience' to mean the 'receipt of sensory information.' Still the point seems clear enough: He takes it to be beyond question that human beings have cognition and that such cognition begins with sensory stimulation. Since the goal is to defend *a priori* concepts, the presumption of *a posteriori* cognition would be a uniquely appropriate opening assumption.

Despite the textual evidence for seeing the transcendental deduction as regressing from the possibility of empirical cognition, Carl presents a powerful case against this interpretation. His argument is historical, philosophical, and textual. The textual case is straightforward. In several key passages, Kant explains that his goal is not to demonstrate merely that the categories apply to all objects of empirical cognition, but to prove that they apply to all objects of sensory intuition. So as he sets up the problem he explains that

> the categories of understanding . . . do not at all represent to us the conditions under which objects are given in intuition. Therefore objects can indeed appear to us without having to refer necessarily to functions of the understanding, and hence without the understanding's containing *a priori* conditions of these objects. (A 89/B122)

The contrast case is the forms of intuition. There is no mystery about why anything that appears to humans must appear through the forms of their sensibility. What needs to be argued is that anything that appears to humans must also be in accord with the principles of the understanding. Kant returns to the theme in the crucial section 26 of the B edition:

> We should [*soll*] now explain how it is possible, through **categories**, to cognize *a priori* whatever objects **our senses may encounter** . . . [Otherwise] one would fail to see how everything that our senses may encounter would have to be subject to the laws that arise *a priori* from the understanding alone. (B159–60)

Given these texts, the philosophical argument seems to follow directly. If the conclusion to be established is that the categories must apply to any object that appears to the human senses, then there is no point in regressing from object cognition, since the intuitions involved in object cognition could be a subset of all human intuitions.

Carl buttresses his reading with a historical account of the evolution of Kant's thinking on the problem first posed in the letter to Herz. In Carl's view, the letter does not distinguish two possible projects, that of explaining how the rules of the understanding must apply to objects encountered through the senses, and that of explaining how those rules apply to objects cognized through the senses. He thinks that Kant offers a sketch of a solution to the second and easier problem in some Reflections from around 1772–73. Having distinguished '*a priori*' from '*a posteriori*' and 'analytic' from 'synthetic' propositions, Kant notes that humans seem to have judgments such as 'everything that is alterable has a cause' that are synthetic *a priori*. After asking himself rhetorically whether these are revelations or prejudices, he supplies a different answer:

> If certain of our concepts contain only what makes experience possible for us, then they can be specified prior to experience; indeed, they can be specified *a priori* and with complete validity for everything we can ever encounter. (R4634, 17.618, cited by Carl, 1989b, 8)

Carl takes the reasoning in this sketch to presuppose the possibility of experience. He then notes that

> The claim that they [the categories] are related to objects if and only if they are conditions of the possibility of experience does not prove that they are in fact related to objects. We need the further premise that the concept of experience is not empty . . . that there are objects of experience. (1989b, 9)

He believes that Kant introduces the notion of apperception, first in the *Duisburg Nachlaß* and then in the *Critique*, to supply that missing premise, to permit an argument that experience is possible. In his view, the passages cited above from the opening of the transcendental deduction and from section 26 are implicit criticisms of the first sketch of the deduction and also pointers to the more difficult thesis to be proved (1989b, 10–11).

Carl takes the *Duisburg* notes to supply a robust proof of the possibility of experience, because he understands the apperceptive 'I' to be a substantial subject. As such, the 'I' would have a nature and its actions would be directed by that nature. Since its nature is to combine representations in ways specified by particular concepts, the possibility of experience is guaranteed—and the fact that all intuitions that humans have must accord with special concepts is explained. As states of a human, the intuitions are combined in accord with the nature of her mind. Carl believes that the discovery of the Paralogisms forced Kant to change his proof strategy.

In Carl's view these two proof strategies—from the possibility of empirical cognition and from apperception—reappear in the *Critique* in the guise of what Kant describes as the 'objective' and 'subjective' deductions. Scholars have also tried to follow the A Preface clue that the transcendental deduction has both a 'subjective' and an 'objective' side to fathom its structure, but there is little consensus on what the sides are. Carl takes the objective deduction (A92–93, A96, A111, Carl, 1992, 53) to regress from the 'fact of experience,' the fact that humans have empirical cognition, and the subjective deduction to establish that 'experience' is not an empty concept through an exploration of the relation between the unity of apperception and object cognition (1992, 53).[9]

Although I agree with Carl about the centrality of the subjective deduction (i.e., the discussions of apperception), I'm not persuaded that he has captured either the logical structure or the development of Kant's thinking about the transcendental deduction. Let's start with the development issue. In a Reflection almost immediately prior to what Carl characterizes as the first draft of a deduction (R4634 cited above), considerations are raised about the mental actions through which humans

> posit [*setzen*] a representation in and for itself . . . From these [actions] arise all cognitions: namely how we can grasp **data** and form something for ourselves

that is called cognition. <u>In nature no **data** can come before us unless, when one perceives the laws therein, they correspond to the universal kinds according to which we posit something</u>; because otherwise no laws would be observed, or any object whatsoever, but only confused internal alterations . . . (R4631, 17.615, CNotes 148–49, my underscoring)

The claim that nature alone does not produce sensible data understood as such is repeated and partially explained in passages from the *Duisburg Nachlaß* that I repeat (with their labels) for easy reference:

[B.] By a universal concept of a sensible **dati**, in which the reality and at the same time its relation to the sensible condition in general is indicated, we understand the action of sensibly determining an object in accordance with such condition, (R4674, 17.643, CNotes 158)

[D.] Now if a norm for the rule of appearances in general or of experiences is to arise—e.g. everything existence is in substance—then **x** is sensation in general as the **specif[ication]** of reality. <u>By being represented as reality it becomes the material of a rule or sensation becomes capable of a rule</u>, and **a** is only a function of the apprehension of appearance as given in general. Now since everything must be given in time, which therefore comprehends everything in itself, thus **b** is an **actus** of apperception, namely the consciousness of the subject which apperceives as that which is given in the whole of time is necessarily connected with it, for otherwise the sensation would not be represented as belonging to me. (R4676, 17.656, CNotes 166, my underscoring)

Nature can produce sensations, but since the concept of a sensible datum is that of something that both indicates reality and occurs in time, nature could not produce sensations understood as sensible data. Rather, representations must be posited as representations or understood as sensations which are real and which indicate something else. None of these Reflections explains why sensations or representations must be understood as such, but the contrast with animal cognition discussed in Chapter 2 provides an answer. Rational cognition requires that cognizers know the bases of their cognition; since the bases are their sensations or representations, they must recognize these representations as such.

In stressing that perceiving sensible data as such involves finding laws in them according to which humans posit something else (their objects) as real, R4631 (quoted above) anticipates an important theme of both the *Duisburg Nachlaß* and the *Critique*. Sensations contribute to cognition when they are understood as representations that serve as the basis for the application of rules (associated with concepts) (A106, A126, discussed below). The dating of most of Kant's *Nachlaß* is controversial, so my claim is not that this Reflection must be earlier than the *Duisburg Nachlaß*. It is rather that if Carl is right that these notes are earlier, then there seems to be a continuous line of development. The concept of 'apperception' appears in Kant's Reflections on theoretical philosophy for the first time in the *Duisburg* notes. It is introduced there with three 'titles' that present conditions that hold for representations insofar as they are set (*gesetzt werden*) in the mind: belonging to a subject, following each other, and composition (or belonging to a whole) (chapter 6, section 4). But it seems to me that this sketch of a 'formal' introduction of 'apperception' develops the suggestion of the possibly earlier Reflection (R4631, quoted above) that, for cognition to be possible, cognizers must be able to posit representations, including sensations, in the mind as such by proposing explicit constraints on that positing, constraints that may have implications about the rules that need to be found in the sensory data.

Unlike Carl, I do not see two interpretive lines being developed in these notes, one that starts from the assumption of empirical cognition and another that starts from 'apperception,' understood in terms of a substantial subject. It seems more natural to see the hint about apperception in the early Reflection and the explicit discussion of it in the *Duisburg Nachlaß* as part of the exploration of the necessary conditions for empirical cognition. Cognition requires sensible representations that are both indicators of real things and states of a subject. Since there are conditions for being states of a subject—the states must be related in time—it is necessary that the rules 'perceived' in the data be such that the sensory representations can be thought of as meeting those conditions. One advantage of this approach is that it enables us to understand how Kant might have believed that an argument that regressed from the necessary conditions for empirical cognition could reach a conclusion about all the objects that come before the human senses (and thus to honor the weighty textual evidence in favor of the former as the transcendental deduction's opening premise and the latter as its intended conclusion). If the necessary conditions for empirical cognition include a subject recognizing her representational states as such, then any further necessary conditions for the latter will be necessary conditions for the former. In this way, one can start by exploring the necessary conditions for cognition and end up by establishing necessary conditions for any object of which humans can form a sensory representation that is understood as such. And as Carl notes, the deduction's intended conclusion is that any object encountered by the senses must fall under the categories. I have indicated in a general way how the theory of apperception fits into an overall proof of the universal applicability of the categories. The details come in Chapter 9.

4. Apriority and Activity

In characterizing both the analytic and the synthetic methods, Kant describes a step where the investigator reverses course from tracing the possibility of empirical cognition in general back to its sources and argues from the sources to (particular) cognitions. This step is where the 'how possible?' question is answered. Cognition is possible only if the categories can be applied to all the objects encountered through the senses. But how is that possible? The introduction to the Analytic of Concepts presents its project as the dissection of the faculty (*Vermögen*) of understanding. It explores

> the possibility of *a priori* concepts, by locating them solely in the understanding, as their birthplace, and by analyzing the understanding's pure use as

such. For this exploration is the proper task of a transcendental philosophy . . . Hence we shall trace the pure concepts all the way to their first seeds and predispositions in the human understanding, where these concepts lie prepared until finally, on the occasion of experience they are developed . . . (A65–66/B90–91)

This project can seem misbegotten. How can dissecting the understanding into the basic actions required for cognition establish anything about the applicability of even very general concepts? To understand Kant's answer to the question of how experience is possible, we need to figure out how the two seemingly disparate projects of the Transcendental Analytic—dissecting the faculty of understanding and establishing the legitimacy of the use of categorial concepts—relate to each other.

Kant believed that he could establish the legitimate application of the categorial concepts to objects of experience if he could show that the universal and necessary principles embodied in the concepts applied to all objects of experience. The second book of the Transcendental Analytic is entitled the Analytic of Principles. His idea seems straightforward. Exactly what bothered Hume about the ordinary concept of 'cause' is that its use presupposed the necessary and universal principle that 'all events have causes.' Hume attacked the legitimacy of the concept by denying that there are any good reasons for accepting the principle that stood behind it (1739/1978, 78). Correlatively, Kant defends the use of the concept by showing that the principle that underlies it is correct. When he suggests at the beginning of the Introduction that *a priori* concepts might arise through the activities of the understanding (B1), what he means is that the principles presupposed by categorial concepts might arise in this manner.

How can this happen? The solution to the puzzle lies in Kant's arresting claim in the A deduction that

> the understanding is always busy scrutinizing [*durchzuspähen*] appearances with the aim of uncovering some rule in them. (A126)

An active understanding examines sensory representations to see if they could fall under its rules. Here I present a simplified version of the process just to get out the basic idea. Necessary complications are added in Chapters 8 and 13.[10] To take the obvious example, the understanding would run through the representations provided to it by the senses to see if any can be understood as instances of causation, as an instance of an object altering from being in state B to being in state C in the presence of some other object A.[11] However many instances are observed of B-type properties being succeeded by C-type properties in the presence of objects of type A, it is impossible to conclude that the succession from state B to state C in the presence of A is necessary. The law that As cause objects to alter from state B to state C could never be extracted from sensory data. Yet some sensory data can be interpreted as instances of it. The understanding looks for possible instances of causal rules and when it finds candidates, when B-type properties are always followed by C-type properties in the presence of A, it pronounces the relation to be one of cause and effect. The understanding continuously scrutinizes and the only events that it takes note of are those that are candidates for standing in causal connections. In effect, its scrutinizing is governed by the law that all alterations that count as such are caused. Thus, *insofar as they are cognized by the mind*, all alterations will be presumed to stand in causal relations. That is the sense in which *a priori* concepts arise through the activities of the mind: The activities sift through the data seeking instances, thereby (implicitly) excluding any possible noninstances and thereby guaranteeing the universality of the principle associated with the concept. It is legitimate to apply the causal concept to events cognized by humans, because within this realm, the principle presupposed by the concept holds universal sway.[12] If the understanding scrutinizes in accord with all the categorial principles, then they will hold across all cognized events and objects and 'empirical cognition' will not be an empty concept.

5. A 'Transcendental' Deduction

Having considered why the transcendental deduction might be considered a 'deduction,' I turn, finally, to the question of why it is 'transcendental.' I take up this signature piece of terminology last, because it is easier to understand against the background of the goals, argumentative form, and other special concepts of the transcendental deduction. The *Critique* supplies a number of clues that Kant sees his use of 'transcendental' as loosely continuous with the tradition. He equates the 'transcendental' concepts with the 'categories' and he is explicit that he borrows the latter notion from Aristotle. He explains that categories are 'fundamental concepts' that have their seat in the understanding (A81/B107). Paragraph 12, added to the second edition, also refers explicitly to the 'transcendental philosophy of the ancients' (B113). Although his usage draws on that of his predecessors, it also represents a sharp break from them. In keeping with the general project of revealing alleged metaphysical insights as epistemological requirements, he recasts 'transcendental' concepts not as concepts of the most basic kinds of things, but as concepts that are required for cognition of things in general. He differentiates 'transcendental' cognition from both cognition of things in themselves and cognition of the (merely) logical structure of knowledge.

The *Critique* contains several discussions that are intended to bring 'transcendental' into focus. Passages (3) and (6) have already been cited in part.

(1) I call all cognition **transcendental** which is not concerned so much with objects, but with our manner of cognizing objects, insofar as that should be possible *a priori*. (A11/B25, amended translation)

(2) Not every kind of cognition *a priori* should be called transcendental, but only that by which we cognize that—and how—certain representations (intuitions and concepts) can be employed or are possible purely *a priori*. The term 'transcendental,' that is to say, signifies such cognition as concerns the *a priori* possibility of cognition, or its *a priori* employment. Neither space nor any *a priori* geometrical determination of it is a transcendental representation; what

can alone be called transcendental is the cognition that these representations are not of empirical origin . . . (A56/B80–81, amended translation, my underscoring)

(3) Transcendental analytic consists in the dissection of all our *a priori* cognition into the elements that pure understanding by itself yields. In so doing, the following are the chief points of concern: [1] that the concepts be pure and not empirical; [2] that they belong, not to intuition and sensibility, but to thought and understanding . . .

By 'analytic of concepts' I do not understand their analysis, or the procedure usual in philosophical investigations, that of dissecting the content of such concepts as may present themselves, and so of rendering them more distinct; but the hitherto rarely attempted **dissection of the faculty of the understanding** itself, in order to investigate the possibility of looking for them in the understanding alone, as their birthplace, and by analyzing the pure use of this faculty. This is the proper task of transcendental philosophy . . . (A64–66/B89–91)

(4) [An empirical deduction of *a priori* concepts is a labor entirely lost] therefore, a deduction of such concepts . . . must be transcendental.

. . . [Again] a **deduction** of the pure *a priori* concepts can never be obtained in this manner [empirically] . . . For in view of their subsequent employment . . . they must be in a position to show a certificate of birth quite other than that of descent from experiences. (A86–87/B118–19)

(5) Hence the transcendental deduction of all *a priori* concepts has a principle to which the entire investigation must be directed: *viz.*, the principle that these concepts must be recognized as *a priori* conditions for the possibility of experience (whether the possibility of the intuition found in experience, or the possibility of the thought). (A 94/B126).

(6) In transcendental cognition, so long as we are concerned only with the concepts of the understanding, our guide is the possibility of experience . . . The [transcendental] proof proceeds by showing that experience itself, and therefore the object of experience, would be impossible without a connection of this kind [between concepts]. (A783/B811, my underscoring)

The intimate connection between 'transcendental' and '*a priori*' is evident in passages (1) through (5); the link between apriority and originating in the [activities of] the understanding is equally evident in passages (2) through (4); passages (2), (5), and (6) connect 'transcendental' to a mode of proof in terms of the possibility of experience or empirical cognition.

Tying these various elucidations together, 'transcendental' concepts are, as the Ancients claimed, 'pure' concepts that originate in the understanding; they are also concepts that have a special use in that they are required for the possibility of empirical cognition in general. The demonstration that the categories or transcendental concepts are required involves establishing that the principles they presuppose are required for the possibility of empirical cognition. The *Duisburg* notes provide some evidence for how Kant understood the special use of the concepts (and so the principles): The principles provide the standards for observation, a use that could not be established through empirical observation. A 'transcendental' deduction is an argument defending the legitimacy of the use of *a priori* concepts by demonstrating that the principles associated with them are required for cognition in general— because they provide the standards for the observations that are the foundation of empirical cognition. 'Transcendental' cognition is cognition that some aspects of (human) cognition are 'transcendental': These elements originate in the activities of the understanding and provide the concepts/principles that supply the standards for cognition in general.[13]

8

Synthesis: Why and How?

1. Problems to Be Solved

A final preliminary remains. We need to get a lot clearer about the central explanatory concept of the transcendental deduction's theory of cognition, that of 'synthesis.' A number of puzzles surround this notion and threaten to engulf the deduction in a thick fog. The purpose of the chapter is to sort through some basic questions about synthesis, so that we have a clear enough understanding of it to navigate the deduction's reasoning.

Perhaps the most obvious question about the synthesis doctrine is why Kant thinks that he needs this *prima facie* psychological notion. We can begin to address the issue by considering potential reasons that have surfaced in earlier chapters. Kant and many others accepted Leibniz's hypothesis of *'petites perceptions.'* Chapter 3 presents Tetens's account of perception: An image consists of many small feelings that have been joined together in a single sensation by an act of consciousness that thereby distinguishes it as a single or unitary sensation (chapter 3, p. 33). One role for synthesis or combination is joining *petites perceptions* to produce a conscious image. DeVleeschauwer took the A deduction's first 'synthesis of apprehension' to be importantly similar to Tetens's 'joining' of small perceptions in a single conscious representation (1962, 86).

Chapter 6 cites passages from the *Duisburg Nachlaß* where Kant discusses the concatenation of sensations or representations (e.g., passage A, p. 69) and the 'setting' of various representations in the mind as representations of the subject and as following one another (passage F, p. 72). Concatenating or 'setting' representations would involve combining representations. It is fairly obvious why Kant believes that sensations need to be concatenated and so why he regards such a synthesis as necessary. He denies that temporal relations can be sensed. Since people are conscious of the succession of their mental states, the representation of a succession of states must be produced by some process that involves combining representations.

A passage in the *Duisburg Nachlaß* (R4681, 17.668) maintains that all combination comes about through the mind, a doctrine that is forcefully reasserted in the opening paragraph of the B deduction (B130). Although the *Duisburg* notes link combining to the mind, they do not explain why the mind—in contrast to the faculty of sensation— must do any combining. The passage about animals and concept use discussed in Chapter 2 provides a plausible answer. Kant takes the ability to recognize the door as the mark of 'stall' and so the ability to use the concept 'stall' to presuppose the ability to make the judgment, 'this door belongs to this stall' (p. 19). Any such judgment involves the combination of representations, 'door' and 'stall.' Cognition involves concept use and concept use requires combining representations, so we have another reason for emphasizing 'synthesis'—and one that is very evident in the *Critique*.

Section 3 considers hypotheses about further reasons that Kant may have had for emphasizing the notion of 'synthesis.' Even at this point, however, we have a variety of reasons. An appeal to synthesizing seems necessary to explain how cognizers are able to form images out of *petites perceptions*, how they can cognize the succession of their mental states, and how they can use concepts. Under these circumstances, it is not surprising that Kant introduces a broad concept of 'synthesis.' Before turning to that account, it may be helpful to recall the overarching problem to be solved. He needs to explain the applicability of rules or concepts of the intellect (understanding) to objects of sense. Many passages in the *Duisburg* Reflections discuss two sorts of combining, intellectual and the combining of sensory states or sensory materials (e.g., passage A in Chapter 6, p. 69). Such discussions do not solve the problem signaled in the letter to Herz, so much as illustrate it. The same seems true of the list just compiled. Forming images and representing a succession of mental states may involve rules for constructing sensory representations, but more needs to be said to link such rules to rules involved in concept application.

A frequently cited passage in the *Critique* appears to solve the problem by brute force. Kant provides a preliminary characterization of concept application in terms of 'functions' that unite representations:

> Concepts . . . rest on functions. By function, I mean the unity of the act of ordering various representations under one representation. Hence concepts are based on the spontaneity of thought, whereas sensible intuitions are based on the receptivity of impressions. (A68/B 93)

Then he simply asserts that

> the same function that gives unity to the various representations **in a judgment** also gives unity to the mere synthesis of various representations **in an intuition**. This unity—speaking generally—is [*heißt*] the pure concept of understanding. Hence the same understanding—and indeed through the same acts whereby it brought about, through analytic unity, the logical form of a judgment in concepts—also brings into its representations a transcendental content, by means of the synthetic unity of the manifold in intuition as such, and because of this, these representations are [*heißen*] pure concepts of understanding applying *a priori* to objects. Bringing such a transcendental content

into these representations is something that general logic cannot accomplish. (A79/B105, amended translation)[1]

In this passage Kant assumes a process of concept formation that is discussed in greater detail in Chapter 13. His idea is that in forming the concept of a thing (a 'stall') or an event (a 'sailing') an act of understanding uses something like a template that relates to a logical form of judgment. Concepts are not pasted together by experience in the manner suggested by Empiricism. Rather, the 'stall' concept is made on the basis of a template of a thing with properties, so that judgments of a particular form (in this case categorial form) would be associated with it, for example, 'a stall has a door.' It may or may not be analytic that a stall has a door; it is analytic that the concept is associated with categorial judgments. Having been formed on the 'substance' ('thing with properties') template, 'stall' must be able to be the subject of a categorial judgment, because the possibility of having properties will be thought in the concept. The concept 'sailing' would be built on an event template, where the properties of an object change in the presence of something else. The event template is associated with hypothetical judgments, for example, 'when a floating device encounters wind, it moves from one place to another.' His bold claim is that the understanding uses the same rule or function—and even the same act or process of applying the rule—in producing concepts that are associated with judgments of particular logical forms and in uniting representations in intuitions, intuitions that acquire 'transcendental content' through this process. Any account of Kantian 'synthesis' must clarify this crucial claim in such a way that it can be seen to have some plausible rationale. The task is made more difficult by Kant's definition and discussion of 'synthesis.'

2. Kant's Definition

Kant introduces the concept of synthesis in a way that seems backwards. Having contrasted the receptivity of the senses with the 'spontaneity' of the understanding, he considers what the spontaneity of thought requires or demands or indicates (*erfordern*):

> Only the spontaneity of our thought requires that this manifold in order to be turned into a cognition, must first be gone through, taken up, and combined in a certain manner. This act I call synthesis. (A77/B102, amended translation)

Since the transcendental deduction is supposed to examine the necessary conditions for the possibility of empirical cognition, it seems that we should be considering what empirical cognition demands. For example, why does empirical cognition require a spontaneous understanding? Instead he asks his reader to consider the implications of a spontaneous understanding for cognition.

Kant's reasoning appears to be something like this: We know that cognition requires both intuitions and concepts and we know that concepts involve 'spontaneity,' a combining that unites different representations 'in' and/or 'under' a further representation. Granting these points, cognition is possible—concepts can apply to intuitions—only if the ordering produced by the spontaneous combination of elements in a conceptual representation is isomorphic to, or in some way appropriate to, the ordering of materials in intuitive representations. And that implies that the latter materials must be combined in a manner that fits with the spontaneous ordering in conceptual representations. The *Duisburg* notes include a discussion where Kant contemplates the possibility that the rules of intellect might depend on the principles of apprehension:

> [O.] Everything that is given is thought under the universal condition of apprehension. Hence the subjective universal of apprehension is the condition of the objective universal of intellection. (R4675, 17.653, CNotes 164)

He also suggests a dependency of conceptual rules on perceptual representations in his handwritten logic notes:

> What is it then in the representation that is in agreement with the represented things? Since the representation borrows its ground from the represented thing, it agrees with the latter in that it is composed out of its partial concepts in the same way that the whole represented thing is composed out of its parts. E.g., one can say that the notes of a musical piece are a representation of the harmonic combination of the tones—not as if a note were similar to a tone, but because the notes have a combination among themselves like that of the tones themselves. (R1676 16.78, CNotes 35)

By 'notes,' Kant means the musical notations. His point is that even though written music does not resemble the tones it represents, the structure of the notations derives from and is isomorphic to the harmonic relations among the tones. In a similar way, the structure of the concept of an object would be isomorphic to the structure of intuitive representations of objects. More abstractly, there must be an agreement between the concepts and the (intuitive) representations of things, and the latter representations supply the standard.

The *Duisburg* notes also bruit the opposite dependency, where intellectual rules are the conditions of (perceptual) apprehension:

> [P.] rules [of appearance] for the solution of appearances are actually the conditions of apprehension, insofar as it proceeds from one to another of them and conjoins them. (R4678, 17.660–61, CNotes 169)

The preliminaries to the 'synthesis' definition reflect his settled position that, because the understanding is spontaneous, the agreement between sensory and conceptual materials required for cognition is possible only if the latter serves as the standard for the former.

Kant defines 'synthesis' as follows:

> By **synthesis**, in the most general sense of the term, I mean the act of adding [*hinzuzuthun*] different representations to one another and of comprehending

[*begreifen*] their multiplicity in one cognition . . . synthesis [must precede analysis, because it] is what . . . gathers the elements of cognition and unites them to [form] a certain content. Hence if we want to make a judgment about the first origin of our cognition, then we must first direct our attention to synthesis. (A77/B103, amended translation)

The emphasis on the primacy of 'synthesis' over 'analysis' seems to be in tension with the claim made two pages later (A78/B105) that the same understanding that *brought* about the forms of judgment in concepts through analytic unity also *brings* about a synthetic unity in intuitions. There would be no incongruity, however, if Kant's view is that the understanding brings about an analytic unity in concepts, that is, connects the concept to certain forms of judgment, for example, 'sailing' to judgments such as 'when a floating device meets wind, it moves,' by originally forming the concept 'sailing' on the event template. I suspect that the tenses are meant to indicate the primacy rather than the priority of the intellectual synthesis to the intuitive one. Perhaps, though, they just indicate the history of epistemology: It has long been recognized that judgments have determinate logical forms that reflect acts of understanding; the novel claim is that the same acts by which the understanding structures concepts perform a second function of arranging sensory materials. How this is supposed to happen is partially explained below.

Kant's intentionally broad definition of 'synthesis' raises great difficulties for the 'same function, same act thesis.' Because he uses 'representation' to cover a wide range of mental states, and offers no restriction in the definition, synthesizing could be applied to everything from unconscious perceptions to ideas that go beyond the bounds of any possible empirical knowledge (A320/B376–77). The scope of 'synthesis' raises a basic question: Is synthesizing a conscious or an unconscious process?

In both the A and B deductions, Kant ties synthesis to consciousness. An A deduction passage about 'counting' that will be one of the foci of Chapter 9 includes the claim that

This number's concept consists solely in the <u>consciousness</u> of this unity of synthesis. (A103, my underscoring)

A crucial B deduction passage that will be considered at length in Chapter 9 repeats the suggestion that some syntheses are conscious and that these are crucial to self-identity:

Reference to the subject's identity . . . comes about not through my merely accompanying each representation with consciousness, but through my adding one representation to another and being <u>conscious</u> of their synthesis. (B133, my underscoring)

The language of the general description of synthesizing, the act of 'adding,' suggests a conscious process; the transcendental deduction citations are explicit about consciousness in synthesizing.

Yet, Kant continues his general account of 'synthesis' by presenting it as an unconscious process:

> Synthesis, as such, as we shall see hereafter, is the mere effect produced by the imagination, which is a blind but indispensable function of the soul without which we would have no cognition whatsoever, but of which we are conscious only very rarely. (A78/B103)

As a 'blind' function of the imagination, synthesis 'as such' must be unconscious.[2] On the other hand, the very next sentence offers a contrast. In the case of concepts, synthesizing is not blind:

> Only [*Allein*] bringing this synthesis **to concepts** is a function belonging to the <u>understanding</u>; and it is through this function that the understanding first provides us with cognition in the proper meaning of the term. (A78/B103, amended translation, my underscoring)

This passage makes two important points; it also raises obvious problems of consistency.

The first key point is the contrast, the claim that synthesizing concepts requires a nonblind faculty, the faculty of understanding. We have already encountered a rationale for linking concepts to consciousness. Concept use is possible only for rational animals, animals who know the basis of their usage. If a cognizer knows why she calls something a 'stall,' then she must be conscious of her representation, and of its various marks, and conscious that she sometimes applies the concept to the object on the basis of those marks and conscious that she cannot apply the concept if those marks are absent. The second important point is about cognition in its 'proper' sense. Kant is narrowing the focus of his inquiry. His exploration in the transcendental deduction concerns the sort of cognition that is distinctive of human or rational cognizers. 'Cognition' in that sense requires concepts and so consciousness.

Although the links among cognition, concepts, and consciousness are central to Kant's project, the resulting claim of conscious synthesizing seems to lead to contradiction.

1. Synthesis as such (*überhaupt*) is carried out by the imagination.
2. The imagination is a blind faculty of the soul.
3. At least sometimes cognizers are conscious of synthesizing.
4. The understanding carries out syntheses involving concepts.

Claim (4) contradicts claim (1) and, on any plausible construal of 'blind,' claim (3) contradicts the conjunction of claims (1) and (2).

Kant resolves the inconsistency between (1) and (4) by suggesting that the imagination synthesizes sensory representations under the guidance of the understanding (A119, B151). Again, his position is that the rules governing the organization of materials in sensory representations are subordinate to the rules of the intellect or understanding. That is how the fit between the intellectual and the sensory materials is going to be explained. I discuss several aspects of these passages below. For the moment, my concern is just with the basic model. It can be expressed without anachronism and with greater clarity in contemporary terminology. The idea would be that the understanding has an executive function that determines how, in general, the mind is going to solve the cognitive problem before it (of combining representations in a conceptual representation); a lower level system (the imagination) carries out the executive orders in order to produce an intuitive representation that is suitable for the particular conceptual representation. The cognitive subject is blind with respect to this imaginative construction.

The inconsistency among (1), (2), and (3) can be eased by assuming that (3) does not refer to the synthesizing of the imagination *per se*, but to the high level principles of the understanding that direct it. Still it is somewhat misleading to claim that all syntheses are carried out by the imagination—except the syntheses of concepts that are carried out by the understanding. The discussion also undermines the 'same function even same act' thesis of A79/B105. Insofar as the understanding both synthesizes conceptual materials and directs the synthesis of sensory materials, the claim is vindicated. We have also seen the rationale for the assumption that the understanding must do the directing. But it is a stretch to claim that it is the same act, since the synthesizing of sensory materials involves additional steps.

The claim of conscious conceptual synthesis is itself vexed. If the idea is that in each concept use a cognizer thinks about the rules governing the concept, then the claim would be refuted by ordinary experience. As we shall see in Chapters 9 and 13, Kant's view is that concept use involves appeal to implicit rules and to a variably clear awareness of acts of checking off the marks to determine whether the concept can be applied. Although cognizers may be only implicitly aware of the rules and the acts, that will turn out to be sufficient for rational cognition. Nevertheless there is a great gulf between the implicitly conscious synthesizing of representations in concept application and the syntheses of the imagination. Only rarely can the imagination's ways of synthesizing be made explicit is such a way that they could be carried out consciously (see the discussion of mathematical construction below). Given that significant difference, it again seems tendentious to describe both syntheses as involving the 'same act.'

The A and B deductions differ in their accounts of how and why the understanding directs the syntheses of sensory materials. In the A deduction, the synthesis of the imagination is introduced through a consideration of the law of association. Despite its wide scope, the operation of synthesizing does not cover combination by association. Instead, association provides a useful contrast case to synthesis. Synthesizing requires acts of adding representations and of grasping the multiple elements in a single cognition. As characterized in the A deduction, association does not involve acts:

> There is a natural law whereby representations that have often followed or accompanied one another will finally associate and thereby enter into connection with one another. (A100)

The representations do the associating and connecting themselves (*sich vergesellschaften und . . . setzen;* my underscoring). That the presence of an act is the essential difference between synthesizing and other sorts of connections across representations is clear in the opening discussion of the B deduction (B130). Besides providing a contrast for synthesis, introducing the law of association is meant to point up a weakness in Empiricism. Particularly in Hume 'association' is the principal theoretical concept for explaining cognition. Kant tries to raise doubts about its suitability as a foundational process: Suppose there are no similarities across representations that enable the law to operate? He thinks the only way to establish its inevitable operation is to appeal to transcendental idealism. Only the representations of which cognizers are aware in inner sense are candidates for the law of association; and it may well be that such representations necessarily exhibit particular sorts of combination that allow them to be [stored] and reproduced (A101).

Kant never makes clear in the A deduction how the truth of these last two claims would solve the problem of qualitative dissimilarity. The obvious objection is that even if candidates for association must have categorial representational structure, none of the categories bears on the issue of qualitative similarity. Further in the 'systematic' discussion of section 3 of the A deduction he changes argumentative tactics. The focus is no longer on inner sense, but on apperception. All representations are governed by the principle of apperception and thus may involve combinations of representations by categorial principles (A118–119).

> **The unity of apperception [considered] in reference to the synthesis of imagination is the understanding**; and the same unity with respect to the **transcendental synthesis of imagination** is **pure understanding**. Hence there are in the understanding pure *a priori* cognitions that contain the necessary unity of the pure synthesis of imagination in regard to all possible appearances. (A119)

Again, it is unclear how this move has any relevance to the problem of qualitative similarity raised in the preliminary discussion.[3] Although the systematic discussion is superior to the preliminary one in its appeal to the principle of apperception to restrict the field of representations at issue, its lack of reference to inner sense leaves out a key element. As is much clearer in the B deduction, a central *explanandum* for the theory of imaginative synthesis is the representation of succession in inner sense.

A common view that Kant eliminated what he called the 'subjective' deduction (Axvi–xvii) from the B edition is belied by his extensive discussion of the relation between the understanding and the imaginative syntheses in section 24. This passage is not concerned to argue that the categories must apply to objects of the senses, but to provide a plausible story about the faculties that make this possible.

> This **synthesis** of the manifold of sensible intuition, which is *a priori* possible and necessary, may be called **figurative** synthesis (*synthesis speciosa*). This serves to distinguish it from the synthesis that would be thought, in the mere category, in regard to the manifold of intuition as such; this latter synthesis is called combination of understanding (*synthesis intellectualis*) . . . **Imagination** is the power of representing an object in intuition even **without the object's being present**. Now all our intuition is sensible; and hence the imagination,

because of the subjective condition under which alone it can give to the concepts of understanding a corresponding intuition, belongs to **sensibility** . . . This synthesis is the effect [*Wirkung*] of the understanding upon sensibility, and is the understanding's first application (and at the same time the basis of all its other applications) to objects of the intuition that is possible for us . . .

This [synthesis] moreover, we always perceive in ourselves. We cannot think a line without **drawing** it in thought. We cannot think a circle without **describing** it. (B151, 154, amended translation)

Despite the 'same act' thesis, Kant both differentiates the *synthesis intellectualis* from the *synthesis speciosa* and also relates it to the latter. The syntheses of the understanding are not tied to any particular sort of sensory intuition, though they are concerned with the combination of sensory material in general. By contrast, the *synthesis speciosa* is an aspect of sensibility, because it relates to the particular human form of intuition. On the other hand, this synthesis is directed by—is an effect of— the understanding. How the imagination works is by representing something as present in a sensory representation that is not (and, perhaps, was not) present in the sensory materials.

Kant illustrates the directing through mathematical examples. As the concept of a line enables a cognizer (consciously) to construct a representation of a continuous mathematical line by sweeping out the line with a point (or so he claims), the understanding's general ways of combining materials enable a cognizer's particular form of imagination (unconsciously) to produce representations of a continuous space occupied by objects of outer sense and of a continuous time populated by representations of inner sense. The treatment of synthesis is better in the B deduction than it was in the A edition, both because it drops the rationale of avoiding qualitative dissimilarity (which categorial structure doesn't address) and because it links the imaginative synthesis directly to mathematics. It thus enables Kant to elucidate the construction of a representation of a succession of mental states by making an analogy with mathematical construction.

Still, there are clear limitations to what Béatrice Longuenesse calls the 'mathematical' model for the transcendental deduction (1998, 34).[4] Kant's goal is to relate the categories to objects of sense, but the concept most closely related to mathematical construction is something like continuity.[5] The Second Analogy considers the continuity of causal change (A208/B253). That passage occurs, however, after the important task of arguing for the necessity of using the category of causation and its attendant principle of the necessary succession of perceptions. It is merely an elaboration of how causation looks to a cognizer with spatiotemporal forms of sensory representation.

The *synthesis speciosa* is an integral part of the explanation of how the categories apply to objects of sense in the B deduction. The crucial paragraph relating the categories of the understanding to the forms of intuition (§26) explicitly refers back to the discussion of this synthesis (B161n.). However, that section also illustrates its claims by the example of cold causing the freezing of water (B163).[6] Since causal relations involve qualitative similarities and differences, it is not obvious how the example relates to the mathematical model. A second problem with the mathematical model is that it has no obvious role for the 'raw' materials of cognition provided by sense (B1). Unlike mathematics, empirical cognition is constrained by the empirically available materials. These limitations do not show that the mathematical model is unimportant for Kant. He returns again and again to mathematical examples. They suggest that it needs to be supplemented.

Because it deals directly with the relation between data and the categories, an obvious candidate would be the scrutinizing process presented in the A deduction and discussed in Chapter 7 (section 4). In that chapter, I noted that my example of scrutinizing for causal relations in terms of temporal following was oversimplified. A full version will be presented in Chapter 13. At this point, I can indicate in schematic form how scrutinizing might relate to mathematical construction for the central case of causation. Empirical cognition begins with the receipt of sensory data. The understanding scrutinizes those data for some sort of evidence that the category of causation can be applied to particular materials. It then brings the data, x, y, and z, under the rule of causation, the rule that one existent is the ground of the alteration in the property of another existent (A160/B199, A189, B232). So x is represented as A (the representation of an event or causal power)[7] and 'y/z' are represented as B and C (representations of different states of a single object). In this process, sensory data have been posited as representations that are synthesized—combined—in accord with the template provided by an *a priori* category. Since time is the form of human sensibility, the understanding directs the imagination to construct a sensory representation of a continuous change from object in state B at an earlier time to object in state C at a later time in the presence of event or power A.

On the 'scrutinize and construct' model, the 'synthesis of the understanding' is a matter of seeking values for the parameters of its categorial templates in the sensory data, placing the values in the template, and of blindly, with the aid of imagination, constructing sensory representations that are suitable to the particular categorial template.[8] This model combines the A deduction's focus on the relation between data and conceptual rules with the B edition's superior treatment of constructing representations on analogy with mathematical construction. It meets a number of *desiderata* that arise in the course of both editions. It replaces two obscure descriptions ('intellectual synthesis' and 'imaginative synthesis') with two fairly clear ones: parameter filling and constructing. Equally important, it honors the two central claims of Kantian epistemology: Empirical cognition is a combination of *a priori* and *a posteriori* elements and it requires both intuitions and concepts. The model presents Kant as providing a plausibility argument for how *a priori* categories could relate to sensory representations without offering hypotheses about actual mechanisms. It also suggests how conscious conceptual syntheses—syntheses that combine some concepts in a resulting concept—could be made possible through the culling and preparing of sensory data through blind syntheses. Thanks to the unconscious synthesizing, intuitive representations would be available that are amenable to classification under general rules, a point that is developed in Chapter 13.

Despite these advantages, the 'scrutinize and construct' model is not completely faithful to Kant's text.[9] Specifically, it does not honor the 'same function, same act' thesis. As we've seen, however, it is not obvious how that thesis can be honored in the context of Kant's other claims about 'synthesis.' What is helpful about the model is that it captures the key points that both the understanding and the imagination engage in synthesizing and that the former faculty guides the latter.

3. Synthesis and Objective Reference

Section 1 offered preliminary hypotheses about Kant's rationale for believing that human cognition must involve synthesizing. Having looked in some detail at how he thinks synthesizing works, we can return to the issue of why he thought it was necessary for cognition. One recurring suggestion is that he believed that synthesis was necessary if cognizers are to refer representations to objects. In the early 1980s Rolf George offered compelling reasons for believing that Kant would have been aware of Sensationism, the hypothesis that the sensations caused in humans by objects impinging on their sense organs are nonreferential. As he notes, the way Kant constructs the '*Stufenleiter*' of representations suggests that he was not only familiar with this view, but assumed its truth (George, 1981, 239):

> The genus is representation as such (*repraesentatio*). Under it falls representations with consciousness (*perceptio*). A **perception** that refers solely to the subject, *viz.*, as the modification of the subject's state, is **sensation** (*sensatio*) . . . (A320/ B376)

If sensations *per se* are nonreferential, then something is needed to connect them to objects. George hypothesizes that Kant may have been influenced by Condillac, who maintained that objective reference is achieved when various sensations are pulled together in a judgment (George, 1981, 236, 244). As will be evident in the discussion of Hoppe's work below, a number of texts are explicit that the categories are required in order to achieve reference to objects.

George's interpretive approach yields a straightforward answer to why Kant was convinced that representations must be synthesized: He agreed with the solid arguments of the Sensationists that sensations were nonreferential and so realized that sensations must be combined in order to permit the reference to objects required by cognition.[10] Although George has helpfully drawn attention to the Sensationist elements in the *Critique*, I'm not sure they are a major factor in the case for synthesis. It is tendentious to 'argue from absence,' but it seems reasonable to believe that if the nonreferential character of sensations were critical, then it would be evident in the A edition's 'argument from below' for synthesis. The argument should begin something like: 'Because sensations are mere states of a subject' and so forth. In fact, the reasoning turns on a very different consideration:

> What is first given to us is appearance. When it is combined with consciousness, it is called perception. (<u>Without the relation to an at least possible consciousness, appearance could never become for us an object of cognition</u>, and hence would be nothing to us . . .). Because every appearance contains a manifold, consequently [*mithin*] different perceptions are encountered in the mind [that are] in themselves [*an sich*] scattered and single, these perceptions need to

be given a combination that in sense they cannot have. Hence, there is in us an active power to synthesize this manifold. This power we call imagination. (A120, amended translation, my underscoring)

The key point is that nothing can be an object of cognition without relating to a possible consciousness. And the problem is that—considered on their own—different perceptions are scattered and single rather than belonging to a consciousness. This lack was noted earlier, at A107, where Kant remarked on the absence of any constant and enduring self across different representations. That passage will be discussed further in Chapter 9. In this context, my point is that the reason a synthesis of perceptions is required is to connect them to one consciousness. Besides the allusion to A107, the way the argument concludes is strong evidence that the problem arises because perceptions in themselves do not relate to a single consciousness. After veering through a further discussion of the law of association, Kant maintains that a lack of associable materials is impossible.

> For only by classing all perceptions with one consciousness (original apperception) can I say, for all perceptions, that I am conscious of them. Hence there must be an objective basis (i.e. a basis into which we can have *a priori* insight . . .) on which rests the possibility . . . of a law extending through all appearances . . . This basis, however, we cannot find anywhere except in the principle of the unity of apperception in regard to all cognitions that are to belong to me. (A122)

The reason it is crucial to connect different perceptions to a common subject is that that is only way that a cognizer can know the basis of her judgments and so enjoy rational cognition. The driving force behind this argument for synthesis is not the fact that sensations do not of themselves refer to objects; it's the fact that they do not of themselves refer to subjects.

In arguing against the traditional view that Kant's epistemology should be understood mainly in the context of Rationalism and Empiricism as opposed to Sensationism, George moves the focus from the *a priori* notion of apperception. He also slights the role of the categories as *a priori* standards for observation and so cognition that is so clear in the *Duisburg Nachlaß*. If this role is given the prominence it seems to warrant, then we get a different picture of the relation between Kant's project and the doctrines of Sensationism. His goal from early on was to show that *a priori* concepts and principles apply to objects of the senses. It is a crucial part of the *Critique*'s argument that the categories are required to distinguish illusion from reality and so to indicate the real objects of cognition. George considers the possibility that sensations might indicate how they should be combined. As he notes, that possibility would undermine Kant's argument for categorial syntheses (1981, 247–48). But the argument of the *Critique* would also be undermined if sensations indicated the real objects that caused them. So the truth of Sensationism is a necessary condition for him to argue in the manner that he does. But that doesn't imply that his goal was to solve the Sensationist challenge about objective reference rather than to defend the applicability of *a priori* categories to objects of sense.

In his pioneering study of Kant on synthesis, Hansgeorg Hoppe agrees with George that the problem to be solved by synthesis is objective reference. He comes to this conclusion from the other side, suggesting, perhaps, a consilience of the evidence. For Hoppe, it is not so much the deficiencies of sensations in not indicating their referents,[11] as the requirements of cognition, that demand a synthesis of representations. As he puts it, the problem with the Empiricist approach common to Locke and to Hume is

> maintaining, on the one side, the separateness of single representations and maintaining, on the other, the (intentional) reference to objects of such separated representations. (1983, 83)

Hoppe cites Husserl, as well as Strawson and Jonathan Bennett, as agreeing that this situation is impossible (1983, 84–85 and n.). The difficulty is that

> in each perception of an object, including single ones, there is an allusion to other perceptions of the same object that can, for example, expand upon the first perception; certainly they can also reveal [it] as deceptive or mere imagination. (1983, 84)

In Strawson's terminology, the concept of objective cognition, including objective perception, requires the possibility of the 'corrected view' (1966, 250) and that in turn requires the possibility of different perceptions or representations of the same object.

Hoppe notes the Kantian texts that provide ample grounds for attributing the view that it is part of the concept of an 'object of representation' that any perception of an object implicitly directs the cognitive subject to others. I cite them to show how incontestable the evidence is. One occurs in the A deduction, the other in the B deduction:

> We find, however, that our thought of the reference of all cognition to its object carries with it something concerning necessity. It does so inasmuch as this object is regarded as what keeps our cognitions from being determined haphazardly or arbitrarily . . . <u>For these cognitions are to refer to an object, and hence in reference to this object they must also necessarily agree with one another, i.e., they must have that unity in which the concept of an object consists</u> . . . (A104, my underscoring).
>
> Cognitions consist in determinate reference of given representations to an object. And <u>an **object** is that in whose concept the manifold of a given intuition is united</u>. But all unification of representations requires that there be unity of consciousness in the synthesis of them. Consequently the reference of representations to an object consists solely in this unity of consciousness, and hence so does their objective validity and consequently their becoming cognitions. (B137, my underscoring)

Kant maintains that it is part of the concept of objective reference that it is possible to have more than one representation of an object. My disagreement with Hoppe concerns what this doctrine implies about the grounds for his belief in the necessity of synthesis.

The argument can seem very straightforward: It is part of the concept of an object of cognition that diverse representations can represent the same object. Therefore those representations must be able to be connected together (so, e.g., they can be compared and a later representation could give the lie to a first impression). Therefore it must be possible to synthesize them. Although Kant would accept each of these claims, they do not get at his core argument for synthesis, the argument concerning the necessary unity of apperception, a version of which we saw above (A122). To begin to appreciate the problem, it will be helpful to consider how Hoppe locates the need for synthesis in Kant's larger project. Although he recognizes that his reading diverges from the way in which Kant spells out the connections among objective reference, synthesis, and the unity of apperception, he believes that the kernel of insight in his theory can be captured as follows. In the B deduction, readers should skip over the difficult and unsustainable '*Egologie*' of section 16 and turn immediately to the unity of apperception required for object reference in section 17 (Hoppe, 1983, 119–21). 'Synthesis' should not be thought of as a process or procedure for uniting representations, but as the (united) condition in which representations must stand to have an object (Hoppe, 1983, 121).[12]

Similarly, despite Kant's assertion that representations must be brought to the unity of apperception (A108), that unity should not be thought of as something achieved, but as a presupposition of the complex representations required for objective reference:

> For Kant in the first instance, the unity of apperception is the thoroughgoing and original unity of a unitary frame [*einheitlich Rahmen*] that makes possible and contains in advance all particular syntheses. This unity is not brought about afresh in a current judgment . . . (Hoppe, 1983, 171)

Hoppe accounts for the necessity of this unity of apperception by appealing to the 'verse argument' of the Paralogisms. As the different words of a verse cannot be distributed among different subjects, the different representations that the subject refers to the same object cannot belong to different subjects (1983, 125). Finally, although Kant describes the unity of apperception in terms of 'self-consciousness,' the necessary unity across representations is not that of a subject, but that of an object. It is that unity that is necessary for reference to an object (1983, 128).

Hoppe's use of the verse argument to explicate the unity of apperception is somewhat surprising. Kant does not use this argument to establish the necessary unity of the subject in the transcendental deduction; he criticizes his predecessors' use of it in the Paralogisms.[13] Further, Hoppe recognizes that, on his reading, the fact that a representation belongs to the unity of apperception means only that that it belongs with others to the same cognizer or to the same 'unitary frame.' He muses about how the tautology that 'all my representations belong to me' could have any consequences. How could it imply the necessity of the categories to the unity of apperception? (Hoppe, 1983, 22–23). For that matter, how could the truth of a tautology be a necessary condition for objective reference? Hoppe expresses the converse worry.

In many passages, including B137 cited above (p. 110), the unity of apperception appears to be not merely a necessary, but also a sufficient condition for object reference. How could the truth of a tautology be a sufficient condition for objective reference? Further, in trying to avoid Kant's '*Egologie*,' by taking the unity required by transcendental apperception to be nothing more than the unity required for objective reference, he makes the central portion of the transcendental deduction argument otiose. If the necessary unity of apperception just is the unity required for objective reference, then the argument is not that objective cognition requires the unity of apperception, which in turn requires the categories. It is simply that objective cognition requires the categories.

Carl also raises the worry about how the unity of apperception can be a sufficient condition for objective cognition in his brief commentary on the B deduction:

> It is curious that Kant does not ask himself this question [about whether the synthetic unity of apperception testifies to the status of representations as cognitions of objects], for he believes that the circumstance in which the synthesis of representations in a cognition of an object presupposes being accompanied by 'a unity in the consciousness of the synthesis of the object representation,' that this unity is already sufficient for constituting the relation of representations to an object, consequently for cognition. (1998, 197)

He also mentions the issue briefly in his book on the A deduction:

> That the reference of a cognition to an object should be the unity of apperception is hardly comprehensible. (1992, 185)

In that study, Carl maintains that Kant does not offer any ground for transcendental apperception (1992, 178). Under these circumstances, he thinks that the best a commentator can do is clarify the relations among that assumption and related key assumptions. This effort leads him to make the same suggestion for explaining the necessity of the unity of apperception that we have just encountered in Hoppe:

> How does Kant arrive at this thesis [that the identity of the consciousness of our self is a necessary condition for all representations]? . . . A subject who is capable of acquiring knowledge cannot therefore possess only one representation. But why is their combination a necessary condition for representing something? One assumes that one can only represent something if it is possible that different representations can represent the same thing, [for]only then can the relation of a representation to its object be made comprehensible, if [that is] several representations allow of being referred to the same object. (1992, 201)

Carl agrees further with Hoppe that it is a mistake to take Kant at his word that different representations are brought to the unity of apperception. This is just a colorful way of putting the point that they must all belong to the unity of apperception for cognition to be possible (1992, 182). Although he resists Kant's talk of creating the unity of apperception, he explains that that unity is 'synthetic,' because it depends on a synthesis of representations (1992, 202).

Hoppe's and Carl's realizations that, on their readings, Kant's insistence that the unity of apperception is necessary and sufficient for objective reference is rendered inexplicable give them pause, but it does not lead them to revise. I will suggest how they should have revised. The problem comes in trying to avoid a full engagement with the doctrine of the synthetic unity of apperception. Hoppe is explicit that he hopes to work around this troubling aspect of the text. Carl is less explicit and he acknowledges that Kant thinks of the unity of apperception as synthetic because it presupposes a synthesis. In characterizing the doctrine as 'ungrounded,' however, he indicates that he doesn't see much in it. Since Hoppe is self-consciously trying to bracket the '*Egologie*,' I focus on the shortcomings of his proposed shortcut.

The metaphor of a frame is telling. On this account, objective reference is possible only if different representations exist in combination with each other. But how is that to be understood? Carl and Hoppe see clearly that the fact that each representation could be attached to a 'self' doesn't show anything (Carl, 1992, 202, Hoppe, 1983, 125). Placing the representations in a common frame is a metaphorical way of saying that they can all be compared, as is necessary if it is comprehensible that a representation can refer to an object. As Longuenesse notes, Kant wrote in a tradition where representations were regularly described as being compared (1998, 84ff.). A standard view was that a present representation could be compared with something 'stored' in (in the frame of) memory. Expressing this view in terms of contemporary discussions of consciousness, it would amount to the claim that the combination of different representations in the representation of an object, or the comparison of different representations of the same object, requires 'access-consciousness'[14] to all of the representations. They are available somewhere and in such a way that they can be accessed by the active powers of the mind. Access-consciousness is clearly a necessary condition for thinking on Kant's or any sane theorist's view. The problem for Hoppe (and I think for Carl) is that although access-consciousness is necessary for reference to objects, it is plainly not sufficient. Since they more or less identify the unity of apperception with access-consciousness, it too turns out to be insufficient for objective cognition. But Kant claims that the unity of apperception suffices for objective cognition.

Again, Hoppe seems to see the problem. He wonders why Kant raises the possibility of a noncategorially mediated mental life in which cognizers would not even know themselves. He thinks that this material has to be read circumspectly. Kant is not saying that such a scattered mental life is a real possibility; he is trying to describe an impossible condition to illuminate the structure of human mental life (Hoppe, 1983, 132). If the unity of apperception is understood in terms of access-consciousness, then a disjointed mind would be impossible for anyone with an intact memory. Kant raises this possibility twice, once at A112 and once at B134. In the A deduction, he is trying to argue that the categories are necessary for meaningful thought. The B discussion is different. There he maintains that synthesizing is necessary in order to have a single consciousness—otherwise

> I would have a self as multicolored and varied as the representations of which I am conscious. (B134)

Just before this text, he explains that cognizers can recognize themselves as an identical consciousness only through awareness of their acts of synthesizing (B133). This passage will be discussed further in Chapter 9. Even now, however, the general shape of the solution to the Hoppe-Carl sufficiency problem should be evident. If we take Kant at his word that representations must be brought to the unity of apperception, then the obvious suggestion is that the synthesizing that produces the unity of apperception can take place only when synthesizing also produces object cognition. In this way the transcendental unity of apperception would be both a necessary and sufficient condition for object cognition. My criticism of Hoppe's study is that he left out an important aspect of Kant's synthesis theory, the part about how synthesizing produces the unity of apperception. In trying to fill in this piece in the next chapter, I honor his methodological principle that the reasoning should be epistemological rather than psychological (1983, Chapter 1).

4. Five Syntheses and Their Relations

Kant describes three syntheses in the A deduction (those of 'apprehension,' 'imagination,' and 'apperception,' A94) and two in the B deduction (the *synthesis intellectualis* and *synthesis speciosa*, B151). I have presented five different syntheses. First, there are syntheses that are required to produce sensory images from *petites perceptions*. Second, some syntheses must supply the spatial and temporal relations in representations of spatiotemporal arrays. Third, there are syntheses of the intellect required by concept use. Given that cognition requires coordinated conceptual and intuitive representations—and that the former are synthesized into particular structures—there is a fourth synthesis that is needed to arrange sensory materials into suitable intuitions, namely, the *synthesis speciosa* (pp.105–107). Finally we have just encountered the synthesis that is required to bring about the synthetic unity of apperception.

Kant will try to connect the first, second, third, and fourth syntheses, by suggesting in section 26 of the B deduction and arguing, in the Principles chapter, that the *syntheses speciosae* directed in accord with categorial principles work on the canvas of human sensibility, so that there is only one synthesis that produces sensory representations of objects and events in spatial and temporal arrays that are suitable to concept application.[15] As we see in Chapter 9 he also connects the third and fifth syntheses, moving from talk of synthesis according to conceptual or categorial rules to talk of syntheses in conformity with the requirements of the transcendental unity of apperception. Preceding sections have offered rationales and models for the four of the five syntheses; section 2 presented a model for understanding the relation between the conceptual and intuitive syntheses. The fifth synthesis, the synthesis of apperception, has been given neither a rationale nor a model. That is part of the project of the next chapter: to present the argument for the necessity of the synthetic unity of apperception and to try to make this synthesis comprehensible.

9

Arguing for Apperception

1. Introduction

Kant's theory of the transcendental unity of apperception emerges in the course of his argument for the objective validity of the categories. In this central chapter, I try to show how the argument for apperception works and what the resulting theory looks like. My analysis begins with a more precise characterization of the type of cognition from which the argument regresses. I then consider exactly what the principle of apperception says. I examine the argument for apperception where it first enters the (first) text, in the discussion of the 'Third Synthesis' in the A deduction (though with some clarifying interpolations from the second edition). I then turn to the version of the argument presented in the B deduction, which includes some important additional considerations.

Although my focus is on the argument for rather than from the principle of apperception, I show how that argument fits into the overall defense of the categories for the parade case of causation—a clear test for any interpretation. I conclude with a discussion of the relation between empirical and transcendental apperception. On this point I am somewhat critical, arguing that Kant's claim that empirical apperception presupposes transcendental apperception is true, but only half the truth. As his theory stands, transcendental apperception also presupposes the empirical variety.

The preparatory materials in Chapters 7 and 8 were intended to permit a relatively uninterrupted presentation of the transcendental deduction argument here. For similar reasons, I briefly consider two alternatives before offering a continuous line of interpretation. In showing why these *prima facie* attractive approaches should be rejected, I defend and motivate my competing analysis.

2. 'I-Think' as the *'Cogito'*: The One-Step Deduction from Judgment

As I read it, the transcendental deduction examines the requirements of (rational) empirical cognition and argues for the necessary togetherness of different representations for such cognition; from that intermediate result, it moves to a defense of the categories. Two textual clues invite different construals of the argument. First, Kant describes the principle of apperception as the 'first and supreme' principle of his philosophy and he casts it in terms of the possibility that the representation 'I-think' can accompany any representation. Second, in an oft-cited note to the *Metaphysical Foundations of Natural Science*, he claims that he can solve the problem of how the categories relate to experience

> almost through a single inference from the precisely determined definition of a **judgment** in general (an action through which given representations first become cognitions of an object). (4.475–76, C1781 190)

The first clue makes it tempting to think that the argument is very like that of Descartes' *Meditations* and so begins with 'apperception' as the bedrock on which all of cognition rests. The second may suggest that judgment—as opposed to apperception—provides the key to linking intellectual concepts and activities to the manner in which objects are represented by the senses. These clues can mislead. Kant could not have begun with apperception and his musings about judgment do not imply that he ever thought that the transcendental deduction could be completed without a full exploration of apperception, without his '*Egologie*.' It's not that judging isn't of central importance to the deduction; it's that it forges an indissoluble link between judging and apperception.

We've already encountered the contextual and textual reasons for rejecting the suggestion that the principle of apperception is like the *cogito* in being first known and so a suitable first premise for an argument about cognition.[1] Wolff and his followers actively debated Descartes' claim that the *cogito* ranked first in the order of knowing (Chapter 5, section 3). Against the background of this debate, and of the general (unresolved) question of how self-consciousness is possible, Kant should not have assumed that '*Ich denke*'—I am conscious of myself as thinking—was acceptable as a first premise. The debate also suggests a further hypothesis for the transcendental deduction's complex structure. His weaving together of considerations about the requirements of object cognition and about the role of the subject in cognition may reflect his appreciation of the solid arguments on each side that the other side was one-sided.

We have also seen some of the textual reasons for denying that Kant cast his argument in a Cartesian mold. As did many of Wolff's successors, he formulates the *cogito* as an inference—and then rejects it (e.g., A355). 'I exist' could not be established inferentially. In the Anthropology lectures, he claimed instead that it was an 'intuition' (25.10, 244, 473–74). Had he continued to believe that cognizers knew of their existence (as simple and identical beings) through intuition, then he might have offered the principle of apperception as a first premise. In fact, he explicitly rejects intuition as a possible basis for 'I exist' in the *Critique* (e.g., B135). He discusses three types of intuitions, intellectual intuitions, outer intuition of objects in space, and inner intuitions of the mind. Intellectual intuitions are impossible for humans. In the B edition, he is also explicit that

> If I were to think of an understanding that itself intuited . . . then in regard to such cognition the categories would have no signification whatever. (B145)

Not only are intellectual intuitions impossible for humans, if they were possible, then the assumption that humans have an intellectual intuition of themselves would be a uniquely bad premise for a transcendental deduction of the categories. Put positively his claim is that the absence of an intellectual intuition of the 'I' is an essential presupposition in the argument for the categories. That leaves outer and inner sensory intuitions. Outer intuitions can present only bodies, not minds. So, only inner intuition could present a thinking self. But he is clear that inner sense can provide no intuition of a self (A107, B134). Given the historical context and his views about intuition, it is hard to see how he could take the unity and identity of a thinking self as a first premise.

Further, the transcendental deduction texts are evidence against the '*cogito* as premise' hypothesis. Especially in the A deduction, the discussion does not begin with apperception, but works its way to apperception as a necessary condition for cognition. But even the B deduction does not begin with apperception; it begins with the need for combination and unity in cognition. Apperception enters as a solution to the problem of the unity required for combination. Although Kant does not argue from the *cogito*, he tries to situate it in relation to his views in the B edition. Chapter 11 explains how he saw the relation between his 'I-think' and that of his illustrious predecessor.

Kant's speculation about the possibility of a one-step transcendental deduction from a precise definition of 'judgment' makes two different approaches seem attractive. We considered one of them in Chapter 8. Kant's gloss of judging as 'an action through which given representations first become cognitions of an object' strongly suggests that objective reference is the key to the deduction. Chapter 8 argued that objective reference cannot be the whole story, because it cannot explain crucial aspects of the theory. One could also take the focus on judgment to indicate that the 'forms of judgments' are as central to the transcendental deduction as they are to the 'metaphysical deduction.'[2] This seems to be Longuenesse's (1998) view, because she devotes most of her interpretive efforts to explaining how the forms of judgments relate to the syntheses of the imagination, thereby resolving the Critical problem. Her analyses are extremely useful, but they tend to displace the unity of apperception and the categories from their central role in the transcendental deduction.

The *Metaphysical Foundations* reference to 'judgment' is misleading, because it mentions only one aspect of Kant's use of this term—its relation to object cognition. It is a firm part of his general theory that cognition always has two sides, a subjective and an objective side. Under the heading Cognition in General, his (i.e., Jäsche's) *Logic* explains that

> All our cognition has a **twofold** relation, first a relation to the **object, second,** a relation to the subject. In the former respect it is related to **representation**, in the latter to **consciousness**, the universal condition of all cognition in general. (9.33, CLog 544)

Given the generality of this claim, a complete or adequate definition of 'judgment' should have a second, subjective side. He presents that side—indeed only that side—in his definition of 'judgment' in the *Logic*. Under the heading 'Definition of a judgment in general,' he explains:

> A judgment is the representation of the unity of the consciousness of various representations, or the representation of their relation insofar as they constitute a concept. (9.101, CLog 597)

Checking Jäsche's version against Kant's handwritten notes reveals that he offers an abbreviated, but faithful, representation of the Reflections:

> The representation of the way in which different concepts (as such) belong to a consciousness is judgment. They belong to a consciousness according to laws of imagination, thus subjectively, or [according to laws] of understanding, that is [are] objectively valid for every being that has understanding. The subjective connection depends on the special situation of the subject in experience. (R3051 16.633)

In light of these fuller discussions of 'judgment,' the *Metaphysical Foundations* proposal of a 'one-step' transcendental deduction from the definition of judgment does not shift the enterprise away from a study of consciousness and apperception.

The book on science appeared a year before the B edition of the *Critique*. So we may go to that text to see how the 'one-step' deduction was carried out. There we encounter the familiar discussion of the apperceptive principle. The focal point of section 19 of the B deduction—the paragraph about judgment—is the subjective side of the complete definition. It repeats the points made in the notes:

> But suppose that I inquire more precisely into the reference of given cognition in every judgment, and that I distinguish it, as belonging to the understanding, from the relation in terms of the laws of the reproductive imagination (a relation that has only subjective validity); I then find that a judgment is nothing but a way of bringing given cognitions to the objective unity of apperception. (B141)

Hoppe and Longuenesse are well aware of these texts.[3] Hoppe makes an interpretive decision to avoid the '*Egologie*.' Longuenesse uses the close relation between apperception and judgment to interpret apperception—and so the transcendental deduction—through judgment rather than judgment through apperception (1998, 57–58, 69). Below I argue that we can understand crucial moves in the deduction only by recognizing the independent status of the *a priori* representation 'I-think' and its principle. My interpretive point here is that the somewhat autobiographical note in the *Metaphysical Foundations* should not be understood as moving judgment—rather than apperception—to the center of the deduction. Given the subjective aspect of Kant's 'judgment' definition, the note does not undermine, but reinforces, the centrality of the unity of apperception, a centrality that is obvious in the texts.

3. What Kind of Cognition Is at Issue in the Transcendental Deduction?

There is fairly wide agreement that the distinctive feature of the transcendental deduction is that it argues for the legitimate use of the categories by arguing (in the

Principles chapter) that the categorial principles that invest them with meaning are necessary conditions for the possibility of experience.[4] Chapter 7 presents reasons for glossing 'experience' as 'empirical cognition.' But exactly what sort of 'empirical cognition' does Kant propose to investigate? Or better, how does he understand 'empirical cognition'?

One of the most well-known theses of the *Critique* is the claim that cognition requires both intuitions and concepts (e.g., A51/B75). In section 1 of Chapter 1 of the Analytic of Concepts, Kant maps out the relation he sees between intuitions and concepts. A concept is or involves a function of unity among representations. It collects or combines different representations, intuitions or (other) concepts, under a common representation (A68/B93). So, for example, the concept 'dog' collects many intuitive representations of dogs under it. It also can contain other conceptual representations, for example, 'animal,' 'possessing a tail' (A68/B93ff.). He explains further that concepts (and the judgments they make possible) cannot stand in direct relations to objects:

> The only kind of representation that deals with its object directly is intuition. Instead the concept is referred directly to some other representation of the object (whether that representation be an intuition or is already a concept) ... In every judgment there is a concept that is valid [*gilt*] for many representations, and, among them it comprehends [*begreift*] also a given representation that is referred directly to the object. (A68/B93, amended translation)

That is, judgments about objects are possible only when the concepts they contain can be understood as representations that express what is common to many intuitive representations, including an intuition that stands in a direct relation to the object (through that object causing certain changes in the mind, A19/B33).

Although the *Critique* stresses that the cognition at issue is conceptual or discursive, it does not spell out how such cognition should be understood. Fortunately Kant's *Logic* is more explicit about the relations among 'discursive' cognition, concepts, and the 'marks' of concepts:

> From the side of the understanding, human cognition is discursive, i.e., it takes place through representations which take as the ground of cognition that which is common to many things, hence through marks as such. Thus we cognize things **through** marks and that is called **cognizing** [*Erkennen*], which comes from being acquainted [*Kennen*].
>
> A **mark is that in a thing which constitutes a part of the cognition of it**, or—what is the same—**a partial representation, insofar as it is considered as a ground of cognition of the whole representation.** All our **concepts** are marks, accordingly, and all **thought** is nothing other than a representing through marks. (9.58, CLog 564, my underscoring)

(Here Jäsche faithfully reproduces materials from R2277, 2279, and 2281, 16. 297–98.)

The text that Kant used for the course, G. F. Meier's *Excerpts from the Doctrine of Reason*, describes one use of marks (16.296). Marks are a ground of cognition, because they enable cognizers to differentiate the object of cognition from other things (24.113, R2283 16. 299). For example, the object is orange and other things are not. By contrast, Kant maintains that marks not only have this 'external' use but also an 'internal use.' In the latter case marks or partial representations are the ground on which the whole concept is applied to the object, not *via* identity and differences with other objects, but *via* identity of the marks (R2282, 16.298). The internal use of marks is not a matter of differentiation but of derivation (R2283 16.299). So for example, the concept 'body' might include the marks 'impenetrable,' 'extension,' and so forth (2.58, C1755 102, A106) and so be applied through the tacit judgments: 'this thing is impenetrable,' and so forth. Under these circumstances, one could derive 'x is impenetrable' from 'x is a body.'

This material is neither new nor controversial,[5] but I wish to highlight two important aspects of Kant's 'mark' theory of concepts. First, marks are concepts. The part-whole relation is not between intuitive representations and conceptual ones, but between concepts that are part of the content of other concepts and the latter 'whole' concepts. This is not a foundationalist account of conceptual cognition—not an explanation of how sensations or intuitions lead to concepts. The second noteworthy aspect of Kant's mark theory is that for a representation to be a mark, it must be considered as such. It is not that cognizers must have the concept 'mark' or the concept 'concept' or the very abstract concept 'representation.'[6] Rather, they must recognize that a mark—say 'impenetrable'—is a partial ground or basis for their application of the concept 'body.' It is part of why they call something a 'body' or part of what they presuppose in calling something a 'body.' Even when not considered in relation to a complex concept, but just on its own, a mark is still a basis of cognition, because it is the ground of cognition of the objects in its extension:[7]

> As one says of a **ground** in general that it contains the **consequences** under itself, so can one also say of the concept that as **ground of cognition** it contains all those things under itself from which it has been abstracted, e.g. the concept of metal contains under itself gold, silver, copper, etc. (9.96, CLog 594)

'Metal,' for example, is a ground of cognition of copper things, because it classes them together with other metals. In describing a copper kettle as 'metallic' a cognizer implies that it is similar to some things and different from others. To recognize a mark as such is to use the term with that understanding.

Humans not only have sensory systems that detect similarities in the properties of objects, they are also discursive cognizers. As such, they can recognize their representations of, for example, the color orange as presenting a humanly detectable property common to many things and (so) as marks—as things that can be offered in answer to the question of why they group those objects together (and exclude others) and of why they label something as a particular kind of fruit, an 'orange.' Since the cognition at issue in the *Critique* is discursive, conceptual, it should be understood as mediated by marks that are considered as such.

Kant also stresses the importance of marks to human cognition in his objection to Meier's suggestion that animals use concepts, a criticism discussed in Chapter 2. I repeat a portion of the relevant citation for easy reference:

I would go still further and say: it is one thing to **differentiate** things from each other, and quite another thing **to recognize** [*erkennen*] the difference between them. (2.59–60, C1755 103–4)

Having conceded to Meier that an ox can differentiate its stall by seeing that it has a door and so, in a sense, by means of one of its marks, Kant points to the crucial difference with the human case. It is the same point just highlighted in the *Logic*. Something can function as a mark only if it is recognized as the basis of differentiation.[8]

The cognition that is the topic of the *Critique*'s investigation is not merely empirical, that is, linked to sensory representations. It is also conceptual and for Kant that means that it is a matter of 'marks' or grounds of cognition that are recognized as such. This point will be crucial to Kant's argument linking cognition to apperception. Since a standard definition of 'rational cognition' is cognition where the cognizer can give the reason—or ground—of the cognition, I use the slightly odd description 'rational empirical cognition' (or, more briefly, 'RE cognition')[9] to characterize the *Critique*'s project. He does not use the expression 'rational cognition' for two reasons. First, he complains in his Logic lectures about the expression. It is too vague and such cognitions should be called 'cognitions of reason,' because that gives their source (24.151, CLog 119). Second, in the *Critique*, he has reasons for distinguishing the 'higher' faculties of 'reason' and 'understanding.' Given the latter usage, the cognition at issue might better be called 'cognition of the understanding' or, less formally, 'conceptual cognition,' because one of its sources is the understanding, the faculty of concepts. I use 'RE cognition', because it captures more fully the sort of cognition whose source is the 'higher faculties,' *viz.*, cognition where the subject knows the reason.

Kant's interest in RE cognition may suggest that he would be on the 'internalist' side of recent debates.[10] As noted in Chapter 2, however, he lists other varieties of cognition besides the rational. The transcendental deduction does not argue that all cognition requires internal justification, but that the RE cognition of which humans are capable is possible only when certain conditions are met. It is not an argument for internalist justification, but an argument from the assumption that, unlike animals, humans can know the reasons for their cognitions.

4. What Is the Principle of Apperception?

In earlier chapters and earlier in this chapter I refer to the 'principle of apperception.' I have also indicated the general shape of the transcendental deduction by reference to the principle. It regresses from the possibility of rational empirical cognition to the truth of the apperceptive principle; it will then argue that the principle of apperception requires that the categorial principles hold across all possible objects of the senses. Since Kant describes it as the supreme principle of cognition and of his theory, one might expect a fairly clear statement of it. The interpretive issue is complicated because of the two *prima facie* inconsistent treatments in the two editions.

Before turning to these texts, it may be useful to recall the longer and shorter historical context. Leibniz took the soul to be a special sort of monad. As a monad it was a simple substance whose states changed through time *via* the operation of a timeless internal principle. Souls possess not only substantial unity, but also memory and some awareness of the transitions from one state to another (though many perceptions are unconscious). The internal principle is also the ground of the conscious transitions and memories that provide subjects access to their own identities (Chapter 4, section 2). Although it is more nuanced, Leibniz's theory fits the description that Hume offered for the Rationalist accounts that were his target:

> Some philosophers . . . imagine we are every moment intimately conscious of what we call our Self; that we . . . are certain, beyond the evidence of a demonstration, both if its perfect identity and simplicity. (1739/1978, 251)

Lecture notes from his courses in Metaphysics and Anthropology suggest that Kant held something like this position in his pre-*Critique* days. Apparently he maintained that in thinking subjects are conscious of themselves as simple, as substantial, and as continuing subjects (Chapter 4, section 4). In this tradition a cognizer who is aware of his representations is aware of something that, as a matter of ontological necessity, belongs with other representations to a simple, permanent, and continuing self. A Reflection from the *Duisburg Nachlaß* presents a more subtle view. In thinking cognizers are conscious of representations as set in the mind according to three exponents: relation to subject, relation of following, and relation to the whole (Chapter 6, passage F, p. 72). This claim is not ontological. It is not that the representations of which the subject is conscious must belong with others to a subject-substance. It is that, in thinking, cognizers represent their representations as belonging to a subject, as successive, and as coherent.

Given this background and Kant's general program of 'reforming' metaphysics by recasting some of its key doctrines as presuppositions of cognition (most famously, 'all events have causes'), we should expect him to argue that the assumption that different representations all or necessarily belong to a common subject is required for RE cognition. That appears to be just what he is doing at the beginning of the A deduction's 'systematic' presentation of the argument for apperception:

> <u>We are conscious *a priori* of the thoroughgoing identity of ourselves in regard to all representations that can ever belong to our cognition, and are conscious of it as a necessary condition for the possibility of all representations.</u> (For any such representations represent something in me only inasmuch as together with all others they belong to one consciousness; and hence they must at least be capable of being connected in it.) This principle holds *a priori*, and may be called the transcendental principle of the unity of whatever is manifold in our representations. (A116, my underscoring)

A cognizer's consciousness of his identity is no longer a matter of intuiting something that is, as a matter of ontological necessity, a continuing self. It is an awareness of self-identity as a necessary condition for the possibility of representations that can represent something. In a note to the text, he elaborates the point:

All representations have a necessary reference to a possible empirical consciousness . . . But all empirical consciousness has a necessary reference to a transcendental consciousness (a consciousness that precedes all particular experience), *viz.*, the consciousness of myself as original apperception. It is therefore absolutely necessary that <u>in my cognition</u> all consciousness belongs to one consciousness (that of myself). Here, then, is a synthetic unity of the manifold (in consciousness) which is cognized *a priori* . . . The synthetic proposition that all the varied **empirical consciousness** must be combined in one single self-consciousness is the absolutely first and synthetic principle of all our thought as such. (A117n., my underscoring)

Any representation (that can be a part of cognition) must be able to be conscious. Although Kant does not explain why this is so, the rationale is clear from his general view of RE cognition. Were such consciousness impossible, a cognizer could never know the grounds of his cognition and so could not be a rational cognizer.

The 'epistemological turn' comes in the next step. The metaphysical proposition that any representation must belong with all others to a continuing self is replaced by the claim that in human cognition, empirical consciousness has a necessary reference to original apperception, that is, to one (continuing) consciousness. Matters become slightly confusing because the principle that Kant highlights has a complex structure: 'All the varied empirical consciousness *must* be combined in one single self-consciousness (for cognition to be possible).' He describes the proposition as 'synthetic.' Since it is also cognized *a priori*, it appears to be a synthetic *a priori* proposition, which is the same status as that of categorial principles. The principle of determinism is that 'all changes occur according to the law of cause and effect'; the claim that would be parallel to the apperceptive principle for the case of determinism would be: 'All changes must occur according to the law of cause and effect (for cognition to be possible).' The latter is a description of the thesis to be proved in relation to the causal principle. It is not the causal principle itself.

We can sort out the complications here by recognizing that the role of the deterministic principle in transcendental idealism involves two necessities and two apriorities. It is necessary for cognition that events are understood as standing in relations of necessary succession. The concept 'cause' cannot be extracted from experience, but is '*a priori*'; the proof that the causal principle is required for cognition is carried out by reason and so is also *a priori*. Kant is not explicit about the double use of these concepts, because he takes it to be obvious that the only possible proof of a universal and necessary proposition ('all events have causes,' 'all representations belong with others to a single self) would show the necessity of the proposition for cognition. He also takes it to be evident that the only possible defense of the use of an *a priori* representation or principle would have to be *a priori* from reason.

With this background, we can understand the structure of the apperceptive principle and also see that the roles played by the principle of determinism and by the metaphysical principle that 'for anything that is a representation, it must belong with others to some continuing self' are largely parallel. For ease in reference, I call the latter principle the 'I-rule'. I should note, however, that my nomenclature reflects Kant's position that the difficult philosophical problem about the ownership of representations concerns their 'togetherness' and not their 'mineness.' What needs to be shown is how different mental states can be unified in a single self and not how an individual can attribute a particular mental state to himself (which he thinks is *via* inner sense). So he assumes that it is sufficient to show that different mental states belong to a common *self*-consciousness or to the same 'I' to show that they necessarily belong together. At various points below, I take note of the fact that being necessarily connected to each other is only a necessary condition for being referred to a common 'I.'

In the A deduction, Kant rules out the possibility of an *a posteriori* basis for connecting a representation to others in a continuing self (A107). Since he takes representations to be either *a posteriori* or *a priori*, the representation of the unity of consciousness must be *a priori*. The B deduction presents the representation 'I-think' as *a priori* (B132). As in the case of the causal principle, the I-rule is *a priori*. If it is also synthetic, then the only way it can be established by the standards of scientific metaphysics is through an *a priori* argument showing that it too is a necessary condition for cognition. And that appears to be the thesis expressed in the apperceptive principle: 'All representations must (if cognition is possible) belong to a single self-consciousness.' Alternatively: it is necessary for cognition that representations are necessarily connected to a single 'I.' Part of the burden of the A deduction is to establish this highest principle, the thesis that the holding of the I-rule is necessary for cognition. In this way, it makes the same move with respect to the I-rule that the Second Analogy makes with respect to the causal principle. Both are removed from metaphysics and relocated among the assumptions that must hold for cognition to be possible. What is somewhat out of place is the focus on the synthetic status of the claim that cognition requires that different representations belong to a common self.[11] If it is to be established by *a priori* reasoning, then the claim should be analytic.

The A and B deductions appear to conflict on this point. In B, the apperceptive principle is characterized as 'analytic' (B135). The apperceptive principle of the B deduction is, however, a different principle. It is not the famous 'I-think' claim:

> The **I think** must be **capable** of accompanying all my representations; for otherwise something would be represented in [*in*] me which could not be thought . . . (B131–32, amended translation and punctuation)

In this text, as in the 'absolutely first principle' in A, the 'must' is an indication of a requirement of cognition. The principle that is characterized as analytic is presented later:

> All **my** representations in some given intuition must be subject to the condition under which I can ascribe them as **my** representations to an identical self, and hence under which alone I can collect them together [*Zusammenfassen*] as synthetically combined in one apperception through the common expression 'I think.' (B138)

In this principle, the 'must' does not indicate a general requirement of cognition: that is, these representations must be combined together in one identical self for cognition to be possible. It refers instead to the fact that, if different representations are linked to a common 'I,' then they must meet whatever conditions are required for belonging to a common 'I.'

This claim is not as banal as the claim that 'anything classified as green must meet the conditions for greenness,' because the condition of belonging to an 'I' is a matter of belonging with other representations to the same 'I.' Kant says this explicitly (though without the contrast to other sorts of concepts):

> For the manifold representations given in a certain intuition would not one and all be **my** representations, if they did not one and all belong to one self-consciousness. I.e., as my representations (even if I am not conscious of them as being mine), they surely must conform necessarily to the condition under which they **can** alone stand together in one universal self-consciousness. (B132)

Still, the claim that 'all my representations must conform to whatever condition or conditions are necessary for them to be collected together as my representations,' or, more generically, the claim that 'any representation that belongs with others to one consciousness must meet the conditions of belonging with others to one consciousness,' is a tautology. Since a tautology can have no implications beyond logical truths, it is natural to ask about the relevance of this tautology to the *Critique*'s project. Kant showcases its relevance in the dramatic B132 claim about the 'I-think.' For a representation to be of any cognitive use to its bearer it must be possible to think something through it,[12] and to think something through it, it must belong with others to a single 'I-think': It must be possible to attach a communal 'I-think' to it. Hence the opening sentence of section 16 that is rightly thought to be the essential point of the B deduction (the I-think must be able to accompany all my representations) is the equivalent of A's principle of apperception. Although the principle of the necessary unity of apperception in B prepares the way for the argument for the categories, it is a tautology that would be of no interest—because it might have no instances—except for the 'I-think' doctrine of B132. Given that doctrine, if cognition is possible, then there must be instances of different representations belonging to a common 'I.'

Two questions remain. Is the A deduction apperceptive principle/B deduction 'I-think' doctrine synthetic? Is the I-rule synthetic or analytic? Kant does not say clearly in either case. He describes the A edition's apperceptive principle as 'synthetic,' but is silent about the status of its equivalent in B. The formulation of the 'I-think' passage and the apperceptive principle in A both suggest that he thinks of the I-rule as having a synthetic *a priori* status and thus as needing to be established as necessary to cognition. But he doesn't say. Instead, he stresses that although the B deduction's principle of apperception is analytic, it presupposes a synthesis (B134, B135). By this, he means that synthesis is required for there to be any instances that meet the conditions of the I-rule, that is, any representations that belong with others to a single self-consciousness. Since being able to attach representations to an 'I-think' is necessary for cognition, such syntheses would also be necessary for cognition. His silence on the status of some key claims may reflect his belief that these last links among cognition, the I-rule, and synthesis are all that he needs for his argument for the categories. And perhaps his earlier claim that the A edition apperceptive principle was 'synthetic' was only an awkward attempt to express the necessity of synthesis to the possibility of applying the I-rule and so to the possibility of cognition.[13]

Since the proof of the A edition principle of apperception/B edition 'I-think' doctrine is a matter of bringing out the conditions required for RE cognition, the principle must be 'analytic,' even if it takes an enormous amount of work to reveal its presuppositions. The same is true for the I-rule. When 'representation' is understood as something that can take part in RE cognition, it turns out that, on careful analysis, any representation must belong with all others to a single consciousness. In this respect, the I-rule is not parallel to the causal principle. But the difference is not particularly significant for Kant's reform program in metaphysics. He redeploys both allegedly ontological principles as requirements of cognition. The difference between them is that the I-rule is so closely connected to the requirements of RE cognition that the rule itself and not just the principle that cognition requires the rule turns out to be analytic.

In sum, the A and B deductions present four interrelated principles connected to apperception.

1. The principle of apperception in A: 'All the variety of empirical consciousness must be combined in one single self-consciousness' (A117n).
2. The I-rule that is embedded in the A edition principle of apperception and in the 'I-think' doctrine of the B edition: 'Representations . . . [belong] with all others to one consciousness' (A116); 'The **I think** . . . [accompanies] all my representations' (B132).
3. The 'I-think' doctrine of B: 'The **I think** must be **capable** of accompanying all my representations' (B132).
4. The tautological B edition principle of apperception: 'All **my** representations in some given intuition must be subject to the condition under which I can ascribe them as **my** representations to an identical self' (B138).

The last is the least important. What the transcendental deduction is to establish is the I-think doctrine/A edition principle of apperception. In subsequent sections, I use 'principle of apperception' and 'I-think doctrine' interchangeably to refer to that thesis. Since the I-rule is embedded in the principle, it will also be a central topic, particularly in relation to the claim that it can be satisfied only when representations are synthesized.

5. The Apperceptive Synthesis of Recognition in a Concept

With a clearer understanding of the sort of 'experience' or 'empirical cognition' that constitutes the beginning of the regressive argument and of the conclusion to be established, we can turn to the text. 'Apperception' enters the A edition in the 'Third Synthesis,' which is variously described as the 'synthesis of apperception' and as the 'synthesis of recognition in a concept' (A94, A103, A115). My clunky section title—which Kant avoids, presumably on stylistic grounds—reflects the intimate connection between the unity of apperception and conceptual cognition (or judgment) in his theory. I do not begin the discussion with the Third Synthesis just because that is the point of entry for apperception. There are philosophical problems with his discussion of the Second Synthesis. It is supposed to explain the operation of the law of association, but cannot do so (Chapter 8, pp. 104–105). The placement of the synthesis of apprehension first in the A edition is also problematic. Kant's considered view is that apprehension is subject to the rules of the intellect, not vice versa (B161–62). Presenting the synthesis of apprehension as the 'First' in A gives the impression that it operates 'before' the others. The B deduction's treatment, which turns to the *synthesis speciosa* after the argument for the 'I-think' doctrine, is better in this respect. Although I start with the presentation in the A edition, I follow the better order of B. Moreover, I draw on some better formulations of the B deduction to clarify the A edition's line of argument—and some of the more expansive discussions in the A edition to fill in more cryptic moves of the B argument. I also refer to both editions in this section and the next to establish the commonality of some claims.

Kant's discussion of the Third Synthesis is unusual, because it employs a detailed example. The example is counting. Three reasons help to explain the selection. Mathematics and logic are the two obvious counterexamples to his thesis that cognition requires both concepts and intuitions. The example illustrates the role of sensory materials in arithmetic. A second reason is that he believes that construction in mathematical proofs can serve as a model for the constructive activities of the understanding. In this case, the point isn't to illustrate the production of continuous lines, but the fact that mathematical concepts enable cognizers to construct sensory (written or imagined) objects fitting the concepts. The third reason is connected to the second, though it may have a different motivation. In mathematics, cognizers do not have to wait for their senses to supply them with information in order to apply a concept. They can construct the 'data' for themselves. This feature enables him to present the example without having to be concerned about transitions between sensory states caused by perception, which are something that his theory will need to explain.

Although Kant has reasons for choosing a mathematical example, it is meant to illustrate judging or recognizing in a concept in general and this is somewhat problematic. He believes that all concepts are associated with rules (e.g., A106).[14] Since mathematical concepts are usually understood as having definitions, the example may suggest that the associated rules are necessary and sufficient conditions for the applicability of the concept. In fact, he thinks that neither empirical concepts nor categories can be defined (9.141–42, CLog 632, A727/B755–56).[15] The associated rules are not definitions, but expositions (incomplete analyses) of the concept (A728–29/B756–57). He thinks of these rules as universal, but for the case of empirical concepts at least, it wouldn't matter to his theory if the rules were probabilistic.

Once the suggestion of necessary and sufficient conditions is rejected and the rules are allowed to be probabilistic, Kant's assumption that concepts are associated with rules can be seen as a version of the standard contemporary view that concepts stand in inferential relations to other concepts and can be used only by individuals who explicitly or implicitly recognize those relations. The rules indicate some of those relations. In the case of concepts that are either not complex or not clear (where the subject doesn't know the inferential relations), the rule would be that of the external use of marks (above, pp. 119–120)—the rule that the concept indicates a property that can be detected by humans and is common to this object and others.

On Kant's telling, counting is more complicated than one might think. In the context of the A edition's discussion of the Third Synthesis, he explains that it is insufficient for cognition just to apprehend something in intuition (the First Synthesis), and just to be able to recall what has been apprehended (the Second Synthesis).

> Without the consciousness that what we are thinking is the same as what we thought an instant before, all reproduction in the series of representations would be futile. For what we are thinking would in the current state be a new representation, which would not belong at all to the act by which it was to be produced little by little. Hence the manifold of representations would never make up a whole, because it would lack that unity that only consciousness can impart to it. If, in counting, I forget that the units that now float before my mind or senses [*Sinnen*] were added together by me one after another, I should never cognize the amount [*Menge*] being produced through this successive addition of unit to unit; nor, therefore, would I cognize the number. For this number's concept consists solely in the consciousness of this unity of synthesis. (A103, amended translation)

His first point is that the mere ability to reproduce the series of stroke symbols, say four of them in a row, is insufficient for cognition. He does not refer to animals here, but the contrast is useful. An ox could have an image of four stroke symbols, but he could not recognize its contents under the concept '4.'

Using the counting rule (or any rule associated with a concept) involves a number of skills. A counter must be aware of his performance in such a way as to catch possible errors and, in this case, to know where he is in the process. Kant presupposes all this in making his second and positive claim: The counter needs to be conscious that he designates the first stroke symbol as '1', and so forth, in order to cognize the amount. In the terms used in the *Logic*, the counter needs to be conscious of his representations of '1,' '2,' and so on, as 'marks' or 'partial representations' that are the ground or basis of his conceptual representation '4.' (The representation '2' is a partial representation of the whole representation '4,' because any because any group of 4 objects must contain a group of at least 2 objects.)[16] The last sentence of the passage notes that, in this case, being conscious of applying the counting rule to the individuals and subgroups of a group is not only necessary for applying the concept to the group, it is also sufficient.

Kant elaborates and refines the account in the further discussion of this example:

> The very word concept could on its own lead us to this observation. For this one consciousness is what unites in one representation what is manifold, intuited little by little, and then also reproduced. Often this consciousness may be only faint, so that we do not [notice it] in the act itself, i.e. do not connect it directly with the representation's production, but [notice it] only in the act's effect. Yet, despite these differences, a consciousness must always be encountered, even if

it lacks striking clarity; without this consciousness, concepts, and along with them cognition of objects, are quite impossible. (A103–4)

He allows that thinkers do not have to pay much attention to individual steps, adding up the stroke symbols little by little. Still, they must be conscious of the judgment '4' as the effect of applying to the represented units the rule that a group has the size of '4' if and only if it consists in four units.[17] The discussion concludes with the very strong claim that without this consciousness, cognition of objects would be impossible.[18]

Given Kant's view of how concepts are employed, we can understand why he thinks RE cognition requires consciousness in acts of judging. Conceptual cognition requires that partial representations, '1,' and so forth, are not merely representations that float before the mind. They must be understood as partial representations, as the basis of the whole representation '4.' If cognizers did not consciously apply the concept '4' on the basis of the representations of the units, then they would not know the basis of their judgments. They would not know that they judge '4,' because they have already noted '2' units with more to follow. With arithmetical concepts the rules offer necessary and sufficient conditions for the applicability of the concept. So a cognizer could infer that the number of units in the group is '4.' Where the rules are merely partial explications, for example, 'bodies are extended,' the judgment that x is a body has 'x is extended' as its basis or partial ground, but the judgment 'x is a body' is not a valid inference from that ground.

Since the hypothesis of an awareness of mental acts can seem strange to contemporary readers, I offered some evidence for the phenomenon in Chapter 2. It would, however, have been familiar to Kant's contemporaries from the *Port Royal Logic* and from other standard texts. So he needn't elaborate on mental act awareness *per se*. His efforts at clarification take the form of a contrast between 'apperception' and 'inner sense.' Inner sense is introduced in the Transcendental Aesthetic. In arguing that a further faculty of apperception is needed, he rejects his earlier view that Lockean inner sense is the key faculty in RE cognition. We can get a better sense of how he understands both cognition and the active self-conscious faculty of apperception by considering why he no longer believes in the adequacy of inner sense.

Chapter 2 describes Tetens's efforts to explain why 'inner sense' should be understood as a sense (pp.23–23). On his account, inner sense is a sense, because it records acts of thinking. A mere record of having judged would, however, be insufficient for RE cognition as Kant understands it. The proper use of concepts requires the counter to be conscious, not that he has judged '4' or even that he is judging '4' right now. It is not even enough that he be aware through inner sense of his partial representations, '1,' and so on. *He must regard his partial representations as such, as the grounds of his cognition; he must be aware of judging '4' on the basis of his partial representations. To be capable of rational cognition, the subject must be aware—as she makes the judgment—of her act as having the appropriate basis. And that requires act-consciousness.* The creation of impressions of mental actions in a Tetensian inner sense is too little and too late to contribute to the rationality of the judgment.[19]

Locke had introduced 'inner sense' in terms of the awareness of mental states and of mental actions. Chapter 2 presented Kant's canonical account of the difference between inner sense and apperception in the *Anthropology* (pp.22–23). He invites his readers to contemplate being aware of their mental states through inner sense and being aware of their mental acts through apperception so that they may see how very different these awarenesses are. In that chapter, I raised a question: Why can't the difference lie in the objects of awareness rather than in the faculty that is so aware? The answer is now clear. The awareness in judging that is essential to cognition is not a perception of an act that could be separate from it. It is an indissoluble component of the self-conscious act itself.[20] Inner sense will not do, because when properly understood as a sense, it involves perception of having acted, not self-conscious action.

At this point, the A deduction has argued for an active self-conscious faculty of apperception. Chapter 10 examines the faculty of apperception in more detail. This chapter follows the argument for the unity of apperception. After the counting example, Kant broadens the argument to any object of cognition. He also introduces the idea of the concept of an object as providing a rule or standard for what makes something an object (A104–5). At one level, the object-rule is just another example of a rule associated with a concept, because all such rules provide standards for using concepts. For example, something falls under the concept 'dog' only if it falls under the concept 'animal.' On the other hand, the object-rule is extremely broad, because it covers all objects of cognition *per se*. He then makes a *prima facie* peculiar equation:

> We are, however, dealing only with the manifold of our representations. And since that x (the object) which corresponds to them is to be something distinct from all our representations, this object is nothing for us. Clearly, therefore, the unity that the object makes necessary can be nothing other than the formal unity of consciousness in the synthesis of the manifold of representations. When we have brought about synthetic unity in the manifold of intuitions—this is when we say that we cognize the object. (A105)

Since he was describing the unity of an object (the rule is that the representations of an object of cognition must not be haphazard or arbitrary but determined in a certain way), it seems strange suddenly to introduce the unity of consciousness.

Kant's move is more intelligible against the background of the disagreement over the priority of object and self-consciousness. How can one claim that object consciousness (reference to an object) comes first? On the representational theory of perception common to the disputing parties, all that cognizers have available to them are particular representations of sensible properties. How is the cognizer to refer these to a common object? Kant's assumption is that she can do so only if she has available some *a posteriori* or *a priori* object rule that enables her to determine which representations could be representations of the same object. As the discussion of the counting example makes clear, however, applying such a rule requires her to be aware of her partial representations (e.g., the representations of a certain shape and of self-propelled motion) and of her mental act as the basis on which she judges the object to be a 'dog.' This awareness not only permits cognition of the object, however, it essentially involves recognizing a relation across the partial cognitions or mental states and the judgmental state, the relation of necessarily belonging together. Since the partial representations are the basis of the judgment, it could not be a judgment—an example of RE cognition—in their absence. Unless the partial representations could be used in producing such a judgment, they could not participate in RE cognition. It follows that since an object rule can lead to cognition if and only if it can be applied to (partial) representations in such a way that it involves recognizing a relation of necessary connection across states, the functioning of an object rule implies the unity of consciousness. And since cognizers have no way to refer representations to objects by grabbing onto an object independently of their representations, the only way that they can refer them to objects is through an object rule. Hence, oddly enough, the key to understanding how representations can refer to an object are the conditions required for a unity of consciousness.

Beginning with objective reference (alone) makes no sense, because the conditions that permit it also bring about a unity of self-consciousness. On the other hand, understanding this process provides some insight into why cognition could not begin with self-consciousness (alone) either. How is the relation of necessarily belonging together to be established in the absence of the functioning of an object rule? Most important, understanding this process and the mutual dependence of object and subject consciousness it involves tells us why examining the possibility of cognition can lead to the discovery of *a priori* rules or templates for forming '*a posteriori*' rules, rules that can be applied to the data of sense in such a way as to create relations of necessary connection among the representations of a cognitive subject. Neither object cognition nor subject consciousness is possible in the absence of rules, rules that supply standards for objects, and rules whose use creates relation of rational dependence and hence necessary connection across mental states. If *a posteriori* object rules are possible only because they are created on the basis of templates—for example, a template that requires that properties be attached to objects (and ultimately to substances[21])—then both reference to objects and consciousness of a continuing subject require that cognition be mediated by the use of such (categorial) templates.

Before launching a full-scale exploration of the unity of consciousness, Kant underlines the importance of object rules. Concepts serve as rules. So, for example, the concept of a body necessarily involves representations of impenetrability, shape, and so forth (A106). He then explains that a concept can be

> a rule for intuitions only by representing, when appearances are given to us, the necessary reproduction of the manifold and hence the synthetic unity in our consciousness of these appearances. Thus when we perceive something external to us, the concept of body makes necessary the representation of extension, and with it the representations of impenetrability, shape, etc. (A106)

The reference to 'reproduction' is somewhat awkward (see next section) and is dropped in the B deduction. His claim that the materials in the partial representations, 'extended', and so forth, must be 'reproduced' in the resulting representation 'body' repeats the point that the latter representation must be understood as being built up out of the partial representations, which are 'repeated' in it. That is, he maintains that the representation of 'body' must be understood as necessarily connected in consciousness to the representation of 'extended,' and so on. Instead of pursuing 'necessary reproduction,' he turns somewhat abruptly to the claim that any necessity must be grounded in a transcendental condition, so we need to find a transcendental basis for the 'unity of consciousness in the synthesis of the manifold' (A106). By a 'transcendental basis,' he means an *a priori* representation that is required for cognition.[22]

Kant then makes a dramatic pronouncement:

> This original and transcendental condition is none other than transcendental apperception. (A106–7)

We then come to another *prima facie* curious twist in the argument. Having just introduced a crucial theoretical term, he considers and criticizes the possibility that self-consciousness could arise empirically, through the operation of inner sense.

> There is, in inner perception, a consciousness of oneself in terms of the determinations of one's state. This consciousness of oneself is merely empirical and always mutable; it can give us no constant [*stehendes*] or enduring [*bleibendes*] self in this flow of inner appearances. But what is to be represented **necessarily** as numerically identical cannot be thought as such through empirical data. A condition that is to validate such a transcendental presupposition must be one that precedes all experience and that makes experience itself possible. (A107, also cited in Chapter 3)

Introducing the inadequacies of an empirical derivation of the I-representation here serves a number of purposes. Kant's general approach is to clarify classifications by contrasting them with neighboring classifications. Empirical consciousness of states offers an obvious contrast for consciousness of a numerically identical subject; similarly inner sense offers a useful contrast for the faculty of transcendental apperception.

Still the thrust of the passage is less comparative than negative. Hume's and Tetens's failures to provide an empirical derivation of the 'I-representation' provide an opening for Kant's unusual theory that self-consciousness is a requirement for cognition and known through that guise. He appears to exploit that opening in rolling out his theory: Empirical derivations do not establish an enduring or constant self; they could not establish necessary identity. Eberhard had claimed that cognizers were aware of their numerical identity through being aware of constancy (*Stätigheit*) or unbroken continuity in the transition from one state to another. Eberhard could be an object of Kant's criticism. He is a somewhat unlikely candidate, because his general approach is Leibnizian[23] and the target seems to be more straightforward Empiricist accounts. The obvious foils are Hume, the discoverer of the insufficiency of Empiricist accounts of self-identity, and Tetens, who failed to grasp the strength of Hume's demonstration, though the passage may be directed at Eberhard as well.

Kant repeats the criticism that, if one tries an empirical derivation, then one will end up with nothing in more florid language in the B deduction:

Only because I can comprise the manifold of the representations in one consciousness, do I call them one and all **my** representations. For otherwise I would have as self as many-colored and varied as I have representations that I am conscious of. (B134, also cited in part in Chapter 8)

Later in the A deduction, in the 'argument from below,' he considers representations apart from the unity of apperception in terms reminiscent of those in which Tetens presented Hume's view: For Hume there is a crowd (*Menge*) of impressions that follow each other singly (*einzelner*) and are separated (*getheilter*) and scattered (*zerstreut*) and are brought together in a whole subject representation through the faculty of imagination. Kant explains that without relation to apperception

different perceptions are in themselves encountered in the mind scattered [*zerstreut*] and individually [*einzeln*]. (A120)

If the unity of apperception were impossible then

much [*eine Menge*] empirical consciousness could be found in my mind—yet found as separate [*getrennt*] and without belonging to a consciousness of myself. (A122)

He also describes representations as on their own amounting to nothing more than a random 'heap' (*regellose haufen*) (A121), Hume's famously disparaging term for the impressions of an allegedly single mind, a term that Tetens often uses as well (e.g., 1.385, 386, 387).

Kant breaks the flow of his positive argument to criticize other approaches for good reason. It gives him the opportunity not just to contrast his view to theirs and, perhaps, to criticize particular predecessors. It also allows him to showcase the superiority of scientific metaphysics in general, by arguing that Empiricists cannot explain the obvious fact that there are continuing cognizers. Rationalist approaches will be shown to be inadequate in the Paralogisms chapter, thereby completing his case that, in this crucial area, only transcendental philosophy can provide a viable solution. Passages like those cited above led me to suggest in earlier work (1990, Chapter 4, *passim*) that a central goal of the argument for apperception was to defeat Hume's skepticism about personal identity. Given the importance of the unity of apperception to the proof of the categories, which Kant partly saw in the *Duisburg Nachlaß*, prior to reading Tetens, that claim is too strong. Still, the shape of the A deduction demonstrates that he does not introduce the theory of apperception only to establish the categories. It is not just a lemma for that proof, but an important result in its own right, because it offers a way of dealing with the unity of self-consciousness that avoids both skepticism and dogmatism. His theory of apperception has the twin advantages of resolving the contemporary puzzle about the unity of self-consciousness and of providing a bridge to the long-sought argument for the categories.

Having explained how he is about to solve the problem of the human representation of unity of consciousness (by revealing it to be a presupposition of experience or empirical cognition) Kant presents his solution:

> Now there can take place in us no cognition, and no connection and unity of cognitions among one another, without that unity of consciousness which precedes all data of intuitions, and by reference to which all representations of objects is alone possible. Now this pure, original, and immutable consciousness I shall call **transcendental apperception** . . .[24] Now this transcendental unity of apperception brings about, from all possible appearances whatever that can be together in one experience, a coherence of all these representation according to laws. For this unity of consciousness would be impossible if the mind, in cognizing the manifold, could not be conscious of the identity of function whereby it synthetically combines the manifold in one cognition. (A107–8)

What does he mean by the claim that the unity of consciousness precedes all data of intuitions? One possibility is that he is agreeing with Crusius and Merian against Wolff that self-consciousness must precede any awareness of objects that would be provided through the data of intuitions. As Thiel notes, the use of the term 'original' (*ursprüngliche*) may be a reference to Merian's position. Still, the last sentence makes this hypothesis problematic. If the unity of consciousness literally 'precedes' all data of intuition, then how could it be impossible except under certain conditions? As we saw in the preceding chapter, Kant says in a number of passages that the unity of apperception must be achieved, that representations must be brought to or under the unity of apperception.

We can resolve the apparent inconsistency between Kant's claims that the unity of consciousness both precedes cognition and is created in the course of the mind's cognizing activities by recalling that the representation of unity is *a priori* and by turning to his clarification of *a priori* representations in the Reply to Eberhard. When criticized for appealing to innate representations, he explained more precisely how his claims about *a priori* representations should be understood.

> The *Critique* admits absolutely no implanted or innate **representations**. One and all, whether they belong to intuition or to concepts of the understanding, it considers them as **acquired**. But there is also an original [*ursprüngliche*] acquisition (as the teachers of natural right call it), and thus of that which previously did not yet exist at all, and so did not belong to anything prior to this act. According to the *Critique*, these are, **in the first place**, the form of things in space and time, **second**, the synthetic unity of the manifold in concepts; for neither of these does our cognitive faculty get from objects . . . rather it brings them about **a priori**, out of itself. <u>There must indeed be a ground for it in the subject, however, which makes it possible that these representations can arise in this and no other manner, and be related to objects which are not yet given, and this ground at least is</u> **innate** . . . The ground of the possibility of sensory intuition is neither of the two, neither **limit** of the cognitive faculty nor **image** [as Eberhard had suggested]; it is the mere **receptivity** peculiar to the mind, when it is affected by something (in sensation) to receive a representation in accordance with its subjective constitution . . . [T]ranscendental concepts of the understanding . . . are acquired, and not innate, though <u>their acquisition, like that of space is no less original and presupposes nothing innate save the</u>

subjective conditions of the spontaneity of thought (in conformity to the unity of apperception). (8.221–23, C1781 312–13, my underscoring)

On his view there are no innate representations of spaces, causes, or anything else, presumably including 'I's. Rather, there are ways of arranging sensory data and of forming concepts that depend on innate tendencies of the mind's receptive and active faculties. In the latter case, the tendencies order conceptual representations in such a way that representations of both categorial concepts and the unity of apperception arise in consciousness.

Presumably the innate ground of the original acquisition of causal representations is the tendency to scrutinize the data of sense for patterns that could be instances of causal relations.[25] According to the passage, this tendency is governed by what appears to be a further consideration. The representations so formed are subject to the unity of apperception. This suggests an extra layer of scrutiny. Cognizers not only come with innate tendencies to scrutinize the contents of representations for indications of causal relations; they also have innate tendencies to scrutinize not the contents of representations, but representations themselves to find representations that meet some other principle. Given that the 'I-think' is *a priori* and that *a priori* representations and principles arise through the (scrutinizing) activities of the mind (B1), this must be his view. If so, it resolves the 'prior to' and 'produced by' problem. The tendency to scrutinize by a principle associated with the 'I-think' precedes cognition; the representation of the unity of consciousness would be produced by that scrutiny.

Still, this resolution raises two obvious questions: Where do cognizers get the idea of 'representation' *per se*? By what principle do they scrutinize representations? Kant's official answer to the first question is straightforward and disappointing. Humans are aware of the world around them through outer sense and aware of the condition of their 'inner world' through inner sense (A22/B37). This answer is not only disappointing, but also in tension with the picture of judging presented through the counting example. Mathematics in general and counting in particular are taken to require some sort of sensory representations (real or imagined stroke symbols), but the faculty that judges '4' on the basis of adding up the stroke symbols one after another is not inner sense but apperception. By the time of the *Critique*, inner sense is no longer the faculty that enables cognizers to know the basis of their judgments. Apperception performs that crucial function. But Kant does not make any effort to reconcile his new view with his continuing claim that cognizers know about their mental states through inner sense. As I suggest below, however, some type of reconciliation might be possible.

The answer to the second question is more helpful. For reasons we have seen, the principle according to which representations are scrutinized cannot be the apperceptive principle, because that principle states that the unity of apperception is necessary for cognition of objects. The principle in question must be the one embedded in the principle, the I-rule that 'all representations must belong to a single consciousness.' This rule is also in tension with the inner sense theory, since, for all we know, inner sense might divulge a condition of the inner world that could not be understood as belonging with others to a single consciousness—and hence could not be a representation. On the other hand, the rule indicates a possible avenue for representing representations as such apart from inner sense. In rational cognition, some states that are representations (judgments) come to be understood as depending on other states that are representations (partial representations that are combined in the whole). It is not possible to represent that dependency or that necessary togetherness without representing the states as such. So this capacity must come along with the capacity for rational cognition. Unlike the case of causation, the unity of apperception is produced through the creation of relations of necessary connection across representational states—and the states thereby come to be recognized as such. More briefly, the activity of thinking produces relations of necessary connection across representations, which thanks to scrutiny *via* the I-rule, enables the cognizer to represent her representations as such and as states of an 'I.'[26] Above I characterized the inner sense theory as Kant's 'official' account of humans' cognition of their representations, but the view just outlined is at least a semiofficial second view.

The discussion of A107 concludes:

Hence the original and necessary consciousness of one's own identity is at the same time a consciousness of an equally necessary unity of the synthesis of all appearances according to concepts, i.e., according to rules. (A108)

How can humans be conscious of representations as necessarily belonging to a single self-consciousness? Besides having faculties capable of synthesizing or combining materials from different representations, they must employ concepts or rules in the manner exemplified by counting or by the use of the concept 'body' and thereby bring about a relation between the partial cognitions and the whole cognition or concept application (or judgment). Through the consciousness of the synthesis they are conscious of the relation between, for example, the representation of the first stroke symbol as '1' and the judgment '4.' They can see these representations as exemplifying the relation of necessarily belonging together, since the judgment '4' would be impossible without the representation of the '1,' and the representation of '1' would be impossible as a ground of cognition without the judgment.[27] In recognizing the relation of necessarily belonging together between these representations, they recognize them as exemplifying the I-rule.

We can now see the contours of the central argument of the A deduction: It is necessary for RE cognition that representations can be understood as necessarily belonging together. We can also see why Kant believed that the unity of apperception and object cognition (under concepts) are necessary and sufficient conditions for each other and why his position is plausible—and may be correct. RE object cognition requires partial cognitions that are recognized as such and so an implicit awareness of the necessary togetherness relation across different states. Further, given the absence of any intuition of an 'I' and the impossibility of establishing relations of necessary connection empirically, he sees no way for cognizers to be aware of their representations as belonging to the unity of consciousness—as necessarily belonging together—except by being aware of a relation between partial cognitions and a whole cognition that suffices for object cognition.

Whether or not this was his intent, Kant's theory offers an elegant solution to the self-consciousness versus object-consciousness priority argument between Wolff and his critics. Kant's theory splits the difference between them while criticizing both for not seeing the intimate connection between object cognition and the unity of consciousness. The critics were correct that there is no cognition worthy of the name prior to self-consciousness and that it is impossible to derive a representation of a unified subject from object representations. It is a *sui generis* representation. On the other hand, Wolff was right that Descartes' scenario of an 'I-think' without any object of thought is impossible.[28]

Once the relation between RE cognition and the possibility of a unity of self-consciousness is clear, we can see how an argument that starts by exploring the necessary conditions for the former can end with a claim about the application of the categories to any object that can affect the human senses (B160). An important part of the argument concerns the necessity of ordering human mental states in time, so that they can have the intuitive coherence required by the sorts of (spatiotemporal) cognizers that humans are. But the general argument that is meant to cover any discursive cognizer, regardless of form of intuition, already provides the solution. The transcendental deduction is able to perform the apparently logic-defying feat of arguing from a narrower class (representations that belong to cognition) to a conclusion about a *prima facie* wider class (any representation that can belong to the unity of consciousness) because of the peculiarities of the I-representation.

Different representations do not manifest a constant 'I' representation in inner sense; there is no I-impression or I-intuition. The I-representation is *a priori*. As such, it is tied to a principle, in this case, the I-rule that all representations must belong to a common 'I.' But how can the necessary connections across representations be forged (and recognized)? In Kant's view, the only possibility is through the rule-governed activity of thinking that produces object cognition. Through that activity, the unity of consciousness is created and recognized: Some representations are, and are understood as, rationally dependent on others; the latter representations (intuitive or conceptual) are participants in cognition (and so representations) and are understood as such only through their relation as grounds for the former. Absent this relation none of the representations, conceptual or intuitive, could be referred to a single subject. In particular, intuitions that could not participate in cognition could not be attributed to a common subject. If the object rules needed for rational cognition are built on *a priori* templates, then it follows that any representation that could be understood as such—as the representation of a common subject of many representations—must be suitable for the application of categorial concepts. Kant summarizes these connections in a letter to Herz:

> If we can demonstrate that our knowledge of things, even experience itself, is only possible under those conditions [the forms of intuition and the categories of the understanding], it follows that all other concepts of things . . . are for us empty and utterly useless for knowledge. But not only that; all sense data for a possible cognition would never, without those conditions, represent objects. <u>They would not even reach that unity of consciousness that is necessary for knowledge of myself (as object of inner sense)</u>. I would not even be able to

> know that I have sense data; consequently for me, as a knowing being they would be absolutely nothing. (11.51–52, CLet 314, my underscoring)

Unless a subject engages in object cognition she can have no grasp of a sensory state as belonging to the unity of consciousness and so no understanding of her sensory states as sensory states or as belonging to a common subject.[29]

After arguing that the consciousness of a subject's identity is at the same time a consciousness of the synthesis of appearances according to concepts or rules at A107, Kant seems to shift to a different reason for connecting representations to a common 'I,' a reason that concerns a common act:

> ... For the mind could not possibly think its own identity in the manifoldness of its representations, and moreover think this identity *a priori*, if it did not have the identity of its act before its eyes [*vor Augen hätte*]—the identity that brings all synthesis of apprehension under a transcendental unity, and thereby first makes possible the coherence of those representations according to *a priori* rules. (A108)

What does Kant mean by the 'identity of the act'? One possibility is suggested by the counting: There would be one extended act of adding the units, '1' and so on. The idea would be that the singleness of the act of generation connects the representations so generated to a single self.

Carl stresses the importance of the generation of numbers in a particular order in the counting example. In his view, the purpose of the example is to illustrate how a concept can determine the order of states in intuition (1992, 163). He also sees the generation by a single (extended) act as the source of the belongingness to a common subject.[30] Although the demonstration of ordering states in counting is very important to Kant's project of explaining how the categories can determine the order of states in inner sense, that cannot be all that is intended. His central point is that without being aware of his acts of counting, the would-be counter could not cognize the total amount. The counter needs not just to apply the rule and so to produce representations in a particular order; he needs to grasp the relation between his partial representations and his judgment '4.' Exactly the same point applies to the idea of a single act as producing the varied actions of counting. Unless that act includes the final act of recognizing that the representation '4' depends on the results of earlier phases of the (extended) act, the would-be counter will not have cognized the amount. This point harkens back to the original definition of synthesis, where a cognizer not only adds various representations together, but also comprehends or understands their manifoldness in one (resulting) cognition. The crucial aspect of the synthetic process is not so much a common act or process of synthesizing, but the relation between the synthesized representation and the representations from which it is synthesized in accord with a rule. Bringing some object x under the concept 'body' or judging that 'x is a body' requires that the cognizer grasp that her judgment depends on a further, partial representation 'x is extended.' This 'recognition in a concept' according to a rule permits the object to be rationally cognized. It also demonstrates that the different representations stand in the relation required for being states of a single 'I.'

We are now better able to appreciate the differences between Gareth Evans's discussion of the identity of a person in tracking an object and the Kantian analysis of my keeping track of our puppy Teddy sketched in Chapter 1. For Evans, the identity of the person through the tracking is a function of two features: The tracking activity is the expression of a belief and the belief can be criterionlessly attributed to the subject. On the Kantian account of keeping an eye on Teddy, I judge that Teddy is still in the room, by noting that he is at a particular place in the room. My judgment is rational, because I know its grounds, and because I know its grounds I take the two states, that of seeing Teddy under the window, and that of judging him to be here, to be necessarily connected together and so to exemplify the rule for being states of a common 'I.'[31] As in the case of an extended act, a temporally extended exercise of a disposition would not, by itself, produce either rational object cognition or necessary connection across the temporally diverse states. On Kant's view, for either to occur, the cognizer must possess some rule that enables her to grasp the logical relations across the contents of her representations. So the approaches are very different.[32]

The importance of rules to object cognition and to thinking one's own identity is why Kant begins and ends the long and difficult A108 paragraph by talking about the necessity of laws or *a priori* rules. But, if the central point of A108 is that the concepts and rules are needed to permit the unity of consciousness, why does Kant emphasize the 'identity' of the act? He claims that a subject would be unable to understand his self-identity if he were not aware of the identity of the act that brings all synthesis of apprehension under a transcendental unity. The first question to ask is whether the identity in question is numerical or qualitative. As the basis of a claim of the numerical identity of the self, it seems that it must be a numerically identical act. On the other hand, it is implausible to think that different representations are brought to the unity of apperception by a single act that extends for a lifetime—or at least implausible to think that that is Kant's view.[33]

It may be easier to understand A108 by considering a related observation from the B deduction:

> We readily become aware that this act of synthesis must be in origin single [*ursprünglich einig*] and equally valid (or of equal weight [*gleichgeltend*]) for all combination. (B130, amended translation)[34]

This passage tilts towards a reading of qualitative identity. Although '*einig*' indicates singularity or perhaps uniqueness, what are we to make of the modifier '*ursprünglich*,' which means 'in origin' or 'originally'? The possibility that the act was originally single and later something else seems to make no sense. Further, Kant uses this term to indicate a special sort of origin in the activities of the faculties. Although the question is vexed,[35] I think the most plausible reading is that the act has a singular origin in the distinctive activity of the thinking faculty.[36] The additional and unusual characterization, 'equally valid,' supports that interpretation. Because the act has its origin in the characteristic activity of the thinking faculty, it always has equal weight or is equally valid.

On Kant's theory, representations are attached to a common 'I' through the operation of synthesis:

> This synthesis is called the original synthetic unity of apperception. All representations given to me are subject to this unity; but they must also be brought under [*gebracht unter*] it through a synthesis. (B135–36)

Yet, as we have seen, synthesis is an operation carried out on some representations that yields other representations. It is carried out in accord with rules that are attached to different concepts—the rule for 'body,' for '4,' for 'dog,' and so on. So how can an operation that is carried out according to different rules produce a univocal relation of belonging to a common subject across all representations? Kant's preemptive reply to this objection is to stress the 'identity' of the act or 'singular character' or its 'equal weight': Even if different representations are combined in accord with a variety of rules, there is no difference in the act of combining itself and hence no difference in the relation of necessary connection created across representations. Representations of self-propelled motions and of certain shapes might be combined in the representation 'dog,' and representations of 'extension' and 'impenetrability' may be combined in the representation 'body,' but the act of combining and the relation of 'being combined in' are the same. That 'synthesis' is in origin singular and equally valid for all acts of combination is not sufficient to connect the subject who judges 'dog' to she who judges 'body,' but it is a necessary condition for doing so. As we shall see below, the equal validity of all acts of synthesis is also crucial in explaining how different sorts of mental states, perceptions as well as conceptions, can be understood as standing in the same relation to each other and so to a common 'I-think.'

Although the single extended act of counting does not explain the unity of the representations in a single consciousness, it does explain something very important. Intending to apply the counting rule, the cognizer starts with real or imagined stroke symbols and assigns them number '1' and so forth. The single act explains the transition from one representation to another. No Leibnizian inner principle unfolds the career of a substance; a cognizer intends to carry out an act of cognition. Besides setting up relations of ground and whole cognition across all the representations—and so the relation of necessarily belonging together—the example illustrates how the order of representations in inner sense can be determined by rules (as Carl helpfully points out) thereby also illustrating the transition of a mind from one state to another.

The counting example also shows how the 'chicken-and-egg' problem that divided Kant's predecessors can be solved. It is true that there is no RE cognition without self-consciousness and true that there is no self-consciousness without representations of objects. The solution can be understood in terms of the simultaneous application of two rules, the counting rule and the I-rule. It is a mistake to model the situation as one in which the counter gets to '4' and through his conscious act of synthesis then realizes (through a further act of synthesis) that the states representing '1' and so forth, and '4' stand in a relation of necessarily belonging together and so are instances of the I-rule.[37] He applies both the counting rule and the I-rule prospectively. He starts counting and building up partial cognitions in the expectation that the partial representations will enable him to determine the number and that the judgment will be based on the partial representations produced by counting. In being aware in the mental act of judging '4' on the basis of the partial cognitions, he knows both the amount and relation of necessarily belonging together across his partial representations and the judgmental state.

Towards the end of the A deduction, Kant returns to the representation of a constant and enduring 'I' that eluded the Empiricists:

> For in this constant and enduring I (of pure apperception) consists the correlate of all our representations insofar as becoming conscious of them is so much as possible. And all consciousness belongs to an all-encompassing pure apperception, just as all sensible intuitions belongs, as representation . . . to time. (A124)

Since 'I-think' is an *a priori* representation, the I-rule should work in the same way as the categorial principles, prodding the understanding to scrutinize the perceptions available to inner sense in search for representations that are instances of it. What is different is that since the only representations that the understanding takes note of are those that fit categorial rules, these representations will automatically also fit the I-rule. (In this way, the 'extra scrutiny' by the I-rule considered above would not eliminate any representations, but only allow for the application of 'common subject' across them.) Hence the 'I' will be a ubiquitous feature of representations of which the subject is conscious.

The A deduction somewhat muddies its message of necessary unity by considering the possibility of 'representations' that do not belong to the unity of apperception. One frequently discussed passage dismisses such 'representations' as 'less than a dream' (A112). A second passage raises the possibility of a multitude of perceptions—empirical consciousness—arising in a human mind, but without belonging to the unity of consciousness (A122). Here such 'perceptions' are said to be impossible. Insofar as 'representations' or 'perceptions' are meant to indicate those mental states that enable humans to have their distinctive form of cognition, however, these occurrences of the terms are misuses. Alternatively, Hoppe is right that these passages are not intended to show that such situations are possible—but rather impossible (Chapter 8, p. 113). The B deduction refrains from such speculation, making it clearer from the beginning that the representations at issue are representations properly so-called, representations that are something for a cognitive subject.

Before turning to the somewhat different way in which the argument is cast in the B deduction, it may be useful to summarize the main points in the A edition argument for apperception. As I understand it, there are six essential steps:

1. Cognition requires intuitions and concepts (e.g., 'body').
2. Intuitions can participate in cognition only insofar as they are understood as providing the basis for concept use (they are the states from which the concept was abstracted) and concept application (they are the basis of concept application), hence, only insofar as they are understood as standing in relations of necessary connection to representational states of applying concepts.
3. The use of concepts requires implicit use of rules (e.g., a rule governing 'body,' 'bodies are extended') or the general rule of similarity for simple concepts or concepts used in the manner of simple concepts.

4. In making implicit use of the rules associated with concepts, the cognizer must recognize some of his representational states (e.g., that representing 'body') as depending on others (e.g., that representing 'extended") and so must recognize the states as standing in relations of necessary connection.
5. When representational states are recognized as necessarily connected together, they are recognized as instances of the I-rule.
6. Thus any representational state that can be understood as participating in cognition must also be understood as meeting a necessary condition for belonging to a common 'I.'

6. Combination and Self-consciousness in the B Deduction

Given the hint from the *Metaphysical Foundations of Natural Science*, we might expect the B deduction to begin with an exact definition of 'judgment.' It does not. Kant simply assumes that cognition must involve combination. He needn't spell out why judgment requires combination, because judgments were standardly taken to involve a relation between two concepts (B140–41). Further, cognition requires both intuitions and concepts, and concepts, like judgments, require combination.

The scope of the opening discussion of the B deduction is broader than concept application and judgment. Kant does not consider combination just as a prerequisite for (all kinds of) judging. His topic is all combination or synthesis of representations, whether the combination is conscious or unconscious and whether or not it is carried out on concepts or on sensible or nonsensible intuitions. Again, he does not spell out why intuitions must be combined. He can, however, presume familiarity with his initial discussion of concepts in the Transcendental Analytic where he presented them as 'functions of unity' among intuitions (and other concepts). A concept is something that unites different intuitive (or conceptual) representations under it (A68/B93). Hence insofar as intuitions are understood as being brought under or united under concepts—which they must be to participate in cognition—they too need to be thought of as combined under a conceptual representation that encompasses them all.

Because combination is essential to judgment and concept use, and so too to cognition, Kant proposes to investigate the necessary conditions for combination as such. He begins by implicitly comparing the sort of combination he has in mind with that offered by Empiricism in its laws of association:

> We cannot represent anything as combined in the object without ourselves' having combined it beforehand; and that, among all representations **combination** is the only one that cannot be given through objects, but—being an act of the subject's self-activity—can be performed only by the subject himself. (B130)

According to Empiricism, representations simply associate themselves and so form combined representations. His claim is that the sort of combination relevant to cognition requires that combination not simply be effected in some manner, but that it is represented as such, as combination. Against the background of his views of rational cognition, we can understand this terse observation as presupposing that in proper cognition, the cognizer knows the ground or basis of, for example, his judgments. In that case, however, he must understand his judgment 'x is a body' as combined out of partial representations, for example, 'x is extended.' Further, in proper cognition, a cognizer understands a concept as such—as something that unites different intuitions (or concepts) under it. In which case, he must also understand his intuitions as combined in a certain sense under concepts.

Having specified the sort of combination relevant to cognition, Kant offers a necessary condition for it:

> But the concept of combination carries with it, besides the concept of a manifold and of its synthesis, also the concept of the manifold's unity. <u>Combination is a representation of the **synthetic** unity of the manifold.</u>[n] (B130–31, my underscoring)

He goes on to deny that the unity involved is the category of unity (B131), whose principle is that all intuitions are extensive magnitudes. Rather the unity is qualitative. He explains further that the use of categorial concepts involves combination. Since the categories thus presuppose the unity in question, they cannot be its source:

> We must therefore search for this unity (which is qualitative unity; see §12) still higher up; *viz.*, in what itself contains the basis for the unity of different concepts in judgments, and hence contains the basis for the possibility of understanding, even as used logically. (B131)

When read on its own, the claim that combination is the representation of the manifold's unity is mysterious. What is this unity? Is it the unity of the materials (suggested by the phrase 'the unity of the manifold') or is it a unity of the faculty of understanding that combines them? Fortunately Kant appends a note that dispels much of the mystery, particularly when read in light of his views about rational cognition. He is specifically addressing the case of analytic judgments.

> Whether the representations themselves are identical, and thus one could be thought analytically through the other; that does not come into consideration. Insofar as we are speaking about the manifold [of representations, i.e., the different representations] the **consciousness** of the one is nevertheless always different from the consciousness of the other, and we are here only concerned with the synthesis of this (possible) consciousness. (B131n.)

Even in the case of an analytic judgment, such as 'F = F,' where the contents are identical, combination is required. For a cognizer to be conscious that F is F, that the representations are identical, she must be conscious of one F and conscious of the other, and the states of representing the common content 'F' are different. To make the judgment, the cognizer must combine or synthesize the materials in the diverse states. Alternatively, to understand her analytic judgment as a judgment, she must understand the judgmental state as being based on the states of representing, say, the left-hand-side F and the right-hand-side F. As we saw in the discussion of the A deduction, however, when a cognizer grasps some of his states as dependent on others and so as necessarily connected, he simultaneously grasps them as instances of the I-rule. Thus the unity that is presupposed when combination can be understood as such is the unity of consciousness.

In arguing against taking the *cogito* as the premise of the B deduction, I noted that the discussion of combination as such serves as a prologue to the introduction of the 'I-think' doctrine. Upon closer inspection, we can see that it lays out a rich background and even the beginnings of an argument (in the note) for the claim,[38] which I repeat for easy reference:

> The **I think** must be **capable** of accompanying all my representations; for otherwise something would be represented in [the original German has *in*, which is better translated into English by *in* than by *to*] me that could not be thought at all, which is equivalent to saying: the representation either would be impossible, or at least would be nothing to me. Representation that can be given prior to all thought is called **intuition**. Hence everything manifold in intuition has a necessary reference to the **I think** in the same subject in whom this manifold is found. (B131–32, amended translation and punctuation)

The second portion of the claim (after the semicolon) modifies the first. As in A, the scope of the 'I-think' doctrine in the B edition is the set of representations that can participate in cognition. For an intuition to so participate, it must be thought. That is, it must be able to be brought under concepts in a thought or judgment (about an object, as we learn slightly later). But to bring an intuition under a concept is to combine it with others under that concept. Hence insofar as any intuition is understood as something that can be part of cognition, it must be understood as something that is combined with other representations in a resultant representation. For example, the concept 'orange' can be used in rational cognition only when it is understood as abstracted from various intuitions which are 'combined' in it or collected under it. And to understand intuitions as combined in concepts is to see the intuitive and conceptual representations as necessarily connected to each other and so as meeting the necessary condition for belonging to a single I-think. Given the necessity involved, Kant observes that

> the representation [I-think] cannot be regarded as belonging to sensibility. (B132)

As noted in section 4, the argument is clearer if we are cognizant of the double dose of necessity. Why an Empiricist account of the 'I-representation' would be unavailing (even if it could be given, which it can't) is that it is necessary for cognition that different mental states are understood as combined and so as standing in relations of necessary connection. And no Empirical account could establish necessary connection.

Although Kant does not present it in this guise, the preceding argument undercuts Wolff's view that object cognition precedes self-consciousness. The claim asserted and defended is that any representation (that could serve in object cognition) must also be understood as belonging to a single self-consciousness. After noting that the representation 'I-think' must be spontaneous and *a priori*, he goes on to discuss the possible ramifications of the argument. If any representation that can serve in cognition must be understood as belonging with others to a common I-think then it must meet the requirements for doing so and those requirements could turn out to be significant.

Kant then turns to the problem of how cognizers are conscious of the identity of apperception. One target of his implicit criticism seems to be Locke's Empiricist account. Locke's 'reflection' theory could not explain how a cognizer is conscious of her identity across different representational states:

> The same thoroughgoing identity of the apperception of a manifold given in intuition contains a synthesis of representations, and is possible only through the <u>consciousness of this synthesis</u>. For the empirical consciousness that accompanies different representations is intrinsically sporadic and without any reference to the subject's identity. Hence this reference comes about not through my merely accompanying each representation with consciousness, but through my adding one representation to another and being <u>conscious of their synthesis</u>. Hence only because I can combine a manifold of given representations **in one consciousness**, is it possible for me to represent the **identity of the consciousness itself in these representations.** (B133, my underscoring)

The objection is that the Lockean consciousness—the consciousness that is inseparable from thinking (ECHU 2.27.9, 335)—is momentary or episodic. As such, it cannot provide a basis for representing a common subject. In this passage, he makes the same objection that Merian raised against Wolff: A 'reflecting' consciousness can provide no evidence of a *continuing* self.[39]

Although Kant's criticism agrees with Merian's objection to Wolff, it applies with equal force to his and to Crusius's competing proposal that self-consciousness is prior to the differentiation of objects. The opening sentence of the passage claims that the identity of the apperception of different states contains a synthesis and is possible only through a consciousness of this synthesis. Later in the passage he claims that to be conscious of her identity, a cognizer must add representations to each other—must combine them—and be conscious in the combining or synthesizing.

Chapter 8 dealt with some problems in Kant's view that synthesis can be both a conscious and an unconscious operation. The setup of the B deduction raises an additional puzzle. He stresses that he is going to consider combination in general, whatever the nature of the materials or the conscious or unconscious character of the operation. But at B133, he says that consciousness of the act of combining is essential for linking different representations to a common 'I-think.' His point is that, even though some, indeed many, syntheses are unconscious, there is still something special about conscious syntheses. If a cognizer were never conscious of synthesizing, then she could not be self-conscious: She could not be conscious of herself as the possessor of different states. And that is because she could never recognize any of her states as standing in relations of necessary connection. The counting example in the A deduction makes Kant's claim more vivid and so easier to grasp. Through the conscious act of combining partial representations according to a rule, a cognizer can both cognize the amount and the relation of necessary connection across his states. In B, the argument is completely abstract: A cognizer can recognize that different representations belong to a single consciousness only through a conscious act of combining materials from some representations in a resultant representation. Through the conscious act of combining, he can both grasp the contents of the resultant state and the relation of necessary connection across the states which contribute to and result from the combining and which is essential to the state being the 'proper' cognitive state that it is. Despite the context of a broad notion of combination (of which more below), conscious combination thus plays the same role in B that it did in A. Consciousness in synthesis informs cognizers of the special relation that holds across their representations in thinking and thus of the necessary connection of those representations with one another.

One aspect of Kant's objection to Locke can be applied to his theory as well.[40] He complains that Locke cannot explain the reference of different representations to a common 'I,' but he has given no account of how a representation can be referred to an 'I' at all. Presumably he thinks (wrongly, as we have seen) that the 'mineness' question can be resolved through inner sense: A representation is 'mine' just in case I am aware of it *via* inner sense. By contrast, he notes in the B edition as well as in the A edition that inner sense can provide no representation of a common self or constant 'I' across varied representations (B134), thereby completing his argument that conscious combining is necessary for recognizing a relation of necessary togetherness of different representations in a single 'I.' Nevertheless, he has not provided an adequate account of how cognizers refer to themselves as particular 'I's either.

Kant goes on to observe that asserting that different representations belong to a common subject presupposes a synthesis. Whoever makes the claim is connecting a variety of representations in a representation of an 'I' that has them all: the 'I' with state R_1 and R_2, R_3, and so on.

> The thought that these representations given in intuition belong one and all to me is, accordingly, tantamount to the thought that I unite them, or at least can unite them, in one self-consciousness. And although that thought itself is <u>not [*noch nicht*] the consciousness of the</u> **synthesis** of representations, it still presupposes the possibility of that synthesis. I.e., only because I can comprehend the manifold of the representations in one consciousness, do I call them one and all **my** representations. For otherwise I would have a self as many-colored and varied as I have representations of which I am conscious. (B133–34, amended translation, my underscoring)

We have to be careful about what is being combined with what. My gloss above can mislead. Kant's point is precisely not that someone who asserts that I am the possessor of R_1, R_2, and R_3 manages to make that claim by combining R_1 with a representation of an 'I,' R_2 with a representation of 'I,' and so forth. This is not possible, because inner sense provides no 'I' representation to combine with others, as he notes in the next paragraph:

> Through the 'I,' as a simple representation, nothing manifold is given; only in intuition which is distinct from this representation, can a manifold be given. (B135)

Different representations are not combined with some permanent 'I' intuition. Instead, they are combined with each other and that can come about only through an operation of synthesis that establishes their necessary connection to each other—and so their conformity to the condition for belonging to one consciousness or an 'I-think.' Combination of representations is thus presupposed in any assertion of coconsciousness. It is presupposed because, absent an intuition of an 'I,' representations can be connected to a common 'I-think' only by being understood as necessarily connected to each other and Kant sees no alternative for meeting that condition other than by grasping some representations as combined in others.

The 'I-think' is a very odd representation, because its use depends on the possibility of combining other representations. Its peculiar status is also highlighted in a note appended to the passage about the necessity of being conscious of combining representations to self-consciousness. For easy reference, I repeat the passage to which the note is appended.

> Hence only because I can combine a manifold of given representations **in one consciousness**, is it possible for me to represent the **identity of the consciousness itself in these representations**. I.e., the analytic unity of consciousness is possible only under the presupposition of some **synthetic** unity of apperception.ⁿ (B133)

By the 'analytic unity of consciousness,' Kant means that different representations, R_1, R_2, and so on, are attached to the same representation (though not intuition) 'I': 'I have R_1,' 'I have R_2,' and so forth. This claim is related to the analytic truth that any representation which belongs to the same 'I' as others must meet whatever conditions are necessary for doing so, but in the note, he takes the argument in a different direction:

> The analytic unity of consciousness attaches to all concepts that are, and inasmuch as they are, common [to several representation]. E.g. in thinking **red** as such, I represent a property that can be found (as a mark [*merkmale*]) in something or other, or can be combined with other representations; hence only by virtue of a possible synthetic unity that I think beforehand can I represent the analytic unity. A representation that is to be thought as common to different representations is regarded as belonging to representations that, besides having it, also have something **different**, about them. Consequently it must beforehand be thought in synthetic unity with other representations (even if only possible ones). Only then can I think in it the analytic unity of consciousness that makes the representation a **conceptus communis**. And thus the synthetic unity of

apperception is the highest point, to which we must attach all use of the understanding, even the whole of logic, and in accordance with it transcendental philosophy; indeed, this power is the understanding itself. (B133–34n., amended translation)

The analytic unity of consciousness is unique in that it is not required just to use a common representation 'I.' It is also required by the use of any concepts where the concept is thought of as common to different (complex) representations in which it is contained. Consider a case where a cognizer recognizes that a representation, say 'red,' is common to many representations, 'cardinal,' 'fire engine,' 'tomato,' and so on. She can do so only if she understands her 'abstraction' of the common element as depending on her consciousness of the (different) complex representations. To do that she must grasp that her representation of the abstracted concept, 'red,' and the states representing the complexes as necessarily connected and so as belonging to a common 'I.' Further, to represent the complexes as such, she must see them as having been produced through the combination of partial representation (and hence as themselves presupposing a common 'I'). Since the 'I' must be common, the use of any concept thought of as common to many representations also requires the use of 'I' and so the analytic unity of consciousness. Since Kant believes that all concepts must be understood as representations that are (potentially) common to many representations, he draws the conclusion that all concept use requires the synthetic unity of consciousness.

An important passage in the Paralogisms chapter (A341/B399) describes the 'I-think' as the 'vehicle' of all concepts and hence of the categories. It is necessary for their use, because that use involves combination. In this note, Kant argues that the 'I-think' is the vehicle for all concept use (and so cognition). Were cognizers unable to recognize their states as necessarily connected they could not recognize their concepts as common to many different representations, because they could not recognize complex representations as combinations. In that case, however, they would be incapable of the proper use of concepts. So the 'I-think' is a peculiar sort of representation in that its use both makes possible the use of concepts that are combined with others and also depends on the possibility of combining representations with others.

The crucial 'I-think' section (§ 16) of the B deduction concludes by reiterating the A edition's insistence that the unity of apperception is not only required for the combination presupposed by rational cognition; the unity of apperception is also made possible through the synthesis of representations. The final paragraph of the section makes the claim twice. It does so first in summing up the argument considered above about conscious combination, combination, and referring different representations to a common 'I':

Hence the synthetic unity of the manifold of intuitions, as given *a priori*, is the ground [*Grund*] of the identity of apperception which precedes[41] *a priori* all my determinate thought. (B134–35, amended translation)

The final thought of the section repeats its crucial lesson:

All representations given to me are subject to this unity [the original synthetic unity of apperception]; but they also must be brought under it through a synthesis. (B136–37)

Given the prominence of this doctrine, I disagree with Carl's suggestion that Kant doesn't mean to claim that representations are brought to the unity of apperception, but only that they must belong to a single self-consciousness.

In Chapter 7, I suggested that because cognition is complicated, an argument that examines the possibility of RE cognition will have many strands. We have just seen a number in the crucial opening sections of the B deduction (§s 15 and 16), where considerations about the requirements of judgments, of concept use, of intuitions that can participate in cognition, and even of making claims about representations as belonging to oneself are explored and interrelated. But the main line of argument in the B edition is not very different from that of the A edition. As I understand it, the A deduction argument is that both recognition in a concept (and so object cognition) and self-consciousness require the simultaneous operation of two rules, an object-rule and the I-rule. The focus of the B deduction is on combination. Both cognition and self-consciousness require combination that is understood as such. And for combination to be understood as such, both combination of the materials of representations in further representations and combination of representations in a subject are required. Despite the differences in presentation, the arguments for the unity of apperception in the two editions are thus surprisingly similar, especially when the next section of the B edition (§s 17) explains that cognition requires a particular sort of combination—that of different representations in an object in accord with the concept of an object. The two editions' deductions are similar because they develop the same twin themes of the lack of an intuition of an 'I' and of the mutual dependence of RE cognition and self-consciousness.

In the next three sections of the B deduction, Kant draws some conclusions and turns explicitly the issue of judgment and the unity of apperception. Section 17 repeats the A edition claim that the principle of the original synthetic unity of apperception is the highest principle of the understanding (B136–37). It also explains that the ultimate combination of representations required for cognition is in the representation of an object—that is, according to the concept of an object—thus repeating the doctrine of A105 already discussed. Section 18 concerns the subjective unity of consciousness and will be discussed below in conjunction with the relation between transcendental and empirical apperception.

I have already briefly considered the section about judgment and apperception (§ 19) in looking at the proposal of a 'one-step' transcendental deduction from the exact definition of judgment. This discussion is interesting in part because it resolves a puzzle about the differences between the arguments of the A and B editions. The introduction of 'transcendental apperception' in A is intertwined with a discussion of how cognition of an object is possible and of rules for cognizing objects. At least in advertisement, the B deduction is supposed to take a different approach, one which revolves around the definition of judgment. This approach would produce a tighter link to the metaphysical deduction where the categories are linked to forms of judgment. When we look at section19, however, the project of elucidating what is meant by 'judgment' and what is necessary for judgments to be possible blends seamlessly into considerations about the requirements of object cognition.

> the [relation or] reference of different cognitions in a judgment . . . is nothing but the way of bringing given cognitions to the unity of apperception . . . E.g. [in the judgment] 'bodies are heavy' . . . the representations belong to one another **in virtue of the necessary unity** of apperception in the synthesis of intuitions, i.e., <u>they belong to each other according to the principles of the objective determination of all representations insofar as these representations can become cognition.</u> (B142, my underscoring)

Since 'objective determination' is determination in accord with the rules of concepts of objects, the relation between concepts in a judgment is possible only through the unity of consciousness—which is possible only through the representations belonging to a single self (also) falling under rules for representing objects.

One notable difference between the editions reinforces the importance of object concepts. When stressing the key role of concepts and rules in cognition in A, Kant offered the explicative judgment 'bodies are extended' as his parade case (A106). This was the exemplary case of an analytic judgment in the introduction of the analytic/synthetic distinction (A7/B11). By contrast the example in B is the Introduction's paradigm of a synthetic judgment, 'bodies are heavy.' As he notes in the segment I elide from the citation, although this is an empirical or contingent judgment, the presence of the copula 'is' indicates that it is a judgment about objects (and not about the state of the subject) and so can be made only according to the rules governing objects. The appropriate rule is something like 'objects have properties,' which provides an *a priori* template for any particular claim such as 'bodies are heavy' (have the property of being heavy).[42] The A deduction might have given the misleading impression that only analytic judgments are governed by rules; that possible interpretation is ruled out in B. In brief, the argument is that certain forms of judgments are possible only because certain kinds of object concepts are possible, object concepts that are necessary for the unity of self-consciousness. I discuss the relation between the forms of judgments and the kinds of object concepts (i.e., the categories) further in Chapter 13 and its Appendix. What seems clear in section 19, however, is that the different strategy that Kant may have anticipated using in the B edition *via* the exact definition of judgment turns out not to be very different from the central line of argument of the A edition that object cognition and self-consciousness mutually imply each other.

Although the multifaceted B edition argument for the unity of apperception in sections 16–19 is not fundamentally different from that offered in the first edition, later parts of the chapter represent an enormous improvement on the treatment of perception in the First Synthesis of the A deduction. I follow the argument of the B edition through some of its later stages with an eye to addressing two worries about my interpretation of the argument for apperception. As I have presented Kant's view, he takes judgmental states and, for example, states representing sensory properties to stand in relations of rational dependence: The judgmental state is formed through the appreciation of the rational relations among a rule, the materials represented in sensory states (or in other conceptual states), and the judgment. But if that is how the relation of necessary connection across mental states is to be understood—in terms of relations of rational dependency—how can that relation hold for the case of intuitions? Intuitions don't stand in rational relations to each other. This worry is particularly pressing in the B edition where one thesis to be established is that everything that is manifold in *intuition* has a necessary reference to the *same* I-think (B132).

Kant's general view about the relations between intuitions and concepts offers one argument: Any intuition that can participate in cognition must be understood by theorists and cognizers as standing in relations of necessary connection to the conceptual representations abstracted from them. But what is the basis of the relation of necessarily belonging to a common subject of two particular and unrelated intuitions? Suppose that I am enjoying a peaceful day at the beach and I suddenly hear a gunshot. Both the states of, say, contemplating the sea and hearing the shot belong to a common 'I,' but *prima facie* at least, they stand in no relations of rational connection to each other. Alternatively, how can my account of necessary connection to each other and so to an 'I' be correct for the flow of perceptions as well as for the train of thought? Even if thinking consists of one rational cognition after another, how can that be the case for perceiving? Examining the last few sections of the B deduction will permit me to offer an answer to this important objection.[43]

A second and related worry is how the argument I see in the transcendental deduction for the unity of apperception can supply an appropriate premise for the argument from the unity of apperception to the necessary applicability of the categories to anything that a cognizer can sense. No interpretation of the argument for apperception can be deemed acceptable unless the argument so understood can be seen as part of an overall argument for the ubiquity of the categorial principles in experience. Kant sketches an argument for the category of causation in the last substantive section of the B deduction (§ 26). I analyze that argument in order to show that and how the argument for apperception that I extract from early parts of the text is part of an overall argument for the category of causation. Several caveats are needed. Most important, I don't think his defense of the causal principle succeeds. So I do not try to show that the argument for apperception that I present is part of a sound argument for the necessity of using causal concepts. Rather, I try to show that it is the sound part of a larger argument that he took to be sound.

Further, even Kant's ambitions for the proof of the categories were less than they appear in prospect. The argument for apperception in the early sections of the B deduction abstracts from space and time. It applies to any sort of rational cognizer. By contrast, the later arguments of the Principles chapter and the argument sketch in section 26 do not make this abstraction. So there is no argument from the requirements of rational cognition to the unity of apperception and from that step to the categories *per se* as necessary rules of synthesis. Even if it were successful, showing that temporally interpreted categories are necessary and sufficient for the unity of apperception of spatiotemporal cognizers could be nothing more than a demonstration of the possibility that the categories *per se* are necessary and sufficient for the unity of apperception *per se*. No recourse is available for a defense of the general thesis that cognition requires the categories, regardless of the particular form of intuition, except an appeal to the table of judgments and its link to the table of categories. For reasons I give in the Appendix to Chapter 13, I don't think this strategy works.

To sum up: The goals of the next section are to extend my account of the relations of necessary connection across mental states to the case of intuitions and to show how that account can be understood as part of an overall argument for the categories that Kant understood to be sound.[44]

7. Arguing from the Unity of Apperception to the Necessary Applicability of Categories to Intuitions

Section 20 of the B deduction offers the hypothesis that the categories are just the rules or functions needed to make the unity of apperception possible. Above I suggest that categorial principles might furnish templates for the construction of *a posteriori* rules about objects that make the unity of apperception possible. But neither Kant's hypothesis nor my suggestion bears any resemblance to a demonstration. He seems to believe that he can take the argument no further unless he reintroduces the forms of human intuition in the second part of the argument. His comment in section 21 is a useful reminder of the abstract level at which the discussion has so far been carried out. It is a mistake—that I've tried to make less likely by my wording—to think of some representations, intuitions or partial cognitions, as coming *before* others, conceptual representations, judgments, or whole cognitions. The relation between them is one of partial cognition to whole cognition or element to combination of elements, not past to future. Avoiding this confusion may be Kant's reason for ceasing to talk of the 'reproduction' of representations in the B edition (see above, p. 131).

Although Kant is not explicit about the point in the *Critique*, we know from the *Duisburg Nachlaß* that he takes the states of a spatiotemporal cognizer to be subject to a second necessary condition. Not only must such states be represented as belonging to a common subject, they must also be represented as following one another in time. Having reintroduced the forms of human sensibility in section 24, he sketches an account of how categories of understanding might apply to anything that can be sensed *via* the introduction of a *synthesis speciosa*. This synthesis is supposed to apply the rules of the understanding in directing a synthesis of the imagination on sensory materials.[45] He offers the example of the rule for lines directing the construction of a line in thought. Section 26 illustrates the *synthesis speciosa* with the central category of causation. In this crucial section, previous elements of the argument are assembled in a final effort to show that and how the categorial principles must apply to all objects of the senses (of spatiotemporal cognizers).

Before looking at that argument, it is helpful to recognize that it must have a somewhat different form from the reasoning of the earlier sections. In the first portion of the B deduction, Kant is concerned with cognizers' consciousness of themselves as the same subject across representations. So it is an analysis of, roughly, how cognition looks to cognizers (if they think about it). The discussion of the syntheses involved in perception (the *synthesis speciosa*) must take a different point of view, that of the theorist. This is not an account of what cognizers are or can be conscious of, but of how perception must be understood in light of the theoretical claim that time cannot be perceived. Ordinary cognizers are similar to his predecessors in believing that they are simply aware of the succession of their mental states.

Kant's first point in section 26 is that humans do not just have forms of space and time (forms that organize materials in a certain way). They also have intuitions or perceptions of determinate spatial and temporal arrays, where properties, objects, and events are represented as standing in determinate spatial and temporal relations with each other. Intuitions can be part of cognition only if they can be brought under concepts. Chapter 8 traced Kant's evolving views that the intuitions that are combined in or under a concept must be suitable to that concept. In the *Duisburg Nachlaß* he considered the possibility that the intellectual representations had to be tailored to the sensory or intuitive ones and also the reverse relation. But in the *Critique* and particularly in the discussion of the *synthesis speciosa*, he is clear that the suitability or isomorphism between conceptual representations and intuitive ones that is necessary for cognition could only be brought about through the understanding directing the construction of perceptual representation in accord with its own intellectual rules.

Since section 26 offers only a sketch of the argument to come in the Second Analogy, I fill in a few points from the more extended treatment to make it more comprehensible. The argument does not regress all the way from RE cognition, but only from the requirement (for cognition) that a spatiotemporal cognizer can know herself to be the same spatiotemporal thinker. In the B version of the Second Analogy, Kant is explicit that time cannot be perceived (B233). So intuition cannot supply the need for a cognizer to be able to represent her states as standing in determinate temporal relations. To represent her states S_1 and S_2 as standing in temporal relations—as a temporal array—it is necessary to represent the synthetic or combined whole of which they are parts and hence to represent S_1 as either following or preceding S_2. But how is it possible to represent them in one relation or another, as preceding or as following?

Reading this background into the preview offered in section 26, the reasoning goes as follows. It is a requirement of cognition (and also widely believed) that cognizers can know that their states belong to a single I and stand in determinate temporal relations. Given the inability to sense either an 'I' or time, how is such cognition possible? When a cognizer thinks of something in causal terms—here, the freezing of water—he thinks of the temporal order as determined. Lowering the temperature necessitates the state of solidity, so he must represent the substance as a solid *after* it was in a fluid state. As Guyer has argued in detail (1987, 241–49), for all the controversy surrounding the interpretation of the Second Analogy, the text is clear that the order of the subject's states is derived from that of the object's states:

> In our case, therefore, I shall have to derive the **subjective succession** of apprehension from the **objective succession** of appearances; for otherwise the subjective succession is entirely indeterminate. (A193/B238)

At this point the cognizer can judge that the fluid state was followed by the solid state of the substance and, *via* the causal theory of perception, that his apprehension of the fluid state preceded his apprehension of the solid state. But the latter is a judgment that the subject's states must have come in a determinate order; it is not a perception of temporal order. And what is to be proved is that the categories must apply to anything that is represented in perception.

To move from the judgment of ice after water to a perception of water followed by ice, Kant introduces the *synthesis speciosa*. Perceptual representations must be suitable to conceptual ones. So when the understanding represents something causally, it directs the imagination or *synthesis speciosa* to construct a sensory representation that is suitable to the causal relation. (At this point, the account may seem hopelessly idealistic; I discuss the role of sensory data in limiting cognition in Chapter 13.) In the case of a temporal cognizer, '*propter hoc*' has a suitable sensory representation in '*post hoc*.' The relation of the lowering of the temperature *causing* water to become ice is represented perceptually as the cognizer apprehending the substance as ice *after* apprehending it as water. So the cognizer not only judges ice after water but constructs a perceptual representation of water followed by ice.

Kant compresses the reasoning as follows (with interpolations):

> When I perceive the freezing of water, then I apprehend two states [of the object] (fluidity and solidity) as states that stand to each other in a relation in time. Since the appearance [the subject's perceptual representation] is [belongs to] inner **intuition**, I lay time at the basis [the representation must be understood as containing temporal relations]. But in time I necessarily represent synthetic **unity** of the manifold [to represent a temporal array the cognizer must combine representations, since time cannot be perceived]; without this unity [this combination by the *synthesis speciosa* directed by the understanding as it grasps causal relations], that relation [of temporal sequence] could not be given **determinately** (as regards time sequence) in an intuition [and the state could not be understood as being the state of a spatiotemporal cognizer]. (B162–63)

Since only the causal relation can determine temporal relations (or so Kant believes), it follows that the contents of any sensory state that can be understood as such (as belonging to a subject and as standing in the following relation to other states) must be such that they can be understood through the category of causation. The perceptual array acquires its needed temporal relations in being constructed to be suitable to causal relations, so this result is inevitable for all perceptions that involve temporal relations—which they all do—and so for all perceptions. In particular the case of *prima facie* 'unrelated' intuitions, perceiving the calm sea and hearing a gunshot, can be understood in the same way as the water to ice case. In this case a larger object, the overall scene I am contemplating, is altered by the firing of a shot and, again, I derive the order of my states from my rational appreciation of the causal relation among objects: An area changes from being quiet to containing a piercing noise when a gun is fired in it.

I do not endorse Kant's theory of the perception of time or his argument for the causal principle. My purpose in running through the argument sketch in section 26 is to defend my interpretation of the first half of the transcendental deduction, the argument from cognition to apperception, by showing how it fits into the argument *from* apperception. It is easy to read the Second Analogy as pursuing a different and simpler line than that of the A and B deductions. Cognizers must be able to understand their mental states as standing in relations of following; allegedly, only a causal law can determine necessary succession; one mental state can be understood as coming after another, because the order of objects represented by the states is determined through the causal law. This approach ignores material that is crucial to both the argument for the causal principle and the doctrine of the unity of apperception. The important feature of causal laws is not just that they refer to temporal succession, but also that they are rules. It is the latter feature that makes the operations performed on representations by the imagination to be syntheses. These are not accidental groupings of representations, but combinations of them according to rules.

The *synthesis speciosa* is not understood as such by the cognizer. But for the theorist it is clear that the relation between intuitions in a temporal array—the representation of perceiving ice after perceiving water—depends on rational considerations. The perception of ice is not rationally dependent on the perception of water; but the perception of ice after the perception of water depends on a rational appreciation of the relations among the representations of 'water,' 'ice,' and a causal rule. The first part of the B deduction argues that it is only the use of an object rule that permits the I-rule to be satisfied in the case of judging; section 26 and the Second Analogy argue that it is only the use of an object-rule that permits the construction of representations of temporal arrays that meet the second condition for apperception, the requirement that the states of a spatiotemporal subject be represented as following one after another. One advantage of my interpretation of the first part of the transcendental deduction argument is that it enables us to appreciate that and how object-rules are necessary for representations to meet both the 'belonging to a common subject' and the 'following' requirements on representations. It offers a univocal account of how the two key elements that cannot be acquired through the senses are supplied through the activities of the mind. Intuitions that can stand in determinate temporal relations must be constructed through the use of object rules, and any intuition that can be thought must be thought under a concept whose use sets up a relation of rational dependence across different representations that makes them states of a common 'I.' Since any intuition that is anything to a thinker must be able to be thought, it follows that it must be possible not just to order representations in time, but to connect them to a common subject.

Kant claims that the bond created across states through the action of synthesis is the same whether the synthesis is conscious or not. It is the same in being the result of the mind's rational activity. At least from a theoretical perspective, representations must be understood as connected to each other in the flow of perceptions as well as in the train of thinking through the mind's rational activities. At first glance, my interpretive claim that the necessary connection across mental states of a single cognizer is one of rational dependence looks implausible for the case of intuitions. When we consider the role of the *synthesis speciosa* in the construction of temporal arrays and so in the argument of section 26, however, we can see that Kant is committed to the view that an appreciation of rational relations is the source of all the connections—conceptual and temporal—that bind mental states to each other.

Matters do not appear that way to cognizers. For them, the transition of their minds from perceiving a ship upstream to perceiving it a bit downstream, for example, appears to be a single experience in the specious present. Because they grasp this experience as a whole, they take themselves to perceive the connection between the two representations as well as their order. Arthur Melnick has argued that the denial of the awareness of succession in the specious present is a serious weakness in the argument of the Second Analogy (1973, e.g., 85). As far as I can tell, however, the specious present is a consequence of Kant's theory rather than a problem for it. He agrees with his predecessors that it seems to cognizers as though they are aware of a succession of representations and aware of those representations as belonging to a common self. Those are the data that his theory must explain in light of what he takes to be the philosophical discoveries that humans can sense neither time nor a common self.

Having shown (I hope) how my account of the argument for apperception fits into the overall transcendental deduction, as Kant understood it, and how it can be applied to the case of intuitions, I return to an issue put aside in section 5, that of mental transitions (for spatiotemporal cognizers). Leibniz took awareness of transitions from one state to another to be essential to the consciousness of an enduring subject. Both Henrich and Carl read Kant as basing the argument for the categories on the need to guarantee that transitions from one mental state to another can be understood as such (Wunderlich, 2005, 228). In section 5, we considered one sort of transition in the counting example: the counter's transition from designating a stroke symbol as '1' to designating the next stroke symbol as '2.' These transitions—representing '2 after 1'—are driven by and grasped through the intention to follow the counting rule. The argument of section 26 (and the Second Analogy) provides an account of other transitions, those brought about through actions of external objects on the perceptual system. In both cases, the understanding determines the order of the contents of 'inner sense' and so the transition from state to state. It does so either intentionally, through a construction of representations in thinking, or in response to the actions of external objects on the senses, where it directs the imagination to build a suitable sensory representation of causal relations using the contents of the representations, for example, a sensory representation of 'water followed by ice.'

Kant's theories of mental unity and of mental transition are remarkably uniform: The active power of understanding that combines materials from sensory data according to rules accounts for both the unity and the transitions. His theories are as uniform as the Empiricist and Rationalist theories that they were intended to replace. For Locke, an unusual sort of sense, inner sense or reflecting consciousness, informs subjects of both their transitions from state to state and of their continuing identity through those transitions. Leibniz's metaphysical theory also offered a unified account. He took the mind, as substance, to have both an intrinsic unity and an internal principle that accounted for the unfolding of its perceptions in a particular order. Kant saw this theory as paradigmatic of the sort of metaphysical theory that blocks progress in science. He does not offer a scientific hypothesis in its place, but a theory of how the mind must function to meet the demands of RE cognition. A cognizer *per se* must have unity, but not a substantial unity. Rather it is a transcendental (*a priori* and required for cognition) unity—a relation of necessary connection across representations that is understood as such—and that is produced in the course of cognition by faculties that combine representations according to rules. It is only his theory of this strange nonsubstantial unity that must be produced through acts of combination involved in thinking that makes it possible for him even to try to argue from the necessity of apperception to the necessary use of object rules for combining representations.

8. Transcendental Apperception, Empirical Apperception, and 'Mineness'

Despite all that has been accomplished to establish the unity of apperception and the necessary applicability of the categories, there is still a large hole in the transcendental deduction's theory of the thinker. For all Kant's efforts to show that the activity of thinking or synthesizing brings about a relation to a common 'I-think,' he still needs to explain how an individual cognizer is able to say '*I*-think.' The obvious place to look for an answer is in his theory of inner sense or empirical apperception. Empirical apperception is supposed to explain how a particular thinker self-ascribes particular representations at particular times (B158). Kant also introduces the notion of 'empirical apperception' to provide a clarifying contrast for the 'transcendental' unity of apperception. I've already considered some important aspects of that contrast in relating his early view about 'inner sense' to his later conception of 'apperception' as an active self-conscious faculty. I conclude my study of the argument for apperception in the B deduction by looking at several other systematic discussions of empirical apperception and by considering again the 'mineness' problem.

Kant's strategy of clarification would be more successful if his notion of 'empirical apperception' were clearer. As we look at some key texts, however, it will be hard to disagree with the interpretive consensus that he left this notion too undeveloped to do any serious work in his theory. His main point about empirical apperception is that it is dependent upon transcendental apperception. Since 'apperception' refers both to a faculty and to the unity of consciousness (produced by that faculty), the contrast can involve four different items: the faculty and unity of transcendental apperception and the faculty and unity of empirical apperception. I have deferred a systematic discussion of the faculty of transcendental apperception until the next chapter, but discussing the relations between empirical and transcendental apperception will require me briefly to consider the faculty as well as the unity of transcendental apperception.

The introduction of 'inner sense' or 'empirical apperception' in the *Critique* seems inconsistent with later claims. 'Inner sense' is introduced as the faculty

> by which the mind intuits itself, or its inner state. (A22/B37)

This description and later ones (B158) suggest that empirical apperception provides representations of a state of the mind at a time: I am tasting something sweet now; I was thinking about the properties of a body earlier. But this claim is inconsistent with a central thesis of the Transcendental Aesthetic that time cannot be sensed and with a central thesis of the transcendental deduction that the 'I' cannot be sensed.

Chapter 2 proposed handling the apparent discrepancy between Kant's claims that time cannot be perceived and that it is the form of inner sense by making a distinction between inputs to and outputs from inner sense (p. 25, section 5). We now have a somewhat fuller account of how temporal relations get 'added' to the raw materials of inner sense. The understanding, which he equates with the 'faculty of (transcendental) apperception,' directs the *synthesis speciosa* to produce a sensory representation suitable to the intellectual representation of a causal relation. In this way, the faculty apperception 'affects' the outputs of inner sense (B153–54). Time cannot be sensed, but it does not seem that way to cognizers. Due to the complex processing needed to produce cognition, a subject is aware of his states through inner sense as following one another in time. On Kant's account, cognizers do not intuit their states as states of a continuing subject through inner sense either. Again, it doesn't seem that way to cognizers, however, which may be why so many (including himself at an earlier time) take the 'I' to be an intuition. As he now understands the situation, a cognizer is aware of states through inner sense as belonging to a common subject only by virtue of his activities of thinking about objects.

When read against the background of the theory he goes on to develop, Kant's introduction of the faculty of inner sense or empirical apperception can be understood as nonparadoxical (though, perhaps, somewhat misleading). Further, as we reconcile the apparent inconsistencies, we come to appreciate his central claim that the ability of the faculty of inner sense to provide representations of the mind and its states is thoroughly dependent on the faculty of understanding or transcendental apperception.

In his focal discussion of the 'subjective' or 'empirical' unity of apperception in section 18 of the B deduction, Kant argues that it depends on the 'objective' unity of (transcendental) apperception. He contrasts the two unities in three different and not obviously compatible ways. The subjective unity is contingent as opposed to the necessary objective unity; the objective unity is related to determining the time sequence whereas the subjective is not; the subjective unity of empirical apperception is derived from the objective unity in particular conditions (B139–40). If the subjective unity is just a special case of the objective unity, as the third condition suggests, then it seems that it cannot be so different from it in the first two respects.

One clue to resolving the tensions in section 18 is that the 'subjective' unity rests on the law of association (Allison, 1983, 156). Kant accepts that even conscious representations are subject to the law (A100), so he wants to explain how representations that must belong to the unity of apperception can be understood as also subject to irrational forces. Locke's original use of 'association' was to explain superstitions such as the 'connection' between goblins and darkness (ECHU 2.33.10, 397–98). A surfeit of fairy tales in childhood leads adults to associate darkness with danger, but this 'relation' is entirely contingent and cannot be used to determine the order of anything in time. The linkage between darkness and danger is subjective in a number of ways. There is no logical connection between the ideas; their connection depends on a contingent history; because of these factors, there is no place for intersubjective agreement. That my history leads me to make the connection cannot be checked by asking you whether you also make the connection. However you answer it is irrelevant to the existence of my association. Despite the thorough contingency of this connection, it would be impossible if I could not represent darkness. For the law of association to operate on conscious representations (as well as on unconscious ones, which aren't Kant's concern here) the cognizer must have conscious representations.

This is the basic sense in which the subjective unity is derived from the objective unity and is a special case of the objective unity. The implied contrast is that the relation could never go the other way. No amount of irrational or accidental association among representations can produce the necessary connections across representations that are required for RE cognition. In section 18, the B deduction finally makes good on the project attempted in the Second Synthesis in the A edition: It explains how the law of association can hold while still being irrelevant to cognition and while presupposing the active faculties that make cognition possible.

So the unity of empirical apperception depends on the transcendental unity of apperception as much as the operation of the faculty of empirical apperception depends on the activity of the faculty of understanding or transcendental apperception. Kant never entertains the possibility of the reverse dependence. But since RE cognition requires that the cognizer know the basis of his judgments and that basis is his representations, however, isn't empirical apperception also necessary to RE cognition? How can the cognizer be aware of combining some of his representations in others unless he is aware of the representations? Kant seems committed to giving empirical apperception or inner sense this crucial role of enabling cognizers to be aware of their representations as such. In that case, however, he should regard the operation of empirical apperception as necessary for the operation of transcendental apperception. He never concedes this point, so perhaps he held the semiofficial view already discussed. Perhaps he believed that the actions of the mind in thinking not only create relations across representations, but also require a cognizer to use her capacity to understand representations as such. But he doesn't say this.

Finally, as noted at the end of Chapter 2, empirical apperception or inner sense seems necessary to solve the problem of how humans use the terms 'I' and 'my'. They call a sensation 'mine' or claim that '*I* think that water turned into ice,' because they are aware of their sensations and judgmental states through inner sense. Given his theory, Kant should acknowledge that rational cognition also depends on empirical apperception. But he doesn't concede this point either. Konrad Cramer has suggested that Kant is able to extract the '*I* exist' from 'I think' because thinking is a self-conscious act (1987, 171). The fact that an act directs a series of subactions is, however, insufficient to establish the 'togetherness' of the representations involved. Cramer well understands that there is a great difference between establishing that a representation must belong to an I-think and showing that different ones must belong to the same I-think (1987, 174). Still even if the act-awareness on its own could not establish the 'togetherness' of representations, it seems well-suited to provide an account of their mineness.[46] Representations are mine because I am conscious of creating some from others—conscious in making judgments. Since this is not Kant's official theory of 'mineness,' but an emendation of it, I postpone further discussion until Chapter 15 where I propose a Kantian alternative to current views on the self-knowledge of belief.

9. Summary

The argument of the transcendental deduction for the unity of apperception consists in an examination of the necessary conditions for RE cognition. Alternatively, it involves a regression from the assumption that humans have such cognition, which sketches how such cognition is possible. It is possible because humans can be aware of their representations as such and can combine representations through self-conscious acts that enable them to grasp the relations of necessary connection across their representations. The transcendental deduction also argues for RE cognition from the assumption that humans know themselves to be identical selves across different representations. The back and forth character of these arguments is possible, because a central thesis is that RE cognition and self-consciousness mutually imply each other.

Since the argument proceeds by an analysis of the normative requirements of RE cognition, the resulting theory of the 'I-think' is not metaphysical but epistemological. It establishes only weak and conditional metaphysical claims, for example, if RE cognition is possible, then some creatures must have the capacity to recognize their representations as such and to engage in conscious synthesis of representations. Given the result that it is a requirement of cognition that different representations be understood as belonging to a common subject, however, the transcendental deduction offers a deflationary defense of the alleged metaphysical principle that all representations inhere in a common substance. Since this principle cannot be established on metaphysical grounds, the deduction provides the only way of defending what seems to be the obvious truth that different mental states necessarily belong to a single thinker.

The transcendental deduction reveals several unusual features of thinkers. Since the necessary connection across diverse states specified by the I-rule can only be established through engaging in thinking, the thinker is, in a real sense, created by his acts of thinking. Absent these, the various capacities required for thinking would lie dormant and never produce thought or the necessary connections that thought requires. Further, thinking and the self-consciousness it enables require an act-awareness in combining representations that is hard to fit into either Kant's system or contemporary theories of mind. In a passage that will be discussed at greater length in Chapter 10, he can only offer a negative characterization of the awareness at issue:

> when the understanding is considered by itself alone, then its synthesis is nothing but the unity of the understanding's act: of which the understanding is conscious as such even apart from sensibility . . . (B153, amended translation)

Finally, despite Kant's enormous efforts to limn the contours of the thinker, the resulting theory contains a large hole. The transcendental deduction is all about the 'I-think,' but it does not work out a good theory of how cognizers are able to use the representation 'I.'

10

The Power of Apperception

1. Introduction

Kant uses the term 'apperception' to refer both to a unity of mental states that is necessary for RE cognition and to a power or faculty that helps produce such cognition. Although the previous chapter focused on the unity issue, it also gave the argument for an active self-conscious faculty of apperception: The faculty enables cognizers to combine or synthesize representations in whole representations according to rules, thereby producing both cognition and necessary connections across representations or mental states. Having introduced the faculty in passing there, I take a systematic look at it in this chapter.

Kant makes a number of claims about apperception that have led commentators to assimilate his views to those of the Rationalist metaphysicians whom he criticizes. Further, in addition to his doctrines of the unity of apperception and of the power of apperception, he offers another theory related to the 'I-concept,' that of the 'Psychological Idea' of a single soul. Some interpreters read him as proposing a theory of a noumenal thinker. It is easy to run these various notions together, since all concern the 'I' and all derive from a Rationalist metaphysics of the soul. This chapter charts the relations among them, so that we can distinguish Kant's insightful positive account of thinking from his insightful criticisms of his predecessors' ways of thinking about the cognitive subject.

In order to lay out the argument of the transcendental deduction, Chapter 9 largely ignored alterative readings. In this chapter I defend and clarify my accounts of the unity and of the power of apperception by contrasting them with the same sounding, but more metaphysically charged, interpretations offered by Henry Allison and Eric Watkins. I also use my analyses to unpack a confusing Reflection that explores the nature of thinking, 'Is it an experience that I think?' Although only an unpublished note, this discussion can be read as revealing the metaphysical underpinnings of Kant's views about thinking. I argue that insofar as it concerns thinking, the considerations involved are purely epistemological.

2. What Is the Power/Faculty of Apperception?

The A deduction's discussion of 'recognition in a concept' introduces 'transcendental apperception' and the 'unity of apperception' into the argument of the *Critique*, but the 'transition' to the deduction foreshadows the arrival of 'apperception.' In this first mention 'apperception' is presented as the name of a faculty:

> Now there are three original sources (capacities [*Fahigkeiten*] or faculties [*Vermögen*]) that contain the conditions for the possibility of all experience, and that cannot themselves be derived from any other faculty of mind, namely, **sense**, **imagination**, and **apperception**. On them are based (1) the a priori **synopsis** of the manifold through sense; (2) the **synthesis** of this manifold through imagination; and (3) the **unity** of this synthesis through original apperception. All the **faculties**, besides having their empirical use, have in addition a transcendental use that deals solely with form and is possible a priori. Above, in Part I, we talked about this transcendental use **in regard to the senses**. Let us now endeavor to gain insight in the nature of the transcendental use of the other two faculties. (A94–95, amended translation)

Kant's trio of faculties is somewhat surprising. The Transcendental Analytic begins by claiming that cognition has two, rather than three, sources and lists them as sensibility and understanding. He may believe that his basic 'two-faculty' theory is consistent with this richer account for a reason we have seen. To create a suitable relation between concepts and percepts, the understanding must direct the operations of the (transcendental) imagination. Still, this trio is not what a reader has been led to expect, because the faculty of apperception rather than understanding is presented as the third faculty.

On Kant's account, there are three mental faculties, with two uses each, an 'empirical' and a 'transcendental' use. His focus is on the 'transcendental' use, but we can understand the 'empirical' use by contrast. He needs to argue for a 'transcendental' use, where faculties 'add' *a priori* elements to representations that are needed for cognition. No argument need be given for the 'empirical' use of these faculties, because these are the uses on which all participants to the debate agree: Humans can receive information through the stimulation of their sensory organs; they can reproduce sensory perceptions through a faculty of 'reproductive' imagination. Further, insofar as the faculty of 'apperception' is identical with that of 'understanding,' all would agree that humans have an ability to form concepts (in part) through the receipt of information from their sensory faculties, and perhaps through the aid of imagination. Insofar as the emphasis is on apperception or self-consciousness rather than understanding, all would agree that humans can be conscious of their various mental states. Having argued for a transcendental use of the faculty of sensibility in the Transcendental Aesthetic, the task of the Transcendental Analytic is to show why humans must also make a transcendental use of imagination and apperception/understanding. He may use 'apperception' in this introductory text instead of 'understanding' to signal something about the nature of its transcendental use. As with human sensibility, human understanding has a particular form, the form that all representations belong to a common subject.

Having presented apperception as a faculty, Kant later characterizes it as a 'root faculty' (*Radikalvermögen*, A114). In the Appendix to the Transcendental Dialectic, the Regulative Use of the Ideas (of Pure Reason), he illustrates reason's search for homogeneity by the example of the faculties or powers of the human mind. In this case, reason looks for a fundamental power (*Grundkraft*) of which the different powers would be varieties (A649/B677). These passages raise an obvious question: Is the 'root-faculty' of apperception the same as a 'fundamental power' of apperception?

I don't think the issue can be resolved just by looking at the way Kant uses the terms 'faculty' and 'power.'[1] Chapter 4 presents Wolff's account of the relation between 'faculties' and 'powers.' He took a 'faculty' to indicate the possibility of doing something. By contrast, reference to a 'power' is supposed to indicate the actual cause of alterations. Were Kant using Wolff's scheme, then the fundamental power of apperception might be what carries out or realizes the capacity or faculty of 'apperception.' The problem with this hypothesis is that his usage simply vacillates. The First Introduction to the *Critique of Judgment* looks Wolffian in that it distinguishes faculties from powers, though his real interest in the discussion lies in the fact that all the higher faculties operate according to principles (20.245–46, CJudge 44–45).[2] In the published introduction, however, the 'power of judging' is listed as a species of the 'faculty of cognition' (5.198, CJudge 83). And, again, his real interest seems to be in the claim that the higher faculties contain constitutive principles of cognition. Given the fluctuating usage, terminology alone seems an inadequate basis for understanding the relation between the root faculty of apperception and the fundamental power of apperception. To make progress on the question, we need to look at the contexts in which they are used.

The 'root faculty' of apperception is introduced at a dramatic moment in the A deduction when Kant considers how his theory might strike a reader. Why should anyone believe the central claim of transcendental idealism, the

> strange and quite preposterous [claim] that nature should conform to our subjective basis, apperception—indeed that nature should in its law-governedness depend on this basis[?] (A114)

In reply, he does not offer new doctrines, but reminds the reader of what has already been established. Any representation that is an empirical cognition of nature must belong to the unity of apperception; but representations can belong to the unity of apperception only insofar as their contents can be combined by rules. Hence it follows that nature insofar as it is able to be known by humans will exemplify laws.

> But we must bear in mind that this nature is intrinsically nothing but a sum of appearances, and hence is not a thing in itself but is merely a multitude of the mind's representations. If we bear this in mind, then we shall not be surprised that we see nature in its unity merely in the root faculty [*Radikalvermögen*] for all our cognition, *viz*., in transcendental apperception; we there see nature in

that unity, *viz.*, on whose account alone it can be called an object of all possible experience, i.e., nature. (A114, amended translation)

Transcendental apperception is a 'root faculty,' more fundamental than sensibility, imagination, or even understanding (but see below), because whatever the contents of sensory or conceptual representations, they must all, as representations, belong to the unity of apperception. More briefly, transcendental apperception is a 'root faculty,' because the principle of apperception is the supreme or highest principle governing cognition. The idea of a 'fundamental power' is offered as a solution to a different problem: not why transcendental idealism is true, but how to make progress in science.

3. Does the Faculty of Apperception Endure? Is It the 'Inner Principle' of a Substance?

Some of Kant's claims about the faculty or power of apperception make his views seem more a continuation than a repudiation of Rationalist metaphysics. One text laying out the apperceptive theory suggests that the faculty of apperception is 'permanent' and thus substance-like if not substantial:

> Now there can take place in us, no cognition, and no connection and unity of cognitions among one another, without that unity of consciousness which precedes all data of intuitions, and by reference to which all representations of objects is alone possible. Now this pure, original, and immutable [*unwandelbar*] consciousness I shall call **transcendental apperception** . . . (A107)

The claim that transcendental apperception is 'unchanging' seems to imply the endurance of a numerically identical thing through time. In the A deduction Kant is explicit that transcendental apperception is numerically identical (A107).

Student notes from the period between the editions present Kant as maintaining that the faculty of apperception does not alter. In discussing empirical psychology in his Metaphysics lectures of 1783 (*Metaphysik Mrongovius*) he is reported as claiming:

> This I remains [even] when everything has changed, when bodies and principles have changed. Now what this identity of his self consists in is difficult to know; everything is related to this, everything can change, only consciousness and apperception, or the faculty for referring representations to one's self remain. (29.878, CMet 248)

The claim that it is difficult to know what the identity of the self consists in is puzzling, since the later part of the sentence implies that it is a matter of a continuing ability to refer representations to a self. Perhaps the difficulty relates to an issue I will consider in Chapter 11, that of conversion. In any case, the lecture notes are helpful because they specify the reason why the faculty of apperception must remain through all changes in body and principles (presumably maxims). A subject must be able to refer representations to a common 'I' (if she is to be a cognitive subject at all). Because of the ongoing necessity of referring to a common 'I,' subjects must always have a faculty for doing so. That does not imply that the faculty must be the same—whatever exactly that would mean—but only that there must always be a faculty or capacity to refer different representations to the same 'I.'

In the run-up to the discussion of an 'unchanging' faculty of apperception in the A deduction, Kant's focus is on the need to find a constant and enduring self (or 'I') in inner appearance. So his claim of an unchanging and numerically identical faculty of transcendental apperception probably expresses nothing more than the necessity of having a faculty through which different representations can be referred to a common 'I.' This reading is supported by the fact that the term *'unwandelbar'* does not recur in the A deduction and is never used in the B deduction.[3] The expression 'numerical identity' is also dropped in the second edition. The view that what is really at issue is a continuing ability to refer different representations to a common 'I' is also confirmed by the parallel passage in the B deduction, at least in the Kemp Smith and Guyer and Wood translations:[4]

> Original apperception, because it is that self-consciousness which, while generating the representation **I think** (a representation which must be capable of accompanying all other representations, and which in all consciousness is one and the same) cannot itself be accompanied by any further representation. (B132, Kemp Smith)

It is not the faculty that endures or is the same across different representations, but the representation 'I think' that is one and the same. Given this text, the Metaphysics notes and the changes from the A edition to the B edition, Kant's considered position seems to be not that the power of apperception is unchanging or numerically identical, but rather that subjects must always have a power of apperception, because they must be able to refer different representations to one and the same 'I-think.'

Kant's remarks about mental powers in other passages might suggest not that they are permanent, but that they are similar to substances in having a single principle of operation. The *Critique of the Power of Judgment* maintains that

> no use of the cognitive powers may be permitted without principles. (5.385, CJudge 257)

Taken out of context, this normative claim seems to echo the Leibnizian doctrine discussed in Chapter 4. Leibniz objected to Lockean 'bare powers' on the ground that it is unintelligible or mere abstraction to refer to a bare faculty independently of the acts that it performs. Any power, properly so-called, must have a disposition, rooted in a substance, to act in one way rather than another. Kant's concern is not with the impossibility of bare powers, however, but with the fact that the cognitive faculties must contain the constitutive principles of cognition (20.245–46, CJudge 44–45, 5.148, CJudge 83).

Further, Kant could not simply take over Leibniz's position without betraying his commitment to scientific metaphysics. Instead, he accepts a version of it as an epistemological norm. It is frivolous to introduce faculties, unless one is in a position to specify the principles by which they must operate in producing cognition or, as in the case at hand in the *Critique of the Power of Judgment*, in contributing to cognition indirectly, by aiding the faculties in reflecting on a kind of object (5.385, CJudge 257). Faculties should be differentiated from each other by their modes of operating. Hence 'one power-one principle' or, more accurately, 'one principle-one power' would be a good maxim, not because a power must be based in a single inner principle of a substance, but for almost the opposite reason: Faculties are introduced only in specifying the principles by which thinking must operate if empirical cognition is to be possible.

We can use this analysis to sort out Kant's *prima facie* confusing claim that the power/faculty of transcendental apperception and that of understanding are one and the same. The understanding would appear to be a counterexample to the one-principle-one-power norm. Since there are twelve categories, it seems that the understanding would combine representations in twelve different kinds of object-concepts and/or in twelve different forms of judgment. It seems to have twelve different modes of operation. By contrast, we might think that a faculty of apperception combined representations in one way, according to the principle that different representations must belong to a common 'I-think.' Yet Kant clearly identifies understanding and apperception:

> The synthetic unity of apperception is the highest point, to which we must attach all use of the understanding . . . indeed this power is the understanding itself. (B133–34n., also cited at greater length in Chapter 9)

In light of the argument of Chapter 9, we can see both why Kant makes the identification and why there is no inconsistency in the claims that there are twelve categories of understanding and that the understanding and apperception are but one faculty. Cognition is possible only when representations are in accord with the I-rule. But that condition can be achieved only when sensory materials can be combined according to the basic rules for representing objects, namely, the categories. Since achieving cognition of objects and self-consciousness always occur together and by the same process, there is only one faculty, which may be characterized either as 'understanding' or as 'apperception' depending on whether one wishes to stress the objective or subjective requirements of cognition. The way it acts, most fundamentally, is in accord with the I-rule.

On my interpretation, Kant argues that the power of apperception must consciously combine representations to bring about both cognition and the unity of apperception. His considered position is not that this power endures or that it reflects the metaphysical disposition of a substance. He characterizes it only in terms of the role it must play for cognition to be possible: A power of apperception must always enable a subject to refer representations to a common 'I'; its operation is understood in terms of a particular principle (the 'I-rule') and the categorial rules that permit the application of the 'I-rule.'

4. Does the Power of Apperception Initiate Causal Chains or Provide Impressions of Necessary Connection?

In this section, I clarify and support my reading of how Kant thinks self-conscious combination works and how it relates to the unity of apperception by contrasting it with the views of Henry Allison and Eric Watkins. My interpretation takes Kant's theory of the unity and power of apperception to be purely epistemological; both Allison and Watkins believe that the epistemological analysis is intertwined with metaphysical considerations. I begin with Allison's influential account of Kant on apperception and judging, a reading that Watkins takes as his starting point.

Allison's interpretation has four pieces. He starts with a gloss of Kant's claim about combination:

> The first step is to note that any representation of a manifold *as a* manifold is a single complex thought. In Kant's terms, it involves a 'synthetic unity of representations.' I regard this claim . . . as obviously analytic: it serves merely to clarify the formal nature of the thought of a manifold, regardless of its particular content. Consequently it should not be confused with the claim that such a representation requires an act of synthesis. (1983, 138)

His point is just that it is analytic that a complex representation is a complex of (simpler) representations. The next step lays out the need for a single subject:

> The next step is to show that a single complex thought requires a single thinking subject. The point here is essentially the same as the one that was noted by William James: a set of distinct thoughts of the elements of a whole can never be equivalent to the thought of the whole itself. Thus, while each of the representations that collectively constitute the single complex thought could conceivably be distributed among a multiplicity of thinking subjects, the single complex thought could not be so dispersed. I take this claim to be likewise analytic. (1983, 138)

Prima facie, it seems odd to invoke the argument that Kant criticizes in the Second Paralogism, though, as we saw, Hoppe also makes this move. The idea would be that Kant's criticism doesn't apply to the argument itself, but only to the conclusion that Rational Psychologists draw from it about the simplicity of the subject. Although an invalid argument for simplicity, it succeeds in establishing unity. As Allison understands the argument, the key is that it is not enough to have the elements of a verse; rather, the elements must be grasped or held together in a unity. As far as I can tell, however, this argument is still vulnerable to the criticism of the Second Paralogism (A352).

> For since the thought consists of many representations, its unity is collective and can, as far as mere concepts are concerned, refer just as well to the collective unity of the substances cooperating on the thought . . . as it can refer to the absolute unity of the subject. (A353)

The unity of the different elements would be a collective unity and Kant denies that such a unity requires the absolute unity of the thinking subject.

By contrast, the operation of conscious synthesis creates something new. Various representations are not just grasped or held together. A whole judgment is constructed out of partial representations thereby creating a relation of necessary connection across the representations. When thought is understood in this way, it is analytic that the I of apperception cannot be a plurality, but must be understood as singular (B407). Alternatively, the form of apperception is a subjectively necessary condition for cognition (A354). However, the analysis of thought that yields these results goes considerably beyond the requirement that all the elements of a verse must be contained in the same frame (Hoppe) or grasped as a unity (Allison). The analysis makes essential appeal to the power of apperception's self-conscious synthesis.

The third step of Allison's account deals with Kant's claims that apperception requires synthesis and a consciousness of synthesis. He tries to clarify the view through an example. Consider

> the simplest possible case: where a subject has two representations, A and B, each of which is accompanied by a distinct awareness of 'empirical consciousness.' In other words, there is an 'I think' A and an 'I think' B pertaining to a single subject. Clearly in order for the subject of both these thoughts to become reflectively aware of its identity, it must combine A and B in a single consciousness. Only by so combining A and B can it become aware of the identity of the I that thinks A with the I that thinks B. (1983, 142)

On Allison's reading, Kant's insistence on the necessity of conscious syntheses for apperception should be understood as part of reflective account of a subject's knowledge of her self-identity. A subject becomes aware of the identity of the 'I' in 'I think A' with the 'I' in 'I think B,' by reflecting on her combining A and B in the thought 'I think A and B.' But both Merian and Kant criticize 'reflective' theories of the self-consciousness. As they would see the situation, if there is a thought 'I think A,' and another thought 'I think B' and a third thought 'I think A and B,' then there is no more reason to assume a common 'I' between the first and third or second and third thoughts than to assume that a common 'I' between the first two thoughts. When a common 'I' is not divulged in the representations, then no amount of reflection will produce such a representation.

Matters are different if the thought 'A and B' is understood as synthesized from (partial) representations 'A,' 'B.' Perhaps Allison assumes this and thus infers that the combination is possible only because the same subject has access to both representations—which thereby shows that they belong to a common subject. His claim would be: Combination establishes sameness of subject, because upon reflection the subject can appreciate that it is a necessary condition of his combining that he has access to the representations to be combined. This is true, but it presupposes a condition that already establishes that representations belong to a single 'I-think': For combination to be understood as such, the whole representation must be understood as rationally dependent on its parts, which establishes a relation of necessary connection across them. Without that presupposition, the argument for common access cannot get off the ground, but with it we already have a relation of necessarily belonging together across diverse representations—and that is the relation indicated by the 'I-think.' Further, the awareness of necessary connection does not require reflection; implicit awareness of the connection is an integral part of RE cognition *per se*.

The fourth part of Allison's analysis of apperception and judgment turns metaphysical, because it links the cognitive analysis to transcendental freedom. In the B deduction, Kant is explicit that combination and (so) judgment are acts that the subject must perform for himself (B130). In Allison's view, this shows that Kant takes the cognitive subject to be transcendentally free. All admit that human beings enjoy what Kant calls 'practical freedom' (A533–34/B561–62). Unlike animals, human beings have the power to resist sensory impulses. They can determine their actions independently of coercion by their senses. But Kant takes morality to require something more than practical or psychological freedom. It requires 'transcendental freedom,' the freedom to be an absolute beginning in the order of causes.

Allison has long maintained that Kant's claims about the spontaneity of judging imply that he thinks that the cognitive as well as the moral subject enjoys transcendental freedom. He provides an especially clear account of how he understands the spontaneity of judging (often referred to in the literature as the 'taking-as' theory) in a recent essay:

> The basic point is that to consider oneself as a cognizer is to assume such spontaneity [transcendental freedom]. This is because to understand or cognize something requires not simply having the correct beliefs and even having them for the correct reasons, it also involves a capacity to take these reasons (whether rightly or wrongly) as justifying the belief. (2006, 389)

In many ways, my current analysis[5] agrees with Allison's. As I understand Kant's dissection of recognition in a concept or judging, the cognizer recognizes (or can recognize) the elements or partial cognitions as grounds of her judgment; otherwise she would not enjoy RE cognition. It is not simply a matter of having representations that would instantiate a rule for bodies, for example, 'bodies are impenetrable,' but of grasping the logical relations between the concept that is used, 'body,' and the partial representation, 'impenetrability.' Still, although our readings overlap on the claim that Kant believes that cognition requires that reasons be understood as such, we disagree about how he understands the necessary conditions for that requirement.

Allison's 'transcendentally free' interpretation would sever the connection between cognition and apperception that Kant labored to explain. We can see this in another simple example, the inference: 'if p, then q,' 'p,' therefore 'q.' Insofar as a transcendentally free cognizer sees his judgment 'q' as a new beginning, he would not see it as dependent on his other representations, and hence would not through the exercise of his cognitive faculties come to understand his states as belonging to the unity of apperception. He would have no grounds for seeing his states as necessarily connected. Partly through Allison's influence, the relation between the spontaneity of thought and that of action in Kant has been a topic of recent interest and I return to it in the broader context of the ethical theory in Chapter 14. In regard to the current project of understanding the argument for the unity of apperception, I will just add that Kant explicitly rejects a Cartesian voluntaristic view of belief in his *Logic*:

> The will does not have any influence immediately on holding-to-be-true; this would be quite absurd. (9.73–74, CLog 577, cf. R2508, 16.398)

In the case of judging or 'objective' holding-to-be-true (A822/B850), the absurdity would be twofold. The 'judgment' would not be an instance of rational cognition, because the 'thinker' wouldn't understand his conclusion 'q' as based on his rational grasp of the premises; and for this reason, the 'thinker' would not understand her states as necessarily connected to each other and so would not understand herself as a thinker.

To sum up, as Allison understands Kant, he maintains that apperceptive consciousness arises through reflection and that taking reasons as such requires a new beginning of a causal chain; as I understand Kant, RE cognition involves the use of rules that enable the subject to grasp the logical relations between the content of her judgment and the contents of other states so that she is in the same act aware both of her reasons as such and of the necessary connection of representations in a single subject. Far from implying a transcendentally free cognizer, Kant's argument for the necessary unity of apperception to cognition is inconsistent with that assumption.

In *Kant and the Metaphysics of Causality*, Eric Watkins highlights the centrality of activity, and consciousness of activity, to Kant's discussions of apperception. On one key point our interpretations agree. Watkins takes the activity of synthesis to produce connections across representations:

> Without these [synthetic] activities, there would be no connections between our representations. Specifically, these activities would seem to be instances of a particular kind of activity, namely an activity whereby a connection between representations is brought about as its effect. (2005, 278)

On the other hand he takes the problem addressed at B132–33 to be

> how we can explain the fact that various representations are mine. (2005, 276)

Although he characterizes the issue in terms of 'mineness,' he links that issue to the 'togetherness' problem. He thinks that B133 presents the solution: Different representations are connected to the same 'I-think' through awareness of synthesizing activities.

> [Kant] argues that the identity of apperception 'contains a synthesis of the representations, and is possible only through the consciousness of this synthesis' (B133). The basic idea behind Kant's argument is that I can know that representations are mine only if I know that one and the same I has each one, but this can be known only if (1) I connect them . . . and (2) if I am aware that I am connecting them (since only my awareness of my connecting them allows me to know that each representation is being had by one and the same self). (2005, 276–77)

Watkins assumes that a solution to the 'mineness' problem depends on a solution to the 'togetherness' problem, which is what Kant addresses in B133.

Watkins's interpretation is a variant of Allison's, which he references (2005, 277). Where Allison takes the important move to be that representations 'A' and 'B' can be combined only if they belong to a common subject, Watkins takes it to be that the representations can be combined only if the subject that acts on 'A' is the same as the subject that acts on 'B.' He sees the move from the consciousness of the act of combining representation A and representation B to the assumption of a common self as inferential.

> Kant [as opposed to Hume] thinks that we can be aware of the self and its identity indirectly, that is, by being aware of the activity of the self when it connects its various representations and by then inferring that it is one and the same self that does the connecting. (2005, 276–77, 278)

His idea seems to be that consciousness of combination establishes sameness of subject, because one can infer from that consciousness to the necessary condition of combining that the representations are acted on by a common subject. This interpretation is also vulnerable to Kant's argument against reflective consciousness. Whether a consciousness accompanies various representations or acts on them, there is no warrant for taking the reflecting or acting consciousness to be the same across representations. One consciousness grasps representation A, another grasps representation B, another is conscious of combining two representations, A and B, in a representation 'A and B.' Where is the identity across these acts unless the combination is understood as depending on and so as necessarily connected to the partial representations? If the cognizer understands her combining activities as such, however, then she also understands her various representations as necessarily connected and so as belonging to a single thinker—with no further inference required. The text of B133 that Watkins cites is fairly clear that cognizers are not aware of their identities just through acting on representations or even by being conscious of the acting, though these are necessary. They must be conscious of producing the combined representation from the elements of the combination:

> This reference [to my identity as a subject] comes about . . . through my **adding** one representation to another and being conscious of their synthesis [*der Synthesis derselben*]. (B133, my underscoring)

A power of apperception could be active in trying to combine representations. But even if that power could somehow be attributed to the same subject (or substance, which seems to be Watkins's model [2005, e.g., 235]), there would be no warrant for characterizing the situation in terms of a single *thinker* unless the activity succeeds in producing combinations according to rules and so the unity of apperception. Under those circumstances, the act of combining can be said to be that of a single thinker. Alternatively, unless the power of apperception produces the unity of apperception, neither it nor its acts belong to a cognitive subject. These considerations depend on the analysis of cognition; they neither require nor are advanced by assumptions about the sameness of a power and/or the substance in which it inheres.

In Watkins's view, conscious synthesis does not just enable Kant to rebut Hume's attack on personal identity. It also offers a non-Humean model of causation as a 'causal power' or 'active ground' that allows him to answer to the skeptical challenge to find a necessary connection between cause and effect (2005, 246ff.). He focuses on the claim at B153 that, in cognition, cognizers are conscious of their synthetic acts, but not through inner sense:

> Now in us human beings the understanding is not itself a power of intuitions; and even if an intuition were already given in sensibility, the understanding cannot take it up **into itself**, in order—as it were—to combine the manifold of [what would then be] **its own** intuition. Hence when the understanding is considered by itself alone, then its synthesis is nothing but the unity of the understanding's act: <u>of which the understanding is conscious as such even apart from sensibility</u> . . . (B153, amended translation, my underscoring)

Watkins takes this passage to be crucial in revealing Kant's deeper (than the regularity account of the Second Analogy) understanding of causation:

> Since Hume consistently denies that he has any internal impression of a necessary connection or causal activity within himself, it is important to investigate this point with great care. (2005, 274)

On this view, 'conscious synthesizing,' synthesizing where the subject is conscious of what she is doing, should be understood as 'consciousness of synthesizing,' where the cognizer has a something like a nonsensory impression of synthesizing and of necessary connection. Alternatively, on Watkins's model, apperceptive awareness is similar to inner sense in being a kind of awareness.

In presenting the understanding as conscious of its act (or perhaps of the unity of its act), and in contrasting this consciousness with sensibility, the language of B153 may suggest this sort of reading. On the other hand, it comes in the middle of a section and a chapter where Kant stresses that apperception/understanding is not a receptive, but an active faculty. In keeping with the emphasis on activity, the mention of sensibility can be read as asserting that the consciousness of the understanding is not receptive. It is not a kind of nonsensible receptivity, but a self-conscious act that does not involve receptivity.

The distinction between conscious synthesizing and consciousness of acts of synthesis is crucial in understanding Kant's view. Had he tried to reply to Hume on causation as Watkins suggests—by finding an impression of necessary connection across mental states—then his argument against Hume on personal identity would fall apart. In earlier discussions I have noted that rational cognition requires an appreciation of rational dependence and *so* of necessary connection. Recognition of necessary connection is part of what is involved in recognition of rational dependence. But this is not an impression of necessary connection. Nor is it possible to argue from an impression of necessary connection to a recognition of necessary connection and then to a recognition of relations of rational dependence. If what the power of apperception does is divulge an impression of necessary connection, then it could not be the fulcrum of the transcendental deduction's argument from the requirements of conceptual or rational cognition, to the unity of apperception. In viewing Kant's analysis of thinking as implying either transcendental freedom or a non-Humean causal bond,

Allison and Watkins introduce metaphysical considerations that would serve only to undermine the argument for the unity of apperception.

5. 'Is It an Experience That I Think?'

One of Kant's most explicit and extensive discussions of thinking occurs in a Reflection (1788–90), 'Response to the Question: Is it An Experience that I Think?' Since it is a Reflection—and a very obscure one—it cannot be presumed to express his considered views or, perhaps, even any coherent views. I discuss it, because I think I can make some sense of it and because it can be read as offering an argument for a noumenal thinker.

Given the topic, the most obvious target is Locke, who took humans to be aware of their thinkings, doubtings, and so forth, through inner sense. Kant begins with the relevant definitions. An empirical representation of which the subject is conscious is a 'perception'; 'experience' is empirical cognition of an object (18.318, CNotes 289). His argumentative strategy is to present variations on a case until the precise thesis in question is in view. His example is from geometry. First he compares thinking about a square in the abstract with apprehending a drawn square. In the latter case, perception is involved and the cognizer is instructed by what he perceives. The thought that brings the perception under the concept of a square yields a representation that is experienced. A cognizer could be aware of his condition of judging 'that is a square.'

Kant then considers just thinking of the *a priori* concept square (with no drawn or imagined model).

> The consciousness of having such a thought is not an experience, for the very reason that since the thought is not an experience, consciousness itself is nothing empirical. (R5661, 18.319, CNotes 289)

This *Gedanken* experiment consists in thinking the concept square, but not in thinking about any square. He seems to beg the question and just assert that since such thought involves no sensory impression, the consciousness involved in thinking cannot be of a state of having (or perhaps receiving) an impression—and so cannot be an experience.

Kant proceeds by teasing apart various claims that might be muddled together in the idea of 'experiencing thinking':

> Nevertheless, this thought brings forth an object of experience or a determination of the mind that can be observed, insofar, namely, as it is affected through the faculty of thinking; I can thus say that I have experienced what belongs to grasping a figure with four equal sides . . . in thought in such a way that I can demonstrate its properties. This is the empirical consciousness of the determination of my condition in time through thought. (R5661, 18.319, CNotes 289)

Suppose my entertaining of the concept of a square is productive. Even without the benefit of a drawn or imagined exemplar, I figure out that the diagonals of a square must be equal. The thought 'the diagonals are equal' would be a determinate event and reportable through inner sense as a mental episode. His next claim is confusing:

> This is the empirical consciousness of the determination of my state [*Zustandes*] in time through thought. The thought [the thinking] itself, <u>although it also occurs in time</u>, takes no regard of time when the properties of a figure are to be thought. But experience is impossible without a connection to the determination in time. (R5661, 18.319, CNotes 289, amended translation, my underscoring)

I take his point to be not just that the judgment or thought, 'the diagonals are equal,' occurs at a time, but that the thinking or grasping of it occurs in time. Yet the thinking cannot be connected to a determinate time. Since any experience must, as an episode of mental life, be assigned a time, it cannot be an experience that we think.

The counting example can make the problem of the lack of a determinate time assignment for thinking more vivid. Suppose I count some stroke symbols. Where should I place an awareness of my act of thinking? The obvious possibilities are these: the awareness of an act of thinking comes first, just before I begin to check off, '1,' and so on, or it comes as I conclude '4.' This sort of account cannot be correct. An awareness of the act of thinking cannot be placed first, because I need to be conscious through the whole process.[6] Nor can the awareness of the act be given a time slot 'between' partial representations contained in the steps and the judgment. For the judgment to be rational, the cognizer must both look 'back' to the representations of the numbers and 'forward' to the judgment '4' to understand the relations between them; awareness of an act of thinking cannot occur after the last step and stop right before the judgment is pronounced (verbally or in thought), or combination would be not understood as such. Reflecting on the properties of a square exhibits the same features. Although the thought that the diagonals are equal can be a mental episode with a determinate time slot, the thinking about the triangles contained in a square, the relations of their sides and angles, and so forth, must continue through the whole process if I am to judge on the basis of my thinking that the diagonals are equal—rather than seeing this claim as something like an alien intrusion in my mind. It follows that a self-conscious power of combining cannot be understood on the model of the awareness of inner states.

Kant makes an abstract and subtle discussion all the more difficult by introducing considerations about transcendental idealism.

> The consciousness when I **institute an experience** is the representation of my existence insofar as it is temporally determined, i.e. in time. Now if this consciousness were itself in turn empirical, then this temporal determination, as contained under the conditions of the temporal determination of my state, would in turn have to be represented. Yet another time would therefore have to be given, **under** which (not **in** which) the time that constitutes the formal condition of my inner experience would be contained . . . <u>The consciousness of instituting an experience and also of thinking in general is</u> **transcendental consciousness, <u>not</u> experience**. (R5661, 18.319, CNotes 289–90, my underscoring)

Suppose we now consider the fact (in his view) that the power of apperception *via* the *synthesis speciosa* introduces temporal ordering into representations. The thinking that produces such an order could not occur in time (at all, since it produces the representation of time). So, if Locke were an idealist about time, then he would see that the thinking that brings about temporal order could be understood as an experience only if there were a second time in which it took place. But a second time is absurd.

By invoking transcendental idealism, Kant can make an additional argument against the claim that subjects have impressions of their acts of thinking—because these impressions would have to take place in a second time. As far as I can see, however, the preceding argument about thinking is independent of transcendental idealism. (In the last sentence of the 'transcendental idealist' passage, which I underscore, he notes that instituting an experience—and also [just] thinking in general—require transcendental consciousness, i.e., apperception.) He explains why he is right in rejecting the then common belief that cognizers are aware of their activities of thinking through inner sense, by showing that the view reduces to absurdity: An inner impression of thinking would have to take place at a particular point in time, but there is no point at which it can take place and be an 'episode' of rational thought. Yet it is also crucial to rational cognition that cognizers understand what they are doing in combining representations. So some syntheses must be conscious even though they cannot be understood as conscious episodes reportable through inner sense. Further, except when thinking is considered as instituting temporal relations, it is understood as taking place in time. His view is not that thinking takes place outside of time in some noumenal realm or that the subject is the limit of the world (at least when we are not concerned about the ideality of time).[7] It is that rational activity is pervasive throughout mental life. Since it is not episodic, it cannot be understood as a datable episode reported on by inner sense, but requires instead a conscious faculty of transcendental apperception.

6. Root Powers, Scientific Ideals, and the Ground of Appearances

With a more detailed understanding of what the faculty or power of apperception does and does not involve, we can return to the issue of the relation between the 'root faculty' of apperception of the Transcendental Analytic and the 'fundamental power' of apperception that is part of the Psychological Idea of the 'soul.' The context of the discussion of the 'root faculty' is the role of the principle of apperception as the highest principle of cognition. The context of the discussion of a 'fundamental power' of mind is different.

Philip Kitcher (1984), Paul Guyer (1990), and Hannah Ginsborg (1992) have laid out the positive message about reason in the Appendix to the Transcendental Dialectic. Kant's aim is to show that, even though they can be abused, the systematizing tendencies of reason play an important role in the advancement of science. Through the prodding of reason, scientists try to find generality in diversity and diversity in generality. In seeking the homogeneous among the diverse, they look, for example, for a fundamental power that is the basis of all other mental powers. This is the same tendency that leads them to seek a fundamental salt that is the common genus of the (then) two main genera, the acidic and the alkaline, and a fundamental earth that is common to the most basic species of earths (A653/B681). This tendency is unrelated to the requirement of rational cognition that all representations belong to a single 'I-think.'

Although Kant's discussion of a fundamental power of mind is comprehensible in context, it raises some puzzles. The most obvious is why he 'happens' to use the fundamental power of the mind to illustrate the general tendency of reason to seek homogeneity that makes science possible. In some ways, it is not an obvious choice. His 1763 essay 'The Only Possible Argument for God' characterized the union of different faculties in a mind as contingent. The contrast was with aspects of nonorganic nature, which all flow from a common and small number of laws. Although the latter arrangement shows the perfection of the Creation, it differs from that encountered in plants and animals, where the organs operate by diverse principles even though their union aims at perfection. In such cases, it appears that artifice is required (2.106–7, C1755 148–49). Perhaps this essay can be dismissed as early, but the First Introduction to the *Critique of the Power of Judgment* explicitly rejects a unitary mental power:

> It can easily be demonstrated, and has already been understood for some time, that this attempt to bring unity into the multiplicity of faculties, although undertaken in a genuinely philosophical spirit, is futile . . . (20.206, CJudge 11)

Given that the impossibility of finding a fundamental power of the mind has been understood for some time, why does he use mental powers to illustrate the operation of the regulative idea of homogeneity?

Two interconnected explanations seem likely. First, Kant may wish to offer an implicit criticism of Wolff's theory of a unitary power of representation.[8] This theory exemplifies the general error of previous metaphysics that the Transcendental Dialectic is supposed to diagnose. By Kant's lights, Wolff misunderstands a regulative idea of reason as a substantive or objective claim about reality. Second, the example smoothes the way for introducing 'soul' as a necessary idea of reason in the subsequent Final Aim section. Then the question becomes, why is he concerned to present the 'soul' as a necessary idea of reason?

When we turn to that discussion, the motivation is fairly evident. Kant casts the soul as an idea of reason in order to criticize his metaphysical predecessors for confusing a regulative idea with an actual object. The Psychological Idea is a means through which the varied appearances of the mind can be systematically studied. Rationalists err when they take a regulative idea that guides the search for knowledge of the mind to be a characterization of metaphysical reality that is the underlying explanation of the existence of those appearances:

> If I want to search for the properties with which a thinking being exists in itself, then I must consult experience; and I cannot even apply to this object any one of the categories except insofar as the schema thereof is given in sensible intuition. But with this experience I never arrive at a systematic unity of all appearances of inner sense. Hence instead of this experiential concept (of what the soul actually is)—which cannot carry us far—reason takes the concept of

the empirical unity of all thought; and by thinking this unity as unconditioned and original, reason turns this concept into a rational concept (idea) of a simple substance that, in itself immutable (personally identical), stands in community with other actual things outside it—in a word, the idea of a simple independent intelligence. In so doing, however, reason has before it nothing but principles of systematic unity that are useful to it in explaining the appearances of the soul. These principles tell us, *viz.*, to regard all determinations as united in a single subject; to regard all powers as much as possible as derived from a single basic power; to regard all variation as belonging to the states of one and the same permanent being; and to represent all **appearances** in space as entirely different from actions of **thought**. This simplicity of the substance, etc., was meant to be only the schema for this regulative principle, and is not presupposed as if it were the actual basis of the soul's properties. <u>For these properties may also rest on quite different bases, with which we are not at all acquainted.</u> (A682–83/B710–11, my underscoring)

Other passages reinforce the warnings. Although science must take a simple soul as its goal, such a being could never be met in perception (A784/B812).

The point of the Psychological Idea is not to

> derive the internal appearances of the soul from a simple thinking substance, but to derive them from one another according to the idea of a simple being. (A673/B701)

It is a serious error to postulate the object of the idea as an existent,

> as if it were are real ground of the properties of the soul (A683/B711)

Such a procedure

> [is] indeed very easy for reason, but it also entirely ruins and destroys all natural use of reason according to the guidance of experiences. [But it leads the 'dogmatic spiritualist' to bypass] . . . for the sake of his convenience, but with the forfeiture of all insight—the sources of cognition that are immanent in experience. (A690/B 718)

This procedure is antithetical to the purpose of regulative ideas, which is to aid in the progress of science, not to stop it in its tracks (A671/B699). Real explanation must advert to experience:

> For the explanation of given things no other things and grounds of explanation can be adduced than those which are connected to the given appearances by already known laws of appearances. (A772/B800)

Kant's reasonable view is that the assumption that all the denizens of inner sense are determinations of a single (if not simple) thing leads scientists to look for relations among these determinations. It will help the scientists to find whatever connections exist across representations and so to discover psychological regularities—but only so long as they assume that one determination is connected to another. The hypothesis that the determinations are all states of a simple substance, which 'explains' why they all belong to a single thing, in fact explains nothing, but serves only to block the progress of science.

At this point, the Transcendental Analytic's 'root faculty' of apperception may appear to have no relation to the Psychological Idea. That is both true for Kant's positive theory and false for his criticisms of his Rationalist predecessors. In his account of thinking, the role of the root faculty of apperception and the principle of apperception is totally different from that of the Psychological Idea. The former is a constitutive principle of cognition, the latter a regulative idea of reason that is useful in science. But Kant believes that Rational Psychologists become confused by the unusual features of the 'I-think' into believing that, for the case of the soul, they have found the simple and identical ultimate substance for which their reason compels them to seek. I'll present his specific diagnoses of their errors and their relations to his positive theory in the Paralogisms in the next chapter.

The last piece of the discussion of the Psychological Idea (which I underscore in the citation) puts the issue slightly differently. In treating the 'soul' as designating an existent rather than as a regulative idea, Rational Psychologists present it as the basis or ground of mental appearances. This way of proceeding not only preempts science, but falsely suggests that human beings can determine the ground or basis of appearances in some way other than by looking for the laws that govern appearances. Kant agrees with his Rationalist predecessors that appearances must have some ground—there must be some reason why appearances are as they are—but he maintains that human beings have no means of discovering what that basis is. That basis, of which cognition is impossible, would be the 'noumena' in one sense of that term (A251–52, Bxxvi, A542–43/B 570–71). In this passage, he explicitly rejects the claim of his predecessors that a simple and identical noumenal substance is the basis of the properties of the thinking self. When he refers to an intelligible or noumenal subject in the *Critique*, it is always in the context of action. Humans are acquainted with their intelligible characters not through their attempts to make the world intelligible in thought, but through their actions (A545/B573ff.).[9]

Even before looking at the details of the Paralogisms' criticisms, we now have a fairly good sense of what has happened to the Rationalist notion of a thinking substance in Kant's hands. The metaphysical principle that all representations must belong to a common subject ends up playing two different roles in his theory. In the Transcendental Analytic, it is revealed as a necessary condition for cognition; in the Transcendental Dialectic, it is presented as a regulative principle of reason for the investigation of nature. He teases the Rationalists' 'I-concept' apart into four different concepts of the 'I' or 'soul.' First and foremost is the *a priori* 'I-think' representation that cognizers must use if they are to be capable of RE cognition. A second useful concept is that of the Psychological Idea of the 'soul' that provides a goal towards which psychological research can be perpetually directed. The crucial third concept is that of a 'noumenal' agent whose special status is divulged through his recognition of the moral law. It is this recognition that informs such an agent that he could do differently from what he may end up doing—and so that he can be the initiator of a causal chain.

Finally, Kant rejects as detrimental to science, mistakenly assimilated to the 'I-think,' and incapable of rational justification the idea of a noumenal self that is the ground of the powers and states of human thinkers. Since the message in the discussion of the Psychological Idea is that the disparate elements in the I-concepts of his predecessors are serviceable only when carefully separated, it seems contrary to both his positive and negative aims to try to reunite them in interpretations of his theory.

11

'I-Think' as the Destroyer of Rational Psychology

1. Understanding Kant's Criticisms

Through Strawson's influential reading of the critique of Rational Psychology in the Paralogisms, Kant's negative claims about the 'I-think' have become more celebrated than his positive theory. Although I disagree with Strawson about the basis of the critique of Rational Psychology, I agree with him about its effectiveness. The Paralogisms chapter lays bare the pretensions of Rational Psychology to knowledge of the soul—although it also leaves a sufficient opening for his more modest claims about immortality in the *Critique of Practical Reason*. I take the basis of this devastating analysis to be the theory of the necessary unity of consciousness that Strawson saw as the main action of the chapter.[1] That is, I take the criticisms of the Paralogisms chapter to be a further working out of the positive theory presented in the transcendental deduction.

This interpretative approach is controversial. To my knowledge the contemporary view that the 'I-think' of the Paralogisms should be connected with that of the transcendental deduction originated with Wilfrid Sellars (1972/2002). Ameriks interprets Kant's attack on Rational Psychology against the background of Rationalist metaphysics (2000, vi) and others have pursued similar lines.[2] The interpretive divide reflects an odd fact about the Paralogisms chapter. It is introduced under the banner of the Psychological Idea (A334/B391, cf. 4.333, C1781 125) and that is a regulative principle of scientific discovery of looking for the most basic substance in dealing with the subject of cognition. By contrast the 'I-think' is an *a priori*, but 'constitutive' representation of all empirical cognition. Cognizers do not merely aim at self-consciousness. They must be able to recognize their representations as theirs in any cognition. Since these two successors to the metaphysicians' I-concept are very different, it is reasonable to conclude that the Paralogisms relate to the regulative 'I' and not to the constitutive 'I-think.' Given this assumption, the most important background would be the contemporary theories of Rational Psychology—as, for example, the crucial background materials for the critique of Rational Theology are the proofs for the existence of God. On the other hand, the texts of the Paralogisms arguments do not contain a whiff of the regulative idea. They are all about the necessary unity of the thinking subject.

Kant's discussion of the Psychological Idea in the *Prolegomena* provides a clue about how he saw the relation between these two 'I's that can help make sense of the disparity between the Paralogisms chapter's project description and its execution:

> It has long been observed that in all substances the true subject—namely that which remains after all accident have been removed—and hence the substantial itself, is unknown to us . . .
> Now it does appear as if we have something substantial in the consciousness of ourselves (i.e., in the thinking subject), and indeed have it in immediate intuition; for all the predicates of inner sense are referred to the **I** as subject, and this I cannot again be thought as the predicate of some other subject. It therefore appears that in this case completeness in referring the given concept to a subject as predicates is not a mere idea, but that the object, namely, the **absolute subject** itself, is given in experience. But this expectation is disappointed.³ For the I is not a concept . . . (4.333–34, C1781 125)

In the psychological case, the case of the 'I', the search for an ever more basic substance seems to halt. Under these circumstances, what is, in fact, merely a regulative idea is mistakenly understood as constitutive. The reasoning that supplies the mirage of a target reached concerns the necessary conditions for thought. Hence the way to unmask the illusion that, for example, a substantial 'I' is constitutive is through a better understanding of what an analysis of the necessary conditions for thought implies about the subject of thought: It is not a concept, and so on. Although Kant is not completely explicit, the clear implication is that the better understanding is supplied by his analysis of the necessary conditions for thought in respect to a subject.

Given this clue and the many references in the text to the necessary unity of the subject of thought, I read Kant's criticisms of the Rational Psychologists as flowing from his positive theory of the transcendental deduction. This does not mean that Ameriks and others are wrong to stress the importance of the then contemporary context—something I failed to do in earlier treatments of the subject (1982b and 1990, Chapter 7). Understanding the Paralogisms requires both knowledge of the tradition and detailed knowledge of the position from which Kant criticizes it.

Despite the disagreement about whether the Paralogisms should or should not be read against the background of the 'I-think' of the transcendental deduction, there is considerable interpretive consensus about three themes of the criticisms. First, the Rational Psychologists are mistaken in believing that an analysis of the necessary conditions for cognition can provide information about the nature of the thinker: The representation 'I-think' is unique in being 'empty'. Second, their arguments err because they mix premises that are transcendental with those that are empirical, thereby committing the fallacy of ambiguous middle (A402, cf. B428–29). Third, although limited 'formal' conclusions can be drawn about the 'I-think', the Rational Psychologists try to extract extravagant conclusions that are not supported by their premises. There is also agreement about the general framework for the discussion. As in other parts of the Transcendental Dialectic, the Paralogisms chapter is intended to supply an 'indirect proof' of transcendental idealism (A506/B534), by revealing the philosophical errors that can be prevented by a proper appreciation of the theory. My interpretive argument is that we can follow Kant's diagnosis of how, exactly, intelligent men fell into these errors only against the background of his positive theory of the role of the 'I-think' in cognition.

Although the arguments about individual Paralogisms are directed against Wolff and his followers, the chapter's overarching theme is the *cogito*. After examining the arguments of the A and B versions of the Paralogisms, I turn to the question of how Kant saw his 'I-think' in relation to the *cogito*. This discussion also takes up a vexed question that is internal to his view. Since he regards 'I exist' as a contingent, empirical proposition, how and in what sense can he maintain that his analysis of rational cognition implies that thinkers exist? Finally, I consider the basis of his insistence that nothing can be known about the thinking self and whether that doctrine makes his position untenable.

2. Kant's Earlier and Later Treatments of Rational Psychology

One way to gain insight into the Paralogisms' critique of Rational Psychology is to compare it with Kant's earlier treatments of the subject. The best source for the latter is L_1, Metaphysics lectures that were given some time between 1777–78 and 1779–80. While there is always risk in relying on student notes, it is somewhat greater in this case. My argument is that we can understand what he came to see as the systematic error of the Rational Psychologists by contrasting what he says in the *Critique* with what he does *not* say in L_1. The change is explained by the fact that his later discussion can draw on the working out of his I-theory in the transcendental deduction. Another possibility would be that the students merely omitted this information. Although that alternative cannot be ruled out, it seems unlikely, so I press ahead with the available sources.

The discussion of Rational Psychology in the L_1 Metaphysics lectures is largely given over to the 'proof' of spontaneity and the countervailing problem of created beings exercising real freedom.[4] According to the student reports, when Kant took up the arguments that are criticized in the Paralogisms, his focus was on simplicity. Apparently the thesis of substantiality was presented with little argumentation. All he is reported as offering for support is the claim that 'I' is the general subject of all predicates, of all thinking and all acting, and is not a predicate of anything itself (28.266, CMet 79).

By contrast, in presenting the Rational Psychology argument for substantiality as paralogistic in the A edition, Kant is expansive about why the 'I' is taken to be something which is always represented as subject and hence why the minor premise is so attractive.

> That whose representation is the **absolute subject** of our judgments and hence cannot be used as determination of another thing is **substance**.

> I, as a thinking being, am the **absolute subject** of all my possible judgments, and this representation of myself cannot be used as predicate of any other thing.
> Therefore, I, as thinking being (soul), am **substance**. (A348)

In the minor premise

> we have merely inferred permanence from the concept of the reference that all thought has to the I as the common subject in which it inheres ... <u>for although the I is in all thoughts ... one can indeed perceive that in all thought this representation occurs again and again</u>, but not that it is a constant and enduring [*stehende und bleibende*] intuition wherein the thoughts as mutable vary ...
> for the constant [*beständige*] logical subject of thought is passed off by it as the cognition of the real subject of the inherence of thought ... <u>For consciousness alone is what turns all representations into thoughts, and hence solely in it as the transcendental subject must all perceptions be found; and apart form this logical meaning of the</u> I we are not acquainted with the subject in itself. (A350, my underscoring)

Kant is being a generous critic. His predecessors have excellent reason for believing that the 'I' is a constant subject. They appreciate that all thought must belong to the unity of self-consciousness or apperception. Their error arises because they assume that the 'I' is an empirical representation (of Empirical Psychology, the necessary precursor to Rational Psychology). But it is not. In language echoing the A deduction, he points out that there is no constant and abiding I-intuition.

Although more extensive than the discussion of the argument for substantiality, Kant apparently presented the argument for simplicity in L_1 as, roughly, the first half of the treatment it receives in the A Paralogisms: If the different parts of a verse were divided among different subjects then no subject would contain the whole representation (28.266, CMet 79, A351–52). When presenting this argument as a Paralogism, he tries to explain the source of the mistake:

> A thing whose action can never be regarded as the concurrence of many acting things is **simple**.
> Now the soul, or the thinking I, is such a thing. Therefore, etc. (A351)

What, again, needs to be explained is the support for the minor premise.

> The so-called **nervus probandi** of this argument lies in the proposition that in order for many representations to amount to one thought, they must be contained in the absolute unity of the thinking subject ...
> Hence <u>here, just as in the previous paralogism, the formal proposition of apperception</u> **I think** <u>remains the whole basis of which rational psychology ventures to expand its cognitions. But this proposition is, of course, not an experience, but is the form of apperception.</u> Although this form attaches to and precedes every experience, it must still always be regarded only as concerning

a possible cognition as such, *viz.*, as **merely subjective condition** of such cognition . . . (A353, A354, my underscoring)

That is, the problem with the Paralogism of simplicity is exactly the same as that of substantiality. The confusion is not about simplicity, but about unity. Indeed, the emphasis on the unity of the subject is so strong in the Second Paralogism that it leads Allison and Hoppe to take the verse argument to be Kant's argument for the unity of apperception. I've argued against that reading, but we can now appreciate its textual basis. The error of the Rational Psychologists lies in mistaking a transcendental condition and representation, 'I-think,' for an experience or intuition of Empirical Psychology.

In Chapter 4, we saw that in L_1 Kant apparently does not accept Wolff's argument from simplicity to immateriality. Instead he maintains that the argument for immateriality depends on the expression or concept 'I,' but he doesn't elaborate. We find the same pattern in the argument about identity, the topic of the Third Paralogism. In L_1, he reportedly offers a very brief and weak argument: I am not conscious of myself as several substances. He then goes on to note that

> The I expresses oneness: I am conscious of myself as one subject. (28.268, CMet 80)

Again, however, he doesn't elaborate.

In one respect, the A edition treatment of the Third Paralogism is just like its treatment of the First and Second in its focus on the unity of the subject of thought. It continues the discussion of the problem of unity.

> What is conscious of the numerical identity of itself in different times is to that extent a **person**.
> Now the soul is, etc.
> Therefore, it is a person. (A361)

Kant explains that the personality of the soul should have been established by considerations about substance:

> It is noteworthy, however, that the personality of the soul and its presupposition, permanence, and hence the soul's substantiality must now first of all be proved. For if we could presuppose the latter, then there would follow from it, not yet indeed the continuance of consciousness, but still the possibility of a continuing consciousness in an enduring subject; and that is already sufficient for personality. (A365)

But the proof of substantiality is flawed.

> There is nothing through which this permanence is given to us prior to the numerical identity of ourselves that we infer from the identical apperception; rather, this permanence is first inferred from the numerical identity. (A365)

The proper order of proof for Rational Psychology would be from permanence to substantiality to numerical identity to personality. That is, it would be from experience, which gives permanence, through an analysis of Ontological categories to conclusions about Empirical substantiality and personality, the unending existence of the person. But that is not what happens. Numerical identity, personality, and permanence are all inferred from the unity or identity of apperception. Again, the starting point of the paralogistic argument is the sound recognition of the identity of apperception, but the reasoning goes astray in inferring substantial permanence and personality from apperception.

Although it continues the theme that the errors of the Rational Psychologists can be traced to their failure fully to understand the transcendental unity of apperception, the Third Paralogism also introduces a new theme, one that is absent from both L_1 and the first two A edition Paralogisms. The theme is announced in the major premise, which does not come from Rational Psychology but from Locke. Leibniz believed that a satisfactory answer to any one of the questions about personal identity, about how subjects know their identities and about the nature of the underlying metaphysical reality, must be part of a uniform account of them all. Locke tied moral identity to mental continuity, though not to substantial identity. In the Third Paralogism, Kant breaks both connections. He denies the inference from mental unity to substantial identity—and to personal identity.[5]

Kant borrows Locke's definition of 'person' for the major premise only to deny its implications:

> Hence the identity of the consciousness of myself in different times is only a formal condition of my thoughts and of their coherence, but does not prove at all the numerical identity of myself as subject. In this subject—regardless of the logical identity of the I—there may after all, have occurred such change [*Wechsel*] as does not permit us to retain its identity ... <u>For in any different state of the subject, even the state of its conversion [*Umwandlung*], this</u> I <u>would always preserve the thought of the preceding subject</u> and thus could also pass it on to the subsequent one. (A363)

Identity of apperception does not suffice for identity of moral subject or 'conversion'—change of heart—would be impossible. As is clear in *Religion within the Bounds of Mere Reason*, written a dozen years later, Kant feels a great pull to honor the possibility of redemption. However wretchedly a person has lived, perpetually considering his self-interest above the moral law, change of heart is always possible. If conversion is to be taken seriously—if someone can become a 'new man' in the terminology of the Gospels—then it must be possible for him to become a new moral person (6.48, CRel, 92).[6] As is also clear in *Religion within the Bounds of Mere Reason* he has great difficulties reconciling conversion with standard Lockean account of personal identity and its links to punishment and reward. It is inconsistent with Divine justice to punish the new person:

> **After his conversion**, however, since he now leads a new life and has become a 'new man,' the punishment cannot be considered appropriate to his new quality (of thus being a human being well-pleasing to God). (6.73, CRel 113)

> The demands of Divine justice are honored, because the conversion itself can be understood as a sort of punishment—indeed death—of the old person. (6.74, CRel 114)

Human justice operates in a different way. Even after someone has become, morally, a different human being

> **Physically** (considered in his empirical character as a sensible being), he is still the same human liable to punishment and he must be judged as such before a moral tribunal of justice and hence by himself as well. (6.74, CRel 114)

In a discussion of the grace involved in God's forgiveness, the matter of self-judging is explained further. Humans can only judge

> (according to the empirical cognition we have of ourselves), so far as we know ourselves (estimate our disposition not directly but only according to our deeds) so that the accuser within us would still be more likely to render a verdict of guilty. (6.75–76, CRel 115–16)

Kant's position does not seem consistent. He wants to maintain at once that the convert is a new person and yet that it is just for him to be punished for the deeds of the old person. Inconsistency arises if 'person' is a moral term to which punishment and reward are attached.

Setting this problem to one side, for the moment, it is clear that Kant's position on conversion implies that he must reject both Locke's and Leibniz's theories of personal unity—and also carefully circumscribe his own theory of the unity of apperception. Memory could be present through a 'person-change.' Leibniz's position errs, not by giving the wrong verdict in cases of conversion, but by ruling it out altogether. On his view, a substance contains all its future states from the beginning (*Monadology* §22, 645), so the sort of change implied by conversion would be impossible in the natural order of things. Since Kant wants to make room for conversion, he has to dismiss not just substantial identity, but also memory continuity and sameness of cognitive subject—the logical I—as sufficient for sameness of person.

Interpreting the Third Paralogism as disputing the sufficiency of mental continuity for personal identity seems inconsistent with its conclusion:

> However, just as the concept of substance and of the simple remained with us, so we may keep also the concept of personality (<u>insofar as it concerns the unity of the subject . . . in whose determinations there is a thoroughgoing connection through apperception</u>). And to this extent the concept of personality is, indeed, needed and sufficient for practical use (A365–66, my underscoring)

On the other hand the gloss of 'personality' in terms of the apperceptive subject relieves much of the tension. Further, the last sentence of the citation is consistent with the view of *Religion within the Bounds of Mere Reason*, because both put forward 'apperceptive personality' as the basis of human forensic practice. Identical apperception is both necessary and sufficient for the *practical* use of the concept of personality. And, given human epistemic limitations, that is all that can be used. Nonetheless, it is shocking that Kant does not find this practice a mark against human justice. Since it cannot see into the hearts of men, human justice lacks the means to track the truth and is, in this sense, completely arbitrary.

Because it is not an argument of Rational Psychology and because it is dropped in the Second Edition, I don't consider the A edition Fourth Paralogism. Summing up the differences in treatment between L_1 and the first three A edition Paralogisms, where the former hints that these issues revolve around the concept or expression 'I,' the Critical treatment argues that the Rational Psychologists err because they mishandle the unity of consciousness that the 'I' represents. Their project is to argue from an Empirical representation through the intellectual categories of Ontology to the nature of its object. In fact, they start with the intellectual conditions required for thought—which should not be understood as Ontological but as Epistemological or transcendental—and on that basis take themselves to have an unusual, but nonetheless Empirical representation of the 'I.' The Third Paralogism adds a *caveat* about his own position. Despite the natural inference from the Lockean tradition, do not identify the unity of apperceptive consciousness with the continuity of the moral person.

As noted at the end of Chapter 3, Kant apparently injected a note of doubt into his presentation of Rational Psychology in L_1. He is reported as observing that nothing in the chain of reasoning is solid unless the main category (i.e., substantiality) proves the consciousness of a subject, a subject that has states and is distinct from the body and can therefore be called a 'soul.' So he seems to see that there is a systematic problem with these arguments in L_1 that centers on the 'I' as subject. Apparently, however, either he did not know how to spell out this insight or he did not choose to do so in this setting. As Julien Wuerth emphasizes, his handling of these arguments in the Metaphysics lectures is fairly negative.[7] In particular, he criticizes the idea that they can accomplish their goal of establishing immortality (28.272, CMet 84ff.). What changes between L_1 and the *Critique* is not that he comes to doubt the teachings of Rational Psychology, which he already did, but that he is in a position to criticize them in a systematic way.

3. 'I-Think' as the Vehicle of the Categories

At a general level then, the difference in Kant's situation between L_1 and the *Critique* is clear. He can mount a principled diagnosis of the errors of Rational Psychology, because he can draw on his theory of transcendental apperception. In this section, I try to pinpoint a key aspect of his new theory that provides much of the basis for the criticisms. We can locate that element by comparing the theory of apperception as first presented in the *Duisburg Nachlaß* with the way in which the topic is introduced in the Paralogisms chapter.

In the *Duisburg* notes, 'apperception' is introduced in terms of three 'titles' or 'exponents': relation to a subject, relation of following each other, and composition. As Guyer observes, the 'titles' of understanding in Kant's *Nachlaß* standardly refer to rules that govern the concept of an object and are forerunners of the categorial principles (e.g., 1987, 41ff.). The titles of apperception would be rules for the representation of a subject of cognition. Since the second title would characterize only spatiotemporal cognizers, there is not much mystery about why it doesn't reappear in the *Critique* where the goal is to characterize rational cognizers in general. It does play a role after the forms of intuition are reintroduced in the later parts of the B deduction. The third title was not much developed in the notes.[8] But the pattern that Guyer sees between the titles of the *Duisburg* materials and the categories of the *Critique* would seem to be repeated in the case of the first title, that of relation to subject. It appears to be a forerunner of the crucial claim of the A deduction that

> all the varied empirical consciousness must be combined in one single self consciousness (A117n.)

and the central thesis of the B deduction that

> everything manifold in intuition has a necessary reference to the *I think* in the same subject in whom this manifold is found. (B132)

That is, it appears to be the forerunner of the 'I-rule.'

Yet the introduction to the Paralogisms chapter that is common to both the A and B editions explicitly denies this point:

> We now come to a concept that was not entered in the above general list of transcendental concepts, and that must yet be classed with them . . . This is the concept—or, if one prefers, the judgment—**I think**. But we readily see that this concept is the vehicle of all concepts as such[9] and hence also that of transcendental concepts, and that it is therefore always also comprised among these and hence is likewise transcendental; <u>but that it cannot have a special title</u>, because it serves only to bring forward all thought as belonging to consciousness. (A341/B399–400, my underscoring)

I assume that Kant brings this point to the fore because it is crucial to understanding the reasoning that follows.

Kant explicitly rejects of any special 'title' for apperception to signal the unique way in which the 'I-rule' functions. The I-rule cannot be applied on the basis of intuitions. This is so for two reasons. There is no intuition of the 'I' and the I-rule can be applied only when some object-rule is applicable to the manifold of intuitions so that the understanding combines some representations in others, thereby creating a relation of necessary connection across them. Categorial rules cannot be applied on the basis of intuitions of, for example, substances and causes either. They can be applied only *via* schematized rules. But the 'I-think' is different. It does not apply through a schema, but through the application of an object rule. Despite its being the highest and most general rule of cognition, it is not an independent rule. It depends for its application on the use of an object-rule. Because the 'I-think' does not apply through its own title in virtue of particular representational contents, but piggybacks on the object-rules, it discloses nothing about the nature of thinkers. It does not apply to a manifold of its own, but serves only to indicate that, through the fact that their contents fall under other rules, representational states stand in relations of necessarily belonging to a single consciousness. This is the basis for Kant's claims that the 'I-think' serves only to introduce all thought as belonging to consciousness and is, itself, a completely 'empty' representation (A341–42/B400, A345–46/B403–4).

Although the peculiar way in which the I-rule functions does not make the Paralogistic inferences inevitable, it shows why they are very likely. Only a philosopher who examines the *a posteriori* and *a priori* sources of representations is in a position to agree with Hume that there is no intuition of an 'I,' without falling into his evident mistake of denying that humans have any I-representation at all. And only a philosopher who considers the necessary conditions for empirical cognition is in a position to see the true source of the necessity and ubiquity of the representation. Without this background, but with some appreciation that the 'I' must always be present, it is natural to think that the ubiquitous 'I' is a permanent feature of representations.

This mistake dominates the discussions of the A Paralogisms and explains how empirical premises become mixed with transcendental ones. A proper understanding of the source of the 'I-think' reveals the claim that different representations must belong to a common 'I' to be transcendental—it states a necessary and *a priori* feature of human cognition. Because the representation 'I-think' always appears as a subject and never as a predicate, it meets the definition of a substance, so the minor premise of the First Paralogism is assertable. The error lies in misunderstanding the ground of the assertion. Correctly understood as transcendental, it permits only the identical conclusion that the 'I' is the absolute subject of all judgments. When a philosopher fails to appreciate that the 'I-think' has no special title, he naturally assumes that the ever-present representation is applied under the title for empirical substances, namely, 'substances are permanent.' From this further erroneous conclusions about immortality quickly follow. A general problem with the Paralogisms is that they mingle transcendental and empirical claims. The minor is assertable only if understood as transcendental. So understood it has no implications whatever about the nature of 'I's. But the conclusion is interesting only if understood as asserting that the soul is a permanent empirical substance. Since the basis of the minor premises of the Second ('the soul is something whose action can never be regarded as the concurrence of many acting things') and of the Third ('the soul is conscious of the numerical identity of itself at different times') is also the transcendental unity of apperception, and their conclusions also purport to be about empirical simple substances and immortal persons, they commit exactly the same fallacy.

4. 'I-Think' as Analytically Contained in the Concept of Thought

Kant begins the much briefer treatment in the B Paralogisms by rehearsing his view that no cognition of objects is possible without intuitions. He then segues from his doctrine that no object can be cognized merely through thinking to the particular problem with the arguments of Rational Psychology:

> Hence I do not cognize myself by being conscious of myself as thinking, but I cognize myself when I am conscious of the intuition of myself as determined with regard to one of the functions of thought. All the **modes** of self-consciousness in thought as such are, therefore, not [*noch keine*] understanding's concepts of objects (categories), but are mere functions that do not allow thought to cognize any object at all, and hence do not allow it to cognize myself as object. (B406–7, amended translation)[10]

In the B edition, Kant separates the different aspects of apperception that are employed in the three different Paralogisms. 'Apperception' involves a constant subject, a singular subject, and an identical subject. When he asserts that these modes do not permit the cognition of any object, he does not mean that they are not, in fact, necessary conditions for object cognition. His point is, again, that these necessary conditions for a subject of thought should not be confused with schematized categorial principles that would enable the subject to cognize himself as an object.

When we understand how the I-rule works, we can see both that 'I-think' can be asserted and that it yields no cognition of the nature of the subject. It applies to representations and to representations that have content—but that content concerns the nature of the object represented and not that of the subject of representations. This central point is explained in more detail in the B edition's succinct account of the First Paralogism:

> Now in all judgments I am always the **determining** subject of the relation that makes up the judgment. But that I, who think, must be considered in such thought always as a **subject** and as something that cannot be regarded as merely attaching to thought like a predicate—this is an apodeictic and even **identical** proposition. But this proposition does not mean that I am, as an **object**, a **being subsisting** by myself or **substance**. This latter goes very far, and hence it requires data that are in no way found in thought. (B407)

Kant's point is not just that in judgments preceded by 'I think' I am the subject of the judgment in the sense that I am she who has the judgment, rather than the subject or topic of the judgment—what the judgment is about. Rather, I am the determining subject who makes a judgment by bringing about a relation between a subject and a predicate. As he has explained, the transcendental deduction, combining representations in a judgment requires at least implicit consciousness of the combining and so an understanding of the representational states as necessarily belonging together (and so, to a common and active subject). Since the analysis of RE cognition reveals the necessity of such a subject for judgment, it is analytic that 'I am the determining subject of any judgment'. But although 'I' meets the definition of a 'substance,' it is not brought under this category in the way that objects are, namely, through finding something permanent in intuition. Further (and unavailable) evidence would be needed to establish that the referent of 'I-think' is a being capable of subsisting on its own—even though it is analytic that 'I-think' is a constant subject of thought.

As in the case of the First Paralogism the B edition discussions of the Second and Third drive home the result of the B deduction that the representation 'I-think' is analytically implied in the concept of rational thought. The Second Paralogism emphasizes the contrast between analytic and synthetic judgments.

> That the I of apperception, and hence in all thought, is a **singular** that cannot be resolved into a plurality of subjects and therefore designates a logically simple subject—this lies already in the concept of thought and hence is an analytic proposition. But this does not mean that the thinking I is a simple **substance**; that would be a synthetic proposition. <u>The concept of substance always refers to intuitions that, in me, cannot be other than sensible</u> . . . Indeed it would be miraculous if what otherwise requires so much effort for distinguishing what is substance in what intuition displays—but even more for distinguishing (as with the parts of matter) whether this substance can also be simple—were here in the poorest of all representation given to me thus straightforwardly, as if through a revelation, as it were. (B407–8, my underscoring)

Here, as in the A edition, the mistake of the Second Paralogism is a repeat of that of the First: It is analytic that a common subject is in all thought, but that in no way establishes that the 'I-think' represents a simple substance. The 'I-think' is the 'poorest of all representations,' because although it can be and must be able to be attached to judgments, it is not applied to an intuition of an 'I' or to any special intuition of its own. It is applied to representations on the basis of contents that make possible judgments about objects.

The focus of the B edition Third Paralogism is also substantiality and permanence. Its dependence on the B deduction's argument for apperception is especially clear:

> The proposition of the identity of myself in all the manifold whereof I am conscious is likewise a proposition that lies in the concepts themselves and hence is analytic. <u>But this identity of the subject, of which I can become conscious in all representations of this subject</u>, does not concern the subject's intuition whereby it is given as object. <u>Hence this identity also cannot mean [*bedeuten*] identity of the person, by which we understand the consciousness of the subject's own substance as a thinking being in all variation of its states</u> . . . (B408, my underscoring)

This discussion indicates a shift from the position taken in the A edition. Perhaps Kant realized that he was trying to do too much in introducing worries about conversion.[11] In any case, he offers a simpler argument: The consciousness of the identity of the 'I,' which is necessary for thought, does not imply consciousness of sameness of substance. As we know from the B deduction, a subject can be conscious of her identity *only* through being conscious of adding different representations together (B133–34). The consciousness of identity which comes about through an implicit consciousness of synthesizing representations does not involve any intuition of the subject or any intuition of anything other than that of the objects of judgments. And that is the source of confusion. (Failing to grasp how the representation of an identical I is possible) the Rational Psychologists assume that it must depend on the awareness of a permanent or continuing being through all the variations in its states.

As far as I can see, although the discussion of the B edition Fourth Paralogism fits part of the mold of the others—it is analytic that I distinguish my own existence as a thinking being from the existence of other things, since other things are distinct from me—it exposes a simpler mistake, a mistake that was obvious to Descartes' earliest critics. That my idea of myself as thinking is distinct from my idea of other things does not imply that I can exist separately from other things (Descartes 1640/1984, 2:141–43).

The B edition also offers a systematic account of the mistake of the arguments of Rational Psychology. Using the First Paralogism as the model, the problem is that

> In the major premise one talks about a being that can be thought in general, in every respect, and hence also as it may be given in intuition. But in the minor premise one talks about it insofar as it considers itself, as subject only relatively to thought and the unity of consciousness, but not simultaneously in reference to the intuition whereby it is given as object for such thought. Therefore, one is inferring the conclusion **per sophisma figurae dictionis** . . . (B411)

It is not clear why such a procedure should be invalid: The scope of the major premise appears to include both beings that are intuited and others that are not; the minor concerns a being that is not given in intuition. Unless the conclusion, which Kant omits, concerns a substance that is given in intuition, there is no fallacy.

Perhaps seeing the problem, he adds a clarificatory note:

> Thought is taken in two entirely different meanings in the two premises. In the major premise it is taken as it applies to an object as such (and hence as it may be given in intuition). But in the minor premise it is taken only as it consists in the reference to self-consciousness; hence here one thinks of no object whatever, but represents only the reference to oneself as subject (as the form of thought). In the first premise one talks about things that cannot be thought otherwise than as subjects. <u>In the second premise, however, one talks (by abstracting from any object) not about **things** but about **thought**, in which the I always serves as the subject of consciousness</u>. Hence in the conclusion it cannot follow that I cannot exist otherwise than as subject, but merely that in thinking my existence I can use myself only as the judgment's subject. And this is an identical proposition that reveals absolutely nothing concerning the way in which I exist. (B411–12n., my underscoring)

According to the note, the major is to be taken as applying to any sort of object that can be a subject (topic) of thought, but the minor does not refer to any object, but to the subject of thought in a very different sense, namely, to the I of apperception. This clarification returns us to the theme we have already encountered in discussing the A edition Paralogisms, *viz.*, that in using 'I-think' one is not referring to something in anything like the way that one refers to objects; rather the use of 'I-think' is governed by the necessary conditions for thought. The note goes beyond previous discussions in highlighting the fact that thinking about the structure of thought in this way involves an abstraction from objects. Abstraction is necessary for reasons that we have seen. RE cognition of objects is a necessary condition for the possibility of consciousness of self-identity; so any assertion that makes reference to oneself as a subject must involve object cognition—or an abstraction from the object or objects of cognition.

According to Kant's critique, Rational Psychology contains a number of errors that can be seen perspicuously only from the perspective of his theory. One difficulty with interpreting the chapter is that since the criticisms are deeply intertwined, he piles one on top of another in a dense argument. As I understand them, this is how they interrelate. As with the entire Dialectic, the overarching diagnosis is that the Rational Psychologists do not grasp the truth of transcendental idealism. This leads them to argue inconsequentially from an alleged Empirical awareness of the soul, through purely intellectual considerations about the necessity of an 'I' in thought, to the conclusion that Empirical subjects of cognition would be simple, identical substances and so immortal. One way to see the mistake from the perspective of transcendental idealism is to see that no Empirical evidence could establish that the soul is simple or substantial. This is so, because there can be no spatiotemporal representation of a simple substance (A784/B812). A further error is that the Rational Psychologists misunderstand the nature of the arguments about the 'I-think' in two complementary ways. First, they do not see that the conditions established as the necessary intellectual conditions for thought are merely transcendental, that is, conditions for the organizing the data of intuition. Failing this, they see those conditions as noumenal—as establishing purely intellectual claims. Second, because they fail to appreciate that time is the form of human intuition, they believe that claims that are purely intellectual can involve time, in particular, the endless time of immortality. A related way to see the error is to see that all cognition requires intuitions. Since the Rational Psychologists don't accept this point, they do not address the Humean question of the lack of an intuition of an 'I.' If they had, they would have seen that they were not following their program of arguing from the discovery of the 'I' in Empirical psychology *via* basic Ontological categories to the characteristics of its referent. Rather they are arguing from the transcendental requirements of thought to the nature of an object of an allegedly 'Empirical' representation. In so doing, they mistake the analytic implications that can be teased out of the concept of rational thought for a synthetic claim of Empirical psychology. Although the diagnosis is complex, the most fundamental reasons for the error are the Rational Psychologists' failure to see that time is a form of intuition and their failure to appreciate the unusual character of the transcendental 'I' representation.

5. Does the Analysis of Cognition Imply the Existence of a Thinker?

Although the common introduction casts the Paralogisms chapter in terms of the *cogito*, the A edition does not return to the argument itself. In the B edition Paralogisms and in the B deduction, Kant tries to deal with the implications of his 'I-think' for existence and for (possible) immortality in relation to Descartes' *cogito*. An obvious explanation for the new-found concern with these issues would be his intention to include of a postulate of immortality in the *Critique of Practical Reason* which appeared a year after the B edition.

Kant agrees with many of his predecessors about the form of the Cartesian argument (see Chapter 5, section 3). It is an inference and wrong for that reason. He claims many times that 'I exist' cannot be an inference from '*cogito*' (e.g., A355). No intermediate premise is needed to move from '*cogito*' to 'I exist,' because the latter is analytically contained in the former. In the setup to the Paralogisms chapters, he explains that he will discuss the '*cogito*' without its existential implication, by regarding it merely 'problematically.' He will consider '*cogito*' not as tied to any perception of an existent, but merely as a function that could be so applied (A347/B405). In this way, he can consider the implications of the concept or representation itself, rather than its implications when applied to something that exists—since the latter approach must involve an existent.

On the other hand, both the B deduction and the B edition Paralogisms suggest that Kant came to understand that his 'I-think' implies not just the (continuing) existence of actual cognizers, but the possibility of a continued existence for any cognizer *per se*. Despite his critique of Rational Psychology, he thus came to appreciate that Descartes was nearly right about *cogito ergo sum*, that thought alone could establish existence. According to several aspects of his cognitive theory, any existence claim must be synthetic and so rooted in intuition. In passages added to the second edition, however, he seems to link continued existence to mere thought.

The notion of a strange nonphenomenal type of existence for the apperceptive 'I' is bruited in two enigmatic passages of the B deduction.

> In the synthetic original unity of apperception, I am not conscious of myself as I appear to myself, nor as I am in myself, but am conscious only that I am. This **representation** is a **thought**, not an **intuition**. (B157)

Besides the apparent conflict with the cognitive theory that requires perception for any cognition, including that of existence, this passages seems to burke the exclusive and exhaustive metaphysical distinction between the phenomenal and the noumenal. Which is the unity of apperception? Kant appends a note intended to clarify his position:

> The **I think** expresses the act of determining my existence. Hence the existence is already given through this **I think**; but there is not yet given through it the way in which I am to determine that existence, i.e., posit a manifold as belonging to it . . . I represent only the spontaneity of my thought, i.e., of the determination, and my existence remains determinable always only sensibly . . . But it is on account of this spontaneity that I call myself an **intelligence**. (B 157–58n.)

The note doesn't so much clarify as deepen the mystery. Instead of explaining what type of existence something enjoys which is neither phenomenal nor noumenal, it seems to raise the possibility of some type of 'bare' existence that is of no determinate kind.[12]

A long note in the B edition Paralogisms helps to remove some of the confusions generated by these remarks:

> The **I think** is an empirical proposition, and contains the proposition **I exist** ... The proposition **I think** expresses an indeterminate empirical intuition, i.e., perception (and hence it does prove that sensation, which as such belongs to sensibility, underlies this existential proposition). But the proposition **I think** precedes the experience that is to determine the object of perception through the category in regard to time; and the existence here is not [*noch keine*][13] a category. The category of existence has reference not to an indeterminate given object, but only to an object of which one has a concept and concerning which one wants to know whether or not it is posited also outside of this concept. An indeterminate perception here signifies only something real that has been given—and given only for thought as such, and hence not as appearance nor as thing in itself, but as something that in fact exists and is marked as such in the proposition **I think** ... when I called the proposition **I think** an empirical proposition, I did not mean that the **I** in this proposition is an empirical representation. Rather, this representation is purely intellectual, because it belongs to thought as such. Yet without some empirical representation that provides the material for thought, the act **I think** would not take place; and the empirical element is only [*nur*] the condition of the application or use of the pure intellectual power. (B 422–23n., amended translation)

Given the contexts, this note (and the previous passages) should be approached in terms of the *cogito* and of Kant's cognitive theory or, more precisely, in terms of how the *cogito* looks through the lens of that theory.

The note does not deny or even waffle on Kant's basic claim that cognition requires the application of concepts to materials originally provided by sensation. In the last sentence, he reaffirms the doctrine with which he begins the Introduction: No thinking can precede the receipt of sensory materials. With nothing to combine, the intellectual powers would lie dormant. How can Descartes' thought experiment in Second Meditation be understood in light of this theory of cognition?

Since no thought is possible without materials to combine, when Descartes imagines that the world and all bodies are nothing, he can only be considering thinking in abstraction from any particular materials to think about. Kant notes that one error of the Rational Psychologists is their failure to recognize that in discussing thought *per se* they must be abstracting from thought of any object. The mistake lies in assuming that this exercise involves cognizing a subject as object rather than considering acts of thinking in abstraction from combining particular materials in any object representation. In the long note, we learn how Descartes' *Gedanken* experiment is possible. We are reminded that 'I-think' is an *a priori* representation that does not need to be acquired through particular sorts of experiences. For this reason, it is possible to imagine along with Descartes that the world as we know it is nothing, and so to abstract not just from the combination of particular materials by thought, but also from all past sensory experience.

What is interesting in the experiment is that humans can abstract from the world as they know it without thereby eliminating the way in which they are conscious of their unity in and through apperceptive act-consciousness. The need for some sensory materials to think cannot be abstracted from. Nevertheless, since the 'I-think' refers only to the form of cognition in general (A346/B404), and not to any particular cognition or to any particular kind of cognition (i.e., cognition tied to a specific form of intuition), on its own it expresses only an indeterminate perception. Having abstracted everything from his sensations or, perhaps, perceptions except their givenness—and their ability to be thought—a human cognizer can consider thinking something through such 'bare' perceptions. That is, he can consider combining them according to some rule or other and of being conscious of that combining. Cognizers can thus imagine being continuing thinkers whose states are mutually dependent as partial and whole cognitions and so are necessarily connected. In this way, they can imagine themselves existing as thinkers, but not as spatiotemporal or as any other determinate kind of thinkers.

In light of the Paralogisms note, we can see what Kant was getting at in the odd claim of the B deduction that in the synthetic unity of apperception, humans can be conscious of themselves not as they appear, nor as they are in themselves, but just conscious that they are. He is not suggesting some odd sort of existence that is neither phenomenal nor noumenal nor determinate in any way. He is maintaining only that when considered in abstraction from any particular form of intuition—as it can be—but not from all given perceptions (which it can't be), self-conscious thought implies existence, though not any particular kind of existence. There is no indeterminate form of existence, but merely abstraction from determinate forms. The note appended to the B deduction passage elaborates that the 'I-think' expresses the act of determining one's existence. Given the later note, we can see the sense in which this is true. The act literally brings into to being the relations required for a 'continuing' self; yet this act which determines existence does not determine the sort of existence, exactly because it is thought of as occurring in abstraction from any particular kind of intuition. The Paralogisms note is also helpful in dispelling any suggestion in the earlier passages that it is possible to consider thought alone, thought without any sensation or perception at all. Some indeterminate perception is required to supply materials for thinking.[14]

Through the device of an indeterminate perception,[15] Kant can offer what he takes to be an acceptable version of Descartes' *cogito*. His predecessor's idea that pure thought could establish the existence of the thinker was mistaken, but it was not far from the truth. Thought can establish the existence of a thinker—but the thought has to take place. Kant's analysis of the requirements of cognition reveals that the basis of a cognizer's knowledge of his thinking and of his continuing existence rests on his conscious acts of synthesizing. Thinking and the relations it produces across states can thus take place regardless of any particular forms of intuition, including the human spatiotemporal form, and that thinking suffices for the existence of a continuing thinker. It cannot take place independently of any perception at all. The analysis of cognition does not imply the existence of thinkers; it implies that cognizers can understand themselves as existing as thinkers independently of their particular forms of intuition. On Kant's reading of Descartes, the Second Meditation presents an imaginative exercise that shows how humans can think of themselves as 'continuing,' atemporal, and spontaneous thinkers. It is thus useful for his larger purposes in writing the *Critique*, because it makes the possibility of immortality intelligible.

6. Why Can't Thinkers Know Themselves as Such?

Kant's argument that thinkers cannot know themselves as substances, as simple, or as continuing persons seems to have a much wider implication: They cannot know their natures as thinkers *per se* at all. Before trying to assess his reasons for denying any knowledge of the thinker as such, we should be clear about exactly what he is denying. In the B deduction, he explains that:

> now **cognition** of ourselves requires not only the act of thought that brings the manifold of every possible intuition to the unity of apperception, but requires in addition a determinate [*bestimmt*] kind of intuition whereby this manifold is given. Hence although my own existence is not appearance (still less mere illusion), determination of my existence can occur only in conformity with the form of inner sense and according to the particular way in which the manifold that I combine is given in inner intuition. Accordingly, I have no **cognition** of myself as I am but merely cognition of how I appear to myself. (B158)

His use of 'appearance' to characterize empirical cognition can easily lead to the impression that he maintains that humans don't know themselves at all. But that is not his position. On his view, humans have knowledge of themselves. They know that they have various mental states; they know that they have various bodily and mental capacities. Further, 'empirical' apperception is like 'empirical' cognition. Empirical cognition is possible only through the application of the *a priori* categories; empirical apperception involves the *a priori* representation 'I-think' as well as particular representational contents (contents that are, again, admixtures of *a priori* and *a posteriori* elements). Humans know that they exist as empirical subjects of cognition with mental states and faculties. There is nothing indeterminate or questionable about this knowledge. It is on a par with their knowledge of the world around them. What they cannot know is what they are like as active thinkers.

Kant realized that the doctrine that cognizers know themselves only as appearances, as objects of inner and outer sense, was a great stumbling block for the acceptance of his theory. Although it is a fairly direct consequence of his widely admired criticisms of Rational Psychology in the Paralogisms, the view that the thinker *per se* is unknowable is as unpopular today as it was when he was writing. Manfred Frank characterizes the doctrine as 'disastrous' for the transcendental deduction, since he takes it to imply some sort of naked being, a being lacking in any qualities or properties (2007).[16] For reasons given above, I don't think this is Kant's position.

Still, it is easy to be impatient with what seem to be Kant's arguments for the necessary ignorance of the active thinker as such. The common introduction to the

Paralogisms presents, and the general discussion in the second edition repeats, an unimpressive argument: Any knowledge presupposes a subject (A346/B404). Why does the fact that in any cognition there must be a subject imply that a cognitive subject cannot occupy both the subject and object position in a knowledge claim? The question he needs to answer is why the cognitive subject *per se* cannot be a cognized object. Kant's procedure also seems open to criticism. If one abstracts from the particular way in which humans exist and just considers thinking on its own (or, better, in conjunction with an indeterminate perception), then perhaps it is unsurprising that one cannot learn anything except the bare fact of a thinker's existence. One reason that he uses this approach is that Descartes and his followers believed that it could be used to establish various properties of thinkers *per se*. He wants to deny that, while still using the thought experiment to establish the conceivability of immortality.

Even if Rationalist attempts to establish that thinking *per se* requires substantiality, and so forth, fail, why does Kant maintain that is it impossible to know anything about what a thing must be like just to be the subject of acts of thought? We can address this question more adequately if we turn briefly to the Transcendental Ideal. There Kant observes that the criterion of the possibility of a thing is compete determination. Any real object must be characterized by one member of each of pair of contradictory predicates (at a time) (A573/B601). Most cognizers have very gappy knowledge of the complete determinations of objects, but to have any knowledge of any object they must have access to a determinable—a respect in which that object can have one or another determinate value. In the classic example, 'fire engine red' would be a determinate of the determinable 'color'. In the case most relevant to Kant's discussion, a particular moment would be a determinate of the determinable time. His claim in the passage above is that cognition of the self requires a determinate kind of intuition, a kind that could have particular determinate values.

Determination and determinables are also themes of the B deduction note that discusses the *cogito*. I cited it only partially in section 4. In the previously elided section, Kant explains why only the 'empirical' states of a cognizer can be known and not the 'determining' subject:

> [In order to determine the way in which I exist] self-intuition is required; and at the basis of this self-intuition lies a form given *a priori*, *viz.*, time, which is sensible and belongs to the ability to receive the determinable. Now unless I have in addition a different self-intuition that gives, prior to the act of **determination**, the **determining** [*Bestimmende*] in me (only of its spontaneity am I in fact conscious) just as **time** so gives the determinable, then I cannot determine my existence as that of a self-active being; instead I represent only the spontaneity of my thought, i.e., of the [act of determination] and my existence remains determinable always only sensibly . . . (B157–58n., amended translation)

Humans can have cognition of themselves as appearances, as spatiotemporal cognizers, because the form of intuition provides a determinable in which states can be assigned determinate locations. 'Time gives the determinable' in the sense that it provides a dimension along which mental states can be assigned particular values.

Kant suggests a way in which cognizers could know themselves as self-active beings, as 'determining' subjects. That would be possible if there were a second form of self-intuition, one that was similar to time in being a dimension that 'gave the determinable' in which determinates could be determined. As I understand his denial of knowledge of a thinker *per se*, it is more or less an internal criticism of Rationalism. The Paralogisms show in detail why none of the determinables proposed by the Ontology of Rational Psychology, substance or accident, simple as oppose to complex nature, continuing identity, and so on, can be used in the case of the thinker. Rational Psychologists would reject space out of hand as a determinable for an immaterial soul. That leaves no option standing but time—their preferred option—and he thinks it cannot work. This is so both for reasons of transcendental idealism (that they don't share), since it involves a form of sensory intuition and so is unsuitable for thinkers *per se*. But it is also true for reasons unique to the activity of thinking itself. As we saw in the discussion of the Reflection 'Is it an experience that I think?' rational thought cannot be understood as taking place at a determinate moment in time.

Kant agrees with the Rationalists that the predicates of materialism are inadequate for characterizing a thinker. He does not see how the necessary connections across the mental states involved in rational cognition can be modeled by the interactions of spatially distinct bodies (B419, cf. 20.308, C1781 395). For this reason he thinks that the considerations raised by the Rational Psychologists should be understood not as offering a doctrine, a body of accepted knowledge, but as providing a discipline which guards against the dangers of materialism (B421). But he argues in the Paralogisms chapter and in the B deduction that their ontology is also inadequate for describing thinking *per se*. It provides no determinable for the determinations of an active thinker. His arguments thereby provide a discipline against the fanaticism of spiritualists (e.g., B415–16n).

Given this context, Kant's claim that the active thinker is unknowable should not be read not as a doctrine, but as a discipline or challenge to potential theories of the nature of mind. He uses his positive theory both to support the Rationalists in their attack on materialism and to demonstrate the fallacies in their immaterialist approach to understanding the mind. In Chapter 15, I argue that his theory of the necessary conditions for rational cognition also poses a challenge to some contemporary ways of thinking about consciousness and rational thought.

Chapter 15 will also return to this piece of the Transcendental Dialectic to examine an important claim not considered here. Kant maintains that the ability to generalize about thinkers has an odd source:

> It must, however, seem strange at the very outset that the condition under which I think at all, and which is therefore merely a characteristic of myself as subject, is to be valid also for everything that thinks; and that upon a proposition that seems empirical we can presume to base an apodeictic and universal judgment, viz: that everything that thinks is of such a character as the pronouncement of self-consciousness asserts of me. The cause of this,

however, lies in the fact that we must necessarily ascribe to thing *a priori* all of the properties that make up the conditions under which alone we think them A346/B404–405)

Although he makes this claim as part of the setup to the analyses of the Paralogistic arguments, it doesn't seem to play any role in the analyses. So I consider it only in relation to contemporary views. His theory that attributing mental states to others is crucially dependent on a first person understanding of thought offers a plausible alternative to current theories of 'mind-reading.'

Part III
Evaluation

12

Is Kant's Theory Consistent?

1. The Old Objection

Having laid out Kant's theory of the thinker, I take up two major and perennial objections to it. If sound, the objections would be reasons to cast the theory aside, whatever its seeming attractions. I begin in this chapter with the older objection: His cognitive theory is inconsistent with the transcendental idealism that it is supposed to support. According to the cognitive theory, empirical cognition is a compound of *a posteriori* representations that come in through the senses and *a priori* representations that arise through the activities of the understanding and imagination. According to transcendental idealism, the world is divided into two exhaustive and exclusive classes, phenomena and noumena. Given the metaphysics, the objects that produce *a posteriori* representations by touching the senses and the transcendental faculties that combine the raw materials of sense must be either phenomenal or noumenal. It seems, however, that they can be neither.

This objection is virtually coeval with the publication of the *Critique*. In 1787, between the editions, F. H. Jacobi argued that transcendental epistemology could not consistently be applied to itself.

> I cannot enter the system without that presupposition [of affection by noumena] and with that presupposition I cannot remain in it. (1787/1983, 222)

The beginning of the 'transcendental story,' to borrow John McDowell's pejorative description (1994, 41–42), cannot advert to noumena, since it is possible to speak of causal relations only among phenomena. Yet the objects that move the senses cannot be understood as phenomenal, because, by Kant's argument, the relation of causation is 'added' to object representations only after they have been 'worked up' through the activities of the understanding and imagination (B1). In the nineteenth century, Hans Vaihinger gave the objection its classic trilemma form: How is the beginning of the story of transcendental epistemology to be told, with noumena affecting a noumenal self, phenomena affecting a phenomenal self, or some monstrous 'double affection' that combines the vices of the first two?[1] Strawson's classic portrayal of the 'metaphysics of transcendental idealism' as a story about the 'affecting relation' between noumenal objects and the noumenal self is a twentieth-century version of the same objection (1966, Part 4). To honor its most famous proponents across the centuries, I call this the 'Jacobi-Vaihinger-Strawson' (or just 'JVS') objection.

The idea that Kant's cognitive theory implicates noumena flourishes beyond the Strawsonian tradition. In a recent essay, Robert Adams maintains that the actions that produce empirical cognition cannot be understood as part of that cognition:

> The *third* [role of noumena] has to do with Kant's transcendental psychology ... The actions that . . . determine the content of our experience can hardly be identified with the causal actions of objects of our experience, for the latter actions are part of the causal structure supposedly imposed on experience by our understanding. It seems to follow that these actions are accomplished outside of our experience, by things as they are in themselves rather than as they appear in experience. And Kant is willing to embrace this conclusion, speaking, for example, of 'a ground, to us unknown, of the appearances' of inner and outer sense.' (A380) (1997, 2–3)

I discuss the cited text below (pp.212-13). Lorne Falkenstein makes the argument in a slightly different way:

> How can something that can only be supposed to exist in a phenomenal world postulated by a subject—something that is denied any independent existence in itself and supposed to exist in the theories constructed by the subject—be identified with the subject that constructs the theories? Were it the case that our postulates merely discovered some antecedently existing thing in itself, then there would be no problem. But, if it is asserted that the objects we postulate do not exist in themselves, but only in our theories, then we end up confronting the absurd result that something that only exists in our theories is what makes our theories, thereby bootstrapping itself, and ourselves and the entire phenomenal world along with it, into experience. (1995, 348)

If Adams, Falkenstein, and others are right, then Kant's criticisms of the mistake of his predecessors in positing an intelligible subject as the true ground of cognition are naïve.[2] When seen in light of his phenomenal/noumenal distinction, his cognitive theory also implies such a subject.

My goals in this chapter are limited. I do not try to show that Kant's cognitive theory is consistent with transcendental idealism, when that theory is understood as denying the reality of space and time.[3] Nor will I revisit the suggestions that the activity of thinking is noumenal because it must take place outside of time or because it must be free.[4] My focus is just on the issue of 'noumenal affection.' If, in Kant's view, cognition begins with the affection of the cognitive subject by noumena, then seemingly, that subject must be a noumenon. Resolving this issue is important because concern to avoid a noumenal thinker who conjures up the phenomenal world leads contemporary sympathizers to downplay or ignore the subject's activities in producing the *a priori* elements in empirical cognition. But those activities are an essential part of Kant's theory; they are what make the theory an interesting alternative to contemporary views.

Given the lineage of the JVS objection, it is reasonable to expect that it is based on solid evidence. The most important text is one that Kant deleted from the second edition. Still, it was there for Jacobi and later interpreters to read and its doctrine seems to be echoed in other passages. As far as I can tell, Kant became confused on an issue that has confused many: how to describe the precursors of cognition without using the cognitive repertoire whose existence the precursors are intended to explain. What I will argue is that despite this error, his cognitive theory does not imply noumenal affection of a noumenal self. Nor did he concede that it did. He is clear that cognition begins with affection by phenomena.

2. The Most Problematic Passage (A251–52)

I begin with the text deleted from the B edition. In section 3 I turn for guidance to another text that seems to support the Jacobi-Vaihinger-Strawson objection and then return to the deleted text.[5] Section 4 offers further support for my diagnosis of the confusion about the causes of sensible representations by considering part of Kant's criticism of Leibniz in the Amphiboly of the Concepts of Reflection.

The deleted material considers reasons for establishing

> the objective reality of **noumena** and . . . the division of objects into **phenomena** and **noumena**, and thus into a world of the senses and of the understanding (**mundus sensibilis & intelligibilis**). (A249)

Kant rejects two possibilities. The first was his view in the *Inaugural Dissertation* (2. 392, C1755 384) that if the senses just represent something as it appears, then this something must also be in itself a thing and an object of nonsensible intuition, that is, understanding (A250).

> Hence there would be, besides the empirical use of the categories (which is limited to sensible conditions) also a pure and yet objectively valid use of them (A250)

He does not endorse this conclusion, but immediately rejects it. If this were true, then

> we could not assert what we have alleged thus far, *viz.*, that our pure cognitions of understanding are nothing more at all than principles of the exposition of appearance. (A250)

Next he considers and rejects the possibility that cognizers must acknowledge noumena, because the understanding always operates by referring properties to objects. This reasoning does not deliver the desired conclusion, because, as he notes slightly later, the concept of such an object—the 'transcendental object'—is not the concept of a 'noumenon':

> The object to which I refer appearance as such is the transcendental object, i.e., the wholly indeterminate concept of something as such. This object cannot be called the **noumenon**. (A253)

(I return to this text below, p. 212.)
Kant is clear that the preceding considerations are not probative. The A edition case for noumena rests exclusively on a different line of reasoning:

> But as for the cause why one, being not yet satisfied by the substratum of sensibility has added to the phenomena also noumena that only the understanding can think, it rests exclusively [*lediglich*] on the following. Sensibility—and its realm, *viz.*, that of appearances—is itself limited by the understanding so that it deals not with things in themselves but only with the way in which, by virtue of our subjective character, things appear to us. This was the result of the entire Transcendental Aesthetic; and from the concept of appearance as such, too, it follows naturally that to appearance there must correspond something that is not in itself appearance. For appearance cannot be anything by itself and apart from our way of representing; <u>hence if we are not to go in a constant circle, then the word appearance already indicates a reference to something the direct representation of which is indeed sensible, but which in itself—even without this character of our sensibility (on which the form of our intuition is based)—must be something, i.e., an object independent of sensibility.</u> (A251–52, my underscoring)

With its worries about avoiding circularity, the passage I underscore is about as direct evidence as one could find for the JVS assumption that the causes of representations or appearances must be noumenal. It seems to say, borrowing Falkenstein's terminology, that appearances could not bootstrap their way into existence.

3. Confusions about the Causes of Sensations

To get a better sense of what Kant is asserting in the deleted passage, it will be helpful to consider a second text, one that occurs in his summing up of the implications of transcendental epistemology in section 6 of the Antinomy of Pure Reason. At first, it too appears to give strong support to the JVS reading. It revolves around a technical term which is crucial for sorting out his views about the phenomenal/noumenal distinction, the concept of a 'transcendental object.'[6] As we saw above, he explicitly denies that the transcendental object can be called a noumenon.

> Our power of sensible intuition is, in fact, only a receptivity, i.e., a capacity to be affected in a certain way with representations. The relation of these representations to one another is a pure intuition of space and time (which are

nothing but forms of our sensibility); and insofar as these representations are connected and determinable in this relation according to laws of the unity of experience, they are called **objects**. With the nonsensible cause [*Ursache*] of these representations we are entirely unacquainted, and hence we cannot intuit it as object. [1] For such an object would have to be represented neither in space nor in time (which are merely conditions of sensible representation), and without these conditions we cannot think of any intuition at all. We may, however, call the merely intelligible cause of appearances as such the transcendental object, just so that we have something that corresponds to sensibility, which is a receptivity. [2] To this transcendental object we may attribute the whole range and coherence of our possible perceptions, and about it we may say that it is given in itself prior to all experience. But appearances are given, in conformity with the transcendental object, not in themselves but only in this experience. For they are mere representations, which signify an actual object only as perceptions; they do so, *viz.*, if such a perception coheres with all others according to the rules of the unity of experience. (A494–95/B522–23, my numbering)

This passage is helpful in assessing the issue of noumenal affection, because Kant is rarely concerned with 'received' data. They were not a bone of contention with his Empiricist opponents. The passage is clear that the relation in question is causation.[7]

Nonetheless, Kant's theory of the *a priori* forms and categories raises a question about how to characterize the objects that cause sensations. In one sense at least, the 'cause of sensations' cannot be understood as an 'object.' In the *Inaugural Dissertation*, he explains that objects do not strike the senses in terms of their (spatial and temporal) form (2.393); at B130, he makes the parallel claim about the combination of sensations in a manifold:

But a manifold's combination (*conjuntio*) can never come to us through the senses.

Since the representations that comprise the representation of an object involve combination, his view is the slightly paradoxical one that objects do not strike the senses in terms of their 'objecthood,' in terms of the combination of representations in the representation of an object. How then can his empirical realist story about the dependence of human knowledge on perception be told?[8]

Kant resorts to a dummy expression, the 'transcendental object,' to designate the correlate of sensibility, that is, that which gives or causes what sensibility receives. This is the sense of 'transcendental object' that he uses in the passage I mark as (1).[9] Given his theory, it is easy to draw the conclusion that insofar as one is thinking about what in an object causes sensory data in the subject, the transcendental object cannot be characterized as spatial, temporal, and so forth. And that is the source of the confusion that is manifest in the passages that appear to support JVS. As Allison notes, since all sensible objects are represented spatially and temporally for Kant, the transcendental object is nonsensible (1983, 250). Although one can see why Kant says this, there is something odd, if not perverse, in describing that which is the correlate of sensibility—the stimulus for the stimulations received by sensibility—as 'nonsensible.'

Since Kant describes the transcendental object as 'nonsensible' in segment (1), it is somewhat shocking that he then claims in the segment I indicate as (2) that humans attribute to it the whole range and coherence of their possible perceptions. This abrupt change leads Allison to claim that two very different senses of 'transcendental object' are at work, although both are nonempirical (1983, 252). One difficulty with Allison's hypothesis is that Kant's discussion flows seamlessly from the occurrence of this expression in (1) to its occurrence in (2). The second usage is explicitly tied back to the first by the anaphoric description 'to this transcendental object.' Here is a simpler hypothesis. What Kant means by 'transcendental object' in the Antinomy is basically what he meant by the 'transcendental object = X' at A105, namely a formal description of an object of cognition. A transcendental object is not a sensible object, because it is not an object at all, but an abstract description of objects of experience.[10] Since, roughly,[11] any object of empirical cognition must (a) cause sensory representations in subjects and (b) have properties that could all belong to one object both characteristics are part of the description. When Kant says that we may attribute the whole range and coherence of our perceptions to the transcendental object, he means the following. Since 'transcendental object' is an abstract description of empirical objects, what happens in a particular instance of perception is that the object causes representations in a subject and, on the basis of those representations and its *a priori* forms and categories, the subject then attributes a variety of coherent properties to the object: for example, it is extended, heavy, and made of wood. Since 'transcendental object' applies to all such objects, it must be a very abstract characterization, so that it can encompass the myriad types of empirical coherence of objects that experience reveals.

Apparent support for the JVS picture of noumenal causes of empirical cognition comes from the (a) rather than from the (b) part of the representation of the transcendental object. The passage, however, contains no mention of noumena. Further, at one level, there is no mystery about why the transcendental object is nonsensible. It is not a thing, but an abstract description of an empirically cognizable object. Kant is clear on this point in the text just before the most problematic passage:

> This transcendental object cannot be separated at all from the sensible data, for then there remains nothing through which it would be thought. It is, therefore, not in itself an object of cognition, but is only the representation of appearances under the concept of an object as such—a concept determinable through the manifold of these appearances.
>
> Precisely because of this, too, the categories represent no special object given to the understanding alone, but serve only to determine the transcendental object (the concept of something as such). (A250–51)

Proponents of JVS might argue that Kant uses 'transcendental object' to indicate *both* the abstract concept of the object of cognition and the abstract concept of a nonsensible cause of the object of cognition. To see more clearly where the problem of characterizing the causes of perceptions lies, it may be helpful to consider a particular case, say smelling a rose. Kant's claim would be that, although olfactory sensibility is stirred by the rose, the rose does not strike the senses in terms of either its spatial properties or its objecthood.

Neurophysiologists now know a lot more about how smell works, but there is nothing in the current account that Kant couldn't easily have imagined (indeed, contemporary views are close to the then standard key and lock metaphor for sensory perception). The olfactory system contains as many as one thousand different types of odorant receptors, receptors that bind odorous molecules (Kandel and Schwartz, 2000, 625ff.). Humans smell a rose when the molecules that are given off by the rose are received by the appropriate receptors. This account belies Kant's view that the cause of sensations is 'nonsensible.' At least with the aid of a microscope, humans can perceive the odorant molecules and describe them in terms used for sensible objects. The olfactory system does not represent odorants as tiny objects with particular molecular structures; it simply binds them, thereby beginning a complex series of neural activities that culminates in the perception of a distinctive smell. Together, however, the two modes of access to odorants, the olfactory and the (*via* microscope) visual, allow sensibility both to receive odors and to represent the properties of the rose that stir the senses—the molecular structure of the odorant.

Similar accounts could be given for touch, sound perception, and so forth.[12] Kant is thus wrong in claiming that the causes of *a posteriori* representations are 'nonsensible,' in the sense that they cannot be represented by terms used for sensible properties. This is the fundamental confusion that stands behind others noted below.[13] Although it is a mistake, it does not lead him to support noumenal causation. Further, while avoidable, the error is also understandable.[14] Since he holds that (empirical) objects do not strike the senses in terms of their spatial, temporal, and objecthood properties—but in terms of other properties—it is not difficult to see why he thinks that the former concepts should not be used in describing those aspects of an object that give rise to sensations. In perceiving my desk, for example, I am unable to receive information about its spatial dimensions (directly). My senses can inform me about its color, impenetrability, and hardness (A20/B35). As in the case of the rose, the description of how the information transfer takes place could be in terms of the reception of light by neurons with a certain structure without contradicting Kant's doctrine that humans cannot directly perceive shape by vision or touch. Richard Axel didn't explain how the olfactory nerves perceive shapes; he used descriptions of molecular configurations to explain how they perceive odors.

Because Kant believes that cognition involves a great deal of processing before it reaches the level of conscious perception or judgment, it is not surprising that he finds the task of describing the causes of sensations daunting. Seemingly, conceptual as well as spatial and temporal descriptions would be ruled out. The situation is, however, nowhere near as dire as he believed. Psychophysicists can use the full range of sensory and theoretical concepts to describe the objects that are stimuli for the human sensory system, without contradicting his claims about the limited receptive capacities of those systems. They could, for example, explain color perception by appealing to the ability of cones to receive different wavelengths of light—thus using a variety of categorial concepts and spatial concepts—without denying his claim that, although colors can be received by the senses, the senses can receive neither spatial nor categorial properties.

Faced with what he takes to be an insoluble descriptive problem, Kant sticks to his empiricist principles: Even if humans can neither perceive nor conceive them, they can still think in an abstract way about aspects of empirical objects as the causes of sensations. As indicated in condition (b) above, at the end of the cognitive process, subjects attribute a range of sensory and other properties to empirical objects. The ordinary person has no qualms about characterizing the causes of sensations as objects with various properties. By contrast, the scientifically informed epistemologist who knows the limits of the senses is circumspect in characterizing the correlate of sensibility, falling back on an abstract description, 'transcendental object.' In introducing the concept of the 'transcendental object' Kant thus saves the phenomena as causes of sensations (even though he incorrectly believes that it is impossible to characterize those causes through 'normal' phenomenal concepts). What he does not do in the passage is appeal to noumenal causes.

It will not have escaped notice that, for all his eschewing of spatial, temporal, and object descriptions, Kant helps himself to a crucial category. The transcendental object is the nonsensible *cause* of sensory representations.[15] How can he say that, particularly when he thinks that he can say nothing else? Again, the answer is relatively straightforward and runs directly against the noumenal causation reading. Kant knows that philosophers and psychologists have excellent reasons for accepting the causal theory of perception and, thus, of cognition. It is a well-established empirical theory that perfectly fulfills the normative requirement that cognition of objects depends, in crucial ways, on the objects. In this case, he thus easily slips into the second mode of access. When a subject receives a bit of sensory data, his receptive faculty does not also receive an impression of causality. Epistemologists (and for that matter, ordinary cognizers) have another mode of access to this process, however, because they can observe the constant correlation between the presence of objects and perceptual reports. Hence they take objects to be the causes of perceptions (though they also note that some features of object representations cannot be transmitted through any sense). Under these circumstances they are justified in saying that something in the object is causing the sensations, even if they cannot say exactly what (and, on Kant's view, never could provide a specific description).

4. A Second Look at the Most Problematic Passage

The apparent support that the Antinomy passage offers for the Jacobi-Vaihinger-Strawson objection is illusory. It has nothing to do with noumenal causation. It is, on the contrary, a discussion of the causation of the *a posteriori* elements in cognition by empirical objects, albeit empirical objects described in a very abstract way. With this clarification of how Kant understands the reception of sensible properties by sensibility, we may return to the deleted and highly problematic passage from the A edition. I repeat the key section for easy reference:

> For appearance cannot be anything by itself and apart from our way of representing; hence if we are not to go in a constant circle, then the word appearance already indicates a reference to something the direct representation of which is indeed sensible, but which in itself—even without this character of our sensibility (on which the form of our intuition is based)—must be something, i.e., an object independent of sensibility. (A251–52, my underscoring)

Since the topic is the causation of sensible representations, it seems reasonable to read it in light of the more extensive discussion just considered. In the Antinomy passage, he is explicit that since space and time are forms of intuition, then it follows (he believes) that whatever it is in an object that causes a sensible representation of itself in cognizers, it is not anything that should be characterized in spatial or temporal terms.

In the above passage, Kant is both less explicit and more extreme. He characterizes the cause of sensible representations as 'an object that is independent of sensibility.' As he sees, this is a very odd usage, since what is known of the object in question is that it is the cause of sensible representations, something that can 'stir the senses' in the terminology of B1. He acknowledges the oddness, noting that its representation is 'indeed sensible'.[16] If he were terminologically consistent with his later discussion, then he would proclaim this independent of sensibility object to be the transcendental object. He does not, but continues

> [n]ow from this consideration arises the concept of a noumenon. But this concept is not at all positive and is not a determinate cognition of some thing, but signifies only the thinking of something as such—something in which I abstract from all form of sensible intuition. (A252)

Kant takes 'noumenon' to have both a positive sense ('creatures of the understanding, including intellectual intuition') and a negative sense ('objects thought independently of human sensibility'). One source of confusion over the causation of sensible representations is that he offers two different considerations for the necessity of a negative use of 'noumenon.' One justification is presented in the first part of the passage:

> But as for the cause why one, being not yet satisfied by the substratum of sensibility has added to the phenomena also noumena that only the understanding can think, it rests exclusively on the following. Sensibility—and its realm, *viz.*, that of appearances—is itself limited by the understanding so that it deals not with things in themselves but only with the way in which, by virtue of our subjective character, things appear to us. This was the result of the entire Transcendental Aesthetic; and from the concept of appearance as such, too, it follows naturally that to appearance there must correspond something that is not in itself appearance. (A251)

The lesson of the Transcendental Aesthetic is that representations of the spatial and temporal properties of objects are dependent on the special features of human sensibility. It follows from the recognition of this dependence that it is possible for there to be objects or aspects of objects that could not be sensed by humans. Following Gerold Prauss, we could call this the 'restriction' argument for a negative concept of 'noumenon' (1974/1989 90ff.). Since the human perceptual system is restricted to properties of certain sorts, it is possible that there are objects that are unknowable through that system.

The first part of A251–52 presents this argument, but the latter part lays out a different route to the negative use of 'noumenon,' an argument from the sensibility-dependent character of the forms of intuition to the alleged impossibility that the cause of sensible representations can be characterized in terms of the forms. Let us call this the 'description' use. The basic circle is as proponents of JVS, and Adams and Falkenstein, would have it: Representations cannot be caused by representations.[17] By itself this point does not imply that the causes of representations cannot be sensible—cannot be understood through the categories and the forms of intuition. Only the epistemological theory that objects do not strike the senses in terms of their spatial, temporal, and categorial properties (plus Kant's failure to see that theorists might have a second mode of access to those elements that do strike the senses) makes it seem plausible that the causes of sensations cannot be described in terms of properties related to sensibility. It is the descriptive route to the negative use of 'noumena' that leads to JVS. Because phenomena have spatial, temporal, and categorial properties, properties that are interpretations of sensations through cognitive processing, the causes of the sensations that begin the process cannot be described in the terms that describe sensible phenomena; so they must be understood as 'noumena' in the negative sense.

One way of sorting out the confusions into which Kant falls in the first edition (and into which he leads his interpreters) is to realize that he makes three inconsistent assertions in regard to the causes of sensations. The Antinomy presents 'transcendental object' as a suitably abstract way of describing the causes of sensations; the deleted A edition passage identifies 'noumena' (in the negative sense of the term) as the cause; but that section also explains that the transcendental object is no noumenon! I repeat the crucial passage:

> The object to which I refer appearance as such is the transcendental object, i.e., the wholly indeterminate concept of something as such. This object cannot be called the **noumenon**. For I do not know concerning it what it is in itself, and have no concept of it except merely the concept of the object of sensible intuition as such—an object which, therefore, is the same for all appearances. (A253)

Far from being noumenal, 'transcendental object' is the concept of a *sensible* object in general.

The passage that Adams cites from the A edition's Fourth Paralogism can be understood in the same way. Kant is concerned to show that dualism can only be understood as a feature of the phenomenal world. He continues:

> I, as represented through inner sense in time, and objects in space outside me are indeed appearances quite distinct in kind, but they are not thereby thought as different things. The **transcendental object** which underlies outer appearances, and likewise that transcendental object which underlies inner intuition is in itself neither matter nor thinking being, but is, rather, a basis—with which we are unacquainted—of appearances that provide us with the empirical concept of both the first and the second kind. (A379–380, my underscoring)

Adams appeals to this passage in discussing Kant's various uses of 'noumena' (1997, 2–3), though the term does not appear in the text. It would be strange if it did given what he is claiming. He would then assert that the noumenal cause of inner and outer representations is the same. By his own theory, he could be in no position to offer any such hypothesis. On the other hand, his claim that the same 'transcendental object' underlies and is the basis of the objects of both inner and outer intuition makes sense if what he is saying is that humans have a single abstract description of what something must be to be an empirical object—whether a material object or a human being who is also aware of her representations. The different states must be coherent, and so forth. That is, the passage makes sense only if its topic is understood not as the 'noumenon' but as the 'transcendental object'—the concept of the object of (inner or outer) sensible intuition as such.

Although Kant deletes the material from A251–52 and all reference to the transcendental object from the B edition phenomenal/noumenal chapter, he leaves enough remnants of his former position in the second edition to fuel JVS, for example, A288/B344:

> Accordingly, the understanding limits sensibility . . . [I]t does think an object in itself. But the understanding thinks it only as transcendental object. This object is the cause [*Ursache*] of appearance (hence is not itself appearance) and can be thought neither as magnitude nor as reality nor as substance, etc., (because these concepts always requires sensible forms wherein they determine an object). Hence concerning this object we are completely ignorant as to whether it is to be found in us—or, for that matter, outside us and whether it would be annulled simultaneously with sensibility or would still remain if we removed sensibility. If we want to call this object noumenon, because the representation of it is not yet sensible, then we are free to do so.

This passage is odd. What does it mean to say that we are *free* to call the transcendental object 'noumenon'? It's up to us—even though the transcendental object might be annulled with sensibility, a possibility that would seem to show its dependence on sensibility?[18]

Although Kant's considered position is that 'transcendental object' and 'noumenon' are different theoretical concepts, two terminological links between them lead to disconcerting shifts in his usage.[19] Both 'transcendental object' and 'noumenon' are used to characterize elements that could not, he believed, be characterized in terms of sensible properties. As such, both could be said to be 'noumena' in the negative sense. Second, the *intelligibilia* of the Rationalists were the ground [*Grund*] or rational basis of phenomena and the transcendental object is the cause of sensations. Under these circumstances, there are solid terminological reasons for representing both noumena and the transcendental object as 'the nonsensible basis of appearances.' The problem is that while the terminology might be justified in each case, the resulting conflation of doctrines gives his theory the appearance of gross inconsistency first flagged by Jacobi.

5. Criticizing Rationalist Confusions

Kant could see the error of conflating noumena with what he would characterize as the 'transcendental object' quite clearly—in the theories of his Rationalist opponents.

In the Amphiboly he criticizes Leibniz for maintaining that cognition is possible through the understanding alone. What follows is a relevant part of his case:

> Matter is *substantia phenomenon* . . . On the other hand, the character of matter that would be intrinsic absolutely, i.e., according to pure understanding, is a mere fancy. For matter is not at all an object for pure understanding. <u>The transcendental object, however, which may be the basis of this appearance that we call matter, is a mere something, about which we would not understand what it is even if someone were able to tell us. For we cannot understand anything except what carries with it, in intuition, something corresponding to our words</u> . . . Observation and dissection of appearances penetrate to the intrinsic character of nature, and one cannot know how far this penetration may in time go. But those transcendental questions that go beyond nature we would, despite all this, still never be able to answer, even if all of nature were uncovered for us. This is so because <u>we have not been given [the ability] to observe even our own mind for in it lies the secret origin [*Ursprung*] of our sensibility—by means of an intuition other than that of our inner sense.</u> Sensibility's reference to an object, and what may be the transcendental basis of this objective unity, this doubtless lies too deeply hidden so that we, who are acquainted even with our own selves only through inner sense and hence as appearance, might with so unfitting an instrument of our investigation discover anything other than what are always in turn appearances—whereas it was the nonsensible cause [*Ursache*] of those appearances that we hoped to explore. (A278/B334, my underscoring)

At first look, this passage also appears to commit Kant to a nonsensible, noumenal cause of appearance. But he is not stating his view so much as criticizing the Leibnizians.

The passage opens by noting that 'matter' is phenomenal, meaning that it exists in some parts of space and exerts its force there. Kant complains that, nevertheless, someone (Leibniz) purports to explain this phenomenon by reference solely to intellectual concepts. This is folly. He precedes the introduction of his own concept, 'transcendental object,' with a 'however' (*aber*) to indicate the contrast between his view and Leibniz's idea of an intelligible ground of phenomena. The transcendental object is the basis (*Grund*) of the appearance of phenomenal matter. He then elaborates the contrast with the Leibnizian *intelligibilia* or noumena (in the positive sense), objects of pure understanding. Because concepts get reference (and so meaning in one sense) from their connection to intuition, there is a sense in which it is impossible to understand what a transcendental object is. This would be so for the reason we have already seen, *viz.*, that Kant doesn't see that there could be a second mode of access to that in objects which causes *a posteriori* representations and which could be understood in terms of spatial, temporal, and categorial properties—that is, which could be understood even if it were presented to humans. He is not agreeing with Leibniz that phenomena must be backed by hidden rational causes; he is criticizing him for confusing the indescribable in phenomenal terms cause of representations, the transcendental object, with a purely intellectual (noumenal) cause.

After the second ellipsis, Kant offers several reasons for denying that Leibniz is in a position to propose a monad hypothesis. With objects, one can continually investigate ever more 'hidden' causes. Matters are different with the interaction between objects and mental faculties. Nothing can be gleaned about that in objects which is the cause of their sensible appearance (or so Kant believes). In the second underscored passage, he turns from considering what in the object causes sensations to considering what in the subject receives sensations. Here too, investigation and understanding are stymied. First, cognizers have access only to their mental states in inner sense and not to their receptive faculties. Second, even if humans had a second 'inner sense,' that sense could discover only sensible properties, whereas the project was not to find further sensible representations, but the nonsensible cause of the phenomenal world—the explanation of why it is as it is. In this passage, Kant again errs in maintaining that transcendental epistemology reveals the hopelessness of the project of understanding the production of representations through sensibility, but the error is not one of assuming a noumenal cause. That is the faulty reasoning that he attributes to Leibniz and his followers.

In effect, the first part of the citation offers a diagnosis of how his clever predecessor went wrong. Were Kant right in assuming no second mode of access, then there is a nonsensible cause of representations of phenomenal objects. But such causes are not at all what Leibniz thought—intelligible entities. The transcendental object is not an *intelligibilia*, a noumenon, but the object of sensible intuition as such or in general. At least when considering his predecessors Kant was very clear about the danger of confusing 'transcendental object' with 'noumena.'

6. What Kant's Epistemology and Metaphysics Imply

Kant's cognitive theory implies the possibility of noumena. Insofar as the objects of human cognition are recognized as objects whose properties are represented through forms of sensibility and the categories of understanding, there is an open possibility of cognition of objects through the categories and some nonsensible intuition. This is not a possibility for human cognizers, but it is a consequence of his epistemology that it cannot be ruled out altogether. In the conclusion of the chapter on Phenomena and Noumena that is common to both editions, he gives this basic argument for the introduction of the concept of 'noumenon':

> The concept of a **noumenon**, i.e. of a thing that is not to be thought at all as an object of the senses but is to be thought (solely through a pure understanding) as a thing in itself, is not at all contradictory; for we cannot, after all, assert of sensibility that it is the only possible kind of intuition . . . (A254/B310)

Given the introduction of 'noumenon' and the rationale for it, it is reasonable to characterize the objects of human cognition as 'phenomena.' But this does not mean that phenomena exist only in human theories as Falkenstein suggests—at least this is not an implication of the cognitive theory.[20] It means only that the human representation of phenomena includes *a priori* elements. If this feature is taken as implying that phenomena are not real, then Kant's project of vindicating the use of *a priori* concepts was doomed from the start. As long as phenomena are allowed to be real, however, then Jacobi and Vaihinger and Strawson are wrong that once we know the full extent of Kant's cognitive theory, we are unable to enter it as he proposes in the Introduction. The opening claim that objects touch the senses and thereby create some elements that are used in cognition can be recast within transcendental epistemology as follows: Humans' sensory data from external objects and their data from sensory representations (which might be in the form of reports on representations or of behavior that is guided by contact with objects) are so regularly correlated that when they scrutinize their data looking for relations that can be interpreted as causal, they find sufficient regularity across them to interpret objects as the causes of sensory representations. Phenomena can be understood as the causes of some elements of cognition both at the beginning of the account and at its conclusion. Given this result, we are free to consider the activities of the mind in creating cognition, without worrying that we have embarked on the bootless enterprise of describing the creation of the phenomenal world itself.

13

The Normativity Objection

1. Psychologism or Noumenalism?

Kant makes two claims about the categories and the 'I-think':

1. The categorial principles are, in the terminology of the *Duisburg* notes, 'rules for the solution of appearances' (R4678, 17.660–61, CNotes 169). They provide standards for observation. The I-rule is the standard for the use of the I-representation.
2. These principles lie *a priori* in the mind, meaning that the source of the principles are activities of the mind.

Since it defends 'objective' standards by tracing them to psychological activities, the *Critique*'s cognitive theory has perennially been subject to the charge of 'psychologism.'[1] Where the JVS objection would rule out the theory as inconsistent, the normativity objection would reject it on the grounds of irrelevance. It fails to address the topic of (normative) cognition.

Some scholars believe that Kant's clear recognition that experience is incapable of furnishing norms leads him to place the cognitive subject among the noumena. Robert Brandom[2] attributes this view to Kant while pointing to its obvious shortcoming:

> One of Kant's great insights is that judgments and actions are to be distinguished from the responses of merely natural creatures by their distinctive *normative* status, as things we are in a distinctive sense *responsible* for . . . Kant, however, punted many hard questions about the nature and origins of normativity, of the bindingess of concepts, out of the familiar phenomenal realm of experience into the noumenal realm. (2000, 33–34)

As Brandom sees it, the normativity of Kantian principles is clear in one sense and utterly opaque in another. He notes that, if his reading is correct, then Kant would have told us nothing useful about the normativity of cognition. In Brandom's view, that normativity must be traced to social practices embedded in the use of language.

I will not repeat the reasons offered in Chapters 10 and 12 for doubting that Kant understood the cognitive subject as noumenal. And Brandom is clear enough about why the hypothesis of a noumenal subject would be particularly unhelpful for a theory of cognition. Instead I will show how Kant could have understood a phenomenal subject as a 'source of normativity' (in Christine Korsgaard's useful phrase, 1996), thereby avoiding the psychologism or noumenalism dilemma.

Kant addressed one aspect of the problem of the psychological or, in his terms, the 'subjective' character of *a priori* principles in the *Critique*. He presented the task of the transcendental deduction as that of showing how subjective conditions, conditions that originated in the activities of the subject, could be objective—could be rules for objects (A89–90/B122). Its argument is that humans do not just happen to combine data in accord with categorial rules and the I-rule. If they did not use these rules, then they would be incapable of RE cognition. If correct, the deduction would simultaneously answer the question of fact (which rules/concepts are used) and of right (why their use is legitimate).

Although the transcendental deduction is aimed at prerefuting the basic charge of 'psychologism,' a significant problem remains. Even if applying the categorial principles and the I-rule could be shown to be necessary conditions for the possibility of RE cognition, that result would be insufficient to establish their status as cognitive norms. To qualify as a norm, a rule must be used normatively by a subject.[3] Kant does not consider this issue in the case of the categorial principles or the 'I-rule,' but he is clear about two other important classes of *a priori* principles. At the first mention of the categorical imperative in the *Groundwork of the Metaphysics of Morals*, he explains that ordinary cognizers implicitly know and follow this rule (4.402, CPract 57). He is also explicit that ordinary cognizers have some critical understanding of the laws of logic that lie *a priori* in the mind. It would be alien to his understanding of how rules, including *a priori* principles, function in human thought and action to read him as believing that the categorial principles and the I-rule are necessary to human cognition, but utterly unknown to subjects.

This chapter defends Kant against the second aspect of the charge of psychologism by showing how he believes that categorial principles enter human cognition through the activities of the mind and then by appealing to the case of logic to show how he could understand those principles as becoming norms for cognizers. My defense contains significant amounts of offense. Filling in missing pieces of the sketch provided by the *Critique* makes the cognitive theory more plausible by demonstrating that it can be developed in some detail. Although I enlarge on the theory in relation to the categorial principles, my interest is not in defending them as norms of cognition. It is in showing that Kant's claim that a principle is both *a priori* and a norm is coherent and how he would have seen it as coherent. The only norm I defend is the 'I-rule.' In essence, I argue for the opposite of Brandom's position. Kant is right that the *a priori* I-rule is a special cognitive norm, because it must be presupposed as a norm by anyone using any cognitive norm, including those acquired through enculturation.

Before considering how humans come to recognize cognitive norms, we need to see how in Kant's view these principles enter human cognition in the first instance.

Drawing on materials from the Logic, Metaphysics, and Anthropology lectures and various Reflections, I examine four processes. Section 2 presents the initial process of scrutinizing the data in order to attach categories to *a posteriori* representations; it then explains how categorial materials or 'transcendental content' might be added to the *a posteriori* representations (A79/B105). The texts I appeal to do not answer every question about these processes and I offer a speculative mechanism to fill a gap. In section 3, I look at Kant's view of how concepts are formed on the basis of the representations created by the first two processes. This section also looks briefly at his remarks about the acquisition of the I-representation. Section 4 uses the model presented in the Logic lectures to explain how he would have seen normative principles attached to the concepts formed through the first three processes as being made explicit and tested. The last section argues for the indispensability of the use of the 'I-rule.'

2. Scrutinizing Sensations and Adding 'Transcendental Content'

The 'scrutinizing passage' on which I have placed considerable interpretive weight presents the understanding as searching through appearances with the aim of discovering some law in them (Chapter 7, section 4). Just before this discussion—at the dénouement of the A deduction—Kant explains that the understanding can find rules in appearances only because it has 'put them into' appearances:

> Hence the order and regularity in the appearances that we call **nature** are brought into them by ourselves; nor indeed could such order and regularity be found in appearances, had not we, or the nature of our mind put them into appearances originally. (A125)

In the *Critique*, he does not consider how this putting in might happen, but he does so in several Reflections that Carl regards as the earliest draft of the transcendental deduction (1989b, 4, see also his 1992, 63–73).

> In order for our sensations to acquire a determinate position* [Kant's note to the asterisk: a determinate position is different from an arbitrary one] in space and time they need a function among appearances; however, position in space and time is determined by proximity to other sensations in space and time; e.g. from the condition of my sensations that has something in common with the preceding ones another one follows . . .
> Through the determination of the logical position the representation acquires a function among the concepts, e.g., *antecedens, consequens*. Yet the sensitive function is the ground of the intellectual one. (R4629, 17.614, CNotes 148)

These notes include two points that we have encountered before. First, Kant asserts that spatial and temporal position is not simply sensed; it is determined by functions. Second, as in the *Duisburg Nachlaß*, he thinks that the sensitive functions are the grounds for intellectual ones. But he vacillates in the Reflections and maintains in the *Critique* that intellectual concepts determine sensitive syntheses.

Reflection R4629 seems to suggest that sensations are assigned positions in space and time by a logical function that locates them in logical 'space'—as, say, a consequent rather than an antecedent in a proposition. In the next Reflection but one, however, Kant offers the view that logical actions and the functions that guide them depend on a nonlogical or 'real' function:

> [1] Logical actions are *actus* by means of which we place and order the *data* for representations of things *respective* to each other. Representations thereby obtained are logical functions. [2] The real function consists in the way in which we posit a representation in and for itself; thus it is an action (*a priori*) which corresponds to every *dato* (*a posteriori*) and by means of which the latter becomes a concept. <u>These actions are the sources out of which the logical actions are possible.</u> From these arise all cognition: namely how we can grasp *data* and form something for ourselves that is called cognition. [3] In nature no *data* can come before us unless, when one perceives the laws therein, they correspond to the universal kinds according to which we posit something, because otherwise no laws would be observed, or any object whatsoever, but only confused internal alterations. [4] Therefore, since we can represent objects only by means of our alterations, insofar as they have in themselves something in conformity with our rules for positing and negating, the real functions are the ground of the possibility of the representation of things, and the logical functions are the ground of the possibility of judgments, and consequently of cognitions. (R4631, 17.615, CNotes 148–49, my numbering and underscoring)

This Reflection has some confusing elements. The part I label (1) seems to suggest that it is logical actions that somehow take data as inputs and produce representations of things as outputs. Yet the second part seems to say just the opposite: To move from data to representations it is necessary to have 'real' functions perform *a priori* actions on the sensory data, thereby producing conceptual representations. The part labeled (4) explains that the human ability to represent objects *via* the alterations that the objects cause in them depends on the fact that the alterations (sensations) have something in them that conforms to rules. Before post-Sellarsian hackles are raised at the suggestion that a sensation could 'conform' to a conceptual rule, one needs to consider the claims of segments (2) and (3), which imply that Kant understands that sensations or alterations in the mind caused by objects cannot be thought of as conceptual representations that agree with fail to agree with conceptual rules—unless they have first been changed by some *a priori* action.

Postponing the issue of concept formation until section 3, Kant's idea seems to be this:

> Alterations of the mind cannot stand in logical relations to each other except *via* the data they contain and only insofar as something in those data makes them suitable to be the sensory basis of one of the kinds of representations that the mind posits as representations of objects. When there is such an element in the data, then the mind posits a certain type of representation on the basis of the data. That representation is understood as real, as something that represents

objects. Through the *a priori* action, the representation comes to possess elements that enable it to stand in the rule-governed relations required by cognition.

Kant stakes out the same position in his handwritten logic notes:

> The real use [of understanding, as opposed to the formal] is determined with regard to the object, when it pertains to experience . . . But because it therefore pertains to things insofar as they are given through experience, it is predetermining, in that it contains the conditions under which all appearances can be cognized in accordance with a rule. For here it is first or for the first time [*zuerst*] necessary to bring every appearance under of title of the understanding: *realitas, substantia*. (R1608, 16.34–35, CNotes 33, amended translation)

How can the use of the understanding be both determined with regard to the object when it pertains to experience (when the object causes alterations in the mind) and also be predetermining? One way to understand his position is in terms of the familiar key and lock metaphor for the reception of sensory information. Experience or the stimulation of the senses is determining, because it provides the necessary keys and the different 'locks' of the mind can be unlocked only with the 'right' key. The understanding is predetermining in two senses. What sorts of keys are effective depends on the available locks—and, more important, what the key unlocks is a process whereby a representation is posited that is suitable as an instance of a category. The real function of creating this representation enables it to be subsumed under rules and (so also to stand in logical relations).

Kant's (unpublished) account of how the understanding puts its rules into appearances raises two large questions: What are the features of sensations that lead the understanding to posit a representation on their basis? (What is the key)? What is the nature of the representation posited? I start with the first. My initial presentation of the scrutinizing passage offered the following picture: The understanding scrutinizes appearances looking for instances of, for example, causal relations. When it finds a constant succession of C representations following B representations in presence of A representations, it brings the sequence under the causal principle of necessary or universal following and so takes the representations to be representations of a real state of affairs. This simple story cannot be correct, because the senses cannot register succession any more than they can register causal relations. So how is the process of 'putting' laws into appearances possible?

Kant does not say, maintaining only that there must be something in the data that makes them suitable to be brought under one category rather than another[4] and that the result is that the sensation leads to a representation that can be brought under a category. I don't think it is adequate to leave the matter there, because the problem raised is exactly the problem that leads philosophers and psychologists to dismiss the theory of the Second Analogy. The classic criticism is not that his view is psychologistic, but that it is psychologically implausible. He claims that cognizers can determine the succession of their mental states only by appealing to the causal relations among the events represented, but it seems impossible to make such appeal without knowing particular causal laws—which can only be learned through the observation of constant succession (e.g., Guyer, 1987, 257–58, Cheng, 1997, 368). The account seems caught in a vicious circularity and the same circle would doom the hypothesis of scrutinizing as thus far presented: Constant succession is an indicator of causal relations so representations manifesting this pattern are recognized as representations of real events—except that perceiving succession requires that the events represented be understood as standing in causal relations and that is impossible prior to the discovery of causal rules through observation of constant succession.

To break out of the circle, it is necessary to find a feature that can be sensed and that is a reliable indicator of the presence of succession and/or causal relations. Although Kant does not offer a hypothesis about such features for any categorial principle, he would have been aware of the obvious surrogate for causality. Motion, or real motion, was widely understood as a sign of causation—as in the case of the ship moving downstream, an example that was originally Newton's (1687/1934, 1:7). What is different now is that we have some understanding of how the brain detects motions. William Harper (1984) argues for the relevance of this work to the theory of the Second Analogy. As he explains, the nervous system is set up so that some higher level visual cells fire only if the lower level cells to which they are connected fire in a particular order, for example, n_1, n_2, n_3, whereas others fire only when the lower level cells fire in the opposite order. In effect, these assemblies allow the nervous system to register a point of light, say, moving from left to right or from right to left in the visual field (Harper, 1984); hence they also allow it to derive right position *after* left position or vice versa. Although the nervous system makes use of temporal relations—it is set up to take advantage of the time lag in which it receives different information—it does not detect time, but motion.[5]

A motion detection mechanism may seem to give the lie to Kant's claim for the necessity of causal relations in determining temporal position.[6] But it can be incorporated into his overall position. In Kant's view the presence of motion is not merely evidence of causation; the relationship is reciprocal. The presence of a cause is evidence for real motion.[7] A motion detector singles out sensory data that could be involved in three interconnected types of claims: a light *moves* from B to C, the light was at C *after* it was at B, the *succession* of the state of being at B to the state of being at C is *necessary* or rule-governed. It is thus an ideal candidate for the means by which the understanding scrutinizes sensations in order to find materials that are likely to stand in lawful relations. Those alterations that were unrelated to motion (or to other surrogates for categorial principles) would fail to be posited as representations.[8]

We may now turn to the second question: What is the nature of the representation that is posited by the understanding when presented with a sensation that includes a surrogate for one of the categories? Alternatively, what does the *a priori* act do in producing a representation that accords with a categorial principle? Staying with the central category of causation, the obvious suggestion is that it directs the imagination to form a perceptual representation of light at C *after* light at B, or of ice *after* water. This activity is presented by Kant as the *synthesis speciosa*, but it cannot be the only activity involved. It wouldn't capture his insistence in Reflection R1608 cited above that the representation be posited as an instance of a categorial principle (it is 'brought under' a categorial principle). To be an instance of causation, the succession of the representation of ice after that of water must be understood as necessary, as an instance of a universal rule. For a posited representation to meet this criterion a second phase of 'scrutiny' is needed—something like the scrutiny I originally presented. Tentatively posited representations of events will be surveyed to see if they contain similar successions of representations in the presence of another representation, say of A, and only those which do will be retained as representations of real events.[9] It is not obvious how to understand this second addition of content. One possibility is simply to think of the understanding as tagging those perceptual representations that potentially represent causal relations as requiring a particular kind of further scrutiny before being posited as representations of something real.

As Kant presents scrutinizing in the A deduction, it does not fully explain his striking claim that the understanding can find rules governing the objects and events that appear to humans only because it has put those rules into appearances. The double-scrutinizing process I describe on the basis of his notes (and some recent psychological results) would do the job. Representations posited as those of real events (and of properties and objects) would all be instances of categorial principles—even though they would also reflect differences in the alterations of the subject and so honor his Empiricist principles.

3. Forming Concepts and Acquiring the I-Representation

It's probably easiest to consider Kant's theory of concept formation in relation to Locke's. Locke understood concept formation traditionally, as involving operations of comparing, reflecting, and abstracting. He highlighted abstraction. Children manage to abstract from time, place, and distinguishing properties to form, for example, the general idea 'man' that can be denoted by the general concept 'man' (ECHU 3.3.9, 412).

Kant often presents the usual trio of operations. This passage comes in Jäsche's version of his *Logic*. I add a piece from Kant's original notes that Jäsche omits:

> The logical *actus* of the understanding, through which concepts are generated as regard to their form are:
>
> 1. *Comparison* of representations among one another in relation to the unity of consciousness.
> 2. *Reflection* as to how various representations can be conceived in one consciousness [as identical or not, (R2876, 16.555)]; and finally
> 3. *Abstraction* of everything in which the given representations differ. (9.94–95, CLogic 592, my interpolation from Kant's notes, Cf. R2853, 16.547, R2876, 16.555)

Yet he limits the role of abstraction. The so-called Blomberg Logic lectures report him as saying

> one cannot make any money by stealing it from someone, and in the same way one cannot make any concepts by abstraction. Through abstraction our representations are only made universal, as already indicated above. If we have no

representations of things, then no abstraction will be able to make concepts for us. (24.255, CLogic 204)

The idea seems to be that representations of things are not the result of an abstractive process, but its precondition. It might seem to follow that Kant takes concept formation to be solely a matter of comparing and reflecting.[10] This is Longuenesse's (1998) position, which I discuss in a brief Appendix to the chapter. In this section, I offer evidence that he holds that comparing requires 'given' representations of things, representations that have already been worked up from sensations through much processing.

In the Jäsche logic, Kant explains that comparison, reflection, and abstraction relate only to the *form* of concepts:

> Since universal logic abstracts from all content of cognition through concepts, or from all matter of thought, it can consider a concept only in respect of its form . . . Hence universal logic does not have to investigate the <u>source of concepts</u>, not how concepts arise as representations, but merely <u>how given representations</u> become concepts in thought; these concepts, moreover, may contain something that is derived from experience, or something invented, or <u>borrowed from the nature of the understanding</u> (9. 94, CLogic 591–92, cf. R2839, 16.540, R2851, 16.546, and, especially, R2856, 16.548, my underscoring)

I take the underscored texts to indicate that the logical operations do not produce content borrowed from the nature of the understanding, but take such content for their inputs.

The same point is made in an excerpt from his handwritten logic notes:

> 1. In logic we deal not with the origin of concepts, whether from the senses or other grounds . . . : that belongs to metaphysics.
> 2. Not with subjective rules (psychological laws . . .): how the understanding thinks, but with objective ones, how it should think, i.e., what is to be thought in accordance with the rules of the **understanding in general** . . .
> 3. Not with (cognitions insofar as they distinguish themselves by means of things) the relations and determinants of things, but with the relations of concepts . . .
>
> The relation which logic considers is that of comparison. <u>For it cannot be that of connection, neither objective, n.3, nor subjective, n.2.</u> (R1599, 16.30, CNotes 31, see also R2851, 16.546)

Kant distinguishes logic and its operation of comparison from metaphysics, representations of objects, and the operation of connection. He is explicit that logic does not deal with the cognition of things, which he relates in the last part of the text to objective connection.

According to student note-takers, Kant also firmly distinguished the logical operation of comparison from that of connecting representations in the 'Mrongovius' metaphysics lectures that are nearly contemporaneous with the A edition (1782–83):

The intellectual cognitive faculty is the faculty for thinking or for making concepts for ourselves . . . (. . . Here the question is whether we can arrive at general representations only [*nur*] through comparison. But [concerning the claim] that for us general concepts arise in comparison, it is rather the opposite that is correct. Thus we arrive at, e.g., the concept of a triangle not through comparison; rather, when we see one for the first time we are immediately aware that its magnitude does not restrict us at all from conferring the name triangle on all three-cornered figures which we see in the future.) (29.888, CMeta 256)

Upon the presentation of a triangle, the understanding recognizes it as falling under the triangle rule. It does not form the concept by comparing triangles; it compares the figure to the rule. Having seen the rule in the instance, a cognizer can see that it would apply equally to other figures with dissimilar magnitudes.

In section 2, we saw an analogous, though different relationship. Through the presence of a sensory surrogate, the understanding is alerted to the presence of a possible causal relation. It then directs the imagination to construct a suitable perceptual representation—of light at C following light at B—and also tags that representation as being posit-worthy only if scrutiny reveals it to be an instance of a general rule where one kind of representation always follows another in the presence of a third type of representation. In this way, the representation is brought under one of the categorial concepts. The categorial rule is not formed through comparison, but the instances are posited as real only if they accord with the rule. As in the case of mathematics, the rule is not made through comparison of instances. Nor in the case of concepts is the putative 'instance' compared to the rule. Rather, it is posited as a representation of an object or event in accord with the rule.

I've illustrated the double scrutinizing model only through the category of causation. Since concept formation is often illustrated through the properties of objects rather than through causes, it will be useful to consider a second case. Jäsche has Kant presenting concept formation through the example of comparing the trunks, leaves, and branches of different kinds of trees. A person is to compare her representations of a spruce, a willow, and a linden with respect to these properties (9. 94–95, CLog 592). But how did the representation of a linden tree, which includes representations of its trunk, branches, and leaves, come to be posited as a representation?

The linden representation would be posited through being brought under the concept of 'substance.' Kant's discussion of 'substance' focuses on its being that which perdures through change, but he also understands a substance as something that has different properties.[11] I will not speculate on a possible sensible surrogate for the relation of properties belonging to a common object.[12] In parallel with the case of causation, the idea would be that when sensations of the color and texture of a trunk indicate that these are sensations of properties of a common object, the understanding directs the imagination to construct a representation of the different properties 'on' a filled and bounded region of space. It would also tag the perceptual representation as requiring an additional scrutiny to be posit-worthy, but a scrutiny of a different sort from that used in cases of possible causes. Since any real property must belong with others to a common object, the representation of the cluster of properties will be taken to represent real properties only if scrutiny determines it to be an instance of a rule that representations of members of that cluster always occur together. Many things can be brown and furry, so the idea is not that each element of a cluster can only occur with every other element in that cluster. Rather, it is that the representation 'brown,' for example, is such that clusters in which it occurs must be multiply instantiated. Again, the transcendental principle that any property belongs with others to a substance would not arise through comparing one representation to another. Representations of possible properties would be posited only when some surrogate of co-belonging is registered and only if the perceptual representation of co-occurring properties is an instance of a rule.

On Kant's view, it is not just abstracting, but also the logical action of comparing that operates on 'given' complex representations—representations in which several representations are connected. If comparison did not operate on complex representations given to it from some other source, then it could not form concepts that have the requisite internal structure to permit rational cognition. Hence, he claims in R4631 (cited above, p. 220) that it is the actions of real functions that make logical actions possible. It is central to his view that concepts are general representations. They must be formed by comparison, because the understanding is looking for elements common to different representations. Having found common elements, it follows of necessity that everything classed under the concept possesses those elements. But the logical act of comparing succeeds only because real *a priori* acts have 'predetermined' the representations that are compared.[13] Further, the representations are not only guaranteed to possess commonalities, they are guaranteed to possess commonalities of particular forms. For representations brought under the titles of 'substance' and 'cause,' they will contain qualitatively identical co-occurring representations and qualitatively identical successions of representations. As a result, the concepts formed by comparing posited representations will be of objects with different properties and of states that follow one another in regular succession. More briefly, the act of comparing to find commonalities succeeds in part because the understanding has put laws into appearances.

The I-rule differs from categorial principles, because it does not enter human cognition through a scrutiny of the appearances of objects and events. It comes into play when a cognizer is conscious of combining some representations in others. In this case, the cognizer recognizes the connection and dependency of the combined state on others as an instance of the *a priori* I-rule. In the *Anthropology*, Kant offers a rare developmental hypothesis about when this capacity arises.

> It is curious that the child who already has a quite complete linguistic facility nevertheless first begins to speak in terms of 'I' quite late (perhaps even a year later), where for some time he spoke of himself in the third person (Charles wants to eat, leave, etc.), and that at the same time a light seems to dawn on him, if he begins to speak in terms of 'I': from that day he never turns back to his former way of speaking—Before he merely felt himself, now he thinks himself.—The explanation of this phenomenon may be quite difficult for anthropologists. (7.127, see also 25.473)

The claim that children have a reasonable vocabulary prior to acquiring the ability to think about themselves may seem to contradict the claim that concept use is possible only for those who can also see the connections among their representations as such. Since the latter thesis is central to the *Critique*, a more likely hypothesis is that he believes that tiny children do not use words as names for concepts. Rather, they merely associate certain sounds with objects and events that they have segregated from their mass of sensations. This hypothesis is consistent with his slightly later remark that very young children have no early memories, because in those pre-I times, they have only scattered perceptions that have not yet be brought under the concept of an object (7.128).

It is disappointing that Kant turns the task of explaining why I-users never revert to earlier forms over to anthropologists and perhaps even more disappointing that he contrasts thinking of oneself with feeling oneself—and leaves it at that. Although the cases of feeling and thinking are contrasted, it is possible to read him as suggesting that a feeling of self is something like a preliminary stage of thinking of self. This reading could be further supported by appealing to a note in the *Prolegomena* that connects the 'I' to a feeling of existence[14]:

> Were the representation of apperception, the 'I,' a concept through which something could be thought then it could be used as a predicate of other things, or could contain such predicates within itself. But it is nothing more than a feeling of existence without the least concept, and is only a representation of that to which all thinking stands in relation. (4.334n., C1781 125)

On the other hand, the context makes clear that Kant's primary purpose in bruiting the feeling possibility is to reinforce his view that the 'I' cannot be understood as a predicate. I don't know why he doesn't simply repeat the Paralogisms' claim that the representation 'I' is empty. In any case, it is hard to see how a 'feeling of self' could be a step in the direction of the 'I-think.' Some of his predecessors and contemporaries tried to solve the problem of personal identity through appeal to a common or fundamental feeling across different states. But this empirical surrogate for an 'I' could not capture the essential claim of his position that different representations are necessarily connected to a single self and there are no half-steps to necessity.

4. Making *A Priori* Principles Explicit and Testing Instances

At this point, we have some sense of why Kant believes that there are rules to be found in the representations through which objects and events appear to humans. To get a sense of how he might think these rules could become norms, we can turn to his treatment of the related issue of the rules of logic, although we'll also look at an important discussion of empirical cognition from the *Prolegomena*.

Kant distinguishes between natural logic and scientific logic. Scientific logic is similar to transcendental philosophy and to grammar. Transcendental philosophy is concerned only with principles that are necessary for the possibility of any cognition of objects, grammar with principles necessary for any language, and scientific logic with principles necessary for any thinking at all (24.792–93, CLog 253, 24.693, CLog

431, 9.11, CLog 527). In characterizing natural logic, he refers to both healthy (*gesund*) and common (*gemein*) understanding (*Verstand*) and reason (*Vernunft*) (e.g., 24.18–19, CLog 6–7). There seems to be no difference between these terms except emphasis. A 'healthy' reason is one that has been properly exercised and is not corrupted; a 'common' reason is one that is shared by all. Since the main contrast is with an understanding or reason that is specifically applied to the task of determining its own rules, and so has the skills and knowledge of the trained logician or grammarian, I use the term 'ordinary' to mark the other half of the contrast. An 'ordinary' understanding or reason is a capacity that is shared by all and that has not been corrupted.

In his handwritten logic notes, Kant criticizes professional logicians for misunderstanding their lay brethren:

> All application of the power of understanding without rules is faulty [or insufficient, *Mangelhaft*], (16.11)

> One is not allowed to object that one can use his reason correctly but without rules in ordinary cognition. That is the word from learned cognition, i. e., that which is somewhat removed from everyday experience (R1572, 16.11)

The latter passage is easier to understand if we consider Kant's frequent distinction between two sorts of rules, instructions (*Vorschriften*) that must be learned and rules according to which the mind or one of its faculties operates without explicit knowledge of the rule (e.g., R1573, 16.13, R1579, 16.17, 19). His criticism is that from the point of view of logicians (or grammarians) ordinary people do not think according to rules, because they do not know the laws of logic or grammar. In fact, however, like Molière's nobleman, they speak in prose (or think) in conformity with rules without explicit knowledge of them (R1620, 16.39).

In the so-called Vienna Logic lectures, which are from the early 1780s, Kant reportedly repeats the point that ordinary cognizers think in conformity with rules:

> every man observes the rules before he can reduce them to formulas. Gradually, however, he attends to what he does. (24.791, CLog 252)

By observing the rules, he means both that performance follows rules and that mistakes in particular cases, caused perhaps by tiredness or inattention, can be caught and corrected. However, he also thinks that 'lay' logicians gradually come to have a more explicit understanding of what they are doing.

Kant sees ordinary cognizers not only as using rules, but as evaluating them through 'common' as opposed to real 'scientific' logic. Despite their important differences, both logics must begin with use:

> Logic is necessarily derived from use, because it contains the first actions of the understanding and we could not think these actions unless we employed [*brauchen*] the understanding in acts (in concrete, examples), this [employment] however could not be learned without exercise and thus these actions would be as little known as speech [without its exercise]. (R1602, 16.31–32)

Although the passage is cryptic and choppy, the point seems reasonably clear: If the mind did not think, combine representational materials, then it would not be a fit subject for any sort of logic, because there would be no judgmental or inferential acts to study. In a similar way, a mind that had the capacity for speech, but no actual speech, would offer no materials for grammarians to analyze.

We know, at least at one level of description, how scientific logic is to proceed from these data. It must determine those rules without which no thought is possible. Kant explains in some detail how 'natural' logic proceeds from the data of judgments and inferences. The ordinary person abstracts his rules from his use of them in particular cases.

> The faculty of universal cognition . . . is the understanding. If the universal cognition is borrowed from particulars, it is ordinary understanding, ordinary sense . . . Universal *in concreto* . . . In [this] case, one acts according to rules of which he is not conscious, and the rules are abstracted from use (natural use of rules). (R1579, 16.18).

> Ordinary understanding is the faculty of judging according to laws of experience or from cognition *in concreto* to that *in abstracto* or to advance from the particular to the universal. (R1575, 16.14)

Because ordinary cognizers tacitly use rules in making judgments or applying concepts and because they have the capacity to recognize particulars as instances of general rules, they can make the rules that they use explicit. Further, since Kant takes empirical concepts to be particular specifications of categorial rules (A126), any judgment will also exemplify some categorial principle. Because ordinary reason is able to see particulars as instances of general rules, it could, in principle, abstract both empirical and *a priori* rules from its natural use.

In a passage from the *Prolegomena*, Kant explains why things do not go in exactly this way.

> What is **ordinary understanding**? It is the faculty of cognition and of the use of rules *in concreto*, as distinguished from **speculative understanding**, which is the faculty of cognition of rules *in abstracto*. The ordinary understanding will then hardly be able to understand the rule: that everything that happens is determined by its cause, and it will never be able to have insight into it in such a general way. It therefore demands an example from experience, and when it hears that this rule means nothing other than what it has always thought when a windowpane had broken or a household article had disappeared, it then understands the principle and grants it. Ordinary understanding therefore has no use further than the extent to which it can see its rules confirmed [*bestätigt*] in experience (although these rules are actually present in it *a priori*); consequently to have insight into these rules *a priori* and independently of experience falls to the speculative understanding, and lies completely beyond the horizon of the ordinary understanding. (4.369, C1781 158)

Ordinary understanding is not adept in handling highly abstract principles or in handling any principles abstractly. Ordinary cognizers would not normally extract such high level principles as the categorial ones. Even when presented with the determinist principle, ordinary understanding will move to something more specific, a principle such as 'a heavy impinging object always causes a window to break' or, perhaps, 'someone always causes a household item to be removed.' These particular causal rules are confirmed by partial enumeration. Such methods could never prove the universality or necessity of particular causal rules, let alone prove the abstract causal principle. Nonetheless, they provide some confirmation for both.

The *Prolegomena* passage is interesting, because even when Kant's purpose is to emphasize the weakness of the methods of ordinary understanding in relation to transcendental philosophy and to castigate his colleagues for thinking that the former sort of 'proof' could be adequate to defang Humean skepticism, he gives ordinary understanding its due.[15] Ordinary people do not operate blindly by the *a priori* principle of causation; they have some grip on the abstract principle through particular causal laws and can partially confirm it and them through examples. Presumably the same would go for other categorial principles and the I-rule.

Having been confirmed, more particular principles become norms of ordinary cognition. As opposed to scientific logic, which produces an organon, the rules of common logic are merely a discipline, explicit reminders of rules one already knows implicitly:

> The rules of common cognition serve only as a discipline, to make one attentive to everything in rules that one already knows, and to guard against eluding these. (R1579, 16.19)

Having consciously extracted the rule that 'someone always causes a household item to move,' for example, I can remind myself *not* to believe that something has disappeared if I realize that it was impossible for anyone to have removed it. I should opt instead for faulty memory, perception, or the like. Since the object is not present at the remembered location and couldn't have been taken, then it couldn't have been there in the first place.

Kant describes further means by which abstracted rules of judgment are tested. In the *Logic*, he takes up the theme of the criteria of truth through which a judgment is tested, not for its material truth, but for its possibility of being true. These include the principle of noncontradiction, the law of the excluded middle, and the principle of sufficient reason. The latter is further explicated as testing a cognition to determine if it is logically grounded, that is,

> if it (a) it has grounds and (b) does not have false consequences ...
>
> From the truth of the consequences we may infer the truth of the cognition as ground, but only negatively: if one false consequence flows from a cognition, then the cognition is false. (9.51–52, cf. R2178, 16.260)

He is not explicit that these tests are performed by ordinary understanding in the passage, but it seems fairly clear that we are not dealing with logical specialists. These are means of testing individual cognitions, not principles of logic; and he describes the logic of ordinary understanding as a 'discipline' and a 'critique'; by contrast, scientific logic is 'doctrinal' or an 'organon' (R1579, 16.18, 19), that is, a study that leads to a set of principles.

Although Kant makes a distinction in kind between natural and scientific logic, he does not draw any limit for the former. Jäsche portrays him as uncertain about the line between the ordinary and scientific uses of the understanding.[16]

> There is some difficulty in determining where the **ordinary** use of the understanding ends and the **speculative** begins, or where the ordinary cognition of reason becomes philosophy.
>
> Nevertheless there is a rather distinguishing mark here, namely the following:
>
> Cognition of the universal *in abstracto* is **speculative** cognition, cognition of the universal *in concreto* is **ordinary** cognition. Philosophical cognition is speculative cognition of reason, and thus it begins where the ordinary use of reason starts to make attempts at cognition of the universal *in abstracto*. (9.27, CLog 539–40)

Both the first paragraph and the curious claim in the third that the line comes where ordinary reason *starts* to try to cognize the universal *in abstracto* suggest that there is some vagueness here. The contribution of the middle paragraph is equally puzzling. How can something be somewhat (*ziemlich*) of a distinguishing mark?

Kant's position is not as contorted as Jäsche's presentation suggests. Since ordinary understanding can see the universal in the particular and so can abstract rules, there is no determinate limit to how far this activity could go. Ordinary cognizers could evaluate particular causal rules, the general causal principle, and formal logical principles. The difference in kind comes in how the resulting principle is treated. Is it then tested and confirmed in *concreto*, in particulars, or is there an attempt at a proof of it in its full generality? The latter sort of proof is beyond the abilities of laymen, so the ultimate justification of categorial principles must rest on the arguments of experts. On the other hand, ordinary understanding need not be blind to its principles at any level, except the earliest where the principles by which it scrutinizes sensations and adds transcendental content to representations are unconscious. For the principles associated with concepts, laymen can make them explicit, appreciate their role as principles and engage in a limiting kind of testing and confirmation of them.

5. Normativity and the I-Rule

At this point, I hope it is clear how *a priori* principles could come to be used as cognitive norms—and that Kant would have seen this development as possible. Still, it is reasonable to complain that I have not adequately defended his view: He holds that cognitive rules and so norms must be *a priori*. He would also argue that the most basic rules that make perception and judgment possible must be *a priori*.

I have not tried to defend Kant's entire epistemological project, but only his claims about the status and function of the 'I-think,' and that is also my goal here. Whatever the fate of his categorial principles as standards of observation, he is correct that the I-rule must be an *a priori* norm for cognition. This can be shown by exactly the same considerations that demonstrate the necessity of an *a priori* representation 'I-think' for RE cognition.

The rules associated with concepts are tacit norms for the concepts' use. An RE cognizer knows the reason for her judgment, both the rule and the partial representations. She knows that these are the reasons and, through her conscious synthesizing, knows that the judgment was produced through a mental act that took account of these reasons. Hence she recognizes these representations as necessarily connected and so as falling under the I-rule.

Now consider a case where a cognizer makes explicit use of a cognitive norm, say the norm that 'if a household item has disappeared, then someone has removed it.' Suppose that only Fritz was in a position to remove the item and the cognizer judges that he did so. For the norm to function as such, she must know that the norm is a partial ground of her cognition, and that her judgment 'Fritz took it' was produced through a mental act that took account of that norm (as well as other factors). In the absence of these conditions, she would not be using the principle normatively or engaging in RE judging. It is not enough that her mental behavior is in accord with a standard—as a pigeon's would be that pecked at the size and shade of yellow disk on which it had been trained; nor is it enough for her to recognize her judgment, 'Fritz did it,' as an instance of the normative principle. She must be aware of judging 'Fritz did it' on the basis of the norm and other information. In that case, however, she would recognize the judgment as dependent on her representing (thinking) of the norm. She would also recognize that representing (thinking) of a norm could be understood as such—as thinking of a *norm* only insofar as it led to judgments that depended on it. In short, a cognizer can use a principle normatively only if her thinking of, or representing, the norm and her judgment are also understood as necessarily connected and so as instances of the I-rule.

Since the I-rule asserts a necessary connection, it could not be learned through empirical observation. What the preceding argument shows is that it could not be acquired through enculturation either. Uninitiated members of a society could not be taught to make normative use of the 'I-rule,' because they could not use any rule normatively unless they already implicitly grasped the I-rule. The remaining possibility is that it is acquired *a priori*. For this reason, Kant's argument for the necessary conditions for RE shows something very interesting about the sources of normativity: The *a priori* representation 'I-think' must be the vehicle not just of concepts but of any cognitive norms.

I conclude with a final piece of defense. Whatever the character of the arguments, it may seem that the conclusion that ordinary cognizers operate with an *a priori* I-rule is too fantastical to be believed. It may seem to be just another episode in the intellectualist myths put about by Rationalist epistemologists. To push back against this reaction, I offer three mundane pieces of evidence.

The first is the familiar reaction of students to Locke's prince and cobbler case. As Locke imagined, those presented with the case see immediately that the mental states of the cobbler-body-prince-mind person do not depend on the mental states of the cobbler-body person before the switch—and that that is the basis of their denying copersonality (when they do). A more recent example of this usually tacit norm is offered by the 1987 movie *Broadcast News*. An airheaded newscaster gets ahead, because an earpiece feed from seasoned journalists enables him to ask clever questions. The plot succeeds only because the average moviegoing audience—a reasonably low bar—understands immediately that, given their lack of dependence on his earlier mental states, the questions are not his. Finally, consider an eyewitness in a trial. If pressed to explain why he claims that Lefty was the assailant, he might respond, 'I seen him with my own eyes.' Presumably even the most intrepid cross-examiner would not press on and ask whether the witness judged Lefty to be the perpetrator, *because* he saw him with his own eyes. To concede that the witness is truthful in what he claims to see and honest in expressing his judgment, and yet to question any relation of dependence between perception and the judgment would immediately be recognized as an accusation of mental incompetence. But what these simple examples show is that anyone who is mentally competent understands the rational dependence of human judgments on other mental states.

Appendix to Chapter 13

Longuenesse on Concept Formation

In *Kant and the Capacity to Judge* Béatrice Longuenesse offers a sophisticated account of concept formation and Kantian cognition that focuses on the operations of comparing, reflecting, and abstracting. Longuenesse's analysis is important in its own right and it provides a useful contrast to mine.

Comparing, reflecting, and abstracting were widely regarded as activities of the understanding,[1] so it is plausible to think that when Kant claimed in the Introduction to the *Critique* that the receipt of sensory data prompted the understanding to the activity of 'comparing,' 'connecting,' and 'separating' representations, he was referring to these familiar logical operations (B1). Further the Jäsche Logic passage cited in the main portion of the chapter (p. 223), the passage linking the unity of consciousness to the operations of comparing and reflecting, can be read as a further spelling out of a cryptic and well-known claim from the B deduction's discussion of judgment (§19). If I distinguish the reference of given cognitions in a judgment from the relations engendered by the reproductive imagination:

> I find that a judgment is nothing but a way of bringing given cognitions to the objective unity to apperception. (B141)

How given cognitions are brought to the objective unity of apperception would be by comparing and reflecting on representations (Longuenesse, 1998, 84ff.).

Longuenesse makes several claims about the advantages of seeing the categories through the logical forms of judgment and the operations of comparing and reflecting:

> If we disregard the priority of the logical forms of judgments over the categories, Kant's whole argument is rendered incomprehensible. (1998, 78)

> So, far from determining the form of judgment, each category, on the contrary, derives its meaning from its relation to the corresponding logical form. (1998, 79)

> It is only by paying sufficient attention to the acts of comparison in judgment that one can hope to understand how judgments formed by comparison of representations may eventually lead to the subsumption of appearances under categories. (1998, 123)

With regard to the first and third advantages, the scrutiny model gives Kant a comprehensible argument for the conclusion that appearances can always be subsumed under the categories.

Longuenesse elaborates the standard logical comparison picture in two important ways. Although Kant is explicit only about comparison in regard to sameness and difference and agreement and disagreement, she appeals to then contemporary logical work to suggest a third type of comparison, comparison in relation to external or internal 'condition.'[2] Wolff had differentiated categorical from hypothetical judgments on the ground that in the former, the condition under which the predicate can be asserted lies within the subject whereas in hypothetical judgments, the condition must be added (1998, 99). She reads Kant's discussion of the impossibility of converting hypothetical judgments into categorical ones (as Wolff tried to do) as indicating that he took these judgments to be importantly different, because

> one form is essentially different from the other *with regard to the act of* thinking. (1998, 102)

Clearly Kant thought that these forms were not convertible:

> The two [categorical and hypothetical judgments] are wholly different from one another as to their nature. In categorical judgments nothing is problematic, rather, everything is assertoric, but in hypotheticals only *consequentia* are assertoric. In the latter I can thus connect two false judgments with one another, for here it is only a matter of the correctness of the connection—the form of the *consequentia* on which the logical truth of these judgments rests. There is an essential difference between the two propositions, All bodies are divisible, and, If all bodies are composite, then they are divisible. In the former proposition I maintain the thing directly, in the latter only under the condition expressed problematically. (9.105–6, CLog 601–2)

Although Kant does not mention acts of thinking, Longuenesse's interpretation is plausible, because he seems to be indicating different ways of thinking about or relating the elements in a judgment.

My difficulty with Longuenesse's interpretation is that if this is how Kant understands the relation between inner and outer conditions, then he could not have seen these judgmental forms as providing meaning to the categories. As Guyer has emphasized, Kant went to great effort to distinguish logical and real relations throughout his career. In particular, he always took the relation of real connection to be central to causal thinking (187, 99). Even if judgers think about a predicate as assertable of a subject only problematically, only under an added condition that lies outside the subject concept, that in no way implies that they are envisioning the state characterized by the predicate as really dependent on the state characterized in the added condition. His illustrative example is not one of causation, but of an additional attribute for a substance, that of being composite.

Longuenesse makes a second addition to the logical comparison account. She takes Kant to understand the comparison of concepts (not just as)

> *comparison in the narrow sense*, [but also] *logical comparison in the broad sense*, a comparison of *concepts* (and thus a *logical* comparison), but under sensible conditions. (1998, 127)

In particular, she thinks that this comparison takes place in relation to the schemata by which images of sensible objects are synthesized (1998, 127). Kant asserts that cognizers bring objects under common concepts such as 'man' not by comparing their images of, for example, thin and fat men, but by comparing their activities of bringing different representational elements to an image (A140–41/B180). Longuenesse's idea is that comparing is done in part through comparing the image forming processes of schematizing. She maintains further that the logical comparison of representations in relation to same or different—or agreement or disagreement—or inner or outer conditions—depends on the sort of schematizing to which the data are amenable.

The differences between Longuenesse's account and mine may seem slight, because both add an essential process to the mere or narrow comparison of ideas. In particular, both stress that concept formation does not float free of sensory materials. But the similarity would be genuine only if Longuenesse sees the schematizing processes as involving some type of scrutiny of sensory materials, a scrutiny that looked for indicators of potential instances of a categorial principle. And that assumption would be alien to the thrust of her argument that the meaning of the categories derives from the forms of judgment.[3] My view is the exact opposite. Kant regarded transcendental logic as a necessary supplement to general logic, in part because it explained how logic was possible.[4] It also explains why a particular form of judgment should be used in relation to particular representations:

> The only thing that I still want to do before we start is to **explicate the categories**: they are concepts of an object as such whereby the object's intuition is regarded as **determined** in regard of one of the **logical functions** in judging. Thus the function of the **categorical** judgment—e.g., All bodies are divisible—is that of the relation of subject to predicate. But the understanding's merely logical use left undetermined to which of the two concepts we want to give the function of the subject, and to which the function of the predicate. For we can also say, Something divisible is a body. If, on the other hand, I bring the concept of a body under the category of substance, then through this category is determined the fact that the body's empirical intuition in experience must be considered always as subject only, never as predicate. And similarly in all the remaining categories. (B128–29, my underscoring)

I agree with Longuenesse that Kant's concern is not surface grammar (which can take either form), but deep logical form (1998, 79n.). But I take his point to be that the deep logical form of categorial attribution of predicate to subject—where the subject concept contains the condition for asserting the predicate—is uniquely appropriate (determined) in some cases, because the representations can be understood as representing instances of the principle that properties belong together in substances. The hypothetical form is uniquely appropriate to other judgments, because the representations involved can be understood as representing instances of the causal principle. Where Longuenesse has the logical forms of judgment bringing intuitions in relation to categories, the highlighted parts of this passage relate intuitions to the logical forms of judgment through the concepts of an object as such, through the categories.[5]

The idea that the categories are not derived from logical forms, but make logic possible is also asserted in passing in the letter of May 26, 1789, to Herz cited in Chapter 9. There Kant characterizes the categories as

> functions of the understanding ... out of which logic develops. (11.51)

These texts and the passages cited in section 3 of the main portion of this chapter present a fairly clear picture: The functions of the understanding are not merely logical functions, but rules for positing representations as representations of things that thereby make cognition and logic possible.

14

Is Kant's Thinker (as Such) a Free and Responsible Agent?

1. Introduction

Having defended Kant's theory against two familiar and potentially devastating objections, I turn to its implications for some issues that are the focus of much contemporary work. Chapter 15 sketches several areas where his analyses have the potential to change the direction of current thinking. Perhaps perversely, I begin my account of the impact of his investigations on the twenty-first-century philosophical scene with a brief discussion of a negative case.

At least for Kant's mature moral theory, the answer to my chapter title question is obvious: No. In the *Metaphysics of Morals* (1798) he presents 'freedom' as the capacity of the moral law to determine the faculty of choice (6.225, CPract 380). Yet he is explicit in *Religion within the Bounds of Mere Reason* (1793) that

> From [the fact] that a being has reason it does not at all follow—at least as far as we can see—that this reason contains the faculty [*Vermögen*] to determine the faculty of choice unconditionally through the mere representation of the qualifications of its maxim for universal legislation. (6.26n, CRel 74)[1]

Prima facie RE cognition and so the unity of apperception require only basic rationality, so the issue seems closed.

Although I argue that that verdict is also correct on further inspection, the issue is complicated by three factors. First Kant also defines 'freedom' as the ability to originate a causal chain. Second, in the Preface to the *Groundwork of the Metaphysics of Morals*, he presents speculative or theoretical reason, the faculty involved in cognition, and practical reason, the faculty involved in action, as one and the same:

> A critique of practical reason, if it is to be complete, requires, on my view, that we should be able at the same time to show the unity of practical and theoretical

reason in a common principle, since in the end there can only be one and the same reason. (4.391)

This comment has, I believe, misled scholars into assimilating his views about the spontaneity of theoretical reason to the freedom involved in the exercise of practical reason. Further, this interpretive line can be supported by other important passages that seem to link the operation of theoretical and practical reason. Given the tight connection between one definition of freedom and the moral law, the obvious way to develop the assimilation has been in terms of the other definition: Theoretical and practical reason are alike in requiring absolute or transcendental freedom, the ability to initiate a causal sequence.

The third factor complicating the relations between Kant's views of theoretical and practical reason is the theme of the preceding chapter. He regards cognition as permeated by norms. Reading his commitment to the normativity of cognition in light of passages linking the exercise of theoretical and practical reason leads to a further interpretive hypothesis: The normativity of cognition must, in his view, be like that of morality in requiring absolute freedom.

The assimilation can be invoked in both directions. Allison has argued that Kant's unattractive views about the absolute spontaneity required for moral responsibility can be made more palatable by seeing them in light of his claims for the necessary spontaneity of theoretical reason:

> In order to understand Kant's seemingly gratuitous insistence on a merely intelligible moment of spontaneity in the conception of rational agency, we must look not to his moral theory or motivational psychology but rather to his views on the spontaneity of the understanding and reason in their epistemic functions. (1990, 36)

From the other direction Akeel Bilgrami appeals to Kant to support his view that thought must be understood as enjoying a similar freedom to that of action:

> Kant himself is fairly explicit that freedom is a necessary condition for the having of thoughts and not just for actions; that it pervades judgment in the realm of the theoretical . . . as well as the practical. (2006, 170)

Allison has tried to capture the transcendental freedom that he sees as part of Kant's theory of cognition in his 'taking as' account of judging. Chapter 10 presented one formulation of his 'taking as' analysis; here I offer a slightly different one to remind readers of the view:

> A helpful way of explicating what Kant means by the spontaneity of the understanding in its judgmental activity (epistemic spontaneity) is to consider judgment as the activity of 'taking as,' or, more precisely, of taking something as a such and such . . . the key point, is that the activity of 'taking as' is constitutive of judgment . . . we cannot represent to ourselves an x as F without not only doing it, that is, consciously taking it as such, but without also in some sense

'knowing what one is doing.' This peculiar mode of cognitive self-awareness is what Kant terms 'apperception.' As such, it is not another thing that one does when one judges (a kind of second-order knowing that one is knowing); it is rather an inseparable component of the first-order activity itself. (1990, 37)

Much of this account seems both right and faithful to Kant. Judging requires a self-conscious act in which the cognizer appreciates his reasons or grounds for the judgment as such. If he didn't, then he couldn't make the judgment. What is unclear is why this act should be described in terms of absolute spontaneity, the beginning of a new causal chain.

Allison's idea seems to be that rules connected to concepts function as norms for cognizers, because they freely choose to apply them—or not. In this way, cognitive norms would be parallel to the subjective principles of actions, or maxims, that agents freely incorporate into their practical thinking and use in the practical sphere. In Chapter 10, I criticized the 'taking-as' account on the basis of my analysis of Kant's argument for apperception. Since RE cognizers must understand combination as such, they must be able to see different mental states as necessarily connected with each other. In the preceding chapter, I added to that analysis by noting that they must also see their representations of norms as necessarily connected to their RE judgments. Given these results, an RE cognizer could not understand her judgment as the beginning of a new causal chain—because she must see it as dependent on her representations of rules and on other representations. Nor could she see her adoption of a normative standard (a conceptual rule) as a new beginning—since that, too, should be rational and so based on the kinds of tests for the adequacy of concepts that Kant details (9.51–52, B113–15). As far as I can see, Allison's reading of Kant on the spontaneity of judgment is thus inconsistent with the central argument of the transcendental deduction, the argument that the RE cognition and the unity of apperception mutually require each other.

On the other hand, there are a number of texts that lend credence to Allison's view and, more generally, to the assimilation of Kant's theory of the thinker to his theory of moral agency. My goal in the chapter is to look at some key supporting texts so that we may sort out the similarities and differences in his views of cognitive and moral subjects. Although I criticize Bilgrami's and Allison's assimilations, it will be clear below that the fault is not theirs, but his. The two definitions of 'freedom' are symptoms of an evident tension in Kant's position between the perceived need to tie morality to the moral law and the perceived need to tie it to absolute responsibility. In the passages suggesting the unity of operation of theoretical and practical reason, he is struggling to bring both factors under the banner of practical reason. When he finally accepts that he can handle the dual anchors of his moral position only by appealing to two faculties, practical reason and an absolutely free faculty of choice,[2] the previously hazy differences between his theories of the thinker and of the moral agent become stark enough for all to see.

From the perspective of Kant's mature moral theory, recent attempts to view cognitive agents as similar in important ways to moral agents are mistaken. I do not offer this doctrine as a contribution to current debates, since that would require a defense of his moral theory rather than of his cognitive one. I try to show only that his work on cognition should not be understood as supporting the contemporary similarity thesis.

2. Texts Linking Theoretical and Practical Reason

I start with Bilgrami's evidence for assimilating Kant's epistemic views and his ethical ones. His aim is not interpretation, but to find historical antecedents of his position that cognition must be understood from a first person point of view of agency (2006, 170). He appeals to two passages, one from the *Critique of Practical Reason* and one from the *Groundwork*. The Second Critique passage offers Kant's slightly defensive account of the relation between the theories of first two critiques.

> Accordingly, considerations of this kind which are once more directed to the concept of freedom in the practical use of pure reason, must not be regarded as an interpolation serving only to fill up the gaps in the critical system of speculative reason (<u>for this is for its own purposes complete</u>) . . . This remark applies especially to the concept of freedom, respecting which one cannot but observe with surprise that so many boast of being able to understand it quite well and to explain its possibility, while they regard it only psychologically, whereas if they had studied it in a transcendental point of view, they must have recognized that it is not only **indispensable** as a problematic concept, in the complete use of speculative reason [as well as completely **incomprehensible**]. (5.7, CPract 142, cited in Bilgrami, 170–71, my addition [in square brackets] from the original text, my underscoring)

This passage seems to me to assert the opposite of Bilgrami's thesis that Kant regards the concept or even the idea of freedom as necessary for thought. In the text I underscore, Kant denies that the idea of freedom is needed to fill gaps in his critical system of speculative reason. Presumably this is because he believes that he has accomplished his goals of explaining the possibility of empirical cognition and of diagnosing metaphysical error without invoking this notion. Why then is the concept of freedom indispensable in the complete use of speculative reason? A transcendental perspective looks at the sources of cognition. It reveals that reason looks for ever higher causes, a regress that could be halted only with the discovery of a cause that is not caused, but is an original beginning. The concept of freedom is indispensable in the literal sense that it is needed to characterize the strivings of reason that are the source of metaphysical error. What the First Critique left open was not the possibility of a further necessary condition for empirical cognition, but a defense of the idea of freedom as something other than a necessary element in the description of error. It did not answer the gaping question of why reason not only encourages humans to look for ever deeper explanations, but pushes them to look beyond the bounds of empirical cognition. This text echoes a passage from the First Critique already cited Chapter 4: Since none of the three cardinal propositions about the existence of God, the immortality of the soul, and the freedom of the will is necessary for **knowledge** [yet the propositions] . . . are nonetheless urgently commended to us by our reason, then—I suppose—their importance will properly have to concern the **practical**. (A799–800/B827–28)

In both passages, Kant reminds the reader of his basic strategy of limiting cognition, so that it had no say on the matters of God, freedom, and immortality. Neither cognition nor its explanation sheds any light on a positive understanding of these ideas (insofar as God is understood as having moral qualities[3]); hence their study should be shifted from the realm of speculative cognition to that of the practical.

The passage that Bilgrami cites from the *Groundwork* is the crucial discussion of 'thinking and acting under the idea of freedom' and is much more helpful in supporting his assimilation of Kant's theory of thought to his theory of action. Allison also appeals to this material to support his claims about absolute spontaneity in cognition (1996, 128) as well as to an important passage from the discussion of the Third Antinomy (1983, 322).[4] I've already touched on the latter passage in Chapter 4 in disputing Ameriks's view that Kant was ambivalent about whether the spontaneity of thought could establish transcendental freedom in the A edition. Here I take a much closer look at it. Although there are important differences between the *Groundwork* and Third Antinomy texts, it will be both efficient and illuminating to discuss them together.[5]

Groundwork:

1. Now, one cannot possibly think of a reason that would consciously receive direction from any other quarter in regard to its judgments, since the subject would then attribute the determination of his judgment not to his reason but to impulse.
2. Reason must regard itself as the author [*Urheber*] of its principles independently of alien influences. (4.448, CPract 96, my numbering)

Third Antinomy:

1. Only a human being, who cognizes all the rest of nature only through the senses, also cognizes himself through pure apperception and certainly in acts and inner determinations, which he cannot count among the impressions of the senses. He is indeed to himself, one part phenomenon, but another part a purely intelligible object, [and the latter] in respect of certain faculties, because the action of these cannot be counted among the receptive [capacities] of sensibility. We call these faculties understanding and reason. Reason, above all, is quite particularly distinguished from all empirically conditioned abilities, because it examines its objects merely according to ideas and according to these ideas determines the understanding, which then makes an empirical use of its own (although likewise pure) concepts.
3. Now, that this reason has causality, or that we at least conceive such a causality in it, is evident from the **imperatives**, which in all that is practical we impose as rules on the executing [*ausübende*] powers. The **ought** expresses a kind of necessity and connection with grounds that does not otherwise occur in all of nature.

2. Now this **ought** expresses a possible action, whose ground is nothing but a mere concept, whereas the ground of a mere action of nature must always be an appearance . . . Whether the object is one of mere sensibility (the agreeable) or even of pure reason (the good), reason does not yield to the empirically given ground and does not follow the order of things as they exhibit themselves in appearance, but with complete spontaneity makes for itself an order of its own according to ideas. (A546–48/B574–76, my numbering)

I number the elements of the Antinomy passage out of order, because its middle portion has no parallel in the *Groundwork* discussion. I return to it below.

Let's start with the first section of the *Groundwork* passage. Although neither Allison nor Bilgrami includes this material, the lead-in to the cited passage concerns practical reason:

In such a being we think of a reason that is practical, that is, has causality with respect to its objects. (4.448, CPract 96)

So does the subsequent text:

Consequently, as practical reason or as the will of a rational being it must be regarded of itself as free, that is, the will of such a being cannot be a will of its own except under the idea of freedom, and such a will must in a practical respect thus be attributed to every rational being. (4.448, CPract 96)

So there is some reason to believe that the topic is limited to practical reason. Still, the argument could be that practical reason has these features because reason *simpliciter* does.

Proceeding on the latter assumption, the claim is that it is impossible to understand thought (or reasoning) that is directed from the outside as thought (or reasoning). If an alien thought is introduced (perhaps a suggestion from a colleague), then that thought could be evaluated by one's understanding and/or reason and adopted or rejected. That would still be thinking. What Kant seems to regard as impossible as thinking is being conscious of an impulse and then conscious that that impulse has produced another mental state, say, a judgment. Against the background of the transcendental deduction, it is clear why he would hold this view. His theory is that judging requires consciousness of synthesis. Bilgrami is right that Kant dismisses this sort of passive watching of mental states as thinking exactly because the resulting 'thought' has no 'I' attached to it. And, it has no I attached, because of the passivity, because there was no self-conscious act of thinking. But none of this implies that thinking is the beginning of a new causal chain and so free in (either) sense required for moral responsibility.

Let's turn to section 1 of the Third Antinomy passage. It refers to 'acts' and 'determinations' that the subject cognizes, and that he cannot reckon as belonging to the senses. We have already seen this view in the passage where Kant contrasts inner sense and apperception. There he describes the understanding as being conscious 'of' or 'in' its act of combining (B153). The difference between the prepositions is extremely consequential. If this nonsensible awareness is meant to be a second inner sense that records acts of combining, rather than an active conscious faculty of combining, then his cognitive theory falls apart. For it is only through performing self-conscious acts of combination that a cognizer recognizes herself as a unity and as an intelligence. By contrast, she cannot be aware of herself as an intelligible creature operating as the beginning of a causal chain or she would have knowledge of transcendental freedom. At the end of the discussion Kant appends final clarificatory paragraph explicitly denying the latter implication:

> It must be noted carefully that by this contemplation we have not sought to establish the **actuality** of freedom as one of the powers containing the cause of the appearances of our world of sense (A558/B586, also cited in Chapter 4)

To avoid reading this passage in such a way that it offers a direct argument from cognition to freedom—thus giving the lie to Kant's claim that the *Critique* shows that the proper realm of 'freedom' is the practical—it should be understood as asserting just what the earlier discussion asserted. Cognizers are conscious in synthesizing representations or thinking.

We can now turn to the second sections of these passages, which I repeat in part for easy reference:

Groundwork:

> 2. Reason must regard itself as the author [*Urheber*] of its principles independently of alien influences. (4.448, CPract 96)

Third Antinomy:

> 2. Whether the object is one of mere sensibility (the agreeable) or even of pure reason (the good), reason does not yield to the empirically given ground and does not follow the order of things as they exhibit themselves in appearance, but with complete spontaneity [*völliger Spontaneität*] makes for itself an order of its own [*eine eignene Ordnung*] according to ideas. (A548/ B576)

Let's start with the seemingly anomalous Third Antinomy passage. What can Kant mean in saying that reason does not yield to an empirically given ground, even when that ground is an object of pure reason, the good? Presumably the idea is that even if an agent happens to have a representation which instantiates the good in a particular instance—he thinks, for example, 'I should keep my promise'—the mere presence of that idea in his mind is insufficient for the morality of his action. As an occurrence in his mind, it is on a par with a feeling of benevolence towards someone in need. If he acts on it, then he is merely acting on an idea (as opposed to a feeling) that he happens to have. Kant does not fully lay out the opposite case, where the agent is acting instead on the basis of reason's ideas, but it is easy enough to fill in from his ethical views. The moral law lies *a priori* in practical reason and when the consciousness of the law leads the agent to conclude, 'I should keep my promise,' then, if he acts on that thought, he acts morally and reason is creating an order in nature according to its own ideas (A807–8/B835–36). And it does so with 'complete spontaneity.' The question is whether this 'complete spontaneity'—even in the moral case—amounts to 'absolute spontaneity' or a new beginning.

When we look at second segment of the *Groundwork* passage, we face the same issue. In describing reason as the author [*Urheber*] of its principles, the text may assert nothing more than that the moral law lies *a priori* in the minds of moral subjects. But it might also be taken to assert that reason is an 'author' in the sense that it either creates or chooses its principles. On the latter reading, Kant's position would be that reason can be (practical) reason only if it can regard itself as the creator/chooser of its own principles. Since this passage may be part of a general discussion of judgment and the Third Antinomy text refers specifically to the apperception involved in speculative reason, Allison and Bilgrami attribute the same position to him for the case of speculative reason. In cognition as in morality, Kant argues that human agents must be free with respect to the norms or principles that they employ. They must not only understand the cognitive and moral norms as grounds on which they make their judgments, but must also view them as principles that they freely choose. Given these texts, their attributions are plausible.

3. Autonomy and Accountability

Although reasonable, Allison's and Bilgrami's interpretations cannot be squared with uncontroversial aspects of Kant's ethical theory. The first wrong turn in the interpretive chain comes at the assumption that he takes moral agents to be free to choose their principles—as if different moral agents might choose different moral laws. Nothing in Kantian ethics makes sense without the assumption that the same moral law lies *a priori* in the practical reason of all rational agents. Earlier I noted that Kantian cognizers cannot be understood as free to choose their principles or norms either. This is an important respect in which the theoretical and practical cases are similar.[6] In his view, human beings come with various *a priori* cognitive principles and a single *a priori* moral principle. Further, he believed that both moral norms and cognitive ones must at some level be understood as such by subjects. Subjects can be rational cognizers or agents only by seeing their judgments of fact and of obligation, permission, and prohibition as dependent on their consciousness of particular principles. Because these principles reflect the nature of a person's mind, they are, and are understood by the person, as arising through her own acts of thinking and reflecting. In this sense, they are and are understood as autonomous principles. The moral norm also has autonomy for its content: Act only on maxims that you could will as laws.

The problem is that the autonomy of cognitive principles does not involve their content. Nor does their use inform cognizers that they are free to do otherwise regardless of the state of the world up to this point. Only the moral 'ought' can do that. But to be cognizant of the moral ought, a subject must be conscious of the moral law. It follows that a mere cognitive being is not free in either of the senses that Kant thinks a moral being must be: He need not have a faculty of choice that can be determined by the moral law and he has no reason to suspect that he can be the beginning of a causal chain. Hence although his thinking is autonomous in a sense, he cannot be held accountable for it in the deep sense in which Kant thinks agents are accountable for their deeds.

The *Groundwork* passage is confusing because Kant tries to explain three things in terms of a single faculty: The autonomy of thought and action, the freedom that arises from susceptibility to the moral law, and the freedom to incorporate the maxim of morality or of self-interest regardless of the previous state of the world, including one's behavior. If 'complete spontaneity' is understood as 'absolute spontaneity' in the Third Antinomy passage, then that passage can also be seen as an attempt to explain everything that he sees as crucial to morality with one faculty. Reason not only judges actions in accord with the moral law; it also incorporates that law as its maxim of choice thereby creating an order according to its own ideas. In trying to do everything with reason, Kant gives the misleading impression that he thinks that reason is the author *qua* creator or chooser of its principles. But that is not the considered view of this ethical and epistemological Rationalist. For better or for worse, it is crucial to both sides of his work that rational principles are unvarying across time and across agents.

Although Kant does not fully work out his ethical position until *Religion within the Bounds of Mere Reason*, the earlier passages contain many essential elements. In particular the middle section of the Third Antinomy text (that I mark as 3) ties the causality of reason to imperatives, to 'oughts':

> 3. Now, that this reason has causality, or that we at least conceive such a causality in it, is evident from the **imperatives**, which in all that is practical we impose as rules on the executing [*ausübende*] powers. The **ought** expresses a kind of necessity and connection with grounds that does not otherwise occur in all of nature. (A547/B575, my underscoring)

Even in the *Critique* Kant is thus fairly clear that the serious proof of freedom is provided by the agent's awareness of the imperatives of morality. This segment also implies that readers err in following the tendency of the whole passage to assimilate the cases of theoretical and practical reason—since the imperatives of the latter involve a unique kind of necessity.

The last point is also given a canonical formulation in the text just after the passage where Kant explains that rational agency is insufficient for moral personality:

> The most rational being . . . might apply the most rational reflection to these objects (incentives) . . . without thereby even suspecting the possibility of such a thing as the absolutely commanding moral law which announces itself to be an incentive, and, indeed, the highest incentive. Were this law not given to us from within, no amount of subtle reasoning on our part would produce it or win our power of choice over to it. Yet this law is the only law that makes us conscious . . . (of our freedom) and thereby of the accountability of all our actions. (6.26n., amended translation CRel 75)

The consciousness of freedom and the resultant accountability is a special feature of the moral law of practical reason. It is not, *contra* Allison and Bilgrami, something that characterizes reason more generally.

Subjects are made aware of their freedom through the consciousness of the moral law and its 'ought,' but theorists justify the freedom required for ultimate moral responsibility in a much more elaborate way. They posit a subjective principle or maxim either to follow the moral law or to subordinate it to the demands of self-interest. Such a maxim must be both the beginning of a causal chain (to permit imputability) and also be adopted through a free power of choice (also to permit imputability), so this subjective basis of morality cannot be rationally cognized (6.25, CRel 74).

Although theoretical reason lacks the two requirements for freedom and responsibility, it possesses a kind of autonomy that practical reason lacks—or at least a kind of autonomy that Kant could not argue that it possessed. As Ameriks observes, Kant came to accept that he could not provide a deduction for the moral law. Both the moral law and the necessary assumption of freedom are 'established' only through the fact of reason. For this reason, Ameriks characterizes his practical philosophy as 'dogmatic,' as opposed to his 'critical' epistemology (2000, 218). By contrast theoretical reason is autonomous at four levels: Reason thinks in accord with its principles (as opposed to principles borrowed from experience), it makes those principles explicit, it evaluates some of its principles by appeal to others, and specialists can evaluate its most basic principles and establish their legitimacy through a transcendental deduction. Practical reason is autonomous at only the first three levels. In tying human freedom to practical obligation and in recognizing the limits of practical reason to deduce its principles, Kant's considered position is that theoretical and practical reason differ fairly dramatically in what they can accomplish.

4. Intellectual Accountability

Having criticized Allison and Bilgrami for assimilating Kant's views of the cognitive and moral subject despite some fairly clear counterindications from basic aspects of his moral theory, I close by defending my nonassimilation reading against a similar charge. Kant famously criticizes his fellow citizens for intellectual timidity in 'What Is Enlightenment?' (8.35, CPract 17). In his *Logic* he urges the adoption of three maxims for reasoning: Think for yourself, think yourself in the position of someone else, and always think in agreement with yourself (9.57, CLog 563). Intellectual accountability is thus an important aspect of his views and of his legacy. Although this point is clearly correct, it does not imply that he thinks that there is a special sort of accountability involved in cognition. Rather, his view is that cognizers must use their cognitive faculties in accord with the moral law.

In the *Logic*, Kant explains cognitive error mainly by the unnoticed influence of sensibility (9.54, CLog 561). However, he also thinks that sloppy thinking can be imputable:

> In a certain sense, however, one can make the understanding the author [*Urheber*] of errors, namely insofar as it allows itself, due to lack of requisite attention . . . to be misled. (9.54, CLog 561)

In a later passage he offers a system of epistemic errors:

> The **inclination toward passive use of reason, or toward the mechanism of reason rather than toward its spontaneity under laws,** can also be called a prejudice of imitation.
>
> Reason is an active principle, to be sure, which ought not to derive anything from the authority of others . . . But the indolence of many men is such that they prefer to follow in the footsteps of others rather than strain their own powers of understanding. (9.76, CLog 579)

From the perspective of his ethical theory, it is clear why the faults of inattention and indolence are imputable. The individual fails to do his duty, because he is not developing—or even exercising—his talents.

Chapter 10 presents a passage in the *Logic* where Kant dismisses as absurd the idea that the will could directly influence judgment (pp.169–70). He goes on, however, to suggest an indirect role:

> Insofar as the will either impels the understanding toward inquiry into a truth or holds it back therefrom, however, one must grant it an influence on the **use of the understanding**, and hence on conviction itself, since this depends so much upon the use of the understanding. (9.74, CLog 577)

Here the imputable deed is not the thinking, but the decision to pursue truth or not. For example, if out of a desire to gain the good opinion of authorities, a scholar refused to inquire into a matter that they wanted to keep hidden, then his refusal is blameworthy. Again, however, there is nothing distinctively cognitive about the nature of the accountability. It would be the same if the individual decided to curry favor with powerful people by offering them sexual favors or by falsely accusing others.

When Onora O'Neill took on the project of finding the unity of practical and theoretical reason for Kant, she argued that the supreme principle for both must be the categorial imperative (1989, 51). In essence, I have just offered additional evidence for the correctness of her solution. She must be the right, because for Kant there is only one moral law. Where I disagree with O'Neill, as well as with Allison and Bilgrami, is in the belief that Kant left the project of finding the unity of the two kinds of reason as a task for sympathetic readers. His mature position is that the freedom that is common and essential to speculative and practical reasoning—freedom in one sense of 'autonomy'—is less important for accountability than the *differentia* of practical reason, which can also move the will and inform agents of their capacity for new beginnings.

15

Kant Our Contemporary

1. Supporting and Showing Relevance

This final chapter is intended to redeem my opening claim in Chapter 1 that Kant's complex and difficult theory of the cognitive subject is worth exploring because it offers 'new' and plausible perspectives on issues of considerable recent interest. I look at four topics: how a successful transcendental argument works, self-knowledge of beliefs, the *explananda* for theories of consciousness, and the human ability to know other minds.

Although I presented Kant's 'transcendental argument' for apperception in Chapter 9, I did not consider well known objections to this form of reasoning. In section 2, I bring out the strength and uniqueness of his argument for the unity of apperception, by contrasting its ability to withstand the classic objection to transcendental arguments with a sophisticated contemporary argument for the same conclusion, the argument offered by Quassim Cassam. Nor did Chapter 9 consider likely objections to the argument's conclusion, the thesis that RE cognition of objects is necessary and sufficient for self-consciousness. Section 3 focuses on the criticism that object cognition is not sufficient for self-consciousness, though it also considers objections to the claim of necessity. I defend Kant's thesis by arguing that he provides a superior explanation of the self-attribution of beliefs (where the subject knows the grounds) to those currently available and that that explanation implies the sufficiency claim. Sections 4 and 5 consider implications of his theory for current attempts to understand the nature of consciousness and 'mind-reading.' In section 4, I argue that his understanding of thinking implies that cognitive science has been far too sanguine about its ability to explain sapience (as opposed to sentience, where well-known troubles lurk). In section 5 I return to claim of the Paralogisms chapter that humans can understand other thinkers only by projecting their conscious acts of thinking onto them (A346–47/B404–5). I argue that this theory would fill a gap in current theories of how humans can understand the minds of others.

2. Transcendental Arguments

Kant believed that he had discovered a new method in philosophy. Special concepts could be shown to be legitimate, not because the senses registered instances and not because they were necessary to characterize fundamental features of reality, but because they were indispensable for any rational empirical cognition. Following Strawson's lead in the 1950s and 1960s, many philosophers, in essence, accepted Kant's verdict on his achievement. He had discovered a novel and effective way to defend the use of disputed concepts. By the late 1960s critics had diagnosed what they (and many others) took to be a fatal flaw in the method. Barry Stroud offered a classic critique in 1968[1] and has continued to press the issue. There have been many skirmishes about transcendental arguments, where different proposals for defense and attack have been tried, but the central line of objection has standardly been a variant of Stroud's devastating analysis. Stroud believed that Kant's argument was more likely to succeed than more recent versions, though he still had reservations. Below, I show how those reservations can be overcome.

Kant's defense of *a priori* concepts aims to establish their objective reality or real possibility: The goal is to show that they must and how they can apply to objects (or to something)[2]. If the argument for apperception succeeds, then it will show that there are thinkers, that 'I-think' can be applied to something that is empirically real. In his seminal treatment, Stroud stressed the twin goals of Kant's and contemporary philosophers' transcendental arguments. If this form of argument is to be effective against skeptical challenges, then it must demonstrate not merely that cognizers must have certain beliefs and concepts; it must show that concepts such as 'independently existing object' and 'other mind' have instances (1968, e.g., 256, see also his 1994, 234). The nub of his criticism is that contemporary transcendental arguers err by assuming that demonstrating the necessary employment of a concept is sufficient to demonstrate that it has instances. Such a demonstration cannot suffice, however, because it concerns only what cognizers must believe (and so what concepts they must possess) and there is no legitimate way to argue from the necessity of a belief in Xs to the objective validity of the concept 'X.'

Stroud suggests that Kant's distinctive argument might succeed where contemporary attempts fail, because it is supposed to show that some conditions are necessary for the possibility of thought or experience itself. He believes that if the argument succeeds, then it will show that there are some members of a privileged set of propositions—propositions that could not meaningfully be denied by anyone (1968, 252–54). Still he thinks that the skeptic may have a rebuttal even in this case, because pragmatic inconsistency may be avoided just so long as a cognizer *believes* that the member of the privileged class is true (1968, 255). For example, if it can be shown that p is a necessary condition for language use, then a cognizer cannot claim that 'p is false' without engaging in self-refutation. Self-refutation can be avoided, however, just so long as language users believe that p, which leaves the question of whether p is true still open.

There is something odd about Stroud's position. If the truth of p is necessary for the possibility of language-use, then any language use demonstrates p's truth. The oddity arises because of the focus on self-verifying or self-refuting propositions. Stroud's targets—Strawson and Shoemaker—aimed to show that certain propositions were privileged, because they couldn't meaningfully be denied (1968, 251). At bottom, Stroud is claiming that even if such a status could be established, that would not amount to truth. Kant's position is different. It is that the possibility of thought requires that certain conditions be met. Because he takes this approach and because of the special status of the representation 'I-think,' he can show that there must be thinkers and that thinkers must employ the representation 'I-think.'

Strawson rekindled interest in Kant's specific thesis as well as in his method. In his view, Kant was right not just in arguing that subjects can ascribe diverse mental states to themselves only if they are also capable of cognizing objects, but also in what he took to be Kant's 'deeper point' (1966, 97ff., 100) that the ability to recognize some thing, 'a,' as 'F'

> presupposes the *possibility* of referring different experiences to one identical self. (1966, 100)

Without this ability, a cognizer could not recognize particulars (that he experiences) as instances of general concepts. Through Strawson's influence the necessity of the unity of consciousness to cognition has become a theme in recent philosophy of mind and epistemology.

To bring out the unique strengths of Kant's transcendental argument for apperception, I compare it Cassam's, because that is the most developed Neo-Kantian argument for mental unity with which I'm familiar. The essentials of Cassam's wide-ranging account can be captured as follows. Recent Neo-Kantians have argued that it is impossible to think of one's experience as containing objects in the weighty sense (items that can be perceived and that can exist unperceived) unless one can self-ascribe perceptions and grasp the identity of the thing to which these perceptions are ascribed (Cassam, 1997, 36). Because of the resemblance of this line of reasoning to Kant's argument from object cognition to the unity of consciousness, Cassam refers to it as the 'objectivity requires unity' (ORU) argument. He notes that those who raise doubts about the existence of continuing persons will not be impressed. Theirs is a thesis about what those objects who were thought to be persons really are; ORU concerns the ways in which individuals must think of themselves in having cognition (1997, 178–79, 181). He presses on, because he thinks that, thanks to ORU, there is something to be explained—namely, how cognizers use the term 'I'—that may require reference to persons.

At this point, Cassam appeals to Evans's (1982) analysis of the range of capacities that are required for individuals to have 'I thoughts': Such individuals must be able to recognize the connection between 'I thoughts' and their special ways of gaining knowledge of their mental states and physical properties; they must recognize the connection between 'I thoughts' and behavior, and so on (1997, 189). So the argument is that objectivity requires unity, including the possession of 'I thoughts' and—moving from epistemological considerations to the grounding of cognitive capacities in a subject—'I thoughts' can be had only by creatures with various further capacities, who are thus persons, or substantial subjects among other items in the (physical) world (1997, 196–97). As Cassam concedes, this argument is weaker than it might be. It avoids the fallacy of arguing from what cognizers must think they are to what they are, by making a large assumption: Only substantial subjects can have the capacities required to be thinkers of 'I thoughts' (1997, 197).

Kant's version of the argument from cognition to the unity of consciousness includes elements that have no place in the Neo-Kantian repertoire. To return to the counting example, the counter is aware of four stroke symbols to which he applies the counting rule, 1, 2, and so on. When he applies the rule, he recognizes that the antecedent of the rule is fulfilled and so judges '4.' Because he is at least implicitly conscious in the act of synthesizing, he recognizes that he has made the judgment on the basis of applying the counting rule to representations contained in sensory states—and that his act of judging thereby creates a relation of necessary connection between the those representations and the judgmental state. Through the conscious act of judging, the judgmental state comes to stand in the relation of rational dependence to the partial cognitions; from the other direction, through that act, the mental states of ticking off '1,' '2,' and so on, achieve the status of partial cognitions through the rational dependence of the judgmental state upon them. Conscious synthesis is crucial for rational cognition. Without it, conceptual or rational cognition of objects is impossible, because cognizers would not know the bases of their cognitions. With that consciousness, however, the cognizer *creates* a relation of rational dependence across his states in part by being at least implicitly cognizant of that relation. Since cognizers come with an *a priori* representation 'I-think' that they apply according to the I-rule of representations necessarily belonging together, they can always attach 'I-think' to their (partial and whole) representations that participate in rational cognition. They need not do so explicitly in every, or even in many, cases. But they always have the implicit act-consciousness and consciousness of the relation across their states that would enable them to attach the 'I-think,' because the hallmark of rational cognition is that it requires the implicit use of two rules, an object rule and the 'I-rule.'

The next section will consider challenges to Kant's view of the necessity of self-consciousness to RE cognition. If we postpone that concern and provisionally accept his theory of thinking, then we can appreciate how his argument differs from typical contemporary transcendental arguments and is thereby immune to Stroud's critique. Thinking that there are external objects or other minds does not make it so. On the other hand, any act of rational cognition involves a conscious act of combination that brings about the relation of rational dependence across mental states that both requires and permits the cognizer implicitly or explicitly to apply the 'I-rule.' The 'I-think' differs from concepts of external objects and it also differs from self-verifying propositions such as 'I am speaking' or 'I'm alive.' The key point about the representation 'I-think' is not that it is self-verifying, but that it (partially) creates its referent: Given the presence of appropriate representations and mental act awareness, this representation creates the reality to which it refers. In this one case, the ability of cognizers to deploy 'I-think' is part of the complex act that brings about the relation of rational dependence across mental states that constitutes their existence as thinkers. The representation 'I-think' seems to be unique in this respect.[3] If this is right, then the expectation shared by Kant and some of his contemporary followers that transcendental arguments can be applied more widely is mistaken.

3. Must Rational Cognition Involve Self-consciousness?

I turn from the classic objection to Kant's mode of arguing to what I take to be the central and most powerful source of resistance to his conclusions about the thinker. The objection is that not merely 'low-level' cognition but also what can properly be called 'rational' cognition does not require self-consciousness. Tobias Rosefeldt has presented the counterproposal in clear terms:[4] Why can't a cognizer enjoy rational cognition simply through her ability to grasp, for example, the logical relations in an inference? Why must she be conscious of anything other than the premises and the conclusion? On Rosefeldt's plausible proposal, what is crucial in drawing the conclusion that, for example, 'Caius is mortal' are the facts or perhaps the beliefs 'all men are mortal' and 'Caius is a man' and an act of inferring, but not a conscious act of inferring and not an implicit recognition of the relation of necessary connection across representations (2009).

Kant's thesis is a biconditional: RE cognition of objects is necessary and sufficient for self-consciousness. Rosefeldt's objection is only to sufficiency. He is unsure that rational cognition requires and so implies self-consciousness. To support Kant's position, I also consider an objection to the claim of necessity. It seems that humans can achieve some kinds of self-consciousness—knowing that they are in pain, for example—without engaging in object cognition. I take up this problem after dealing with the problem of sufficiency, because recent work by Matthew Boyle can be adapted to show how the solution to the problem of sufficiency of RE cognition for self-consciousness can also provide a way of answering the objection that mere sensation can lead to self-consciousness in the absence of rational cognition of objects.

My strategy for defending Kant's claim that cognition requires and so implies self-consciousness is to situate his position in relation to a debate about the impossibility of self-blindness for creatures that have certain cognitive capacities, a debate that has been going on for about a dozen years and has reached a level of considerable sophistication. Most of the participants whose contributions I discuss believe that Kant's views on thinking have a role to play in the debate. Their focus, though, is on the systematic issues and not on Kantian exegesis.[5] Although my concerns in this chapter are also systematic, I draw on the exegesis given in previous chapters to offer a detailed account of the implications of his work for this issue. In essence I defend Kant's claim of sufficiency by laying out his positive contribution to the discussion of self-blindness.

Starting in 1988,[6] Shoemaker has presented a series of papers exploring self-knowledge. Their principal thesis is that a certain kind of 'self-blindness' is impossible. In particular, it is not possible to have a creature

> who has the conception of the various mental states, and can entertain the thought that it has this or that belief, desire, intention, etc., but which is unable to become aware of the truth of such a thought except in a third person way. (1996, 31)

Shoemaker's discussion of self-blindness is part of his critique of the idea that humans have an 'inner sense' that can be understood on a quasi-perceptual model. On such a model, self-blindness would be possible—but it isn't. The position that I attribute to Kant is related to Shoemaker's thesis: A creature who has the conception of a cognizer (as one whose states are necessarily connected) and can make (conceptual) judgments, where he knows the reason, could not know about the rational dependence and so necessary connection of his states in only a third person way. There is a disanalogy, since it is not obvious how one could learn about such a connection from a third person perspective.[7] A further disanalogy is that the creature does not just have the concept of a cognizer, but also the capacity to make judgments. Still the main thrust of Kant's thesis is strikingly similar to Shoemaker's. It is not possible to have a creature that has particular cognitive capacities and that is also self-blind. In Shoemaker's terminology, Rosefeldt's challenge is to spell out exactly why a creature capable of cognizing where she knows the reason could not be self-blind.

Since the logic of my argument is a little unusual, it may be helpful to lay it out in advance. Rather than looking at the proponents of self-blindness, I'm going to consider Shoemaker's and others attempts to show that self-blindness is impossible in relation to certain cognitive tasks. I argue that these efforts fall short in important ways and that Kant's particular views about rational cognition provide a more compelling case for the impossibility of self-blindness in these tasks. Given just this description, I appear to be defending Kant by reiterating his position. I do not do that, because some of Shoemaker's allies defend the thesis of the impossibility of self-blindness by locating this issue in the context of the self-attribution of belief *per se*. The current dialectical position is that self-blindness is impossible for believers, because the only plausible accounts of how they can self-ascribe beliefs imply that they cannot be self-blind in having beliefs. Assuming that no one who raises the possibility of rational cognition without self-consciousness is prepared to accept the consequence that rational cognizers cannot self-ascribe beliefs, I can defend Kant's view by arguing that his account of rational, conceptual judgments or beliefs offers the only plausible account of how such beliefs can be self-ascribed.[8]

Shoemaker's argument that self-blindness is impossible takes the form of a *reductio*. Appealing to 'Moore's paradox,' that is, the impropriety of asserting, '*p*, but I don't believe that *p*,' Shoemaker considers the case of George, who is allegedly self-blind, but who nonetheless has resources for avoiding such remarks. For one thing, he knows that such remarks are held to be paradoxical. Given those resources, nothing in his behavior will give away his condition. It follows from George's case that we might all be self-blind. Since that conclusion is absurd (1996, 37–38), the hypothesis that George is self-blind must be rejected. This argument has been subject to serious objections (e.g., Byrne, 2005), but perhaps a larger problem with it is that Shoemaker doesn't provide an explanation for the necessity of the claim. He appeals to Grice's work on assertion, but notes that his conclusion is meant to cover a broader range of cases than merely those who are able to make Gricean assertions (1996, 38).

In *Authority and Estrangement*, Richard Moran offers a way of filling in the gap in Shoemaker's case by explaining why self-blindness is impossible for creatures that have the concept of belief and that can form beliefs.[9] Moran draws on Evans's view that self-ascription of beliefs is possible, because belief states are, in Roy Edgley's terminology (Moran, 2001, 60), 'transparent' to the world. In the classic case, I determine whether I believe that there will be a third world war, by considering the evidence for and against this proposition. Evans's approach to self-knowledge has been widely adopted, because it meets two *desiderata* for such knowledge: It is immediate and it is authoritative, in that it is immune to error by misidentification of the subject. Sometimes the latter requirement is presented as the view that self-knowledge is criterionless or groundless. An important project has been to explain why this 'groundless' knowledge is nonetheless in accord with rational principles and so counts as knowledge.

Moran recasts Evans's point in the language of 'transparency':

> With respect to the attitude of belief, the claim of transparency tells us that the first-person question 'Do I believe p?' is 'transparent' to, answered in the same way as, the outward-directed question as to the truth of p itself. (2001, 66)

He also offers an explanation for why the claim of transparency is correct:

> But only if I can see my belief as somehow 'up to me' will it make sense for me to answer a question as to what I believe about something by reflecting exclusively on that very thing, the object of my belief. (2001, 66–67)

Although he adopts Evans's approach, Moran notes the difficulties caused by cases of bad faith and repressed beliefs (e.g., 2001, 121, 131). To borrow a case from Freud, the 'Ratman' could not determine whether he believed his father was still alive by considering the objective evidence of his father's death, funeral, and so on (1909/1975). Still, Moran thinks that Evans's account is broadly correct. Typically subjects can answer the question of whether they believe that p by considering the evidence for p. And, as noted, he has a theory of why Evans's position is mainly right. Determining what you believe is not a matter of discovering some antecedent fact about yourself, but of constituting that fact. A person answers a question about what she believes by making a decision or a commitment of some sort; alternatively, she answers the question by making up her mind (Moran, 2001, 58, 2003, 404). Moran's account would also explain why Shoemaker's impossibility claim is correct. Any creature that can self-ascribe a belief—can determine what it believes—does so through the entitlement provided by the claim of transparency that enables it to move from the belief that p to the second order belief that it believes that p. But since a creature with beliefs and with the concept of belief can always make this move such a creature is not self-blind.

Despite these advantages, Moran's theory has several puzzling features. He notes one of them himself in a symposium discussion of his book:

> The claim of transparency *is* something of a paradox: how can a question referring to a matter of empirical psychological fact about a particular person be legitimately answered without appeal to the evidence about that person, but rather by appeal to a quite independent body of evidence. (2003, 413)

As Alex Byrne notes, Moran's claim of transparency can be recast in the apparatus of epistemic rules as:

BEL If p, believe that you believe that p. (2005, 95)

Cast in this way, the difficulty is clear. 'BEL' is a very bad rule, since the truth of some claim is no evidence that I or anyone else believes it (Byrne, 2003, 95). One way to avoid this problem is to go back to Evans's original formulation. On that view, it is not the truth of p that permits knowledge of one's own belief, but that one has engaged in a process of determining that p that is the proper basis of transparency:

> I get myself in a position to answer the question whether I believe that p by putting into operation whatever procedure I have for answering the question whether p . . . If a judging subject applies this procedure, then necessarily he will gain knowledge of one of his own mental states: even the most determined sceptic cannot find here a gap in which to insert his knife. (Evans, 1982, 225).[10]

Because he recognizes that it is not the truth of p but the act of determining the truth of p that provides the basis, Evans's original version of transparency seems preferable to either Moran's 'self-constituting' or Byrne's 'epistemic rule' account. Both Moran and Byrne make efforts to take into account that it is not the fact that p but the fact that S is trying to determine the truth of p that is crucial, but Evans's view builds this in from the beginning and so is somewhat simpler. As we see in the discussion of a contribution of Kieran Setiya's to this tangle of issues, however, Evans's theory has difficulties in accounting for cases of belief where the subject knows the reason.

There is an additional problem with Moran's 'self-constituting' view of the self-ascription of belief. The paradox he acknowledged concerns the *prima facie* odd fact that we are to determine what we believe not by looking to ourselves, but 'out' at the world. If this seems too impersonal a source of self-knowledge, the self-constituting or 'deliberative' approach to belief formation and (consequently) belief self-attribution (2001, e.g., 32) also seems too personal, because it involves responsibility and commitment. Byrne objects that in many cases, for example, the belief that he lives in Cambridge, Massachusetts, no deliberation is required. He doesn't need to make up his mind on this point, because he already knows where he lives (2005, 85). I'm not sure that this is a serious problem, since he can only recall that he accepts this judgment if he made it at an earlier time (cf. Boyle, 2009, 159–60).

The more worrying aspect of Moran's theory from a Kantian perspective is that he takes beliefs or judgments to be 'up to the subject.' Although Kant takes cognition to involve conscious acts, he does not believe that they are up to the subject. Rather, cognition is a matter of sensory evidence and concepts whose use is largely validated through past sensory evidence. Below, I present a Kantian account of the self-ascription of belief that also implies the impossibility of self-blindness and that avoids making self-cognition either completely impersonal or so personal that it is left to the subject.

In a recent essay, Kieran Setiya (2009) takes a somewhat different approach to filling in what he sees as the gap in Shoemaker's argument for the impossibility of self-blindness. He also casts the defense of the thesis of the impossibility of self-blindness in terms of the proper account of self-attribution of beliefs. He poses the latter problem in an illuminating way. What we need to be asking about beliefs about our beliefs is 'by what rational means are such beliefs acquired?' (2009). The question is pressing, because *prima facie* it seems that they could not be acquired by observation (unless one favors inner sense) or by inference, with the remaining option that they are groundless, and so without an adequate rational basis. He takes Shoemaker's impossibility of self-blindness claim as a *datum* for answering the question of the rational means by which beliefs about our beliefs are acquired. Thus, what he will try to explain is the truth of this conditional:

> If A has the capacity for inference and can ascribe beliefs to others, she has the capacity for groundless knowledge of her own beliefs. (2009, 12)

In explaining why the conditional is true, he will both vindicate and expand Shoemaker's claim that such conditionals must be true.

Setiya begins his account by raising and dismissing a possible line of solution:

> Superficially, at least, the capacity for inference cannot be responsible for groundless and so noninferential self-knowledge. This knowledge must derive from another rational capacity . . . [that is such that] its possession by subjects capable of inference is necessary, not contingent. What explains this necessity? Presumably, that inference exploits and relies upon this prior source of self-knowledge. On this proposal, making the inference from *p* to *q* requires the belief that one believes that *p*, acquired by a capacity distinct from both perception and inference. That is why self-blindness is impossible . . . and why the conditional is a necessary truth. The difficulty for this line is that, while some sorts of epistemic self-management rely on self-knowledge, as when I notice a contradiction in my beliefs, or reason hypothetically, distinguishing what I believe from what I merely suppose, the bare capacity to form one belief on the basis of others does not. (2009, 13)

Setiya makes two assumptions in dismissing the possibility for defending the impossibility of self-blindness that he clearly lays out—and that I will argue is close to, but importantly different from, the Kantian position. One is explicit in the last sentence. Epistemic self-management is not involved in a capacity to form one belief on the basis of others. The second assumption, which is discussed more fully in a subsequent passage, is that if the capacity for inference implies and so presupposes self-cognition, then the self-cognition involved must be prior to the inference. Below I fashion a Kantian argument against the second assumption and briefly indicate why he would also oppose the assumption that belief doesn't require self-management. Before turning to Kant, I raise some difficulties for Setiya's positive proposal for solving the problem of the rational grounding of beliefs about one's beliefs.

Setiya notes that if inference implies but does not presuppose self-knowledge, then it must be the source of such knowledge. As part of his solution, he suggests that we think of

> inference in the ordinary sense—forming a belief on the basis of prior beliefs that offer putative evidence for its truth—as a species of *epistemic rule-following*. (2009, 15)

He then follows Byrne in recasting Evans's 'transparency' account in terms of such a rule:

> Whenever you are in a position to assert that p, you are *ipso facto* in a position to assert 'I believe that p.' (2009, 15)

Setiya's argument is that if you have the capacity for inference then you have the (more general) capacity to form a belief on the basis of others. In that case, you could follow the preceding epistemic rule and so be capable of identifying your beliefs without relying on evidence. Setiya is careful to point out that a move from 'p' to 'I believe that p' is not an inference, since (as we have seen) the truth of 'p' does not offer even putative evidence for the truth of 'I believe that p.' A further problem that he notes, but doesn't really handle, is that seemingly a creature could have the capacity for inference, but lack this particular rule (2009, 16). At least we have been given no reason to believe that that situation is impossible.

Agnes Callard raises a different and important objection to Setiya's proposal.[11] The transparency claim

> does not serve to generate all our theoretical self-knowledge—that is, it doesn't rule out a certain form of theoretical self-blindness. Say I believe that p, and that if p then q, and I conclude that q. I might come to know this, that is, I might come to know that I believe that q *because* I believe that p and that if p then q. Presumably, we frequently have knowledge of this kind—it is the knowledge of the justification of a belief. Now could someone have theoretical rationality, including the ability to see the beliefs of others as justified, but be unable to ever see where his own beliefs came from? I think not, but this scenario is not ruled out by transparency, because the transparency rule only generates self-knowledge in the form of second order beliefs (I believe that I believe that p) and the belief that I believe one thing because I believe another is not a second order belief (2009)

Callard's criticism of Setiya is crucial for the project of defending Kant's version of the impossibility of self-blindness thesis. On that view, what requires self-consciousness is not cognition of whatever degree, but only cognition where the subject knows the reason for her judgment. By Callard's argument, that is just what appeals to transparency cannot explain. Her point against Setiya is not, of course, that he has failed to defend Kant,[12] but that his defense of the impossibility of self-blindness is too limited to deal with important cases.

In a note Setiya suggests, but does not fully work out or defend, an extension of the transparency strategy to explain how cognizers know the reasons for their beliefs. The following rule could be added to handle these cases:

> If you believe that the fact that q shows that p, form the belief that you believe that p, because you believe that q. (2009, 20, n. 41)

I assume that Setiya uses the slightly awkward locution 'believe that the fact that q' to make it clear that we are not already dealing with a belief about your belief. So you believe that the fact that *q* shows that *p* and not that your belief that *q* shows (you) that *p*. Otherwise, we'd already have a case of self-cognition. To make the case more concrete, we may consider an example that Setiya discusses in the text. Suppose that S believes that it has rained because there are puddles on the sidewalk. Translating this belief into Setiya's schema, we get 'S believes that the fact of puddles on the sidewalk shows that it rained.' From this condition, S is to move *via* the proposed epistemic rule to 'I believe that it rained because I believe that there are puddles on the sidewalk.'

But how is S to understand the condition that entitles her to make the move? As noted, Setiya uses the 'fact' locution to be explicit that this is not a belief. But how can one fact *show* another? Alternatively, how can S understand this part of her belief? If we try to avoid self attribution, then the content would have to be something like 'the fact of puddles *shows* that it rained—to those who can grasp the relation between these facts.' Even on this understanding, 'the fact of puddles *shows* (to the typical cognizer) that it rained,' there would not be an adequate basis for S to move *via* the claim of transparency to 'I believe that it rained because I believe that there are puddles,' since S might not understand herself to be a typical cognizer, and so forth. Further, on this understanding, the content of the belief makes implicit appeal to some cognizer or other and so does not honor Evans's basic strategy of explaining cognition of the inner realm by looking outward rather than inward. Setiya offers this as a rough-and-ready account, but it is hardly accidental that he uses 'shows' or some similar locution, since the goal is to capture the content of a belief when a person believes one thing on the basis of something else.

One way to see the difficulty is to recognize that, in the case of beliefs or judgments where the cognizer knows the reason, the content of the belief must include 'shows' or some similar relational term. But if the content of a belief involves a relation, then it must also involve appropriate *relata*. What are the candidates? The obvious candidates are inapt. The belief that *q* doesn't show the belief that *p*. Yet, as we have just seen, the fact that *q* doesn't show the fact that *p* either, unless there is someone to grasp the relation between these facts. A formal system could be developed in which 'p' can validly be derived from 'q.' But this exercise would be beside the point. The *explanandum* is not whether 'p' could be proved on the basis of 'q,' but how a person comes to believe one thing on the basis of another in such a way that he can self-ascribe his belief and its basis. What this 'shows' is that the '*shows*' locution—and anything that could be substituted for it—demands a complex complement that includes facts, a fact appreciator, and facts appreciated: The fact that *q shows that p* to someone who apprehends that fact and grasps its relation to the fact that *p*, and thereby acknowledges the fact that *p*.

At this point, the account of self-ascription of rational belief appears headed for just the sort of regress that Setiya warns against:

> [If] rational capacities rely on beliefs about our mental states, not just the realization of those states . . . [then] groundless [not based on sensory evidence] self-knowledge would be impossible. (2009, 14)

In this case, the belief that 'the fact of puddles *shows* that it rained' would carry an implicit reference to a subject in its key term 'shows' and the question immediately arises about how such reference is possible. As I understand it, Kant's theory of thinking provides a way out of the impasse. We can avoid infinite regress and avoid an impossible reading of 'shows' (that contains no implicit reference to a subject).

On Kant's view, subjects do not self-attribute beliefs or their appreciation of rational relations *prior* to judging. It is not that S can believe 'p because q' only by first attributing to himself the belief that q, and perhaps the belief that q is evidence for p, and perhaps the capacity to appreciate such relations. Rather, in apprehending q and the logical or evidential relation between q and p, a cognizer who has an implicit understanding of the I-rule also grasps that the state of judging that p stands in a relation of rational dependence (and so necessary connection) to the representation of the fact that q, a relation that makes them states of a single thinker. It is in the act of appreciating the rational relations between his representations of q and p that he becomes conscious of himself as an intelligence (B158–59)—comes to represent himself as someone who appreciates rational relations/makes logical moves—and comes to represent his representations as such. On Kant's view, in performing the conscious act of judging 'the fact that q shows that p,' S comes to at least an implicit understanding that the conditions required by the showing relation are fulfilled: The fact that q shows that p to someone, because she is aware of forming the judgment p on the basis of her apprehension of q and her grasp of its relation to p and so of the relation of rational dependency between the states that make them states of a (single) cognizer. That is how she is able to have a belief with the content 'the fact that q shows that p.'

On Setiya's account, the belief that the fact of puddles shows that it rained would be the condition of a claim of transparency that entitles S to form a second order belief that she believes that it rained because she believes that there are puddles. My argument has been that this strategy cannot provide a satisfactory theory of the self-ascription of beliefs in such cases. Either S cannot form the belief 'the fact that q *shows* that p' because she lacks the *relata* necessary for the use of 'show' or if she can form this first order belief, then it incorporates an implicit reference to a subject. On the other hand, as noted earlier, Kant's argument turns on the unity of representations in a single subject rather than on their 'mineness.' So we seem to have two theories that can account for parts of the problem of self-ascribing beliefs where the subject knows the reason, the transparency account that is aimed at the problem of self-ascription but can't account for the belief content in the case of beliefs known through reasons, and Kant's theory of how cognizing objects enables subjects to forge and recognize relations of rational dependence across their states that make them cognizers and that make them conscious of their states as those of a cognizer and conscious of themselves as appreciators/forgers of rational relations, but which does not account for *self*-ascription, the use of 'I' in 'I-think.'

For reasons we have seen, there seems no way to patch the transparency rule that does justice to the content of the belief to be self-ascribed. On Kant's view, the cognizer who judges that it rained because there are puddles could self-ascribe the judgment because she is aware of such states through inner sense. But the inability of the inner sense theory to account for self-ascription is supposed to follow from the impossibility of self-blindness. That failure is also the starting point of the contemporary project of explaining self-ascription through the transparency of mental states to the world. So Kant's way of filling out his account of the self-ascription of beliefs where the subject knows the reason cannot be invoked to complete a Kantian defense of the impossibility of self-blindness.

Nevertheless, despite Kant's reliance on inner sense for reporting states of judging, his overall position offers a further resource that seems to do the job. He stresses both the act of synthesis and its conscious character. When a subject infers, for example, he is at least implicitly conscious of a movement of mind from premises to conclusion. Kant was clear that this act-consciousness could not be understood on the model of inner sense—as a registering of an act by the mind. For the inference to be rational, the cognizer must be conscious (in the act) of inferring the conclusion on the basis of the premises. It is through such consciousness that he understands the judgmental state as rationally dependent on representations of the premises and he understands himself as an appreciator/forger of rational relations. The suggestion would be that self-ascription—mineness as well as togetherness—is grounded in the conscious act of synthesizing or thinking.

How I know a judgment is mine is that I am implicitly conscious in making it. Since I am implicitly conscious in making it, I am implicitly conscious of making it—but not at all in the manner that I would be through inner sense. We can express this point in terms of a different entitlement principle:

> If a cognizer (consciously) performs an act of rational cognition A, then she is entitled to self-ascribe A.

The consciousness involved (which I put in parentheses to emphasize its pleonastic status) is crucially different from that of inner sense, because it is inseparable from the act of judging. Consciousness of making the judgment on the basis of a rational appreciation of the relation between it and various partial representations is a necessary aspect of the judgment being a judgment. And because the consciousness is part of what makes the act an act of rational cognition, the cognizer will always be in a position to self-ascribe the judgment and the self-ascription will always be correct. Although this approach differs from the transparency model in important ways it shares the feature that Evans took to be the hallmark of a successful resolution of the puzzle of self-ascription. Because such consciousness is part of the truth conditions for performing an act of rational cognition

> even the most determined sceptic cannot find here a gap in which to insert his knife. (Evans, 1982, 225)

In the Kantian framework we thus have all that is needed to the explain self-ascription of judgments or beliefs where the subject knows the reason, because if I am implicitly conscious in making a judgment then I am entitled to self-ascribe it.

Although Kant explains human awareness of mental states through inner sense, the preceding elaboration of his theory of apperception to handle self-ascription is in keeping with his views about the close relation between the activity of synthesizing and the subject. In the general discussion of synthesis that sets up the argument of the B deduction, he explains that

> Among all representations, **combination** is the only one that cannot be given through objects, but—being an act of the subject's self-activity—can be performed only by the subject himself. (B130, also cited in Chapter 9)

What is meant by the claim that combining is not merely the subject's activity, but her 'self-activity'? There seem to be two, complementary possibilities. Synthesis or combination is an activity that is distinctively a cognitive subject's activity; combining is an activity that is somehow self-constituting. Putting these together, the idea would be that combining representations in cognition is an activity that is unique to cognitive subjects and that makes them to be cognitive subjects. And that appears to be Kant's view. It is through trying to make sense of sensory data that cognizers come to combine representations and so to create the relations across their states that are the hallmarks of single subjects; it is in performing the same operations that they use their distinctive cognitive abilities that would otherwise lie dormant and unknown. Absent these activities, humans are not thinkers, but only creatures with the capacity to be thinkers. Although Kant takes cognitive acts to constitute thinkers, his view differs sharply from Moran's, because the self-constituting acts, while done by the cognizer, are not 'up to her.'

To understand the Kantian apperceptive view of self-ascription, it is important to recognize both that the subject's awareness in/of judging or believing on the basis of reasons is nothing like the awareness provided by an inner sense and that this awareness preempts any epistemic rule that would have the cognizer moving from beliefs (just) about the external world to beliefs about her beliefs. How a cognizer determines that she believes 'p because q' is not and cannot be purely impersonal, with no reference to a subject. A cognizer who believes that the fact that q shows that p already understands enough about her situation to be able to assert not just 'p because q,' but 'the fact that q shows that p to an I.' For in judging 'p because q' she understands her states to stand in the relation that makes them states of an 'I' and her cognitive abilities to be those that make her an 'I.' All that she needs to move from this understanding to the self-ascription 'I believe p, because I believe q' is an implicit understanding that she may use 'I' when engaging in acts of rational cognition. On the Kantian view, coming to believe that you believe something for a reason is not an exercise that only involves the world; it also involves an implicit (or explicit) consciousness of yourself as a thinker, as a appreciator and forger of rational relations across mental states, which states are brought into relation with each other through those activities. Cognition must be understood as 'agental,' by theorists and cognizers alike, not because it is 'up to the subject,' but because it involves conscious mental activity.

I have now completed my defense of Kant's claim that rational cognition requires self-consciousness. The objection is that cognitive subjects might be self-blind. My argument has two parts and a presupposition. The presupposition is that it is possible for cognizers to self-ascribe beliefs or judgments when they know the reason for their beliefs. In the first part I argue that several attempts to defend Shoemaker's impossibility of self-blindness thesis—including his own—have various defects. I focus on the arguments of Moran and Setiya that argue that, given the only plausible theory of the self-ascription of beliefs (variants of Evans's 'transparency' strategy), self-blindness is impossible. My criticism of Setiya's theory is Kantian: the transparency strategy presupposes that it is possible to be in a state of believing where one knows the reason without simultaneously referring to a cognitive subject. Although my criticism depends on the Kantian insight about the necessary reciprocity of knowledge of objects and of the subject, it does not presuppose the truth of that claim. Rather, it redemonstrates that self-cognition is necessary for object cognition in the case of Setiya's particular proposal. The second part of my argument is the presentation of a successful Kantian explanation of the possibility of the self-ascription of beliefs where the subject knows the reason. Having argued against the widely accepted transparency strategy for explaining self-knowledge in these cases, Kant's theory is left as the only plausible such explanation—and it implies that self-blindness is impossible.

I have offered a defense of only a limited Kantian thesis, the thesis that creatures that are capable of belief where they know the reason must be self-conscious. His claim in the *Critique* is broader: All conceptual cognition involves knowing the reason. In Setiya's terminology, all conceptual cognition is partly a matter of 'self-management,' since cognizers must hew to rules associated with concepts. In Chapter 9, I try to make Kant's position plausible, noting its relation to the widely held view that one cannot be said to have a concept without some appreciation of the inferential relations into which it enters. Since appreciating such relations would involve conforming one's usage to them, some measure of self-management seems required for any concept-user. Still, it would take me too far from my main topic to assess whether the Kantian objection to Setiya's extension of Evans's transparency strategy could be made to work for all cases of (conceptual) belief. Could that be shown it would undermine the general strategy of taking knowledge of the world (plus context) to be the basis on which the subject's knowledge of his beliefs is warranted.

Having dealt with the objection that cognition of objects is not sufficient for self consciousness, I turn to the claim that it is not necessary. One class of problematic cases is that of sensations. *Prima facie* subjects are self-conscious when they are hungry or in pain, and such self-consciousness does not seem to involve rational appreciation or action of any kind. In a recent essay, Matthew Boyle considers a similar objection to Moran's theory that self-ascription of belief can be explained through the use of rational principles of transparency, because humans come to have beliefs through deliberation. The objection, made by David Finkelstein (2003, 155, 162), among others, is that Moran's deliberative or self-constituting explanation of self-ascription cannot be extended to sensations. Boyle's goal is not to defend Moran's theory as providing a complete account of self-knowledge—Boyle thinks there are two different sorts—but to show that Moran was right in claiming that the sort of self-knowledge that he can explain is fundamental. I briefly present Boyle's defense, because it can be applied fairly directly to Kant's theory.

Boyle begins by assuming that any creature who makes an utterance expressing knowledge of her own mental states must understand that utterance (2009, 142). Further, self-knowledge must involve the representation of a mental state and not simply its expression, since the latter could be accounted for merely by the presence of the state (2009, 144). But if subjects are to represent their mental states, then they must be able to combine representations, for example, 'I' and 'pain' in complex representations, 'I am in pain.' Boyle goes on to argue in defense of Moran that the ability to combine representations requires understanding relationships among representations and that making an utterance or representing a state of affairs involves taking a stand on what is true—and so deliberation (2009, 159). If this is correct, then the variety of self-knowledge that Moran explains would be fundamental, because it is impossible to have knowledge of sensations in it absence. At the end of his essay, he crystallizes its central point:

> Unless we recognize that [Moran's] sort of self-knowledge as fundamental, and distinct from our knowledge of what we sense, we will not be able to understand what makes the object of self-knowledge a *self*. For to be a self is to be a thinker and an agent, and to be a thinker and an agent is to be capable of a kind of activity that stands in contrast to the passivity of sensation. Nor is this merely a point that must be acknowledged by *theorists* of self-knowledge. Even to be capable of having such mundane thoughts as 'I am in pain,' we must have an at-least-implicit conception of an active subject to which sensations belong. (2009, 161)

Boyle regards the argument he develops as Kantian (2009, section 6), so it is unsurprising that it can be adapted in defense of Kant's necessity thesis. If an utterance 'I am in pain' is to express self-knowledge, then it must involve representational elements that have been combined in a whole judgment and that relate in systematic ways to other representations. Boyle defends Moran by connecting the ability to use such a representational system to the capacity for deliberation. To defend Kant, the ability to use a representational system where representations can be combined because they stand in systematic relations to other representations must be linked to the representation of objects. But this is familiar territory: The use of concepts requires the ability to distinguish correct from incorrect uses and that requires the possibility of a 'corrected view' (Strawson, 1966, 250), and that, in turn, requires an object to which subjects can have different avenues of access (or which they can access at different times). My claim is not that such arguments have silenced the skeptics, but only that they suggest that there is much to be said in defense of Kant's claim of the necessity of object knowledge for self-knowledge.

Boyle's concluding point gets to the heart of the matter, though it does not go as far as Kant's position, as I understand him.[13] For Boyle, a creature who lacked the capacities to combine representations would not be a self. Kant's point is even stronger: Absent the activities involved in judging and inferring, humans would remain in a state of being potential thinking selves; it is only the exercise of these capacities that creates the relations among mental states that are distinctive of cognitive subjects and that permit them to understand themselves as 'I's. So absent the self-consciousness made possible through thought, a human who is conscious of pain would not be self-conscious, because she would not be a self. In reply to the likely objection that judging and inferring might just concern sensations and not objects distinct from the subject, we can appeal, again, to the line of argument just noted, the argument that judging and inferring require representations and those cannot be deployed unless they include representations of objects. Again, my claim is not that defenders of the Kantian view that self-consciousness requires object cognition have carried the day or even that the debate has ended. It is only that much has been said in Kant's defense on this point where I have tried to offer a somewhat new take on his 'deeper' thesis (Strawson, 1966, 97ff., 100) that object cognition requires self-consciousness.

Boyle's argument concerns only sensations, but it can be extended to cover other cases, for example, self-ascription of position or movement. It is hard to see how an animal could track its prey without representing itself as being at a particular location. In a similar way, it might seem that humans could have self-knowledge of their positions and movements in the absence of judgmental awareness of objects. They must know where they are and what they are doing if they are to go on successfully navigating in the world. But this line of objection will again be turned aside by Boyle's central insight (here in its Kantian version, 2009, 160): In the absence of an adequate representational system, where representations stand in systematic relations to each other and so can play a role in judgment and inference, there is no self to which position and movement can be attributed. To defend the necessity claim I need to add just one piece to Boyle's argument. Such a representational system can be used only when it contains representations of objects.

On a Kantian view, the *self*-ascription of pains and the like would depend on a cognizer's ability to have beliefs about objects. That does not imply, however, that he would take a cognizer's knowledge of his pains to be warranted in the same way in both cases. Kant's concerns in the *Critique* are with cognitive sensations—states that provide the basis for knowledge of objects—and not with, roughly, states that inform the subject of his bodily condition. Boyle argues that it is a mistake to accept the 'Uniformity Assumption,' the presumption that all forms of self-knowledge will be explained in the same way. He cites Kant as a philosopher who correctly distinguishes cases of active thinking from the passive receipt of sensations (2009, 160). Kant's official view, though, is that both judgments and sensations are self-ascribed through inner sense. His analysis of rational cognition and apperception permits interpreters to develop a better 'Kantian' view for the case of judgments. He doesn't address the case of bodily sensations such as pain in the context of cognition. Given both the official theory and the (perhaps resultant) lack of interest in the 'mineness' problem, it isn't clear how one could develop a Kantian account of the self-knowledge for sensations.

4. A Second Hard Problem of Consciousness?

How are we to understand the explicitly or implicitly conscious acts of synthesizing representations that Kant takes to be essential to rational cognition? Recent work in consciousness studies has divided the object of inquiry into several different species. Perhaps the most basic division is between 'creature consciousness' and 'state consciousness' (Rosenthal, 1997). A creature is conscious if he is awake as opposed to asleep or knocked out. But a conscious creature can have many unconscious states, including, for example, states involved in the processing of perceptual information. 'State consciousness' has been subdivided into states that are 'access conscious,' 'phenomenally conscious,' and, roughly, 'monitoring conscious.'[14] Before considering the varieties of state consciousness in greater detail, it is evident in these broad divisions that mental acts have not been taken to be *explananda* for theories of consciousness.[15] This may reflect the influence of a famous dictum of Karl Lashley (1958, 4) that is often cited by cognitive scientists seeking to cast off the yoke of Cartesianism, of introspectionism, or of both: 'No activity of mind is ever conscious.'

'Access consciousness' refers to the availability of a representation for many different uses, including speech, reasoning, and the control of action. By contrast representations would be access-unconscious if they could be used by only one system, as in the case of representations of shading that help the visual system determine the shape of a perceived object (Marr, 1982, 239ff.). Ned Block (1995, 2002) has argued that it is important to separate access-consciousness from phenomenal consciousness ('A-consciousness' and 'P-consciousness'). A state is P-conscious just in case there is something that it is like to be in that state (cf. Nagel, 1974), not P-conscious if there is nothing that it is like to be in that state. From Leibniz onwards apperceptive consciousness has been regarded as quality-less and so, in current terminology, as not P-conscious.

Conscious combining of mental representations does not, however, seem to fit into the mold of A-consciousness any better than that of P-consciousness. A-consciousness is intended to cover ordinary and extraordinary cases where the person denies awareness of any qualities, but clearly has access to perceptual information. The ordinary case is an individual who is driving home while thinking about something else. The driver may claim to have been oblivious to the sunset or the foliage, but she was plainly conscious of both in some sense, because she turned on her lights and steered clear of trees along the road. The unusual case that has aroused much interest is 'blindsight.' Some individuals suffer from scotomas—holes in their visual fields caused by various medical conditions. Scotomas can be detected by experiments which project images onto the affected portion of the retina. Subjects report that they see nothing in part of their visual fields. Yet they are better than chance at guessing what is there when given a forced choice of options. What Block and others find interesting about these cases is the presence of A-consciousness in the absence of P-consciousness (1995, 2002). From the perspective of conscious acts of judging or inferring, however, A-consciousness is no more suitable as a model than P-consciousness. On Kant's theory of thinking subjects must have access to much information. But the key point about rational cognition is not just access to information, but the conscious combining of information so that the subject understands the relations of necessary connection across the information bearing states and understands herself as a thinker.

Of the available varieties, the most promising for dealing with act-consciousness seems to be monitoring consciousness. Block has distinguished three different models of monitoring consciousness. First, it can be understood in terms of metacognition, where being in a mental state is accompanied by the thought that one is in that state. It can also be considered as a kind of self-scanning. Finally, one could think of it as a sort of phenomenal consciousness, an awareness of some sort of phenomenal quality (2002, 214ff.). In the case of concept use, perhaps it would be a feeling of judging. But none of these models of monitoring consciousness provides an apt description of judging or concept use, as Kant analyzes that activity.

We have already seen the difficulty with metacognition. Rational cognition is not simply a matter of knowing that you are in a state, say of judging, but of being conscious of entering that state through a synthetic act. The second option seems equally unpromising. If a sequence of mental states did not involve an awareness of entering the latter state through a synthetic act, then scanning that sequence cannot make up the loss (any more than reflecting on a mental state could provide it with a representation of the self if it lacked one, as Merian and Kant observed). The third option seems even less plausible. Even if we reject the standard view that apperception is quality-less and assume that different mental actions have different feels, judging and inferring do not seem to be centered on phenomenal consciousness in the way that the paradigm cases of feeling pain or seeing purple are. If there is a phenomenal feeling to these acts, it is not their essence, which concerns the grasping of the necessary connections across one's thoughts brought about by one's mental actions in appreciating the logical or evidential relations of their contents.

P-consciousness has been the subject of countless recent discussions in philosophy of mind. The problem, in a nutshell, is that information processing accounts of mentality—which are the stock in trade of the field—seem unrelated to what it is like to see, for example, a purple haze (Levine, 2001). Purple light might register in the visual system and that registration might permit all the behaviors associated with normal purple seers, yet the individual would have no experience of what seeing purple is like. Because it cannot be captured by current information processing accounts of mentality, David Chalmers refers to P-consciousness as the 'hard' problem of consciousness (1996).

A symptom that a type of consciousness falls into the 'hard' category is the susceptibility of the best available accounts to 'Zombie' objections. 'Zombies' are creatures that look and sound like ordinary people, but that are unconscious. The creature described in the last paragraph would be a Zombie with respect to the color purple. If Kant is right that they require conscious acts of combining, then judging and inferring would also be subject to Zombie objections.

We can imagine a creature that takes in perceptual and conceptual information and that produces 'judgments' and 'inferences' as outputs. To accommodate Kant's 'two-rule' point, we can take the creature's information processing system to be jointly satisfying two rules: for example, when previous states have included representations of four stroke symbols, and when the state to be outputted depends on the presence of those states, output not just '4,' but 'I judge 4.' Since all outputs depend on the inputs in information-processing models, however, the second rule must be amended. Otherwise all the conscious and unconscious processing will come out as rational cognition and the creature will immediately be exposed as different from humans. To handle this problem, we could appeal to an 'inner sense.' The amendment would be: Apply the second rule to only those states that can be reported through inner sense. With the aid of Tetens's theory of inner sense, we can envision creatures that are so programmed and that can also give the reasons for their judgments or inferences. They would process information or, in Kant's terminology, combine representations in regular ways, and through a Tetensian inner sense they would have a record of these acts for a subset of cases. If the record were sufficiently complete, they might know which representations they had combined in which other representations. So when asked the basis of their belief that it rained, they could reply, 'I believe that it rained, because I believe that there are puddles on the sidewalk.' When asked why they believed that q, they could point to the belief that p and the belief that 'if p, then q. When asked why they believed they were seeing a 'body,' they could reply that they believe that they are seeing something extended. As Shoemaker's George was trained to avoid revealing assertions such as 'p but I don't believe that p,' they could be programmed to say that their beliefs 'depended' on their reasons.

As Kant understands 'higher' mental processes these Tetensian creatures would be cognitive Zombies. They would act and sound like rational cognizers, but they would be ersatz thinkers.[16] It's difficult to capture exactly what they are missing, so I offer three different formulations. Even though such creatures could connect their judgments to partial grounds, they could not make the connection in the right way. They could not see their judgments as the results of acts of judging based on evidence that they possess. Alternatively, although they would know in a sense that these are judgments that they have made rather than received, they would not see any fundamental difference between thinking for themselves and taking on the opinions of others. Still a third formulation: Although they would connect judgments to their grounds, the connections would seem accidental, because they would not understand the rational dependence of the judgmental representations on the partial representations.

If Kant is right about thinking, then there is a second hard problem of consciousness. Further, if he is right that implicitly or explicitly conscious acts of rational cognition are critical in turning a potential thinker into an 'I,' then there will also be significant and hard-to-bridge gaps in accounts of 'I's.

5. Other 'I's

Kant's argument for the unity of apperception is an exploration of the necessary conditions for cognition. As such, it would seem to support a general conclusion: All thinkers enjoy this unity. Yet, as noted at the end of Chapter 11, he claims that such a generalization must have a different source:

> It must, however, seem strange at the very outset that the condition under which I think at all, and which is therefore merely a characteristic of myself as subject, is to be valid also for everything that thinks; and that upon a proposition that seems empirical we can presume to base an apodeictic and universal judgment, *viz*: that everything that thinks is of such a character as the pronouncement of self-consciousness asserts of me. The cause of this, however, lies in the fact that we must necessarily ascribe to things *a priori* all of the properties that make up the conditions under which alone we think them (A346/B404–405, also cited in Chapter 11)

The conclusion that thinking is possible only under the 'form' of apperception cannot simply be generalized to any thinker *per se*, because a thinker can truly understand it only through understanding the relation of necessary connection or rational dependence across representations, and he can do that only through the act-consciousness involved in synthesis. Since any thinker is act conscious of only his acts of combining representations, he must project how he thinks onto others whom he takes to be 'I's. This move is legitimate, because, in contemporary terminology, a cognizer is 'entitled' to ascribe the *a priori* properties to a thing that make it possible for him to think that thing.

More briefly, what the examination of the necessary conditions for rational cognition shows is that any cognizer must be able to understand his states as necessarily connected. It follows that to think of any (other) cognizer, a cognizer must think of that other 'I' as understanding his states as necessarily connected—but the first 'I' can do that only by projecting his conscious acts of combining onto the other 'I.'

Skeptics are not going to be convinced by this argument. Doubts are to be swept away by the claim that one is entitled to knowledge of other minds on the slender basis of one's own case. How does that remove the possibility that one is surrounded by cognitive Zombies? As a reply to skepticism, Kant's view of knowledge of other minds is ineffective. In the last few decades, however, concerns about other minds have largely shifted from skeptical worries to the issue of how 'mind-reading' is possible or what it involves. As in earlier sections, I evaluate Kant's position on this issue by comparing it to the current options.

Knowledge of other minds involves two subtopics: how one knows that others have minds, how one knows the content of another mind's thoughts.[17] Kant's claims concern only the first. Although recent work has been focused on the second, there is still overlap on the question of the sorts of resources that are brought to bear in understanding that one is in the presence of another 'I.'

Current discussions revolve around two theories of mind-reading. Alison Gopnik (1993) and many others have argued that, as humans come with primitive theories of physics and biology, so too they come with a primitive theory of human psychology that manifests itself around the age of four. According to the primitive theory, humans have beliefs and desires that lead them to act in various ways.

Dramatic evidence for this theory was provided by experiments testing whether small children understood what beliefs were. Following hints from Jonathan Bennett, Gilbert Harman, and Daniel Dennett, psychologists Heinz Wimmer and Joseph Perner (1983) tested children's grasp of 'belief' by seeing whether they understood when someone had a false belief. In the classic experiment, a child observed a puppet, Maxi, place a chocolate in a box and go out to play. A mother puppet then came in and moved the chocolate from the box to a cupboard. The question for the children was: When Maxi returns, where will he look for the chocolate? Children younger than three and one half standardly reply: 'in the cupboard'; children older than four (when they are not autistic) reply: 'in the box.' Because of their potential to shed light on the nature of autism, variants of the Maxi experiment have been repeated many times.

Although interpreting the experiments has been controversial, they are often taken to support the idea that children older than four have a primitive grasp of the psychology of belief. Other experiments have produced similar results for 'desire.' However yucky lima beans might be children understand at a certain age that a person who *likes* lima beans will eat them rather than the tasty goldfish crackers that they could choose (Gopnik, 1993). Given these results, the theory that children (and so adults) understand the minds of others because they are endowed with a primitive theory of belief-desire psychology has been widely embraced. Because the ability to grasp human psychology seems independent of IQ (Down syndrome children acquire the ability at the same age as normals, whereas higher IQ autistic children do not), the view is sometimes expressed in terms of the existence of a 'theory of mind module' that is dedicated to mind-reading. For obvious reasons, this explanation of mind-reading is often called the 'theory theory.'

Robert Gordon (1986) and Alvin Goldman (2006), among others, have proposed a different mechanism for understanding other minds. In their view, how a four-year-old comes to understand that Maxi will look in the box has nothing to do with theories. Rather, she imagines herself in Maxi's situation of having left the chocolate in the box, and she realizes that since she would look in the box, so would Maxi. That is, children and adults read other minds through 'simulating,' through imagining themselves in the situation of the other and determining what they would think and do. More recently, Goldman has suggested that some type of hybrid theory must be right. One weakness in the simulation account is that it cannot provide knowledge of other minds unless it is assumed that one does not merely simulate others, but also that one has knowledge of one's own mind. To fill in this gap, a simulator would need to have some theoretical knowledge.

Viewed in relation to the current debate, Kant appears to hold a hybrid theory. He takes humans to have an *a priori* representation of an 'I-think' as something whose states belong together of necessity. But he thinks that an 'I' comes to understand that her states stand in that relation only through conscious acts of combining. Since I can be conscious only of my acts, I can understand others as 'I's only by projecting the complex consciousness that I have in making judgments and inferences onto them.

Despite its superficial similarity to contemporary accounts of mind-reading, Kant's view is different in a key respect. Partly because he is not concerned with particular contents, he focuses on a very basic question: What is involved in representing another 'I' as such and what resources do humans have to do that? For him, the first step in representing another as an 'I' is representing her as an 'I-think,' as a rational cognizer whose states stand in relations of rational dependence. The ability to represent others in this way must be explained if a theorist is to offer hypotheses about how humans recognize that others have the sorts of beliefs and desires that can be had only by rational cognizers.

I noted that simulation accounts seem incomplete, because they lack an explanation of the base case for the simulation, namely, how someone who has a mind understands her mind. It follows from Kant's theories of thinking and of knowledge of other 'I's[18] that the theory theory is also incomplete. Neither theory provides an explanation for the core *explanandum*: How can humans represent another thinker as such? By contrast, he is poised to answer that question, because he has painstakingly developed a theory of the requirements of RE cognition. Given that theory, his plausible claim is that representing another as an 'I' is possible only if a thinker uses herself as a model.

Chapter 13 showed the implications of Kant's theory of the thinker for the use of norms. Chapter 14 laid out (but did not defend) the Kantian case against understanding cognitive agency as similar in important ways to moral agency. This chapter drew implications from his work for a type of argument that has been pervasive in the philosophy of mind and for theories of the self-attribution of belief, theories of consciousness, and theories of how minds are able to understand each other as minds. Looking back over this material, I still find it surprising how much the *Critique* has to offer to those who are puzzled about cognition and its subject.

Notes

Chapter 1

1. Chapter 15 considers some important additions made by Evans (1982) and Cassam (1997). Even a brief list of influential scholars who have been inspired by Strawson would also include Sydney Shoemaker (e.g., his 1996) and Dieter Sturma (1985). For a more recent examples, see Edmundts et al.'s introduction to a series of papers on the Paralogisms (2006, 261).

2. References to the *Critique of Pure Reason* will be in the text, with the usual 'A' and 'B' indications of editions. In providing English translations, I usually rely on Pluhar (1996), but I also use Kemp Smith (1968), and Guyer and Wood (1998) at points. I do not, however, follow Pluhar rendering '*Vorstellung*' as 'presentation,' but use the more standard 'representation.' When I alter a translation beyond rendering '*Vorstellung*' as 'representation,' I indicate that the translation is amended. References to Kant's works, other than the *Critique of Pure Reason*, will be to Kant 1900—and will be cited in the text by giving volume and page numbers from that edition. These translations will be from the Cambridge edition, where available, or my own; again I'll indicate any substantive alterations. Where I use Cambridge translations, as is or amended, I indicate the volume by 'C' and a short mnemonic, for example, 'CMet' for the Cambridge edition volume *Lectures on Metaphysics* (for the mnemonics and the corresponding works, see the abbreviations list). In all quoted passages I follow the suggestion of Guyer and Wood and indicate Kant's emphasis with boldface type; I use italics where Kant uses Roman (as opposed to Gothic) script for foreign words.

3. 'C1755' indicates Walford and Meerbote (1992).

4. 'C1781' refers to Allison and Heath (2002).

5. Kant is especially clear on this point at B113:

Yet whenever a thought—no matter how empty it seems to be—has maintained itself for such a long time, then it deserves an inquiry into its origin, and entitles us to conjecture that it has its basis in some rule of the understanding that, as often happens, has only be wrongly interpreted.

6. 'CLet' refers to Zwieg (1999).

7. '*Reflexionen*' are Kant's literary remains and so are also sometimes referred to as '*Nachlaß*.' They are published in volumes 14–19 and 20–23 of Kant (1900–) and include

unbound manuscripts and notes that Kant wrote on empty spaces in his class texts and in letters. Here I call these collectively 'the Reflections,' and I use the term 'Reflection' for them individually; I follow standard practice and indicate the numbers assigned to the Reflections by the editors of the Academy edition by 'R.' I abbreviate references to the selection of Reflections included in the Cambridge Edition volume *Notes and Fragments* (Bowman, Guyer, and Rauscher, 2005) by 'CNotes' and the page number. Guyer (CNotes xxiiiff.) explains some of the controversies surrounding the dating of the notes.

8. Klemme (1996, 27, 47–48) and Kuehn (1987, 178–79) provide details of the varied sources of information about Hume that were available to Kant. Kant would have reencountered Hume's denial of personal identity as he was reading Tetens (1777/1979).

Chapter 2

1. Some of the material I elide about 'reflection' is discussed in Chapter 5.
2. References to Locke's *Essay Concerning Human Understanding* will have this form, ECHU followed by book, chapter, and section numbers and the pagination in Locke (1690/1975). See also ECHU 2.21.4, 233–34, where Locke is explicit that bodies afford the mind no idea of thinking at all.
3. Shoemaker has tabulated a list of differences between inner sense and perception (1996, 204ff.)
4. Descartes listed doubting, understanding, affirming, denying, willing refusing, imagining and sensing as the mind's actions in the Second Meditation (1640/1984).
5. It is possible to interpret this passage as claiming that the idea of succession does come from a mental activity, namely the successive apprehending of different ideas. Although I can't pursue that possibility, it seems to be open.
6. I should offer a caveat. In this discussion and others I consider Kant's views of human thinking in relation to the deficiencies he sees in animals. I present this material not because I endorse any of his claims about animal cognition but because he uses the comparison to clarify the cognitive capacities of humans. As far as I can see, these discussions make no contributions to current debates about animal cognition; they are helpful in interpreting Kant.
7. I examine Kant's views about 'characteristic marks' in Chapter 9, section 3.
8. 'CLog' refers to Young (1992). It includes both student lecture notes and the *Logic* text Kant asked Jäsche to prepare for publication. Jäsche did the edition on the basis of Kant's handwritten logic notes (CLog xvi–xvi), which are included in volume 16 of the Academy edition. When I rely on Jäsche's edition, I often cite the relevant portion from the handwritten notes as well, giving the Reflection number and the page(s) in volume 16.
9. The editors to the Cambridge Editions of the various lecture courses provide extensive descriptions of the origins and subsequent treatment of the student 'notes.' See for example, CMet xxi–xxvii.
10. The oft-recounted story from Hamann is that Tetens's book lay open on Kant's desk as he wrote the *Critique*. See Bona Meyer (1870, 56). Kant reports his reading in a letter to Marcus Herz of April 1778:

> Tetens, in his diffuse work on human nature, made some penetrating points; but it certainly looks as if for the most part he let his work be published just as he wrote it down, without corrections . . . After exhausting himself and his reader [in a discussion of freedom from the second volume] he left the matter just as he found it, advising his reader to consult his own feelings. (10.232, CLet 167)

Carl (1989a, 115) discusses additional evidence, including notes in Kant's hand in his copy of Tetens.

11. References to Tetens are to Tetens (1777/1979) and include volume and page numbers.

12. One exception to this claim is the idealistic discussion of the A edition Fourth Paralogism. This material is deleted in the B edition.

Chapter 3

1. Reinhard Brandt argues that Rousseau may have provided inspiration for some of Kant's distinctive views about knowledge and the self. Kant read *Émile* during the 1760s (Kuehn, 2001, 129). Rousseau presents the Savoyard Vicar as engaging in a Cartesian exercise of doubting. His efforts led quickly to skeptical doubt about knowledge of a self distinct from its states:

> Who am I? . . . I exist . . . Do I have particular sentiments of my existence, or do I sense it only through my sensations? This is my first doubt, which it is for the present impossible for me to resolve; for as I am continually affected by sensation whether immediately or by memory, how can I know whether the sentiment of the *I* is something outside these same sensations and whether it can be independent of them? (1762/1979, 270)

Rousseau's question is slightly different from Hume's. Where Hume looked for the empirical basis of the representation of a unitary self, Rousseau asked whether he could know the 'I' to be something outside of sensations and independent of them. Further, he did not remain skeptical. He resolved the problem by pointing to the mind's activities:

> According to me, the distinctive faculty of the active or intelligent being is to be able to give sense to the word *is*. I seek in vain in the purely sensitive being for this intelligent force which superimposes and then which pronounces; I am not able to see it in nature . . .
>
> Therefore, I am not simply a sensitive and passive being but an active and intelligent one; and whatever philosophy may say about it, I shall dare to pretend to the honor of thinking . . .
>
> Having so to speak, made certain of myself, I begin to look outside myself . . . (1762/1979, 270, 272)

Two aspects of this discussion lend credence to the claim of influence. At a general level, Rousseau connects knowledge of self to intellectual activities. As we have seen (and will see in greater detail later on), Kant links the thinking 'I' of apperception to activities. Rousseau also specifically connects activities to the ability to use the word 'is.' In an important paragraph of the B deduction (§19), Kant explains that the ability to use the copula 'is' depends on the (active) understanding and the unity of apperception.

Although these similarities are striking, there are problems with the claim of influence. The evidence is not particularly strong, since the first passage cited above occurs in the margins of one of the student Anthropology lecture notes and not in other notes allegedly from the same course. Further, if Kant took the doubts of the Savoyard Vicar seriously, then it is hard to understand why he would begin the discussion of the self by noting its substantiality, simplicity, and spontaneity, as he apparently did (25.10).

2. My discussion is indebted to the illuminating interpretation offered by Edwin McCann in 'Locke on Identity' (1987).

3. References to the *New Essays* (Leibniz, 1765/1996) are cited with the original section numbers as well as the pagination from the translation.

4. References to Leibniz's works other than the *New Essays* will be to Loemker's edition (Leibniz, 1969). They will be cited in the text by title of work and section number (e.g. '*Monadology* §1'), followed by the pagination in Loemker.

5. Kemp Smith's *Commentary* is the main source of this view (1923/1962, 207 and 207n.). There is also a wider debate about Hume's influence on Kant. H.-J. DeVleeschauwer (1962, 28, 42, though see also 64) and, more recently, Reinhard Brandt (1992, 102ff.) and Wolfgang Carl (1989a, 146ff.) have argued that Kant's claims to have been importantly influenced by Hume should not be taken at face value. It would take me too far afield to look at the arguments on both sides of this issue.

6. Robert Paul Wolff's (1960) discovery of the connection long predates mine. For reasons I don't understand, his own reading of Kant (Wolff, 1963) was unaffected by it and it was not discussed in the literature, which followed Kemp Smith (see the preceding note) in disavowing any direct knowledge of Hume on the self.

7. In 1982a and 1990 (Chapter 4), I assumed too hastily that because Kant provided a rebuttal to Hume's denial of the self that was his intention—rather than promoting his own agenda.

8. Eric Watkins (2009) has recently published an anthology of source materials to the *Critique* that has selections from Tetens, including this passage. He doesn't include the material on inner sense I discussed in Chapter 2. Since the volume just came out, I use the translation I had already made.

9. I presented a two-sentence account of this theory earlier (1990, 98). Falk Wunderlich (2005) provides a clear account of further aspects of Tetens's views.

10. Kant discusses the relations among the properties of continuing, permanence and substantiality in the Third Paralogism. See Chapter 11, pp.184–85.

11. As we shall see in Chapters 4 and 11, however, the presentation of Rational Psychology reported in L_1 is not completely straightforward.

12. The description occurs in a letter to Herz dated May 11, 1781 (10.270, CLet 181).

13. DeVleeschauwer offers the classic argument for this connection (1962, 85).

14. Carl observes that DeVleeschauwer noted that Kant's and Tetens's approaches were very different, without saying exactly where the differences lie. Carl makes good this lack by analyzing a further passage from L_1, when Tetens's influence would have been very great, and showing how completely Kant's investigation differs from Tetens's search for empirical origins (1989a, 120–25).

Chapter 4

1. 'CPract' refers to Gregor (1996).

2. References will be to the Olms edition of 1983 (Wolff, 1751/1983) and will be given in the text as Wolff gave them: abbreviated book title (*Meta[physik]*) with the section number, followed by the page number in the Olms 1983 edition. Watkins (2009) includes this paragraph and other useful material from Wolff.

3. See, for example, Ameriks (2000) and Watkins (2005).

4. Kant is reported as returning to this issue in the 'Volckmann' Metaphysics lecture notes of 1784 and 1785 (28.430–31). There he connects his discussion of 'power' directly to the principle of the Second Analogy, noting that empirical cognition depends on everything happening in accordance with laws. He also reiterates his criticism of Wolff that a power is a relation of a substance to accidents.

5. *Psychologica Rationalis* explains that it is still necessary to attribute different faculties, because

> they are actuated through the force, *which is subject to diverse laws*. (*Psychologica Rationalis*, no. 81, cited in Richards [1980, 235, n. 5], my emphasis)

6. Notes taken by Johann Gottfried Herder are included in volume 28 of the Academy edition in two places, because the latter collection was found after the first had been prepared for printing (CMet xxix). They are quite disordered and present no sustained discussion of Rational Psychology.

7. Chapter 14 places this passage in its broader context.

8. For further discussion of this issue, see Chapter 11, section 5.

9. Chapter 11 contrasts this treatment of the issues with the more expansive discussions of the Paralogisms chapter.

10. Julian Wuerth (forthcoming) traces the long history of this argument.

11. See Chapter 14.

12. Ameriks's general view of the Paralogisms chapter is that Kant's continued attraction to the arguments of Rational Psychology led him to support weakened versions of the conclusions. This doesn't seem correct even for the Second Paralogism. Kant says that in this case, as in that of the First Paralogism, 'the formal proposition of apperception, "I think," remains the sole basis on which Rational Psychology ventures to expand its cognition' (A354). Thus, if the 'verse argument' is the basis of Kant's support for the conclusion of the Second Paralogism, it must be because that argument also stands behind his support for the principle of apperception itself. Allison holds that position (1983, 138), but it is not clear that Ameriks would subscribe to it.

Chapter 5

1. Udo Thiel (1994) argues that Locke was concerned to distinguish 'consciousness' from 'reflection.' In the text, I claim that Locke took reflection to be ubiquitous by appealing to a text where he says that all acts are 'conscious.' Although I believe that Thiel may well be right about Locke's intentions, I think that Leibniz read him as interchanging 'consciousness' and 'reflection' and my interest is primarily in the reaction to Locke's view rather than the view itself. Thiel also thinks that Leibniz read Locke as taking consciousness to be reflection.

2. I'm grateful to Desmond Hogan for the reference to Crusius's highly relevant text.

3. Both Thiel (1996, 220) and Wunderlich (2005, 41–42) report that Andreas Rüdiger also argued that differentiation presupposes consciousness in an essay of 1727.

4. Perhaps Crusius's point is also that differentiation requires not just a power of consciousness, but consciousness of specific items to be compared.

5. Thiel presents this theme as linking Merian to Tetens, as it plainly does. It is also relevant to Kant's view of the 'I think.'

6. Brandt also cites this remarkable claim (1994).

Chapter 6

1. Guyer offers an interesting discussion of this note that considers it in relation to a wider variety of topics (1987, 49–50).

2. I consider some possibilities for these conditions in Chapter 13, section 2.

3. My attention was drawn to this passage from Longuenesse's discussion (1998, 97). She takes 'exponent' to refer to a relation of concepts that belongs to a series. So the idea would be that a particular subject-predicate relation would be part of a series of, for example, subjects that are predicates for other subjects. This may be Kant's view. I emphasize only the notion of an 'exponent' as indicating a relation among concepts, because that is all that the note says and because that seems to be his usage in other notes.

4. Chapter 13, section 2 provides a way of spelling out this mysterious seeming determination of a sensation as an indicator of a particular sort of reality.

5. Besides the passages I cite, Kant addresses the issue of connecting sensory and intellectual representations in eight other *Duisburg* passages: 17.649, 653, 654–55, 660, 663, 664, 666, and 667–68. For this reason, I think that Alison Laywine's (2006) suggestion that these notes are importantly concerned with metaphysical issues from *Inaugural Dissertation* is somewhat overstated. The issue Kant comes back to again and again in these notes is the epistemological problem he diagnosed in the letter to Herz.

6. See Chapter 7 for further discussion of Carl's idea of a 'subjective' deduction.

7. '*Identität*' occurs in one passage (R4676, 17.653), '*identisch*' in two (R4674, 17.645, 17.646). In all three occurrences the topic is logical identity.

8. Another passage of the *Duisburg Nachlaβ* presents conditions for intuitions and perceptions:

> Everything that is **thought** as an object of intuition stands under a rule of construction.
> Everything that is **thought** <u>as an object of perception stands under a rule of apperception, self-perception.</u>
> Experience in general. Either intuition or sensation.
> <u>Appearance is made objective by being brought as contained under a title of self-perception</u> and thus the original relations of apprehension are the conditions of the perception of the real relations in appearance. (R4677, 17.658, CNotes 167, my underscoring)

One might argue that the underscored passages are early statements of the claim that any representation of an object must be subject to the conditions of apperception, including its identity or including the condition (title) that representations relate to a subject (citation F). But the context suggests that apperception's role is that of the source of rules for unifying representations in representations of objects. The faculty of apperception continues to play this important role in the *Critique*. But it is a different role from that of the requirement of the unity (meaning identity) of apperception.

9. We can see these points illustrated in a text that Carl uses to pinpoint his disagreement with Guyer:

> The condition of all apperception is the unity of the thinking being. From this flows the connection of the manifold according to rules and in a totality. (R4675, 17. 651, CNotes 163, Carl, 1989a, 90)

As Carl explains, two readings are possible, because the antecedent of 'this' is ambiguous between the 'unity' of the thinking being and the entire preceding thought. On the first interpretation, the unity of the thinking being would be the source of the connections. The subject, *qua* substance, would bring about the connecting and Carl's view would gain considerable support. And no issue of identity would arise. Now suppose that the antecedent of 'this' is taken to be the whole first sentence. Then the connection of the manifold by the rules would be the necessary condition for the (temporal) unity of empirical apperception, as Guyer believes. Again, however, the temporal unity is only a necessary condition for states to be apperceived as belonging to a subject; by itself temporal unity does not imply an identical apperception.

Chapter 7

1. Tetens suggested rephrasing the question of 'objective' truth along these lines in the *Versuche*:

> Whether the necessary laws of thinking of our understanding are only subjective laws of our thinking faculty or whether they are laws for every thinking faculty in general? (1777/1979, 1:540)

2. See my 1990 (Chapter 1, *passim*), for further discussion.

3. Kant also discusses analytic versus synthetic methods in the published version of his logic lectures:

> **Analytic** is opposed to **synthetic** method. The former begins with the conditioned and grounded, while the latter goes from principles to consequences or from the simple to the composite. The former could also be called **regressive**, as the latter could be called **progressive**. (9.149, CLogic 639)

In describing the analytic method as regressing from the 'conditioned and grounded,' Kant means, I take it, that it regresses from an accepted body of propositions. On that assumption his presentations of the difference between the methods would be consistent.

4. I'm grateful to an anonymous referee for Oxford University Press for reminding me that Kant is clear that the investigation is to proceed from an inquiry into pure reason.

5. Margaret Wilson (1974) was an early advocate of this interpretation.

6. Cf. Strawson (1966, 250).

7. Kuehn (1997, 236–39) also discusses intermediate figures who develop other means of establishing the possibility of a concept, including Lambert and Tetens, whom Kant certainly read.

8. Here I am in agreement with Kuehn (1997, 240) that Allison is mistaken in sharply differentiating 'objective reality' and 'objective validity' (1983, 133ff.).

9. Carl's account of the logical relation between these two arguments conflicts with popular readings of Kant's two most explicit observations on the 'subjective' deduction. On Carl's reading, the subjective deduction is a necessary complement to the objective deduction. But when Kant explains the difference between these sides in the A Preface, he suggests that the subjective one is dispensable:

> This study . . . has two sides. The one side refers to the objects of pure understanding and is intended to establish and make comprehensible the objective validity of understanding's *a priori* concepts, and precisely because of this pertains to my purposes essentially. The other side seeks to examine pure understanding itself as regards its possibility and the cognitive powers underlying it in turn, and hence seeks to examine it in a subjective respect. And although this latter exposition is of great importance for my main purpose, it does not pertain to it essentially. For the main question is always this: what, and how much, can understanding and reason cognize independently of all experience? Rather than: how is our **power of thought** itself possible? This latter question is, as it were, a search for the cause of a given effect, and to that extent there is something about it resembling a hypothesis. (Axvi)

A second well-known observation comes in a note to the *Metaphysical Foundations of Natural Science*. It also suggests that what is crucial for Kant's purposes is only the proof that the categories are principles of any possible experience and not the account of how experience is made possible by them (4.475n., C1781 190).

In Carl's view, Kant caused needless trouble for himself with these comments. He believes that the 'subjective deduction' itself does not inspire worries about unjustified psychological hypotheses, because these passages contain analyses of the interrelations between the unity of apperception and object cognition. Only Kant's remarks raise this specter.

10. The complications are needed because my discussion abstracts from an important fact: cognizers cannot simply perceive the order of their states. Chapter 13 explains how the scrutinizing process might go when that condition is acknowledged.

11. Here I follow Arthur Melnick (1973) and, subsequently Guyer (1987) in interpreting Kant as taking causation to be a three place relation among powers or events, and earlier and later properties of substances.

12. Making the scrutiny process central to the reasoning of the transcendental deduction implies a way of interpreting transcendental idealism that is independently attractive. It offers a fine balance between the idealist and realist elements. The understanding does not ride roughshod over the data 'imposing' various concepts whatever the data. Rather, it examines the data to find sensations that may be represented as the bases for the application of laws. In opposition to the overly idealist 'imposition' model, Guyer has proposed a 'conditional' or 'selection' model (in Falkenstein's terminology [1995, 424, n. 4]). In this model, the categories are not imposed on sensory data; rather they serve as restrictions. If representations meet the conditions specified, then they can belong to a subject (Guyer, 1987, 53–55). Although it avoids excessive idealism, a conditional or 'selection' model gives the false impression that humans could perceive causes and substances and even temporal and spatial relations. The scrutinizing process suggests instead a 'selection-plus-imposition' model of transcendental idealism. When certain patterns are present in the data, the understanding selects the data to be represented as the basis for the application of one of its rules. It then represents the data as such.

13. A discussion added to the second edition makes a finer discrimination between principles that apply to things and principles that apply to cognition. Kant introduces the 'principle of the Schoolmen' that

quodlibet ens est unum, verum, bonum. (B113)

as a potential objection to the completeness of his table of 'transcendental' concepts. His objection to adding them is that

> these supposedly transcendental predicates of **things** are, in fact, nothing but logical requirements and criteria of all **cognition** of things in general, and prescribe for such cognition the categories of quantity, namely, **unity, plurality** and **totality**. But these categories, which, properly regarded, must be taken as material, belonging to the possibility of the things themselves, have, in this further application, been used only in their formal meaning, as being of the nature of logical requisites of all cognition, and yet at the same time have been incautiously converted from being criteria of thought to be properties of things in themselves. (B113–14)

At first glance, these remarks are confusing. Kant seems to say at once that the 'one,' the 'true,' and the 'good' are material—the terms apply to things—and also that they do not designate properties of things. He seems to complain that his predecessors took properties of thought to be properties of things—and also to say that categories must be taken to be properties of things not of thought. Kemp Smith tried to forestall confusion by interpolating '[empirical objects]' after 'things themselves' in line 5.

The unclarity is, however, superficial. Kant's general position is that his predecessors wrongly took categorial or transcendental concepts to apply to things as they are in themselves apart from cognition. In fact, 'transcendental' concepts indicate properties that are found, not in all objects whatsoever, but in all objects insofar as they can be represented in human cognition. What is new in this paragraph is a further distinction between, if I can put it this way, the formal properties of cognition, *per se*, and the 'formal material' properties of objects of cognition. Logical consistency is a formal property of cognition, regardless of particular contents. Kant thinks that qualitative unity and qualitative plurality are also formal properties of cognition without regard to content. So, regardless of content, the different parts of a concept should fit together as the theme of a play (qualitative unity) and it should embrace sufficient marks that it implies the maximum of true consequences about the 'objects' to which it applies (qualitative plurality). By contrast, what he thinks of as true categories do not characterize properties of cognition in general; they characterize objects that can belong to human cognition in general. Understood in another way, as representing 'unity,' 'plurality,' and 'totality,' the Ancient transcendental concepts are categories that apply to objects of cognition. By contrast, in the proposed additional usage, the 'transcendental' concepts do not transcend the differences across objects, because they do not characterize objects, but cognition. Proper 'transcendental' concepts are the *a priori* concepts of objects in general that make human cognition possible.

Chapter 8

1. This rendering is similar to Kemp Smith's.

2. Falkenstein's discussion of the 'blindness' of synthesizing has led me to think more about this operation (1995, 54ff.).

3. As Westphal has also noted (2004, 101ff.)

4. Longuenesse also thinks the model is limited and must be supplemented by a logical reflection model (1998, 33). In the Appendix to Chapter 13, I discuss why I think logical reflection is also inadequate.

5. I say 'something like,' because Friedman has pointed out the one of Kant's difficulties was that he lacked the contemporary understanding of 'continuity' (1992, 72).

6. Longuenesse dismisses the importance of the examples (1998, 213), but that seems a fairly implausible move, both in itself and in light of the centrality of the causal concept for Kant.

7. In this discussion I stay neutral on the debate about whether Kant takes events or powers to be causes. I return to the issue in Chapter 10.

8. My account of the imaginative synthesis or the *synthesis speciosa* raises an obvious question. What is the relation between this synthesis and the *schemata*, which are also characterized as products of the secret arts (A142/B181) of the imagination (A140/B179)? Kant aims to solve a number of puzzles in the Schematism chapter. One problem comes from the 'concept application as image matching' theories of the Empiricists. He will handle Berkeley's famous objection that no image can be adequate to apply the concept 'man' to the fat and the thin or the concept 'triangle' to the scalene and equilateral. The proposal is that cognizers do not compare images, but the imaginative procedures that they go through in perceiving men and triangles (A140–41/B180). Regardless of the plausibility of the solution, the case of the pure concepts of understanding is different, because whereas men and triangles can be perceived, necessary succession cannot. In this case Kant's idea is that cognizers order the materials of sense according to *a priori* rules of understanding, so they have a sensory representation of, for example, a B-property gradually transforming into a C-property in the continuing presence of some condition or power A. Hence the *schemata* seem to perform the same job as the *synthesis speciosa*. Yet, Kant does not identify the processes. Perhaps the reason is that the transcendental deduction and the Schematism Chapter have different *explananda*. The latter is supposed to provide a general account of how object representations are subsumed under concepts (A137/B176). The former is supposed to provide a general theory of how *a priori* concepts relate to objects of the senses, by showing how an intellectual synthesis could both differ from and direct an imaginative synthesis.

To my knowledge, Longuenesse (1998) is the first person to explore in depth the important (and in retrospect, obvious) question of the relation between the *synthesis speciosa* and the *schemata*. I resist her otherwise extremely plausible account, because the *schemata* or *synthesis speciosa* cannot bridge the gap from logical comparison to subsumption under categorial principles (see the Appendix to Chapter 13).

9. The model is also unfaithful because it includes only two processes and so abandons the A deduction's 'three synthesis' theory. Still the B edition seems also to replace a three-step process with two processes, the intellectual and imaginative syntheses. This is not a matter of abandoning the innovation of the productive imagination that was linked to the original second synthesis, but of recognizing that sensory perception requires a productive imagination (a point already noted at A120n.). What is jettisoned is the attempt to provide a transcendental basis for the law of association.

10. As further evidence of Sensationist leanings, George cites the discussion of sensations in the Anticipations of Perceptions:

> Apprehension by means of sensation occupies only an instant, if, that is, I do not take into account the succession of different sensations. Since sensation is that in an appearance which does not involve a successive synthesis proceeding from the parts to the whole representation, it has no extensive magnitude. (George, 1981, 240, A167/B209)

Much of George's case is persuasive, but there are countervailing considerations. In his view, the Anticipations passage would be a premise for Kant's claim that the representation of objects as spatial and extended must be a result of an interpretation placed on sensations, a figurative synthesis (1981, 240). The location of the Anticipations chapter, after the discussion of synthesis and the introduction of the *synthesis speciosa*, makes this argumentative structure less likely.

More important, the particular course of the discussions in the Axioms of Intuition and the Anticipations of Perception suggest that the passage is better read as a conclusion than as a premise. The first line of the proof of the Axioms presupposes that the representations of space and time are *a priori:*

> In respect of form [*der Form nach*], appearances contain an intuition in space and time that lies *a priori* at the basis [*zum Grunde liegt*] of them all [*insgesammt*]. (A162/B202, amended translation)

That is, the opening assumption is that space and time are not sensed but are *a priori* forms. The initial move in the proof of the Anticipations makes the same assumption:

> Perception is empirical consciousness, i.e., a consciousness in which there is sensation as well. Appearances, as objects of perception, are not pure (i.e. merely formal) intuitions, as space and time are (for these cannot in themselves be perceived at all). (A166/B207)

Kant's point is not that, because sensations have neither spatial nor temporal extent, then space and time must be forms of intuitions; it is that, since space and time are merely forms of intuitions and cannot be sensed, cognition requires the presence of something that can be sensed and of sensations. Similarly, the claim above that apprehension by means of sensation takes only an instant and has no magnitude does not seem to be a premise, but a (further) conclusion that follows from the conclusions established in the Transcendental Aesthetic.

One could reply that these passages repeat the claims of the Transcendental Aesthetic— which are supported by Sensationism. The wording of the 'first exposition' of space offers some evidence in favor of this view:

> Space is not an empirical concept that has been abstracted from outer experiences. For the representation of space must already lie at the basis in order for sensations to be referred to something outside me (i.e. to something in a location in space other than the location in which I am). (A23/B38)

Although this passage raises the issue of providing a referent for sensations, the parallel discussion of time does not.

Time is not an empirical concept that has been abstracted from any experience. For simultaneity or succession would not even enter our perception if the representation of time did not lie at the basis [*zum Grunde läge*] *a priori*. (A30/B46, amended translation)

When considered in light of the parallel account of time, the first exposition of space appears to be more focused on the location of objects than on objective reference *per se*. The other three expositions of space do not mention the issue; the second exposition considers the possibility of representing space with no objects in it. Finally, Kant's clear allusions to the Newton-Leibniz debate (e.g., A32/B49) make the traditional hypothesis of the source of his views about the status of spatial and temporal representations more likely than Sensationism.

11. Hoppe discusses the question of atomism in perception, but not the specific Sensationist thesis (1983, 77ff.).

12. Although synthesis is defined as an act, some texts, such as A120 cited above (p. 108–109) present representations as simply containing a multiplicity of perceptions.

13. Hoppe is not alone in making this *prima facie* odd move. I criticize Henry Allison's appeal to the verse argument to establish the unity of apperception in Chapter 10, p. 167.

14. For the canonical account see Block (1995, 2002).

15. See also the discussions of A120 and A120n. that connect the formation of images to the ordering of representations.

Chapter 9

1. At B139, Kant characterizes the synthetic unity as the first principle of human understanding; he also characterizes it as the 'highest principle' of cognition. As we shall see, these characterizations are consistent with his view that it is none the less dependent on the use of categorial concepts and principles.

2. That is, Chapter 1 of Book 1 of Division 1 of Part 2, 'The Clue to the Discovery of All Pure Concepts of Understanding.'

3. Longuenesse offers a 'logical' gloss of these texts (1998, 81).

4. The agreement is not universal, because some take the argument for the categories to come in the 'metaphysical deduction.'

5. See, for example, Howell's helpful presentation (1992, 61ff.).

6. I'm grateful for Christopher Peacocke for urging me to remove any suggestion that Kant takes cognizers to have a meta-cognitive vocabulary of 'marks' and 'representations.'

7. I'm grateful to a comment by Stephanie Grüne that led me to see that I should discuss a wider range of cases of concepts.

8. In a note to the B Paralogisms, Kant also raises the contrast between differentiating and being aware of the basis of the differentiation:

> A clear representation is, rather, one in which the consciousness suffices for **being conscious of the distinction** between this representation and others. If the consciousness suffices for distinguishing between them but not for being conscious of the distinction, then the representation would still have to be called obscure. Hence there are infinitely many degrees of consciousness, down to it vanishing. (B414–15)

Although a human's consciousness of her representations may have degrees, from the obscure to the clear, Kant does not believe that the difference between human and animal cognizers is one of degree. Sometimes humans can act 'instinctively,' with little awareness of what they do. Animals are incapable of being conscious of their representations as such, *a fortiori*, incapable of being conscious of them as the basis of the way they distinguish things (cf. 25.1033).

9. This is not meant to be an appallingly bad pun on 'recognition.'

10. I made this over-hasty assumption in Kitcher (2008).

11. My understanding of the status of this principle was clarified by a workshop hosted by Tobias Rosefeldt at the University of Konstanz in June 2008.

12. Béatrice Longuenesse used this helpful formulation in a conversation in February of 2006.

13. In the B edition Paralogisms Kant characterizes the principle that different states belong to a single subject as 'analytic.' See Chapter 11, section 4, for discussion.

14. I make no effort to defend Kant's appeal to rules associated with concepts. On Kripke's (1982) interpretation of Wittgenstein's discussion of rule-following (1953), it makes no sense to say that concept-users follow rules for or associated with concepts. As far as I understand that argument, Kant's position would be vulnerable to Kriptensteinian skepticism about rules. Whether this skepticism can be mitigated has been a subject of intense debate. Paul Boghossian (2008) offers a recent endorsement and expansion of the argument for rule skepticism.

15. For further discussion see my 1990 (Chapter 8) and Philip Kitcher (1982).

16. I offer this more precise formulation after Béatrice Longuenesse and Robert Howell questioned how '2' could be a partial representation of '4' at a meeting of the German Idealism Workshop on November 20, 2009. I use the term 'group' rather than 'set' in the text, because Kant predates any systematic study of sets. On the other hand, his logic notes contain proto-Venn diagrams indicating the relations of set inclusion for different types of judgments. See, for example, R3036, 16.627.

17. Jen Saugstal pointed out that because numbers can be used in two ways, as ordinals and as cardinals, there is some ambiguity about how exactly to understand Kant's argument. In the text, I assume the 'cardinal' reading, because Kant uses the term '*Menge.*' Still the argument can also be run on an ordinal reading. In this case, it is not that a set of stroke symbols exemplifies the '4' rule, but that the counter has kept track of where he is in number sequence. He designates the next stroke symbol as the 'fourth' not on the basis of the '4' rule, but on the basis of his being aware of where he is in the sequence. In either case, Kant's point is that the use of number concepts in adding or in counting is possible only through an awareness of the judgmental state '4' or 'fourth' as dependent on representations contained in other states.

18. Kant's use of 'faint' in this passage, and his claim at B133–34 that a thought of synthesis is not a consciousness of synthesis (discussed below), led me in (1990) to claim that he vacillated on what I stigmatized as 'synthesis-watching.' As is clear in the cited passage, however, conscious synthesizing—though not consciousness of synthesis—is central to his view.

19. Chapter 15 spells out the problems in greater detail (section 4).

20. I owe this formulation to a very helpful discussion with Sebastian Rödl. Even though the awareness of a mental action cannot be separate from it, when the awareness occurs, it might seem that there are mental actions that are not accompanied by awareness. Chapter 15's discussion of the possibility of rational cognition in the absence of self-awareness also considers the possibility of rational mental action in the absence of awareness.

21. Because he wants to argue that cognition of succession (and so change) in one's mental states requires cognition of change in the world, Kant focuses on a principle associated with 'substance,' *viz.*, that in all alteration, substance is permanent. But he takes the category to be that of the inherence of properties in objects (and ultimately substances), A80/B106.

22. See Chapter 7 (section 5).

23. Wunderlich (2005, 56, n. 193) suggests that Eberhard's claims may have been a target of the Second Paralogism in A.

24. The text I elide concerns the relation between the unity of apperception and that of space and time. This was a doctrine Kant sometimes offered, but did not in the end maintain.

25. See Chapter 7 (pp. 94–95) and Chapter 8 (p. 107).

26. Besides the account of the difference between innate representations and *a priori* ones in the reply to Eberhard, Kant apparently also considered the priority of the faculties and the necessity of data in his set of metaphysics lectures L₁. In reply to the question of whether pre-birth souls have cognitions, he explains that

> the soul . . . already possessed all abilities and faculties; but such that these abilities developed only through the body, and that it acquired all the cognitions that it has of the world only through the body . . . **The state of the soul before birth was thus without consciousness of the world and of itself.** (28. 284, CMet 93)

Although the issue concerns the necessity of embodiment, the position is the same as that offered in the Reply to Eberhard. Humans come equipped with faculties (and so with innate tendencies to operate in various ways), but without sensory data they cannot have cognition or even consciousness of themselves. On his view, the faculty of apperception and its the I-rule precede the receipt of sensory data, but the consciousness of unity of consciousness and perhaps the unity itself, arise only through the receipt of data—and only through the receipt of data that can be handled in such a way that the I-rule can find application.

27. I use the counting example as the parade case of Kant's theory, because he does in the A deduction and because it is simpler. In the case of 'body,' for example, for the judgment to be rational, it might not be based on a partial representation 'extended,' but on some other partial representation such as 'shape.' Or it could even be used as a simple concept such as 'orange' is used, where the rationality of the cognition does not rest on any particular partial cognition, but on the presumption of a set of similar representations from which the concept was 'abstracted.' In the latter case, the cognition is rational—is a case where the subject knows the basis or ground—because she takes the present judgment to be based on the similarity of the present instance to the instances from which she abstracted the concept. Here, too, in making the judgment, the subject is aware of its rational dependence on and so necessary connection to, the earlier states.

28. Several critics saw Wolff's appeal to differentiation as involving too much complexity to provide a basis for self-consciousness—because differentiation implicitly involved judging (Wunderlich, 2005, 41–42). If the critics were right, and Wolff saw object differentiation as requiring judgment, then his claim that cognizers were aware of themselves through being aware of their acts of differentiating or judging would be in substantial agreement with the doctrines of the *Critique*. On that reading of Wolff, Kant would not be criticizing his predecessor's view, but elaborating it.

29. The claim that such possible unconnected sense data would be nothing to me repeats the assertions that any representation that could not participate in cognition would be impossible as a representation (A116, B132) or would be nothing to me (B132).

30. Carl made this point in conversation.

31. As noted in Chapter 1, it is not necessary that I know him to be here on this basis; I might have some other reason for the judgment. The point is that since I do know him to be here on the basis of seeing him by the window, the rationality of my judgment in this case depends on that observation.

32. In Chapter 15, I argue that Kant's view raises a significant obstacle to Evans's widely accepted approach to self-knowledge.

33. See note 35 for defense.

34. Kant elaborates by suggesting that representations that have been synthesized can be analyzed. Presumably the idea is that analysis is more obviously a single (type) of operation. Still, I'm not confident I see his point about analysis.

35. I'm grateful to a referee for OUP for pressing me on how to read this passage. Although *'einig'* strongly suggests a single act, I don't think *'einig'* can be handled separately from *'ursprünglich.'* But reading Kant as suggesting that all of a human's cognition comes out of a single original act moves him too close to a Leibnizean view that the course of (cognitive) life is just the unfolding of a single principle.

36. Cf. the claim about spatial representation reflecting the peculiar character of the receptive faculty in the citation from the Reply to Eberhard above.

37. I'm grateful to Bernard Thöle for raising this objection in response to an earlier description of what the counter does. The relation between these two rules will be crucial in Kant's diagnosis of the errors of the Rational Psychologists in the Paralogisms.

38. Hence I think Allison errs in dismissing this material (1983, 137).

39. See Chapter 5 (pp. 59–60). Henrich argues in a well-known essay that Kant follows many predecessors in adopting an impossible 'reflection' theory of consciousness (1966, 191–93). The criticism of Locke (or of someone who holds Locke's position and/or of Wolff or someone who holds his position) at the pinnacle of the B deduction shows that he well understood that cognizers cannot use reflection, or mere consciousness of representations, to bootstrap their way either to having a self or to being self-conscious.

40. I'm grateful to Robert Howell for stressing the importance of making clear Kant's own difficulties with reference to an 'I.'

41. I argued in section 5 that there is no inconsistency between the claim that the 'I-think' is an *a priori* representation and so, in a sense, 'precedes' actual thought and the claim that the unity of apperception is made possible through the unity (or combinability) of representations.

42. In the setup to this discussion, Kant mentions the other two sorts of judgments, the hypothetical and the disjunctive. Presumably these would work in the same way. In a hypothetical judgment, the relation is not between concepts, but between judgments (B141). These are linked not by the copula 'is' but by the connective 'then' (cf. 9.105–106, CLog 600–601). So in the judgment, 'If cold it applied to water, *then* it freezes' the connective 'then' would indicate a reference to the *objective* unity of apperception. In this case, the object rule 'events or changes are brought about by causes' would be the *a priori* template underlying the judgment 'if cold is applied to water, then it freezes.'

43. Bernard Thöle pressed this objection forcefully—and helpfully—at a discussion at the Max Planck institute in Berlin on December 3, 2007.

44. I'm grateful to an anonymous referee for Oxford University Press for leading me to clarify exactly what I aim to show.

45. Chapter 8 (p. 105–106).

46. My thinking on this issue has been much influenced by discussions with Christopher Peacocke and by chapter 7 of his (2008).

Chapter 10

1. Longuenesse appeals to some of Kant's remarks in the Mrongovius Metaphysics lectures (1998, 7n.) to suggest that he thinks of *'Vermögen'* as indicating the possibility of acting and *'Kraft'* as denoting the actualization of this potential in relation to perceptions (1998, 8). She expresses considerable hesitation about the consistency of his usage. Kant apparently began the discussion in the lectures by noting that it was quite hard to say what the difference between the two is. In the Metaphysics lectures, the topic of power is tied to the issues of basic and derivative powers. I suspect that distinction is the one he is concerned to preserve.

2. 'CJudge' indicates Guyer and Matthews (2000).

3. It does occur in the Transcendental Dialectic in presenting the Rationalist view he opposes, see A682/B710.

4. Pluhar renders the passages as follows:

> I call it original apperception; for it is the self-consciousness which, because it produces the representation I think that must be capable of accompanying all other representations[,] and [because it] is one [*ein*] and the same [*dasselbe*] in all consciousness, cannot be accompanied by any further representation. (B132)

Pluhar has a solid grammatical argument in favor of his translation. 'One and the same' cannot refer to 'the representation I think (*die Vorstellung: Ich denke*) because '*ein*' and '*dasselbe*' must have a neuter antecedent (1996, 77, n. 195). Since 'self-consciousness' (*dasjenige Selbstbewußtsein*) fits the bill, he takes it to be the subject of the description 'one and the same.'

There are, however, stylistic reasons for favoring not the 'representation "I think"' but just 'I think' as the subject of 'one and the same.' Kant often uses the expression 'das Ich denke' ('the I think'), most notably at B131-32. Given that distinctive locution, he may be referring back not to 'representation,' which would require feminine forms, but to its content, 'das Ich denke.' Further, it seems that 'one and the same' must modify 'the 'I think,' because the reference of the last phrase to a 'further' representation 'accompanying' something suggests that the subject under discussion is the content of a representation. Additional support for this reading comes from the *Anthropology*, where Kant digresses to explain cognition. He uses the same phrase, '*ein und dasseble*,' to refer to the 'I', which is said to be one and the same in all judgments, because it is only the form of consciousness (7.141).

5. As noted in Chapter 9, endnote 18, I did not take adequate account of conscious synthesis in earlier work. As I understand his position, Allison does not take cognition to involve act-consciousness; his focus is on the spontaneity of judgments. Where we now agree is in recognizing that cognizers must grasp their reasons as such. On my account it is not just that cognizers have the capacity to grasp their reasons as such but that they do so through their conscious synthesizing.

6. For a more extensive discussion of this issue, see Rödl (2007, Chapter 3). My formulation of this point is indebted to this account.

7. Allison draws this conclusion (1983, 278, 292-93).

8. Chapter 4 (section 4).

9. I'm grateful to a referee for Oxford University Press for leading me to make this point more straightforwardly. I discuss these matters further in Chapter 14.

Chapter 11

1. See Chapter 1 (p. 5).

2. Rolf-Peter Horstmann follows Ameriks's lead and adds that looking to the chapter for enlightenment about Kant's I-theory rather than in relation to the theories of his time may cause one to miss its essential points (1993, 408-9). In his new book, *Kant's Theory of the Self*, Arthur Melnick sets out on his interpretation of the Paralogisms without first considering the positive theory of thinking from the transcendental deduction. On the other hand, Katja Crone (2007, 160) believes that the discussion of the Paralogisms is enriched by the deduction material.

3. Kant's nearly contemporary lecture notes (as reported by students), the 'Metaphysics Mrongovius,' assert exactly what he is denying in his published work:

> If we leave aside all accidents, then substance remains, this is the pure subject in which everything inheres or is the substantial, <u>e.g. I.</u> (29.771, CMet 179, my underscoring)

When presumed to be accurate and read on its own, this passage suggests that Kant believed that cognizers have some cognizance of a substantial 'I.' In the published work, he is clear that this hope of Rationalist metaphysics must remain unfulfilled.

4. See the discussions in section 4 of Chapter 4.
5. I did not appreciate this point in my 1982b or 1990.
6. 'CRel' indicates Wood and Di Giovanni (1996).

Kant also discusses this issue in the 'Pillau' Anthropology lectures of 1777–78:

> The identity of the self is very incomplete. If he has done something bad, anyone can afterwards improve himself, and not, however, for [merely] a short time. [Such a one] is no longer punished in revenge, because he is not the same any longer (though [he is] punished as an example. (25.735–36)

Perhaps the point of the doctrine of the Religion book also has something to do with making the individual an example—or perhaps with not allowing him to be an example of someone who escapes punishment.

7. Wuerth made this observation in a very useful conversation in May of 2009 that also gave me a number of ideas for organizing the materials of this chapter in ways to make my disagreements with others (including him) more perspicuous.

8. Brook (1994), Henrich (1989a) and Longuenesse (1998) think of the unity of apperception in terms of the consistency of the subject's set of representations, which might be a way of developing the title of composition (or coherence).

9. Chapter 9 (pp.147–8 presents his argument for the claim that the 'I-think' is the vehicle of all concepts.

10. Here as in the crucial discussion of the necessity consciousness of a synthesis of apperception at B134–35 (Chapter 9, p. 146) I follow Kemp Smith in translating '*noch keine*' simply by 'not' rather than by 'not yet,' as Pluhar does, because that rendering makes no sense in context. Kant's position isn't that the modes of self-consciousness are 'not yet' concepts of objects, as if they could somehow become such concepts.

11. In the B Paralogisms, the discussion is couched in terms of change (*Wechsel*) of states and not conversion (*Umwandlung*).

12. Here I borrow Manfred Frank's expression 'bare existence' (2007). Frank takes these passages to reveal terrible weaknesses in the theory of the 'I' offered by the transcendental deduction, weaknesses that are somewhat ameliorated by the long note in the Paralogisms that is discussed next. I disagree with his suggestion that Kant resolves the problem in that note by invoking an 'indeterminate' perception as a preintuitive consciousness of the self. As I explain below, the issue seems to concern abstraction from any particular intuition, and even form of intuition, and not a peculiar type of intuition.

13. See note 10 above.

14. The Reflection "Is it an Experience that I think?" (R5661, discussed in Chapter 10, section 5) seems to allow for thought without any perception. Kant considers first drawing a square in thought and then just thinking about one. Since the latter exercise can lead to an episode of thinking of the properties of a square, this unpublished reflection seems to offer a counterexample to the 'no cognition without intuition or perception' doctrine.

15. Manfred Frank takes the 'indeterminate perception' in this difficult passage to be a characterization of the nature of the 'I-think' representation (2007). That is, he takes 'I think' to designate an indeterminate perception. Kant's language (*ausdrucken, bedeuten*) can easily be read as Frank suggests. I resist this approach for two reasons: the indeterminate perception is empirical, and Kant immediately reminds the reader of the *a priori* character of the 'I-think'; the indeterminate perception is introduced as a perception or intuition and Kant is explicit that the awareness in synthesizing is not an intuition (also see below). My

reading is very different, since I take 'indeterminate perception' not to refer to the consciousness of synthesis, but to materials to be thought in abstraction from any particular kind of intuition.

16. Frank modifies the condemnation in light of the note to B422, which he reads as proposing that the categories of quality apply *via* intuition.

Chapter 12

1. Cited in Allison (1983, 247–48).

2. Beyond the Paralogisms, Kant objects to these views in the Final Aim section of the Appendix to the Transcendental Dialectic. See Chapter 10, section 6.

3. Falkenstein, for example, argues that the paradox of the continuum led Kant to believe that space and time could not exist, because then contemporary notions of them were inconsistent (1995, 35–41).

4. These issues are discussed in Chapter 10 (sections 4 and 5). I return to a more extensive consideration of the issue of freedom of thought in connection with of that of action in Chapter 14.

5. Although I disagree with them at points, my discussion is indebted to the extensive work of Gerold Prauss (1974/1989) and Henry Allison (1983) on these texts.

6. Kant's discussions of 'noumena' and the 'transcendental object' often involve a third technical term, 'things in themselves' (*Dinge an sich*). Kant's uses of '*Dinge an sich*' are confusing, because he makes three different distinctions between 'appearances' and 'things in themselves.' One distinction is evident, that between empirical illusions and empirical things in themselves (e.g., A29–30/B45). The second, between phenomena and noumena, is also fairly clear. But he also uses it to make a third distinction, that between an appearance and the 'basis' of that appearance. The potential for confusing the last two distinctions is on full display in the Antinomy text.

7. Prauss notes that Kant's account of empirical affection was thoroughly causal (1974/1989, 208).

8. My thinking about this issue has been greatly aided by Prauss's discussion of the 'problem of empirical affection' (1974/1989, 205ff.). In a sense, my view is the converse of Prauss's. Whereas he thinks that Kant had a solution to the problem of empirical affection that empirical psychologists could not achieve with merely empirical methods, I think that Kant made the problem of empirical affection unnecessarily difficult, whereas psychophysicists well understand how to solve it. (Prauss does not raise the issue in connection with the text on which I focus, A494–95/B522–23.) For Prauss, the difficulty is how one thing, say, a red impression, can be understood both as caused by an object and as the not yet interpreted basis of empirical cognition. In his view, Kant's theory of experience solves this, by looking at the impression in two respects—as the effect of an object upon the subject's faculties and as an impression that the subject uses as the basis of cognition. Although I think that analysis is correct, it seems to me that most psychologists also take this dual view. On my account, the problem with empirical affection in Kant's philosophy is that provides unwitting support to the JVS interpretation. The difficulty arises not from general considerations about the basis of empirical cognition, but from distinctive features of Kant's account, in particular, his claims about the subjective sources of the forms and categories.

9. Allison reads 'correlate' so that it would contrast with cause (1983, 242).

10. Although I agree with Allison on this point, I disagree with his suggestion that the transcendental object is the ground of knowledge taken as a whole (1983, 252). In the discussion to follow, I understand 'transcendental object' to be an abstract description of the causes of particular representations.

11. I say 'roughly,' because I am leaving out objects that cannot be sensed, such as the other side of the moon, or objects that can no longer be sensed, because they existed in the past. Kant takes these sorts of objects to be knowable by a chain of inference from objects that can be sensed (A225–26/B272–73 and A493/B521). The discussion of how to understand receptivity is introduced in terms of the problem of knowledge of the past.

12. Kant offers a very similar analysis of the sense of taste in his handwritten logic notes, though the topic is primary and secondary qualities (R1676, 16.77, CNotes 35).

13. This point represents my basic disagreement with Allison's understanding of this cluster of issues. Allison's analysis is that 'thing in itself' is a way of characterizing an object, as independent of the 'epistemic conditions' required for cognition. Since those conditions include space, time, and the categories, to regard something as a '*Ding an sich*' is to regard it in abstraction from those properties (1983, 250). Although this would be true, it does not explain why Kant believes that a nonsensible object must be the *cause* of perceptions. The explanation is that objects cannot strike the senses in terms of their spatial, temporal, and categorial properties.

14. As far as I can see, Falkenstein makes a similar mistake in his otherwise extremely clear-headed analysis of the Transcendental Aesthetic. In his view, Kant's strategy for 'isolating' the forms of sense is

> hopeless. Even if Kant could succeed in removing everything intellect thinks through its concepts from experience, he would be left with something that, according to blindness ['intuitions without concepts are blind'], would not be an object of knowledge. (1995, 56, see also 149)

On Kant's theory, the subject of cognition needs to add concepts to his intuitions to have cognition. This is, however, perfectly compatible with a cognitive theorist finding a different mode of access to intuitions and describing those representations however he may.

15. Allison tries to explain away this usage on the grounds that Kant means 'cause' only in the purely logical sense, so he is not being inconsistent in characterizing a '*Ding an sich*' as 'causal' (1983, 254). The problem with this solution is that Kant's empirical realism requires that the relation between representations and their causes be real, and not merely logical.

16. Further, Kant suggests at one point (A288/B344) that the transcendental object might be annulled if sensibility were eliminated. I take the problem to be that a key without the lock to receive it would not be a key and so could not be designated as the correlate of sensibility, that is, as the transcendental object.

17. That is, I'm assuming that by 'appearance' in this passage Kant does not mean 'phenomenon' but 'representation'. If he meant the latter, the argument would not work, since phenomena can be causes of other phenomena.

18. See note 16 above, which suggests why the transcendental object might be annulled along with sensibility (because it is the key to which sensibility is the lock).

19. A passage that was deleted with the A Paralogisms chapter is even more peculiar with respect to terminology:

> [S]omething lies at the basis of outer appearances and affects our sense in such a way that this sense acquires the representations of space, matter, shape, etc., And this something, considered as noumenon (or better, as transcendental object), might yet also be simultaneously the subject of our thoughts . . . (A358)

Rather than correct himself, why doesn't he just put the claim correctly and leave it at that?

20. My understanding of this issue is indebted to Falkenstein's discussion of 'empirical affection' (1995, 326–27). I believe that that account of 'empirical affection' brings him very

close to the solution to the long-standing charge of internal inconsistency that I propose here. He does not see it that way, because he believes that Kant's reflections on the puzzles of contemporary theories of the nature of space and time convince him that real things cannot be spatial. As noted, my concern is only with the consistency of the theory of cognition in abstraction from any worries about space and time.

Chapter 13

1. Although Jacobi's objection is older, since he struck between the editions, this objection is nearly as venerable. Karl Leonhard Reinhold, who began to popularize the 'Critical' philosophy in the late 1780s, tried to make up for what he saw as the original's insufficiently critical attitude to its psychological assumptions by providing a 'metacritical' defense of them (my 1990, 6).

2. Allison also holds this view. I discuss his assimilation of the Kantian cognitive subject to the Kantian moral agent in Chapter 14.

3. As in Chapter 9, I do not try to defend Kant's use of rules or norms against rule skepticism.

4. A passage in the *Duisburg Nachlaß* is especially clear on this point:

I will not deem whatever I want in the appearance as either subject or predicate, rather it is determined as subject or respectively as ground. Thus what sort of logical function is actually valid of one appearance in regard to another, whether that of magnitude or of the subject, thus which function of judgments. <u>For otherwise we could use logical functions arbitrarily, without making out or perceiving that the object is more suitable for one than another</u> . . . (R4672, 17.635, CNotes 153–54, amended translation, my underscoring)

5. On this account the perception of motion depends on the lapse of time between the registering of information at different points on the retina. This assumption may seem to be at odds with Kant's denial of the reality of time. On the other hand, he is clear that phenomenal time is real and an omnipresent feature of lay and scientific theories (A36/B54ff.). Hence there are reasons to think the hypothesis is sufficiently congenial with Kant's views to be used as a supplement to them and also reasons to think it is not compatible with his overall position. The issue couldn't be solved except by a thorough investigation of his reason for the ideality of time thesis—which I can't attempt.

6. In my 1990 (263, n. 59), I wondered whether Harper's analysis undercut Kant's claims for causation. The text addresses and tries to remove that concern.

7. See note 9 below. I discuss the relations between time, motion, and causation at greater length in my 2004.

8. My claim is not that motion detectors are useful surrogates for all cases of causation. Kant's examples of freezing water and a (slow-moving) ship could not be detected in this way. I appeal to motion detectors only to illustrate how scrutinizing could work in a way that avoided the circularity regularly imputed to the theory of the Second Analogy.

9. In this way a perception's suitability as an instance of causation is a criterion for its representing a real motion.

10. The Jäsche logic also downgrades abstraction while stressing the importance of the other operations:

Abstraction is only a negative condition . . . the positive condition [for generating a universal representation] is comparison and reflection. (9.95, CLog 593, cf. R2865, 16.552–53)

11. Here I follow a fairly standard practice and take objects to be *prima facie* substances for Kant.

12. Current research—and standard views in the history of philosophy—take common motion to be an indicator of a single object. This indicator is, however, not exactly apt for Kant's example of a tree!

13. This claim is not in conflict with Kant's view in the Transcendental Dialectic that nature must help.

14. Katja Crone draws on some Kant's remarks about the feeling of self to suggest that he has a preconceptual notion of the self (2007, e.g., 162). My discussion in the text raises considerations that cast some doubt on this hypothesis.

15. Kant is more negative about common sense in *Prolegomena* than in his hand-written notes for the Logic lectures. I do not think the difference is significant, but is merely a reflection of his ire in the former with the inadequacy of the school of common sense philosophy.

16. I have not found a source for this passage in Kant's own notes and the concordances of CLog don't list references in any of the available Logic lectures. Young reports that Jäsche may have worked with a set of notes ('Hoffman') that were apparently destroyed during World War II (CLog xviii).

Appendix to Chapter 13

1. Besides Locke's *Essay*, they are included in the *Port Royal Logic* (Arnauld 1662/1964).

2. Longuenesse (1998, 147ff.) also discusses a fourth type of comparison that I don't consider.

3. In replying to criticisms of Sally Sedgwick and Henry Allison, Longuenesse writes:

> To have the category of substance is to have the rule: look for something that remains permanent while its properties change. (2005, 24)

Although this passage sounds very like my 'scrutinizing' account, it is offered in defense of her (1998) claim that the way to read B128 is as claiming that it is the logical functions of judgments that determine the intuition.

4. In the 'Volckmann' metaphysics lecture notes, Kant is said to have claimed:

> The hypothetical and disjunctive judgment presuppose [*voraussetzen*] the categories . . . (28.428)

He makes the same point in the 'Mrongovius' lecture notes, saying exactly the same thing:

> In the case of hypothetical and disjunctive judgments, the categories underlie [them] [*liegen zum Grunde*]. (29.770)

5. Longuenesse suggests that this text is not easy to interpret (1998, 79n.), but it seems reasonably straightforward.

Chapter 14

1. Although I cite the pagination in the Cambridge Edition for easy and consistent reference, I use the translation from Pluhar (2009, 28n.).

2. As Jens Timmerman and Kwan Tze-Wan helpfully reminded me, Kant referred to the faculty of choice in first introducing ethical matters in the *Critique* (A533–34/B561–62). This faculty is, however, noticeably absent from the *Groundwork* and is only presented in its canonical role in his mature ethical theory on in *Religion within the Bounds of Mere Reason*.

3. The idea of a supreme intelligence designing a world that can be understood by human powers is presented in the *Critique* as a regulative idea for the study of nature (e.g. A670/B698), but as unconnected to issues of morality and freedom.

4. Allison also cites a passage from the set of metaphysics lectures L_1:

> When I say: I think, I act, etc, then either the word I is applied falsely, or I am free. Were I not free, then I could not say: **I** do it, but rather would have to say: I feel in me a desire to do, which someone has aroused in me. But when I say: I do it, that means spontaneity in the transcendental sense. (28.269, CMet 81)

This passage seems to have everything that Bilgrami and Allison could wish for to support their interpretations, since the spontaneity of thought is both linked to the 'I' and is transcendental. On the other hand, as I noted in discussing L_1 in Chapter 4, Kant is recorded as being highly skeptical about whether the proof of transcendental freedom from the internal principle of an 'I' is acceptable because such subjects are created.

5. The same theme comes up in a passage in Kant's 1783 review of Schultz. Ameriks appeals to this review to support his claim that Kant was not willing to give up the argument from thinking to spontaneity in the A edition (2000, 200).

> Although he [Schultz] would not himself admit it, he has assumed in the depths of his soul that understanding is able to determine his judgment in accordance with objective grounds that are always valid and is not subject to the mechanism of merely subjectively determining causes, which could subsequently change; hence he always admits freedom to think, without which there is no reason. In the same way he must also assume freedom of the will in acting without which there would be no morals, when—as I have no doubt—he wants to proceed in his righteous conduct in conformity with the eternal laws of duty and not to be a plaything of his instincts and inclinations . . . (8:14, CPract 10)

Here he claims that speculative and practical faculties are exactly parallel—and also free—precisely because they apply objective (unchanging and valid for all) laws across whatever sensory circumstances present themselves. That is, the 'freedom' at issue is, if I can put it this way, the freedom to be bound by the laws of one's own understanding and reason. So while I agree with Ameriks that the passage concerns the spontaneity common to practical and theoretical reason, the spontaneity at issue is not the freedom to begin a new causal chain. For further discussion of this common, but nonabsolute spontaneity, see below, p. 245–46.

6. I'm grateful to Béatrice Longuenesse for making me see that I should be explicit about this similarity between the cases.

Chapter 15

1. Stroud noted that his objection was similar to that offered in Thomson (1964).

2. See Chapter 7 (section 1) and Chapter 13 (section 2).

3. The most likely challenge to uniqueness would come from the realm of agency where humans make themselves agents through intentional action. I touched on this complex topic in the preceding chapter and cannot explore it further here.

4. Rosefeldt (2008) offered the objection in comments given at a workshop at the University of Konstanz in June 2008. Christopher Peacocke offered the same objection in conversation. Tyler Burge considers the possibility of a creature that engages in critical reasoning but does not have the linguistic resources to express the first person point of view. He rejects this possibility, because he thinks that critical reasoning must involve self-knowledge, because it involves

rational review (1998, 260, 262). As I understand Kant's position, he offers a different and more direct reason for rejecting this possibility. See next section.

5. Shoemaker does not refer to Kant in the discussion of self-blindness *per se*, but in connection with many related issues about consciousness and unity. Moran (2001, 127, 138–39) appeals to Kant to support his position, as do Setiya (2009) and Boyle (2009). These authors are explicit that they are taking Kant as inspiration and support and not trying to provide a defensible interpretation of his view.

6. Several of Shoemaker's essays on self-blindness are collected in Shoemaker (1996).

7. As we see in section 5, Kant denies that a person can learn about the necessary connection of different states in an 'I' in a third person way.

8. In this discussion, I take Kant's notion of 'judgment' to be equivalent to contemporary notions of 'belief.' His own notion of 'belief' (*Glaube*) is closer to contemporary notions of 'faith.'

9. Moran does not detail the exact relations of his account to Shoemaker's, but notes early on that his theory is deeply indebted to Shoemaker's discussions of these issues (2001, 2, n. 1).

10. Byrne (2005, 98) cites this passage in order to object that the skeptic can get his knife in. The problem is that one could set this procedure in motion, but arrive at the belief that one has a belief in some other way—say by excessive coffee consumption.

11. In comments on a paper that was an earlier version of Setiya (2009) and which he presented at a conference sponsored by the Lipkind Lecture Fund (and others) in honor of Anscombe's *Intention*. The conference was held at the University of Chicago on April 24 and 25, 2009.

12. Setiya appeals to Kant's 'I think' passage in support of his claims for transparency, but, as noted, does not claim to be offering an interpretation of Kant.

13. I'm grateful to Matthew Boyle (personal communication) for clarifying the space between his position and the position I think that Kant held.

14. In this section I rely mainly on Block (1995, 2002).

15. One notable exception to the neglect of mental actions is Christopher Peacocke (2008, Chapter 7).

16. One way to run the objection that rational cognition does not require self-consciousness would be to propose that Tetensian creatures recognize rational relations. This line is not very attractive, however, because as noted in the text, they are lacking in so much besides self-consciousness that they do not seem to be rational cognizers.

17. I owe this clear formulation to Bonnie Talbert.

18. I borrow this helpful expression (other 'I's) from Peacocke (2005).

Bibliography

Adams, Robert M. (1997). 'Things in Themselves.' In *The Philosopher's Annual*. P. Grim, K. Banes, and G. Mar, eds. Atascadero, CA: Ridgeview, XX: 1–24.

Allison, Henry. (1983). *Kant's Transcendental Idealism: An Interpretation and Defense*. New Haven: Yale University Press.

———. (1990). *Kant's Theory of Freedom*. New York: Cambridge University Press.

———. (1996). *Idealism and Freedom: Essays on Kant's Theoretical and Practical Philosophy*. New York: Cambridge University Press.

———. (2006). 'Kant on Freedom of the Will.' In *Cambridge Companion to Kant and Modern Philosophy*. P. Guyer, ed. Cambridge: Cambridge University Press: 381–415.

Allison, Henry, and Peter Heath, eds. (2002). *Immanuel Kant. Theoretical Philosophy after 1781*. The Cambridge Edition of the Works of Immanuel Kant, P. Guyer and A. W. Wood, gen. eds. New York: Cambridge University Press.

Ameriks, Karl. (1978). 'Kant's Transcendental Deduction as a Regressive Argument.' *Kant-Studien* 69: 273–87.

———. (2000). *Kant's Theory of Mind*. 2nd ed. Oxford: Oxford University Press.

Ameriks, Karl, and Steve Naragon, trans. and eds. (1997). *Immanuel Kant. Lectures on Metaphysics*. The Cambridge Edition of the Works of Immanuel Kant, P. Guyer and A. W. Wood, gen. eds. New York: Cambridge University Press.

Arnauld, Antoine. (1662/1964). *The Art of Thinking*. J. Dickoff and P. James, trans. New York: Library of Liberal Arts.

Bacon, Francis. (1620/1998). '*Novo Organum*.' In *Modern Philosophy: An Anthology of Primary Sources*. R. Ariew and E. Watkins, eds. Indianapolis: Hackett: 4–8.

Beattie, James. (1772/1809). 'Essay on the Nature and Immutability of Truth.' In *The Works of James Beattie*. Philadelphia: Hopkins and Earle, Essays, Vol. 1: 30–360.

Bilgrami, Akeel. (2006). *Self-knowledge and Resentment*. Cambridge, MA: Harvard University Press.

Block, Ned. (1995). 'On a Confusion about a Function of Consciousness." *Behavioral and Brain Sciences* 19: 227–47.

———. (2002). 'Concepts of Consciousness.' In *Philosophy of Mind: Classical and Contemporary Readings*. David Chalmers, ed. New York: Oxford University Press: 206–18. [Abridged and revised from Block (1995)]

Boghossian, Paul. (2008). 'Epistemic Rules.' *Journal of Philosophy* CV: 472–500.
Bona Meyer, Jürgen. (1870). *Kants Psychologie*. Berlin: Wilhelm Hertz.
Bonnet, Charles. (1755/1978). *Essai de Psychologie*. New York: Olms. (Reprint)
Bonnet, Charles. (1755/1773). Des herrns Karl Bonnet psychologischer Versuch als eine Einleitung. Lemgo: Meyerschen Buchhandlung.
Bowman, Curtis, Paul Guyer, and Fred Rauscher, trans. (2005). *Immanuel Kant. Notes and Fragments*. P. Guyer, ed. The Cambridge Edition of the Works of Immanuel Kant, P. Guyer and A. W. Wood, gen. eds. New York: Cambridge University Press.
Boyle, Matthew. (2009). 'Two Kinds of Self-Knowledge.' *Philosophy and Phenomenological Research* 78(1): 133–64.
Brandom, Robert. (2000). *Articulating Reasons*. Cambridge, MA: Harvard University Press.
Brandt, Reinhard. (1981). 'Materielen zur Entstehung der Kritik der reinen Vernunft: (John Locke und Johann Schultz).' In *Beitrage zu Kritik der reinen Vernunft 1791–1981*, I. Heidemann and W. Ritzel, eds. Berlin: de Gruyter: 37–68.
———. (1984). 'Historisches zum Selbstbewusstsein.' In *Probleme der 'Kritik der reinen Vernunft.'* B. Tuschling, ed. Berlin: de Gruyter: 1–14.
———. (1992). 'Buchbesprechung: Lothar Kreimendahl: Kant—Der Durchbruch von 1769.' *Kant-Studien* 83(1): 100–111.
———. (1994). 'Rousseau und Kants 'Ich Denke.'' In *Autographen, Dokumente und Berichte. Zu Edition, Amtsgeschäften und Werk Immanuel Kants*. R. Brandt and W. Starke, eds. Hamburg: Felix Meiner Verlag: 1–18.
Brandt, Reinhard, and Werner Stark. (1997). 'Einleitung der Herausgeber.' In *Kants Vorlesung über Anthropologie*. Akademie der Wissenschaften zu Göttingen, eds. Berlin: de Gruyter: vii–cli.
Brook, Andrew. (1994). *Kant and the Mind*. New York: Cambridge University Press.
Burge, Tyler. (1998). 'Reason and the First Person.' In *Knowing Our Minds*. C. Wright, B. C. Smith, and C. McDonald, eds. Oxford: Oxford University Press: 243–70.
———. (2003). 'Memory and Persons.' *Philosophical Review* 112 (July 2003): 289–337.
Byrne, Alex. (2005). 'Introspection.' *Philosophical Topics* 33: 79–104.
Callard, Agnes. (2009). 'Comments on Setiya.' (Unpublished manuscript)
Carl, Wolfgang. (1989a). *Der Schweigende Kant: Die Entwurfe zu einer Deduktion der Kategorien*. Göttingen: Vandenhoeck und Ruprecht.
———. (1989b). 'Kant's First Drafts of the Deduction of the Categories.' In *Kant's Transcendental Deductions*. E. Förster, ed. Stanford: Stanford University Press: 3–20.
———. (1992). *Die Transzendentale Deduktion der Kategorien in der ersten Auflage der Kritik der reinen Vernunft: Ein Kommentar*. Frankfurt am Main: Vittorio Klosterman.
———. (1998). 'Die B-Deduktion.' In *Kritik der reinen Vernunft*. G. Mohr and M. Willaschek, eds. Berlin: Akademie Verlag: 189–216.
Cassam, Quassim. (1997). *Self and World*. Oxford: Oxford University Press.
Chalmers, David. (1996). *The Conscious Mind: In Search of a Fundamental Theory*. Oxford: Oxford University Press.
Cheng, Patricia. (1997). 'From Covariation to Causation: A Causal Power Theory.' *Psychological Review* 104: 367–405.
Cramer, Konrad. (1987). 'Über Kants Satz: Das: Ich denke, muß alle meine Vorstellungen begleiten können.' In *Theorie der Subjektivität*. K. Cramer, H. F. Fulda, R.–P. Horstmann, and U. Pothast, eds. Frankfurt am Main: Suhrkamp: 167–202.
Crone, Katja. (2007). 'Vorbegriffliches Selbstbewußtsein.' In *Kant in der Gegenwart*. J. Stolzenberg, ed. New York: de Gruyter: 149–65.
Crusius, C. A. (1745). *Entwurf der nothwendigen Vernunft-Wahrheiten wiefern sie den zufälligen entgegen gesetzet werden*. Leipzig: Johann Friedrich Gleditschens Buchhandlung.

Descartes, René. (1640/1984). *Philosophical Writings of Descartes*. J. Cottingham, R. Stoothoff, and D. Murdoch, trans. Cambridge: Cambridge University Press.
DeVleeschauwer, H.-J. (1962). *The Development of Kant's Thought*. New York: Nelson.
Edmundts, Dina. (2006). 'Die Paralogismen und die Widerlegung des Idealismus in Kant's "Kritik der reinen Vernunft,"' in 'Schwerpunkt: Kants Paralogisms.' D. Edmundts, S. Grüne, and U. Schlösser, eds. *Deutsche Zeitschrift für Philosophie Berlin* 54(2): 295–309.
Edmundts, Dina, Stephanie Grüne, und Ulrich Schlöser. (2006). 'Einleitung zur Schwerpunkt: Kants Paralogisms.' D. Edmundts, S. Grüne, and U. Schlösser, eds. *Deutsche Zeitschrift für Philosophie Berlin* 54(2): 261–63.
Evans, Gareth. (1982). *The Varieties of Reference*. J. McDowell, ed. Oxford: Oxford University Press.
Falkenstein, Lorne. (1995). *Kant's Intuitionism: A Commentary on the Transcendental Aesthetic*. Toronto: University of Toronto Press.
Finkelstein, David H. (2003). *Expression and the Inner*. Cambridge, MA: Harvard University Press.
Frank, Manfred. (2007).'Kant über Sebstbewußtsein.' Chapter 7 of his *Auswege aus dem deutschen Idealismus*. Frankfurt am Main: Surkamp: 183–93.
Freud, Sigmund. (1909/1975). 'Notes upon a Case of Obsessional Neurosis.' In *The Standard Edition of the Complete Psychological Works of Sigmund Freud*. J. Strachey, ed. London: Hogarth Press: 10:155–249.
Friedman, Michael. (1992). *Kant and the Exact Sciences*. Cambridge, MA: Harvard University Press.
———. (2009). 'Newton and Kant on Absolute Space: From Theology to Transcendental Philosophy.' In *Constituting Objectivity: Transcendental Perspectives on Physics*. M. Bitbol, P. Kerszberg, and J. Petitot, eds. *Western Ontario Series in Philosophy of Science* 74: 35–50.
Frith, Colin, and Eve Johnstone. (2003). *A Short Introduction to Schizophrenia*. Oxford: Oxford University Press.
Gawlick, Günter, and Lothar Kreimendahl. (1987). *Hume in der Deutschen Aufklärung*. Stuttgart-Bad Cannstatt: Frommann-Holzboog.
George, Rolf. (1981). 'Kant's Sensationism.' *Synthese* 47: 229–55.
Ginsborg, Hannah. (1992). 'Kant on the Systematicity and Purposiveness of Nature.' (Unpublished manuscript)
Goldman, Alvin. (2006). *Simulating Minds: The Philosophy, Psychology and Neuroscience of Mindreading*. Oxford: Oxford University Press.
Gopnik, Alison. (1993). 'How We Know Our Minds: The Illusion of First-person Knowledge of Intentionality.' *Behavioral and Brain Sciences* 16: 29–113.
Gordon, Robert. (1986). 'Folk Psychology as Simulation.' *Mind and Language* 1: 158–71.
Gregor, Mary, trans. and ed. (1996). *Immanuel Kant. Practical Philosophy*. The Cambridge Edition of the Works of Immanuel Kant. P. Guyer and A. W. Wood, gen. eds. New York: Cambridge University Press.
Guyer, Paul. (1987). *Kant and the Claims of Knowledge*. New York: Cambridge University Press.
———. (1990). 'Reason and Reflective Judgment: Kant on the Significance of Systematicity.' *Noûs* 24: 17–43.
Guyer, Paul, and Eric Matthews, trans. (2000). *Immanuel Kant. Critique of the Power of Judgment*. The Cambridge Edition of the Works of Immanuel Kant. P. Guyer and A. W. Wood, gen. eds. New York: Cambridge University Press.
Harper, William. (1984). 'Kant's Empirical Realism and the Difference between Subjective and Objective Succession.' In *Kant on Causality, Freedom, and Objectivity*. W. Harper and R. Meerbote, eds. Minneapolis: University of Minnesota Press: 108–37.
Henrich, Dieter. (1966). 'Fichtes Ursprünglichen Einsicht.' *Festschrift für Wolfgang Cramer*. Frankfurt am Main: Vittorio Klostermann: 189–232.

———. (1976). *Identität und Objektivität: Eine Untersuchung zu Kants transzendentaler Deduktion*. Heidelberg: Winter.

———. (1989a). 'The Identity of the Subject in the Transcendental Deduction.' In *Reading Kant: New Perspectives on Transcendental Arguments and Critical Philosophy*. E. Schaper and W. Vossenkuhl, eds. New York: Blackwell: 250–80.

———. (1989b). 'Kant's Notion of a Deduction and the Methodological Background of the First Critique.' In *Kant's Deductions*. E. Förster, ed. Stanford: Stanford University Press: 29–46.

———. (1994). *The Unity of Reason*. Richard Velkley, ed. and trans. Cambridge, MA: Harvard University Press.

Hoppe, Hansgeorg. (1983). *Synthesis bei Kant*. Berlin: de Gruyter.

Horstmann, Rolf-Peter. (1993). 'Kants Paralogismen.' *Kant-Studien* 84(4): 408–25.

Howell, Robert. (1992). *Kant's Transcendental Deduction*. Synthèse Library. J. Hintikka, gen. ed. Boston: Kluwer Academic.

Hume, David. (1739/1978). *A Treatise of Human Nature*. P. H. Nidditch, ed. 2nd ed. Oxford: Oxford University Press. (Revision of L. A. Selby-Bigge edition of 1888, Oxford University Press)

Jacobi, F. H. (1787/1983). *David Hume über den Glauben, oder Idealismus und Realismus. Ein Gespräch*. New York: Garland. (Reprint)

Kandel, Eric and James Schwartz (2000). *Principles of Neuroscience* (fourth edition). New York: McGraw Hill.

Kant, Immanuel, [1781/1787]. *Critique of Pure Reason*.

———. Kemp Smith, Norman, trans. (1968). New York: St. Martin's.

———. Pluhar, Werner, trans. (1996). Unified Edition. Indianapolis: Hackett.

———. Guyer, Paul, and Allen W. Wood, trans. (1998). The Cambridge Edition of the Works of Immanuel Kant. P. Guyer and A. W. Wood, gen. eds. New York: Cambridge University Press.

———. (1900–). *Kants gesammelte Schriften, Akademie Ausgabe*. Königlichen Preussischen Akademie der Wissenschaften, ed. 29 vols. de Gruyter.

Kemp Smith, Norman. (1923/1962). *A Commentary on Kant's 'Critique of Pure Reason.'* New York: Humanities Press.

Kitcher, Patricia. (1982a). 'Kant on Self-Identity.' *Philosophical Review* XCI: 41–72.

———. (1982b). 'Kant's Paralogisms.' *Philosophical Review* XCI: 515–47.

———. (1990). *Kant's Transcendental Psychology*. New York: Oxford University Press.

———. (2004). 'Kant on Constructing Causal Representations.' In *Representation in Mind: New Approaches to Mental Representation*. H. Clapin, P. Staines, and P. Slezak, eds. New York: Elsevier: 217–36.

———. (2008). 'Kant's I Think.' In *Recht und Freiden in der Philosophie Kants: Akten des X Kant-Kongress*. Valerio Rohden et al., eds. New York: de Gruyter: Vol. 1, 181–98.

Kitcher, Philip. (1982). 'How Kant Almost Wrote Two Dogmas of Empiricism (and Why He Didn't).' In *Essays on Kant's Critique of Pure Reason*. J. N. Mohanty and Robert W. Shahan, eds. Norman: University of Oklahoma Press: 217–49.

Klemme, Heiner F. (1996). *Kant Philosophie des Subjekts*. Hamburg: Felix Meiner Verlag.

Korsgaard, Christine. (1996). *Sources of Normativity*. Cambridge: Cambridge University Press.

Kripke, Saul. (1982). *Wittgenstein on Rules and Private Language*. Cambridge, MA: Harvard University Press.

Kuehn, Manfred. (1987). *Scottish Common Sense in Germany 1768–1800: A Contribution to the History of the Critical Philosophy*. Montreal: McGill-Queen's University Press.

———. (1997). 'The Wolffian Background of Kant's Transcendental Deduction.' In *Logic and the Workings of the Mind*. P. A. Easton, ed. Atascadero, CA: Ridgeview: 5:229–50.

———. (2001). *Kant: A Biography*. Cambridge: Cambridge University Press.

Langton, Rae. (1998). *Kantian Humility: Our Ignorance of Things in Themselves*. Oxford: Oxford University Press.

Lashley, Karl. (1958). 'Cerebral Organization and Behavior.' In *Association for Research in Nervous and Mental Diseases, Research Publication: The Brain and Human Behavior* 36. H. C. Solomon, S. Cobb, and W. Penfield, eds. Williams and Wilkie: 1–4.
Laywine, Alison. (1995). *Kant's Early Metaphysics and the Origins of the Critical Philosophy*. Atascadero, CA: Ridgeview.
———. (2006). 'Kant's Metaphysical Reflections in the Duisburg Nachlass.' *Kant-Studien* 97(4): 79–113.
Leibniz, Gottfried Wilhelm. (1765/1996). *New Essays Concerning Human Understanding*. P. Remnant and J. Bennett, trans. and eds. New York: Cambridge University Press.
———. (1969). *Philosophical Papers and Letters*. L. E. Loemker, trans. and ed. 2nd ed. Boston: Reidel.
Levine, Joseph. (2001). *Purple Haze: The Puzzle of Consciousness*. Oxford: Oxford University Press.
Locke, John. (1690/1975). *Essay Concerning Human Understanding*. P. H. Nidditch, ed. Oxford: Oxford University Press.
Longuenesse, Béatrice. (1998). *Kant and the Capacity to Judge*. Princeton: Princeton University Press.
———. (2005). *Kant on the Human Standpoint. Modern European Philosophy Series*. R. B. Pippin, gen. ed. Cambridge: Cambridge University Press.
Marr, David. (1982). *Vision*. San Francisco: Freeman.
McCann, Edwin. (1997). 'Locke on Identity: Matter, Life, and Consciousness.' *Archiv für Geschichte der Philosophie* 69: 54–77.
McDowell, John. (1994). *Mind and World*. Cambridge, MA: Harvard University Press.
Melnick, Arthur. (1973). *Kant's Analogies of Experience*. Chicago: University of Chicago Press.
———. (2009). *Kant's Theory of the Self*. New York: Routledge.
Merian, Johann Bernard. (1749/1778). 'Ueber die Apperzeption seiner eignen Existenz.' *Magazin für die Philosophie und ihre Geschichte*: 89–132. Available: www.ub.uni-bielefeld.de.
Moran, Richard. (2001). *Authority and Estrangement*. Princeton: Princeton University Press.
———. (2003). 'Responses to O'Brien and Shoemaker.' *European Journal of Philosophy* 11(3): 402–19.
Nagel, Thomas (1974). 'What Is It Like to Be a Bat?' *Philosophical Review* LXXXIII: 435–50.
Newton, Isaac. (1687/1934). *Mathematical Principles of Natural Philosophy*. F. Cajori, trans. Berkeley: University of California Press. (Revision of Andrew Motte, trans., London: Printed for Benjamin Motte, at Middle Temple-Gate in Fleetstreet, MDCCXXIX)
O'Neill, Onora. (1989). *Constructions of Reason*. Cambridge: Cambridge University Press.
Paton, H. J. (1965). *Kant's Metaphysics of Experience*. New York: Humanities Press.
Peacocke, Christopher. (2005). '"Another I": Representing Conscious States, Perceptions and Others." In *Thought, Reference and Experience: Themes on the Philosophy of Gareth Evans*. J. Bermúdez, ed. Oxford: Oxford University Press: 220–57.
———. (2008). *Truly Understood*. New York: Oxford University Press.
Pluhar, Werner, trans. (2009). *Immanuel Kant. Religion within the Bounds of Mere Reason*. Indianapolis: Hackett.
Prauss, Gerold. (1974/1989). *Kant und das Problem der Dinge an sich*. Bonn: Bouvier.
Richards, Robert J. (1980). 'Christian Wolff's Prolegomena to Empirical and Rational Psychology: Translation and Commentary.' *Proceedings of the American Philosophical Society* 124: 227–39.
Rödl, Sebastian. (2007). *Self-Consciousness*. Cambridge, MA: Harvard University Press.
Rosefeldt, Tobias. (2008). 'Comments on Patricia Kitcher, "Unity and Self-consciousness in Kant's Thinking Subject."' (Unpublished manuscript)
Rosenthal, David. (1997). 'A Theory of Consciousness.' In *The Nature of Consciousness*. N. Block, O. Flanagan, and G. Güzeldere, eds. Cambridge, MA: MIT Press: 729–53.

Rousseau, Jean-Jacques. (1762/1979). *Émile or Education*. Allan Bloom, trans. New York: Basic Books.
Sassen, Brigitte, ed. (2000). *Kant's Early Critics. The Empiricist Critique of the Theoretical Philosophy*. Cambridge: Cambridge University Press.
Sellars, Wilfrid. (1972/2002). '". . . This I or He or It (the Thing) That Thinks.'" In *Kant's Transcendental Metaphysics: Sellars' Cassirer Lectures, Notes, and Others Essays*. J. F. Sicha, ed. Atascadero, CA: Ridgeview: 341–62.
Setiya, Keiran (2009, [April 30]). 'Knowledge of Intention.' (Unpublished manuscript)
Shoemaker, Sydney. (1996). *The First Person and Other Essays*. Cambridge: Cambridge University Press.
Strawson, P. F. (1966). *The Bounds of Sense*. London: Methuen.
Stroud, Barry. (1968). 'Transcendental Arguments.' *Journal of Philosophy*: 241–56.
———. (1994). 'Kantian Arguments, Conceptual Capacities, and Invulnerability.' *Kant and Contemporary Epistemology*. P. Parrini, ed. Boston: Kluwer.
Sturma, Dieter. (1985). *Kant über Selbstbewußtsein*. New York: Georg Olms Verlag.
Tetens, Johann Nicolaus. (1777/1979). *Philosophische Versuche über die Menschliche Natur und ihre Entwicklung*. Hildesheim: Olms. (Reprint)
Thiel, Udo. (1994). 'Leibniz and the Concept of Apperception.' *Archiv für Geschichte der Philosophie* 76: 195–209.
———. (1996). 'Between Wolff and Kant: Merian's Theory of Apperception.' *Journal of the History of Ideas* 34: 213–32.
———. (1997). 'Varieties of Inner Sense: Two Pre-Kantian Theories.' *Archiv für Geschichte der Philosophie* 79: 58–79.
Thomson, Judith Jarvis. (1964). 'Private Languages.' *American Philosophical Quarterly* 1(1): 20–31.
Walford, David, with Ralf Meerbote, trans. and eds. (1992). *Immanuel Kant. Theoretical Philosophy 1755–1770*. The Cambridge Edition of the Works of Immanuel Kant, P. Guyer and A. W. Wood, gen. eds. New York: Cambridge University Press.
Warda, Arthur. (1922). *Immanuel Kants Bücher*. Berlin: Verlag von Martin Breslauer.
Watkins, Eric. (2005). *Kant and the Metaphysics of Causality*. New York: Cambridge University Press.
———. (2009). *Kant's Critique of Pure Reason: Background Source Materials*. New York: Cambridge University Press.
Weldon, T. D. (1958). *Kant's Critique of Pure Reason*. 2nd ed. Oxford: Oxford University Press.
Westphal, Kenneth R. (2004). *Kant's Transcendental Proof of Realism*. Cambridge: Cambridge University Press.
Wilson, Margaret. (1974). 'Leibniz and Materialism.' *Canadian Journal of Philosophy* 3(4): 495–513.
Wimmer, Heinz, and Joseph Perner. (1983). 'Belief about Beliefs: Representation and Constraining Function of Wrong Beliefs in Young Children's Understanding of Deception.' *Cognition* 13: 103–28.
Wittgenstein, Ludwig. (1922). *Tractatus Logico-Philosophicus*. London: Routledge and Kegan Paul.
———. (1953). *Philosophical Investigations*. G. E. M. Anscombe, trans. Englewood Cliffs, NJ: Prentice Hall.
Wolff, Christian. (1751/1983). *Vernünftige Gedanken von Gott, der Welt und der Seele des Menschen, auch allen dingen überhaupt*. Hildesheim: Olms. (Reprint)
Wolff, Robert Paul. (1960). 'Kant's Debt to Hume via Beattie.' *Journal of the History of Ideas* 21: 117–23.
———. (1963). *Kant's Theory of Mental Activity*. Cambridge, MA: Harvard University Press.

Wood, Allen W., and George Di Giovanni. trans. and eds. (1996). *Immanuel Kant. Religion and Rational Theology*. The Cambridge Edition of the Works of Immanuel Kant, P. Guyer and A. W. Wood, gen. eds. New York: Cambridge University Press.

Wuerth, Julian. (forthcoming). *Kant on Mind, Action, and Ethics*. New York: Oxford University Press.

Wunderlich, Falk. (2005). *Kant und die Bewusstseinstheorien des 18 Jahrhunderts*. Berlin: de Gruyter.

Young, Garry. (2006). 'Kant and the Phenomenon of Inserted Thoughts.' *Philosophical Psychology* 19(6): 823–37.

Young, J. Michael, trans. and ed. (1992). *Immanuel Kant. Lectures on Logic*. The Cambridge Edition of the Works of Immanuel Kant, P. Guyer and A. W. Wood, gen. eds. New York: Cambridge University Press.

Zweig, A. trans. and ed. (1999). *Immanuel Kant. Correspondence*. The Cambridge Edition of the Works of Immanuel Kant, P. Guyer and A. W. Wood, gen. eds. New York: Cambridge University Press.

Index of Quoted and Cited Passages

Critique of Pure Reason
Axvi 105, 277n9
Axvi–xvii 105
A1–2 83
A9 81
A92–93 91
A94 114, 126
A94–95 162
A96 91
A100 104, 158
A101 105
A103 102, 128
A103–104 130
A104 110
A104–105 130
A105 130, 149, 208
A106 120, 127, 131–32
A106–7 132
A107 32, 37, 62, 109, 117, 124, 132, 164
A107–8 133–34
A108 111, 136, 138–39
A111 91
A112 113, 141
A114 163–64
A115 126
A116 74, 122–23, 126, 283n29
A117n 4, 122–23, 188
A118–119 105
A119 103, 105
A120 108–9, 133, 281n12n15
A120n 280n9, 281n15

A121 133
A122 109, 111, 133, 141
A124 21, 141
A125 219
A126 92, 94, 229
A189 107
A249 205
A250 205
A250–51 208
A251–52 178, 205–6
A252 211
A253 206, 212
A348 183
A350–52 183
A352 167
A353 168m 183–84, 275n12
A354–55 116, 194
A358 288n19
A7/B11 150
A11/B25 95
A19/B33 119
A20/B35 209
A22/B37 15, 35, 157
A23/B38 280–81n10
A30/B46 281–82n10
A36/B54 289n5
A56/B80–81 95–96
A64–66/B89–91 94, 96
A68/B93 99, 119, 142
A77/B102 100
A78/B103 103

A79/B105 99–100, 219
A80/B106 282n21
A81/B107 95
A84–85/B116–17 86
A86/B119 87
A86–87/B118–19 96
A89–90/B122 81, 218
A94/B126 85
A137/B176 279n8
A140–/B179 236, 279n8
A140–41/B180 279n8
A142/B181 279n8
A160/B199 107
A162/B202 280n10
A166/B207 152
A193/B238 45
A204/B250 45
A205/B250 45
A205/B250–51 46
A225–26/B272–73 288n11
A254/B310 215
A278/B334 214
A288/B344 213, 288n16
A320/ B376 108
A320/B376–77 102
A341/B399–400 148, 188
A341–42/B400 189
A345–46/B403–4 189
A346/B404 196, 198
A346/B404–405 200, 249, 268
A347/B405 194
A493/B521 288
A494–95/B522–23 207
A506/B534 182
A533–34/B561–62 169, 290n2
A542–43/B 570–71 178
A545/B573 178
A546/B574 49, 252ff
A546–48/B574–76 49, 243ff
A558/B586 49, 244
A573/B601 198
A649/B677 163
A671/B699 177
A673/B701 177
A682/B710 46
A682–83/B710–11 176–77, 285n3
A683/B711 177
A690/B 718 177
A727/B755–56 127
A728–29/B756–57 127

A772/B800 177
A783/B811 85–86
A784/B812 177, 193
A799–800/B827–28 50, 241–42
A803/B831 50
A807–8/B835–36 244–45
A822/B850 170

Bxxvi 178
B1 89
B1–2 82
B3–4 83
B4 83
B5 84
B19 81
B67 25
B67–68 50
B90–91 93–94
B113 95, 271n5, 278n13
B113–14 278n13
B128–29 236
B130 99, 105, 130, 139, 142, 169, 207, 262
B130–131 143
B131 143
B131n. 143
B131–132 124, 144, 285n4
B132 4, 61, 124, 125–26, 144, 151, 165, 188, 283n29, 285n4
B132–33 170
B133 32, 62, 102, 114, 145, 147, 170–71
B133–34 146, 191, 282n18
B133–34n 147–48, 166
B134 113, 117, 125, 132–33, 146
B134–35 148m 286m b, 10
B135 116, 124, 125, 147
B135–36 140
B136 4
B136–37 149
B137 60, 110, 112
B138 124, 126
B139 281n1
B139–40 158
B140–41 142
B141 118, 234, 284n42
B142 150
B147 89
B151 103, 105–6, 114
B152–53 22, 50
B153 22, 160, 172, 243
B153–54 158

INDEX OF QUOTED AND CITED PASSAGES   303

B157 194
B157–58 50
B157–58n. 50, 194, 198
B158 157, 197
B159–60 90
B160 157
B162–63 154
B232 107
B233 153
B406–7 190
B407 168, 190
B407–8 191
B408 191
B411 192
B411–12n. 192
B414–15 281n8
B415–16n. 199
B419 100
B421 50, 199
B422n 50, 287n16
B429 50

New Elucidation of the First Principles of Metaphysical Cognition
1.411 42
1.412 42
False Subtlety of the Four syllogistic figures
2.58 19, 120
2.59–60 18–19, 120–21
2.60 19
Inquiry into the Distinctness of the Principles of Natural Theology and Morality
2.106–7 176
Inaugural Dissertation
2.283 6
2.393 207
2.39495 67
2.399 20–21
2.400–1 20
2.407 67
Prolegomena to Any Future Metaphysics
4.275 84
4.276 81
4.333–34 181
4.369 229
Groundwork of the Metaphysics of Morals
4.391 238–39
4.392 84–85
4.402 218
4.448 242–44

Metaphysical Foundations of Natural Science
4.472 7
4.475n 277n9
4.475–76 116
Critique of Practical Judgment
5.7 241
5.97 42
Critique of the Power of Judgment
5.148 165
5.198 163
5.385 165–66
Religion within the Bounds of Mere Reason
6.25 247
6.26n 238, 246
6.48 185
6.73 185–87
6.74 186–87
6.75–76 186
Metaphysics of Morals
6.225 238
Anthropology from a Pragmatic Point of View
7.134 22–23
7.141 89, 285n4
What is Enlightenment?
8.35 247
On a Discovery
8.221–23 134–35
Logic
9.11 227–28
9.27 231
9.33 117
9.51–52 230–31, 240
9.54 247
9.57 247
9.58 119
9.64–65 19–20
9.73–74 169–70, 248
9.94–95 223
9.95 289n10
9.96 120
9.101 117–18
9.105–6 235, 284n42
9.141–42 127
9.149 277n3
Correspondence
10.130–31 68
10.232 272n10
10.340–41 6
11.51 237
11.51–52 137–38

Reflections
R1572, 16.11 228
R1573, 16.13 228
R1575, 16.14 229
R1579, 16.17 228
R1579, 16.18 229, 231
R1579, 16.19 230
R1599, 16.30 224
R1602, 16.31–32 228–29
R1608, 16.34–35 221
R1620, 16.39 228
R1676, 16.77 288
R1676, 16.78 101
R2178, 16.260 230
16.296 119
R2277, 16.297 119
R2279, 16.297 119
R2281, 16.98 119
R2282, 16.298 120
R2283, 16.299 120
R2839, 16.398 169–70
R2839, 16.540 224
R2851, 16.546 224
R2856, 16.548 224
R2876, 16.552–53 289n10
R2876, 16.555 223
R3036, 16.627 282n16
R3051, 16.633 118
R3063, 16.636 70
R4629, 17.614 219
R4634, 17.615 91–92, 220
R4634, 17.618 90–91
R4672, 17.635 289n4
R4674, 17.643 68–69
R4674, 17.647 21, 35, 72
R4675, 17.653 101, 276n7
R4676, 17.656 35, 70, 72–73, 92
R4678, 17.660 82
R4678, 17.660–61 35, 72, 101, 217
R4679, 17.662 76–77
R4679, 17.663 75
R4679, 17.664 74, 75
R4681, 17.667–68 21
R4681, 17.668 99
R4686, 17.675 77
R4901, 18.23 36
R5661, 18.318–19 173–75
First Introduction to the Critique of the Power of Judgment
20.206 176
29.245–46 163, 165
What Real Progress has Metaphysics made in Germany since the Time of Leibniz and Wolff?
20.308 199
Student Lecture Notes
24.18–19 228
24.113 119–20
24.255 223–24
24.791 228
24.792–93 227–28
25.10 35, 116, 273n1
25.244 35, 48–49
25.473 49, 226
25.473–74 35
25.859 49
25.1033 281n7
28.224 37
28.226 38
28.239 45
28.261 44
28.261–62 44
28.262 44
28.265 35
28.266 51, 182–83
28.267 49, 51
28.268 41, 42, 52, 184
28.269 41–42, 52, 291n4
28.272 187
28.272–73 52
28.276 20
29.770 290n4
29.771 285n3
29.878 164
29.888 225
29.904 49

General Index

A priori
  vs. a posteriori 82–83, 86
  and activity 93–95, 220, 222
  content *see* transcendental content
  definition of 82ff., 134–35
  marks of 83
  and subjective origins 82ff., 189, 218
  two-fold apriority of categorial principles 123
A priori concepts *see also* categories 6, 35, 66ff., 250, 279n8
  applicability to objects of senses 88–89, 109, 137, 197
  need for transcendental deduction of 86, 97, 215
  and skepticism 86
  as standards for cognition 84, 109, 130
  as universally applicable 86, 95, 96
A priori principles *see* categorial principles
Adams, Robert M. 204, 212
Agents, cognitive and moral 9, Chapter 14 *passim*
Allison, Henry 24, 32, 207–8, 277n8, 284n38, 285n7, 287n5n7n10, 288n13n15, 290n3
  on assimilating cognitive and moral agents 47, 239, 291n4
  on argument for apperception 167–69, 170, 285n5
  on freedom 169
  on reflection 168, 170

'taking as' analysis of judging 169–70, 239–40
  and 'verse' argument 167, 184
Ameriks, Karl 10, 11, 37, 247
  on Kant on freedom 49–50, 53, 291n5
  on Paralogisms 180, 181, 275n12
Animals, Kant on 19–20, 49, 120, 169, 272n6
Apperception
  as constant or unchanging 164–65, 291n5
  in *Duisburg Nachlaß* 70, 71, 72–75
  empirical 157
    as dependent on transcendental 158–59
    and law of association 158
    and mineness 26, 146, 157–59
    necessity of 159
  faculty of
    active 130, 172
    and faculty of inner sense 21–23, 117, 123–24, 129–30, 132–33, 135–36, 146–47, 261–62, 267–68
    identical to faculty of understanding 162–64, 166
    self-conscious 128–30, 172–73
  original 61, 74, 109, 123, 132, 134–35
  principle of 116, 124–26
    in A 122–24
    as analytic vs. synthetic 124–26
    argument for 122, 136
    in B 124–25
  role of in deduction 92–93, 115, 151–57
  titles of 72, 74, 92, 187–88

305

Apperception (*continued*)
    transcendental unity of 122–23, 124, 126, 132–34, 138, 148
        creation of 145–46, 148–49, 171
        as dependent on empirical 159
        as necessary and sufficient condition for objective reference 111–13, 129–31, 134–37, 139–41, 145–46
Association, Law of 104, 105, 127, 158
Autonomy Chapter 14, section 3 *passim*, *see also* freedom

Beattie, James 31, 32, 34
Belief ascription 254–60
Bennett, Jonathan 110, 269
Bilgrami, Akeel 239–43, 245, 246, 247, 248, 291n4
Block, Ned 266, 281n14
Boghossian, Paul 282n14
Bona Meyer, Jürgen 272n10
Boyle, Matthew 253, 256, 263–65, 292n5n13
Brandom, Robert 217–18
Brandt, Reinhard 15, 273n1, 274n5, 275n6
Brook, Andrew 286n8
Burge, Tyler 291–92n4
Byrne, Alex 254, 256, 258, 292n10

Callard, Agnes 258
Carl, Wolfgang viii, 8, 10, 11, 112–14, 138, 140, 149, 158, 219, 274n5, 283n30
    on dating of L_1 36
    on *Duisburg Nachlaβ* 66, 72–75, 76, 276n9
    on proof structure of deduction 74, 90–93, 277n9
    on Tetens 35–38, 272n10, 274n14
Cassam, Quassim 249, 251–52
Categorial Principles 6, 45, 84, 139, 217, 218, 227ff, 231, 245
Categories *see also* a priori concepts
    and intuitions 107, 152ff
    and logical functions 149, 150, 234–37
    objective validity of 115
    templates for 107, 131, 137, 150, 284n42
Causation 71, 106, 123–24, 126, 158, 278n11
    finding causes 94–95, 107
    and motion 222–23
    and power 107, 171–72
    proof of causal principle 42, 46, 135, 151, 153–55
    and necessary connection 21, 172

Chalmers, David 267
Characteristics *see* marks
Cheng, Patricia 222
Cogito
    Kant on 182, 193–97
    Merian on 24, 59–60
    and transcendental deduction 115–17
    Wolff on 58
Cognition
    and consciousness 57–61, 160, 128–31, 172
    degrees of 19–20, 121
    kind of at issue in *Critique* 19, 118–21
    of objects 54, 57–60
    necessary conditions for 109, 130–31, 140, 149, 156, 159, 161, 170, 178, 240, 253ff
    and normativity 218, 232
    rational 8, 9, 19, 25, 92, 104, 109, 121, 129, 143, 144, 148, 151, 159, 170, 172, 175, 199, 226, 252, 253ff
    RE cognition 121–23, 126, 129, 130–31, 136, 137, 140, 149, 156, 160, 170, 218, 238, 253ff
    and self-consciousness 130–31, 140, 149
Combination *see also* synthesis 101, 105, 108–9, 117
    acts of 102, 140, 142, 156
    in the B deduction 139, 142ff
    and concepts 99, 142, 149
    Kant's broad notion of 101–2, 139, 142–44, 146
    unity required for 113, 143–44, 128
Concepts
    and combination *see* combination and concepts
    formation of 100, 131, 223–26
        and comparing, reflecting, and abstracting 223, 226
        Longuenesse on 234ff
        Tetens on 33
    marks of 19, 119–20
    as rules for judging objects 127–29, 30, 131, 136, 139, 140, 141–42, 150
    structure of 131, 137, 224
Consciousness
    Access 113, 266
    and cognition *see* cognition and consciousness
    hard problem of 265ff
    of objects 58, 50–60, 61ff, 64
    monitoring 265, 266

phenomenal 265, 266, 267
    of self *see* self-consciousness
    theories of Chapter 5 *passim*
Conversion 185–86
Cramer, Konrad 159
Crone, Katja 285n2
Crusius, C. A. 58, 59, 60, 64, 77, 134, 145

Deduction 122–24 *see also* Transcendental Deduction
    in A Chapter 9, section 5 *passim*, 146
    in B 124–25, Chapter 9, section 6 *passim*
    conclusion of 81, 83, 90ff
    premise of 89ff., 116–17
    subjective 74, 91, 1–5–6
Dennett, Daniel 269
Descartes, René 17, 24, 47, 57, 59, 64, 137, 192, 193–95
Determinables 198–99
Determinism, principle of 6, 123
DeVleeschauwer, H. J. 66, 98, 274n5n13n14
Duisburg Nachlaß 81–82, 93, 99, 122, 276n5n8
    on apperception 70–71, 72–75, 98, 152, 187–88
    Carl on 72–75, 91
    dating of 66
    on rules for objects, 92, 97, 101, 109, 217, 289n4
    relation to *Critique of Pure Reason* 76ff

Eberhard, Johann August 62, 64, 132, 134, 282n23, 283n26
Edgley, Roy 254–55
Editions of *Critique*, differences between
    on apriority 82–83
    on principle of apperception 122–25
    on Transcendental Deduction 117, 150
Edmundts, Dina 271n1
Epistemology, Kantian
    central claims of 25, 107, 119
    in relation to metaphysics 6–7, 39, 122, 126
Evans, Gareth 4–5, 139, 251, 254–55, 256, 259
Examples
    of concept 'body' 120, 131–32, 138, 142
    counting 127–30, 135, 138, 140, 146, 156, 174, 252, 282n17, 283n27
    freezing of water 153–55
    moving light 222–25
    puddles and rain 259–60. 267–68

Shoemaker's George 254, 268
Teddy 4–5, 139
Tetensian Zombies 267–69, 269
thinking about a square 173–74
tree 225
Experience, possibility of 84, 85, 89–91, 96, 119

Faculties, psychological
    empirical and transcendental use of 162
    endurance of 164–65, 166
    fundamental or basic 163, 164, 175–77
    higher 19–20, 39, 121, 163, 268
    vs. powers 162–63
Falkenstein, Lorne 204, 206, 212, 215, 278n12, 279n2, 287n3, 288n14n20
Feder, Johann Georg 15, 63
Finkelstein, David H. 263
Frank, Manfred 286n12n15
Freedom *see also* autonomy, spontaneity
    Allison on 239
    as belonging to practical reason 39, 238–43, 237
    Bilgrami on 239, 240–42, 246
    and choice 240
    and created beings 42, 50
    and moral law 238, 240, 246
    transcendental 41, 49, 244
    and transcendental apperception 49, 243–44
Freud, Sigmund 17
Friedman, Michael 279n5
Functions, logical and real 220–21, 226, 235, 236, 237, 289n4, 290n3

Garve, Christian 6, 39
George, Rolf 108–9
Ginsborg, Hannah 175
Goldman, Alvin 270
Gopnik, Alison 269
Gordon, Robert 270
Grüne, Stephanie 281n7, 275n1
Guyer, Paul 175, 272n7, 278n12
    on causation 42, 153, 221–22, 235–36, 278n11
    on the *Duisberg Nachlaß* 66, 73–75, 187, 188, 276n9

Hamann, J. G. 31–32, 272n10
Harman, Gilbert 269
Harper, William 222, 289n6

Henrich, Dieter 8, 10, 11, 156, 284n39, 286n8
   on analogy with legal deductions 87–88, 89
Herder, Johann Gottfried 275n6
Herz, Marcus 36, 37, 61, 64, 68, 137, 237, 272n10, 274n12
Hißmann, Michael 63
Hogan, Desmond 275n2
Hoppe, Hansgeog 11, 89, 110–114
Horstmann, Rolf-Peter 285n2
Howell, Robert 281n5, 282n16, 284n40
Hume, David 3, 86, 105, 172
   influence on Kant 11, 31, 32, 105, 230, 274n5
   on personal identity 31–32, 35, 37, 64, 122, 171
      Kant's awareness of 11, 31–32, 33–38, 76, 132–33, 189, 193, 272n8, 274n6n7
Husserl, Edmund 110

I- concept 9, 161, 180 *see also* I-representation
   acquisition of 226
   lack of intuition of 137
   Rationalist versions of 178–79
Idea, Psychological 8, 161, 175, 176–79
Identity of self, *see* identity, personal
Identity, personal 3
   and arbitrariness 28–30, 187
   and conversion 85–86
   Hume on 11, 31–32
   Kant on 48, 184–87
   Leibniz and Locke on, 29–31, 184, 185
   Tetens on 33–34
Identity, substantial 29–30, 185, 186
I-intuition
   absence of 35, 76, 109, 117, 136, 137, 183, 191, 193, 198–99
   early acceptance of 35
Imagination, faculty of
   productive synthesis of 103, 105–6, 109, 152, 154, 162, 203, 279n8, 280n9
   relation to faculty of understanding 104, 106, 107–8, 162, 225
   and representation of time 154, 156, 222
   reproductive 104, 114, 118, 162, 234
   and Tetens 34, 36
Impressions 24, 34, 49, 82, 129, 175, 220, 221, 222, 225, 236
Inner sense
   and apperception 21–23, 24, 129–30
   early views on 18–19, 20
   Locke on 16, 17–18
   materials of 25
   and mineness 26, 124, 146
   as necessary for cognition 159
   Shoemaker on 253–54, 272n3
   Tetens on 23–24
Internal sense *see* inner sense
Intuitions
   in relation to concepts 103–4, 107, 114, 144, 151, 153–54
   and rational relations 150–51, 154
I-representation *see also* I-Concept
   as *a priori* 35, 38, 76, 137
   lack of empirical derivation for 35, 37, 38, 132, 144
I-rule
   and principle of apperception 123–26, 135, 136, 141, 121, 166, 188
   necessity of for norm use 232
   and object rules 136, 137, 140, 149, 160, 166, 188–89
I-think
   as *a priori* representation 124, 135, 144
   vs. the *cogito* 115–17, 193–97
   and cognition 125, 126, 137, 141
   as empty 147, 189, 191
   and I exist 193–97
   neither appearance nor thing in itself 194, 196
   no title for 187, 189
   'one and the same' 165
   peculiarities of representation 146–47, 149, 187–89, 190, 192
   as vehicle of the categories 147–48, 187

Jacobi, F. H. 203, 204, 205, 213
Jacobi-Vaihinger-Strawson objection 204, 205–13
Jäsche, Benjamin 19, 20, 118, 119, 223, 225, 231, 272n8, 290n16
Judgments
   analytic 143–44, 150
   and concepts 19, 119, 120
   definition of 116, 117–18, 142
   forms of 100, 102, 117, 166, 234–35, 237
   and necessary connection of mental states 11, 136–37, 140–41, 143, 149, 150–51, 232–33
   as relation between concepts 99, 142

and self-consciousness 129
synthetic *a priori* 81–82

Kandel, Eric 209
Kemp Smith, Norman 85, 87, 271n2, 274n5n6, 278n13, 279n1, 286n10
Kitcher, Philip viii, 175, 282n8
Klemme, Heiner F. 11, 32, 50, 272n8
Knutzen, Martin 15, 61, 64
Korgaard, Christine 218
Kraus, C. J. 31
Kripke, Saul 282n14
Kuehn, Manfred 15, 61, 273n1, 277n7n8
  on deduction and possibility of concepts 8, 87–89
  on Hume's influence 31–32, 272n8

Langton, Rae 87
Lashley, Karl 266
Laywine, Alison 72, 276n5
Lecture Notes, student
  dating and reliability of 20, 36, 48
  Metaphysics Lecture notes L$_1$
    Carl on 36
    and freedom 41–42, 49
    and the Paralogisms 38, 41, 51–53, 182 87
    on powers 44–46
Leibniz, Gottfried Wilhelm 29–30, 40–42, 55–57
Levine, Joseph 267
Locke, John
  influence on Kant 6, 11, 15
  on internal sense 16–18
  on personal identity 27–28, 185, 186, 187
  on reflection 17, 54–55
Logic
  acts required by 16
  contrasted with metaphysics 224
  natural or ordinary (vs. scientific) 227–31
Longuenesse, Béatrice 9, 106, 275n3, 279n4n6, 281n3, 282n12n16, 286n8, 291n6
  on activities of comparing, reflecting, and abstracting 113, 224, 234, 235, 236, 284n1, 290n2n3n5
  on concept formation 234–37
  on forms of judgment 117, 118, 237
  on schematism 279n8
  on *synthesis speciosa* 279n8

Lossius, J. C. 32

Marks (*Merkmale*) 19, 103, 104, 119–20, 121, 127–28
Marr, David 266
McCann, Edwin 273n2
McDowell, John 203
Meiners, Christoph 63, 64
Melnick, Arthur 156m 278n11, 285n2
Mendelssohn, Moses 36
Mental activities *see* synthesis
Mental acts 9, 11, 24, 30
  a priori 226
  equally valid 139
  extended 138
  identity of 138, 139, 171
  Locke on 17, 18, 64
  and logic 16, 17, 155
Mental states *see also* representations
  'mineness' of 4–5, 26, 115, 124, 136, 146, 159, 170, 260–62, 265
  necessary connection of *see* necessary connection of mental states
  rational connection of 5, 131, 136–37, 139, 146, 150–51, 155, 159, 199, 252, 254, 260, 266–68
  togetherness of 5, 124
  transitions between 29–30, 41, 43, 62, 64, 122, 127, 132, 140, 155, 156ff
Merian, Johann Bernard 24, 59–61, 64, 77, 134, 145
Metaphysical Deduction 117, 149, 281n4
Metaphysics
  in relation to epistemology *see* epistemology
  in relation to metaphysics
  scientific vs. traditional 5–6, 45, 76, 124, 133, 165
Mind as model for objects 74
Mind-reading 200, 268–70
Moran, Richard 254–56, 262, 263–64, 292n5n9

Nagel, Thomas 266
Necessary connection of mental states 131, 136, 137, 140–52, 155, 156, 160, 188
Necessity 4, 22, 83, 110–11, 189, 193
  two-fold of categorial principles 123–24, 144
Newton, Isaac 67, 222, 281n10

Noumena
    argument for existence of 205–6, 211, 215
    and describing causes of sensations 206, 208–10
    as indicating restriction on knowledge 211
    positive sense of 211
    self as 161, 174–75, 178–79, 193, 194, 196, 202–3
    vs. transcendental object 207–8, 212–15

Objective reference as necessary and sufficient for apperception 111–13, 129–31, 134–36, 139–41, 145–46
O'Neill, Onora 248

Paralogisms
    Ameriks on *see* Ameriks on paralogisms
    competing interpretations of 180–81, 182
    discovery of 36–37, 76, 91
    general errors of 189, 192, 193
    relation to 'I-think' 180–84, 188–89, 191
    relation to Psychological Idea 180–81
    Second Paralogism 52, 111, 167–68, 183–84
    Strawson on 3, 5, 180
    Third Paralogism 182, 184–86
    Wuerth on 187
Paton, H. J. 54
Peacocke, Christopher viii, 17, 281n6, 284n46, 291n4, 292n15n18
Perception
    causal theory of 153, 210
    indeterminate 195–96, 198, 286–87n12n15
    unconscious (*petite* or small) 33–34, 41, 102
Permanence and substance 45–46, 183, 184–85
Perner, Joseph 269
Personality *see* identity, personal
Pluhar, Werner 271n1, 285n4, 286n10, 290n1
Possibility, real 88, 250
Powers
    Active 18, 82, 108–9, 130, 156
    vs. faculties 162–63
    fundamental or basic 44, 52, 62
    Leibniz on 43, 47
    and principles 165–66
    Watkins on 170–72
    Wolff on 44, 47–48, 58
Prauss, Gerold 211, 287n2n7n8
Psychologism 217–218

Psychology, Empirical 35, 47–48
Psychology, Rational 35, Chapter 4, section 4 *passim*
    dependence on Empirical 35, 47–48
    Kant's critique of Chapter 11, sections 2,3,4 *passim*
    Kant's presentations of 35, Chapter 11, section 2 *passim*
Psychology, Transcendental vii, 8–9, 11, 203, 204

Rationalism 5–7, 10, 39, 44–45, 46, 72–74, 76, 122, 156, 164–66
    Kant's criticisms of 133, 161, 199
Reason, theoretical and practical 50, 176–78, 245, 247, Chapter 14, *passim*
Receptivity vs. Spontaneity 22, 99, 100, 134, 172, 206–7
Recognition in a Concept *see* Synthesis, of recognition in a concept
Reflection 17–18, 22, 27, 54–55, 57
    Allison on 168, 170
    Henrich's objection to 284n39
    Kant's criticism of 145
    Merian's criticism of 59–60
Reflections (*Reflexionen*), Kant's 271–272n7
Reinhold, Karl Leonhard 289n1
Representations *see also* mental states
    a priori see a priori concepts
    as grounds of cognition 8, 18, 119–20, 121, 128
    partial vs. whole 8, 75, 101, 119–20, 129–31, 136, 138, 140–41, 152
    recognized as such 119, 121, 135, 136, 260
    varieties of 18–20, 108, 121
Rosefeldt, Tobias vii, 253–54, 291–92n4
Rousseau, Jean-Jacques 273n1
Rüdiger, Andreas 275n3
Rules
    for concepts 70, 99, 101, 104, 107, 127, 130, 131, 136, 140, 141, 150
    and implication relations 127
    Kripke's objection to 282n14
    for objects 35, 71–74, 81–82, 84, 90, 99, 139
    and sensible data 92–95
Rödl, Sebastian vii, 282n20, 285n6
Ryle, Gilbert 24

Sacks, Mark vii
Sassen, Brigitte 15
Saugstal, Jen 282n17

Schemata 188, 190, 236, 279n8
Schwartz, James 209
Scrutinizing 93–95, 107–8, 135, 278n12
Second Analogy 124, 153–54, 221–22
Self-blindness 25, 253–62
Self-feeling Chapter 5, section 4 *passim*
Self-Knowledge 5, 25–26, 50
  Boyle on 263–65
  Evans on 254–55
  limitations of Chapter 11, section 6 *passim*
  Moran on 254–56
  Shoemaker on 25, 254
Sellars, Wilfrid 180, 220
Sensationism 108–9
Sensations
  as belonging to subject 72–73, 76, 92
  causes of Chapter 12, section 3 *passim*
  concatenating 68–69
  concept of 69
  as indicators of reality 23–24, 69–71
  nonreferential character of 108–9
  relation to sensory data 69, 92
  rules for positing 70, 75, 91–93
  self-ascription of 26, 263–65
  temporal order of 71, 73, 76, 153
Sensibility, faculty of 15, 69, 73, 90, 105–7, 162–63, 172, 195, 207, 210–15
Setiya, Keiran 256–63, 292n5n11n12
Shoemaker, Sydney 9, 25, 251, 253–54, 255, 256–57, 262, 271n1, 272n3, 292n5n6n9
Simulation theory 270
Smell, theory of 208–9
Smith, Joel vii
Spontaneity, absolute 41–42, 49, 52, 242, 239, 240, 244–46 *see also* freedom
Strawson, P. F. 10, 265, 271n1
  and corrected view 110, 264, 277n6
  on criterionless self-ascription 3–4, 11
  on noumenal affection 204
  on the Paralogisms 5, 180
  and transcendental arguments 250–51
Stroud, Barry 250–52, 291n1
Sturm, Thomas vii
Sturma, Dieter 10, 271n1
Substances 35, 42, Chapter 4, section 3 *passim*, 67, 140, 181–83, 186, 289n11
  see also permanence and substance
  and powers 43–46, 165–66
  template for 100, 131, 225–26, 237, 282n21

Synthesis *see also* combination
  and analysis 101–2
  of apperception [aka: Third Synthesis] 99, chapter 9, section 5 *passim*
  of apprehension [aka: First Synthesis] 34, 38, 98
  blind 103, 279n2
  conscious vs. unconscious 102–4
  definition of 99, Chapter 8, section 2 *passim*
  Hoppe on 11, 110–13
  of imagination [aka: Second Synthesis] 38
  necessary for object cognition, subject cognition 108–9, 110–14
  same function, same act thesis 99–100, 105–6
  and scrutinizing 107–8
  speciosa 105–7

Talbert, Bonnie 292n17
Tetens, Johann Nicolaus
  empirical method of 33, 77
  on Hume 34, 133
  on inner sense as representational 23–24, 129, 267–68
  influence on Kant 35–38, 76–77, 98, 129, 132, 272n10, 274n14, 276n1
  on origins of concepts 33 34, 35
  on personal identity 35, 37, 63–64
  on self-feeling 34
  on synthesis 34
Theory theory 269–70
Thiel, Udo 54, 59, 61, 63, 134, 275n1n3n5
Thing-in-itself (*Ding an sich*) 288n15
Thomson, Judith Jarvis 291n1
Thöle, Bernard vii, 284n37n43
Tiedemann, Dietrich 32
Time 20–21, 70–71, 92, 107, 141, 151
  inability to sense 25, 71, 76, 152–56
Tittel, Gottlob August 15
Transcendental, meaning of term 95
Transcendental arguments 250–53
Transcendental concepts *see* categories, *a priori* concepts
Transcendental Content 162
Transcendental Deduction *see also* Deduction
  Carl on 90–93
  complexity of 87–89, 93, 149
  'one-step' deduction 116, 117–18
  and possibility of experience 85
  transcendental method of 85

Transcendental Deduction (*continued*)
   type of argument
      analogy with legal deductions 87–89
      analytic vs. synthetic 84–85
      Kemp Smith on 85
      Kuehn on 87–89
      as reflective equilibrium 84
Transcendental Idealism
   consistency with cognitive theory 203–5
   models of 278n12
   and representational skepticism 86–87
   and space and time 204, 287n3
Transcendental object 206–15
Transitions between mental states *see* mental states, transitions between

Understanding, faculty of
   identical to apperception *see* apperception, faculty of
   relation to faculty of imagination *see* imagination, relation to faculty of understanding
   spontaneity of *see* apperception, faculty of
Unity of consciousness *see* apperception, unity of

Vaihinger, Hans 203–4, 215–16
Verse argument 52, 184, 275n12, 281n13

Watkins, Eric 8, 161, 170–73, 274n3n8
Weldon, T. D. 24
Westphal, Kenneth R. 279n3
Wilson, Margaret 30, 277n5
Wimmer, Heinz 269
Wittgenstein, Ludwig 282n14
Wolff, Christian
   on immateriality of soul 52, 184
   on mental continuity 58
   on object cognition 47, 54, 58, 59, 64, 137, 283n28
   on possible objects 88
   on powers 43–44, 48, 163
   on Rational and Empirical Psychology 47–48
   on representation 23, 48, 176
Wolff, Robert Paul 274n6
Wuerth, Julian 187, 275n10, 286n7
Wunderlich, Falk 54, 61–62, 156, 274n9, 275n3, 282n23, 283n28

Young, Garry 17

www.ingramcontent.com/pod-product-compliance
Ingram Content Group UK Ltd.
Pitfield, Milton Keynes, MK11 3LW, UK
UKHW041959230426
12048UKWH00008B/428